藤崎　竜

(What's 1+2?)

I'm a little embarrassed about signing autographs. This is because I can't think of myself as a *mangaka* who's worthy of signing them. Someday, when I become a great *mangaka*, maybe I'll be able to sign autographs without hesitating.

Ryu Fujisaki

Ryu Fujisaki's *Worlds* came in second place for the prestigious 40th Tezuka Award. His *Psycho +, Wāqwāq* and *Hōshin Engi* have all run in *Weekly Shonen Jump* magazine, ~~available~~ on DVD in Japan and ~~fiction, literature and~~ *Engi* a mix of genres that ~~imagination.~~

HOSHIN ENGI VOL. 9
The SHONEN JUMP Manga Edition

STORY AND ART BY RYU FUJISAKI
Based on the novel *Hoshin Engi*, translated by Tsutomu Ano,
published by Kodansha Bunko

Translation & Adaptation/Tomo Kimura
Touch-up Art & Lettering/HudsonYards
Design/Matt Hinrichs
Editor/Jonathan Tarbox

Editor in Chief, Books/Alvin Lu
Editor in Chief, Magazines/Marc Weidenbaum
VP, Publishing Licensing/Rika Inouye
VP, Sales and Product Marketing/Gonzalo Ferreyra
VP, Creative/Linda Espinosa
Publisher/Hyoe Narita

Printed in the U.S.A.

Published by VIZ Media, LLC
P.O. Box 77010
San Francisco, CA 94107

SHONEN JUMP Manga Edition
10 9 8 7 6 5 4 3 2 1
First printing, October 2008

THE WORLD'S
MOST POPULAR MANGA

www.viz.com

www.shonenjump.com

HOSHiN ENGi

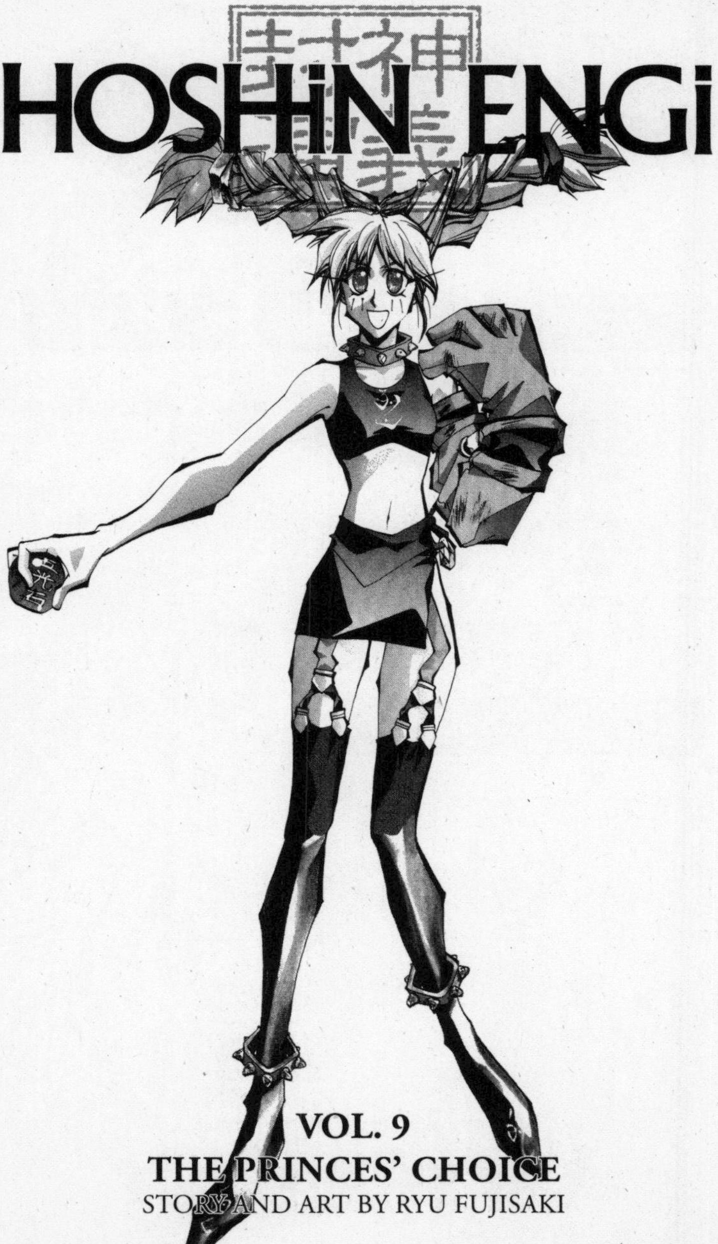

VOL. 9

THE PRINCES' CHOICE

STORY AND ART BY RYU FUJISAKI

THE CHARACTERS

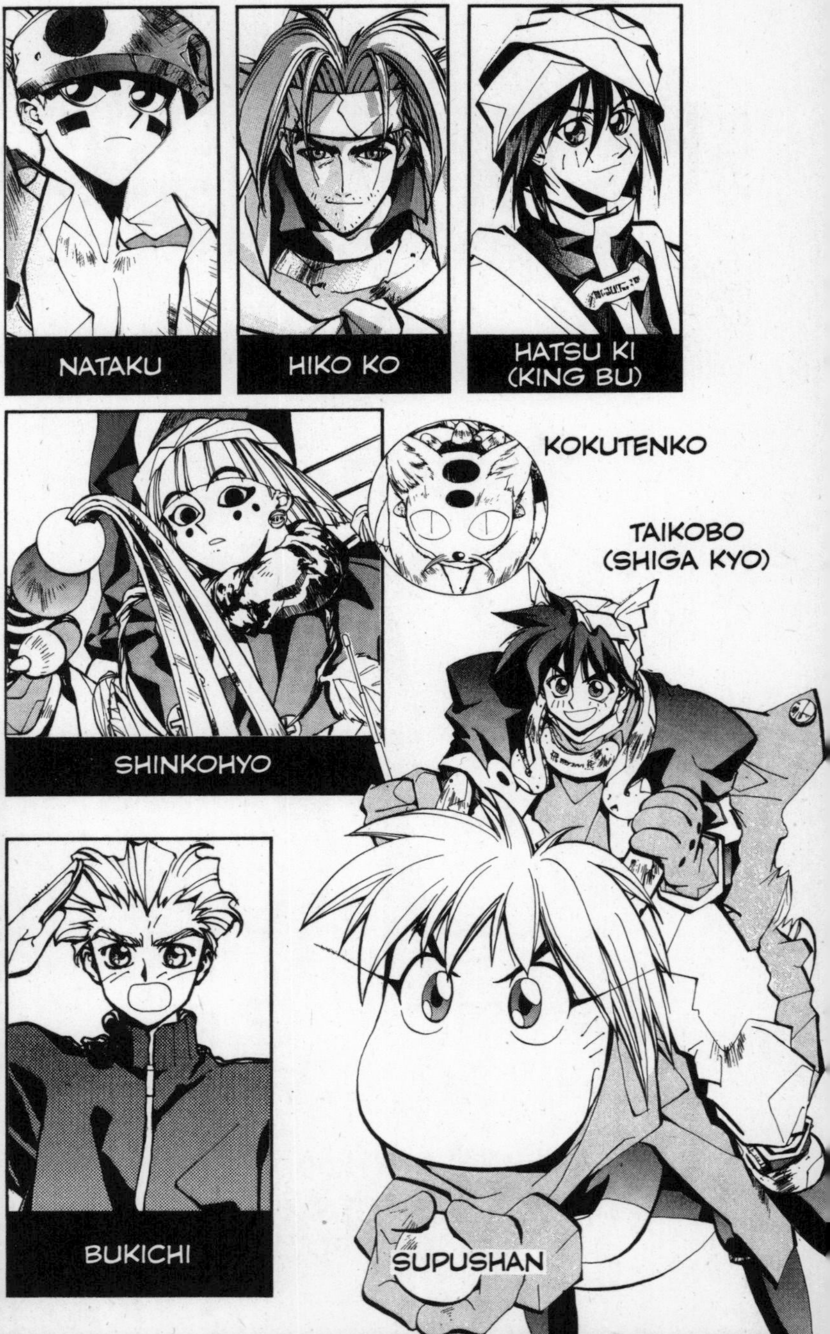
HATSU KI (KING BU)
HIKO KO
NATAKU
KOKUTENKO
TAIKOBO (SHIGA KYO)
SHINKOHYO
SUPUSHAN
BUKICHI

DAKKI

KING CHU

BUNCHU

INCHI

INCHON

The Story Thus Far

Ancient China, over 3,000 years ago. It is the era of the Yin Dynasty.

After King Chu, the emperor, married the beautiful Dakki, the good king was no longer himself, and became an unmanly and foolish ruler. Dakki, a *Sennyo* with a wicked heart, took control of Yin and the country fell into chaos.

To save the human world, the Hoshin Project was put into action. The project will seal evil Sennin and Doshi into the Shinkai, and cause Seihakuko Sho Ki to set up a new dynasty to replace Yin. Taikobo, who was chosen to execute this project, acts to install Sho Ki's heir Hatsu Ki as the next king. Hatsu Ki takes the title King Bu and declares Seiki is now the Kingdom of Zhou, effectively declaring war against Yin. Meanwhile, Taikobo sends Dokoson on a mission to make Yin's spy Toh Sengyoku their ally?!

VOL. 9
THE PRINCES' CHOICE

CONTENTS

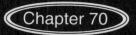

Chapter 70

TOH KYUKO, SENGYOKU AND RYUSHUKO PLEDGE ALLEGIANCE TO ZHOU

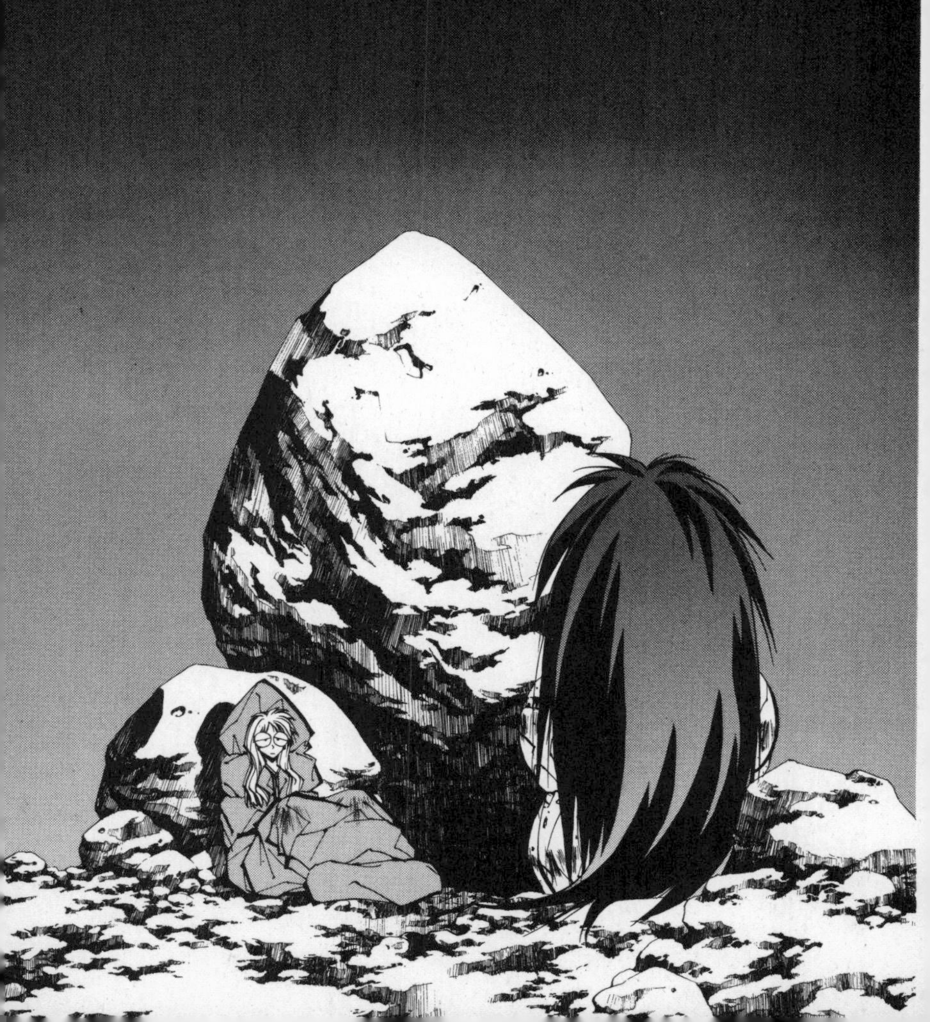

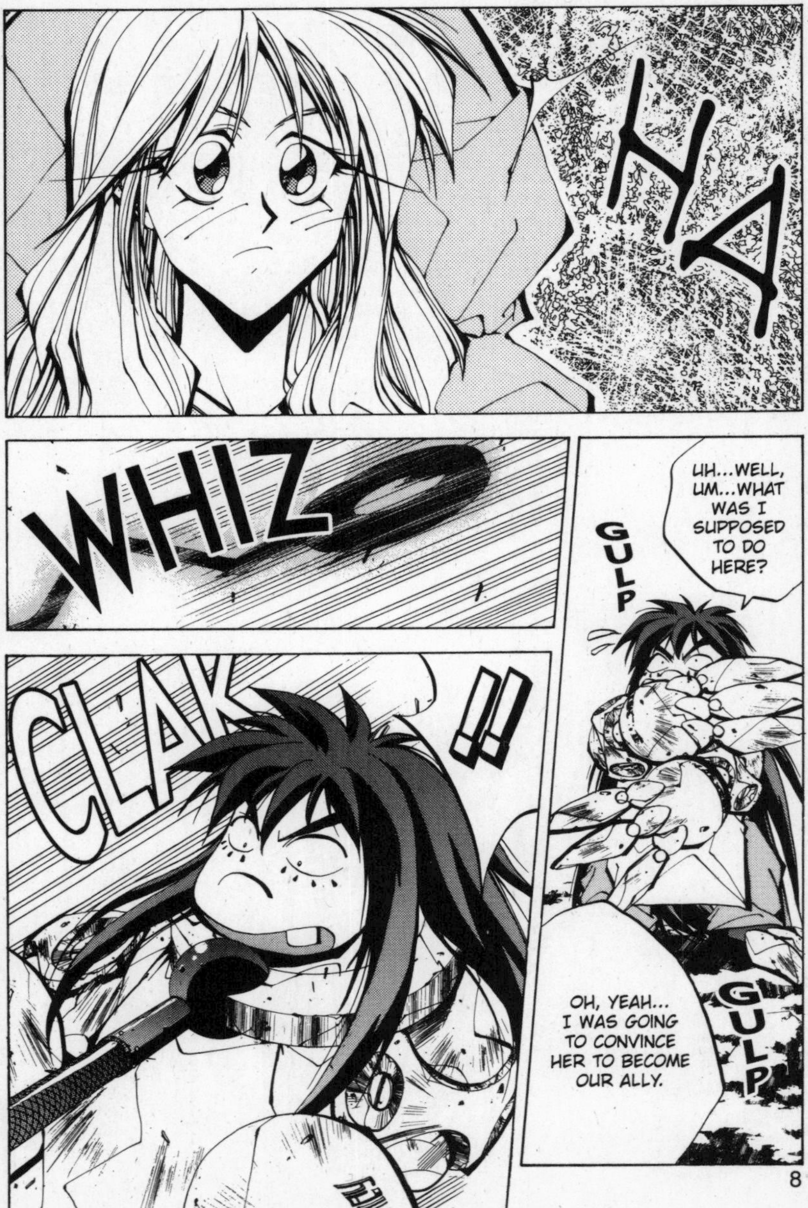
HA
UH...WELL, UM...WHAT WAS I SUPPOSED TO DO HERE?
GULP
OH, YEAH... I WAS GOING TO CONVINCE HER TO BECOME OUR ALLY.
GULP
WHIZ
CLAK
!!

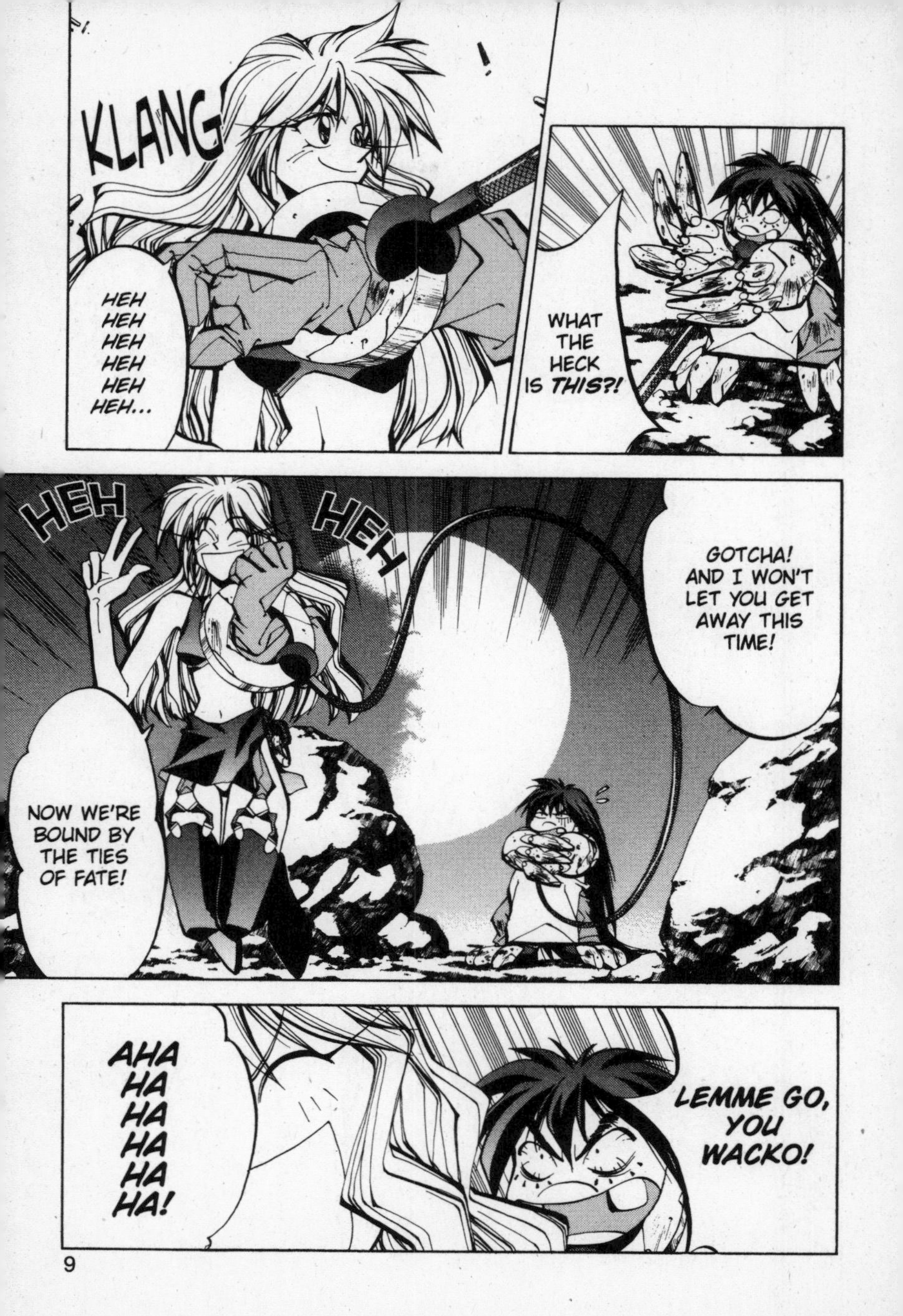
WHAT THE HECK IS *THIS?!*
!
KLANG
HEH HEH HEH HEH HEH HEH...
GOTCHA! AND I WON'T LET YOU GET AWAY THIS TIME!
HEH
HEH
NOW WE'RE BOUND BY THE TIES OF FATE!
LEMME GO, YOU WACKO!
AHA HA HA HA HA HA!

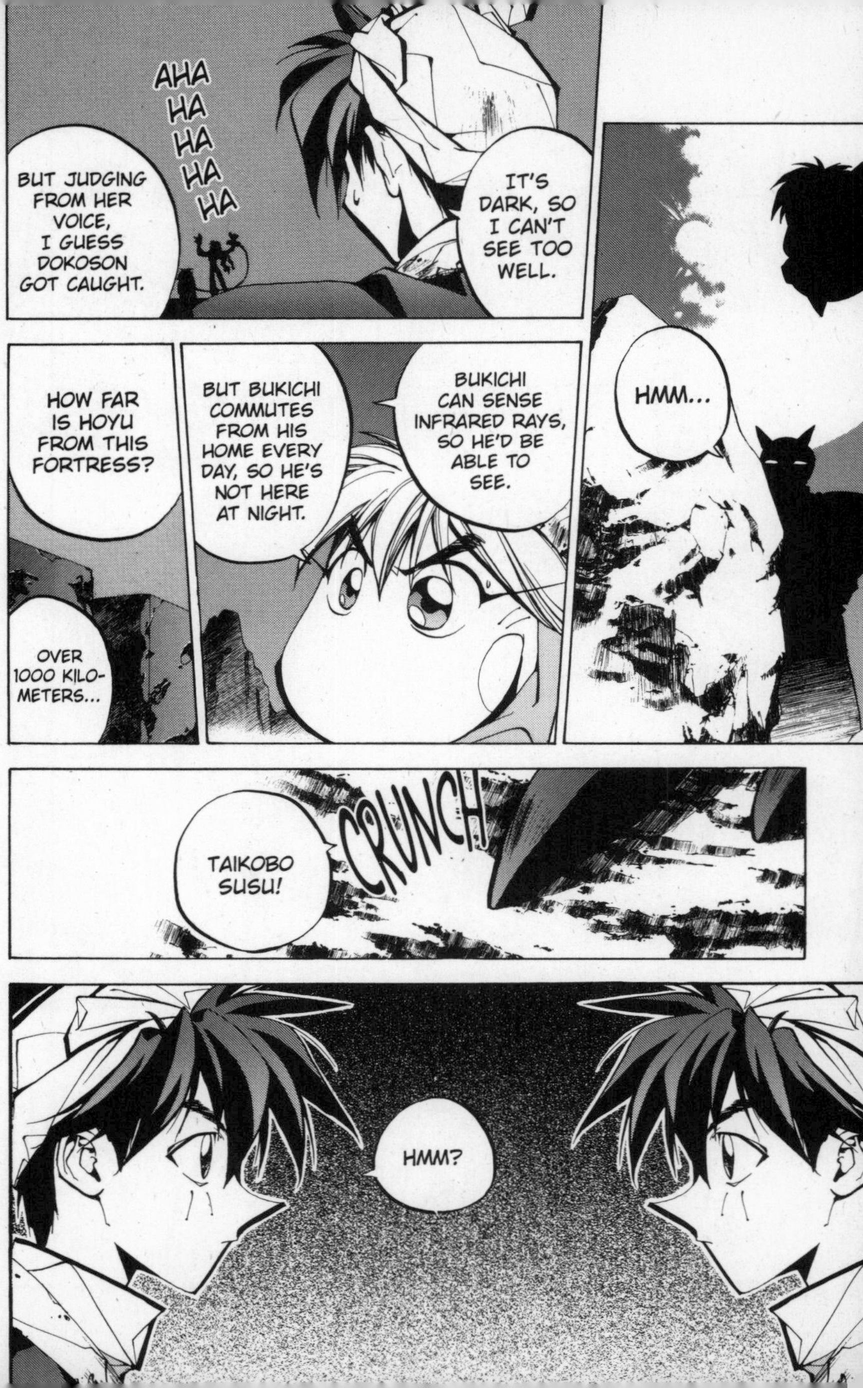
IT'S DARK, SO I CAN'T SEE TOO WELL.
AHA HA HA HA HA
BUT JUDGING FROM HER VOICE, I GUESS DOKOSON GOT CAUGHT.
HMM...
BUKICHI CAN SENSE INFRARED RAYS, SO HE'D BE ABLE TO SEE.
BUT BUKICHI COMMUTES FROM HIS HOME EVERY DAY, SO HE'S NOT HERE AT NIGHT.
HOW FAR IS HOYU FROM THIS FORTRESS?
OVER 1000 KILO-METERS...
CRUNCH
TAIKOBO SUSU!
HMM?

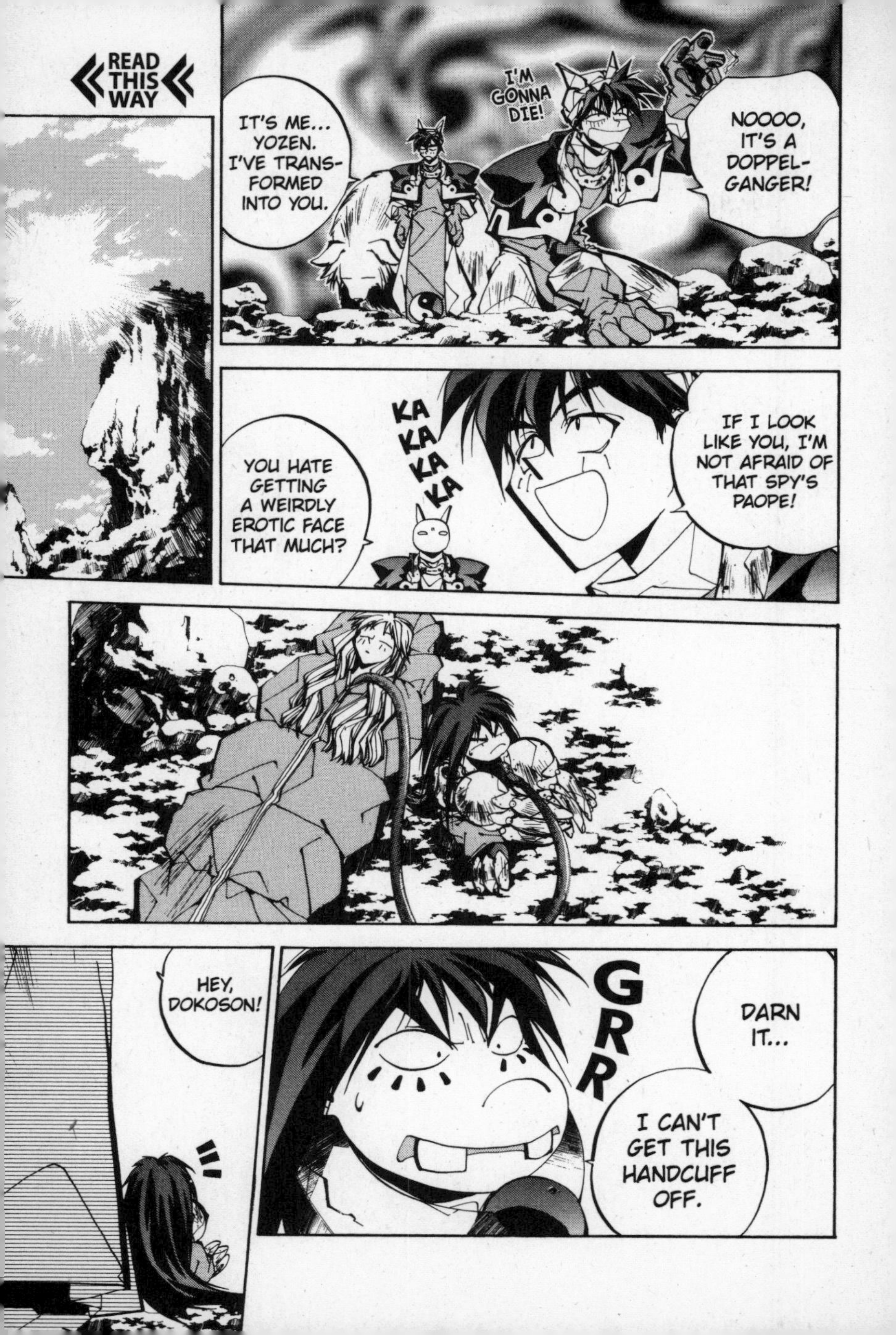
READ THIS WAY
NOOOO, IT'S A DOPPEL-GANGER!
I'M GONNA DIE!
IT'S ME... YOZEN. I'VE TRANS-FORMED INTO YOU.
IF I LOOK LIKE YOU, I'M NOT AFRAID OF THAT SPY'S PAOPE!
KA KA KA KA
YOU HATE GETTING A WEIRDLY EROTIC FACE THAT MUCH?
DARN IT...
GRR
I CAN'T GET THIS HANDCUFF OFF.
HEY, DOKOSON!
!!!

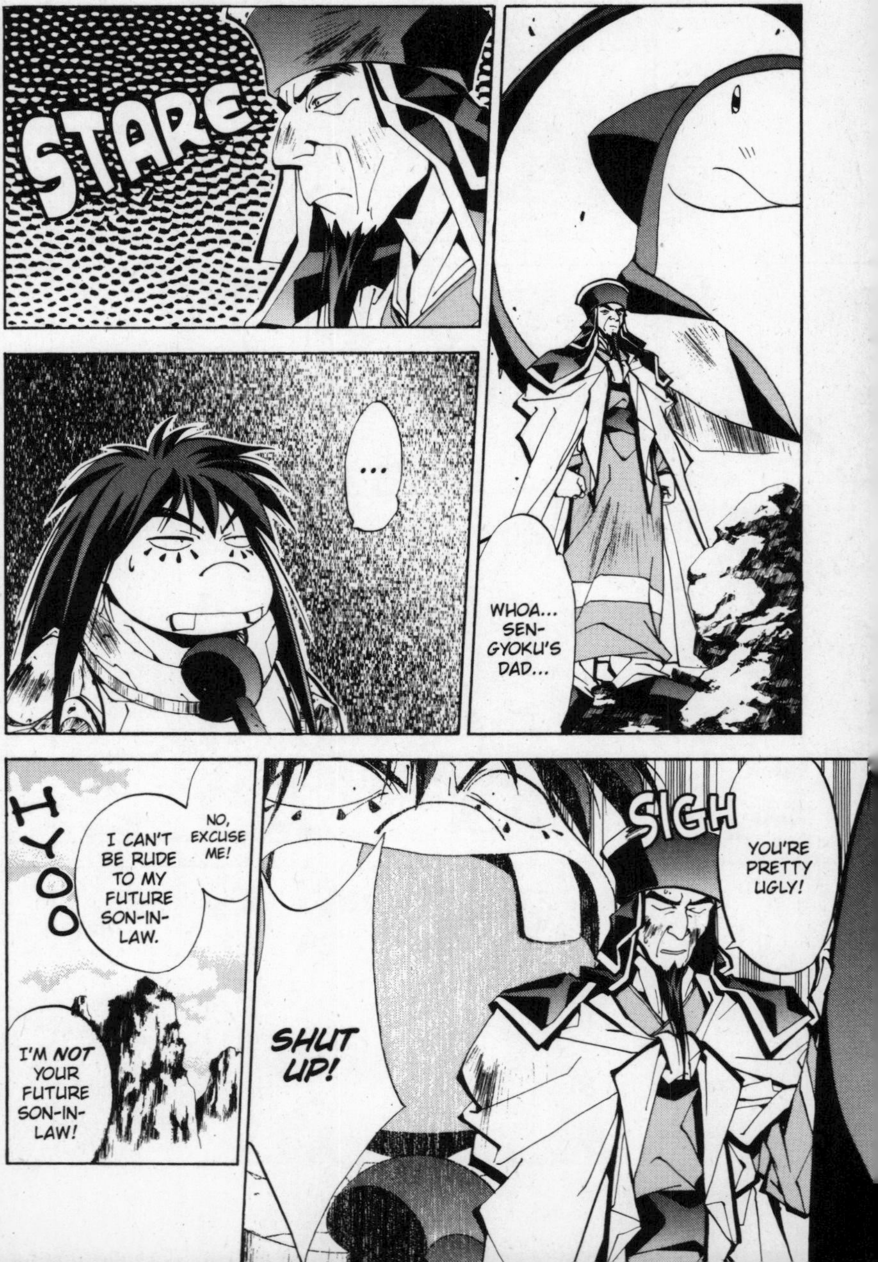
WHOA... SEN-GYOKU'S DAD...
STARE
...
SIGH
YOU'RE PRETTY UGLY!
SHUT UP!
NO, EXCUSE ME!
I CAN'T BE RUDE TO MY FUTURE SON-IN-LAW.
HYOO
I'M *NOT* YOUR FUTURE SON-IN-LAW!

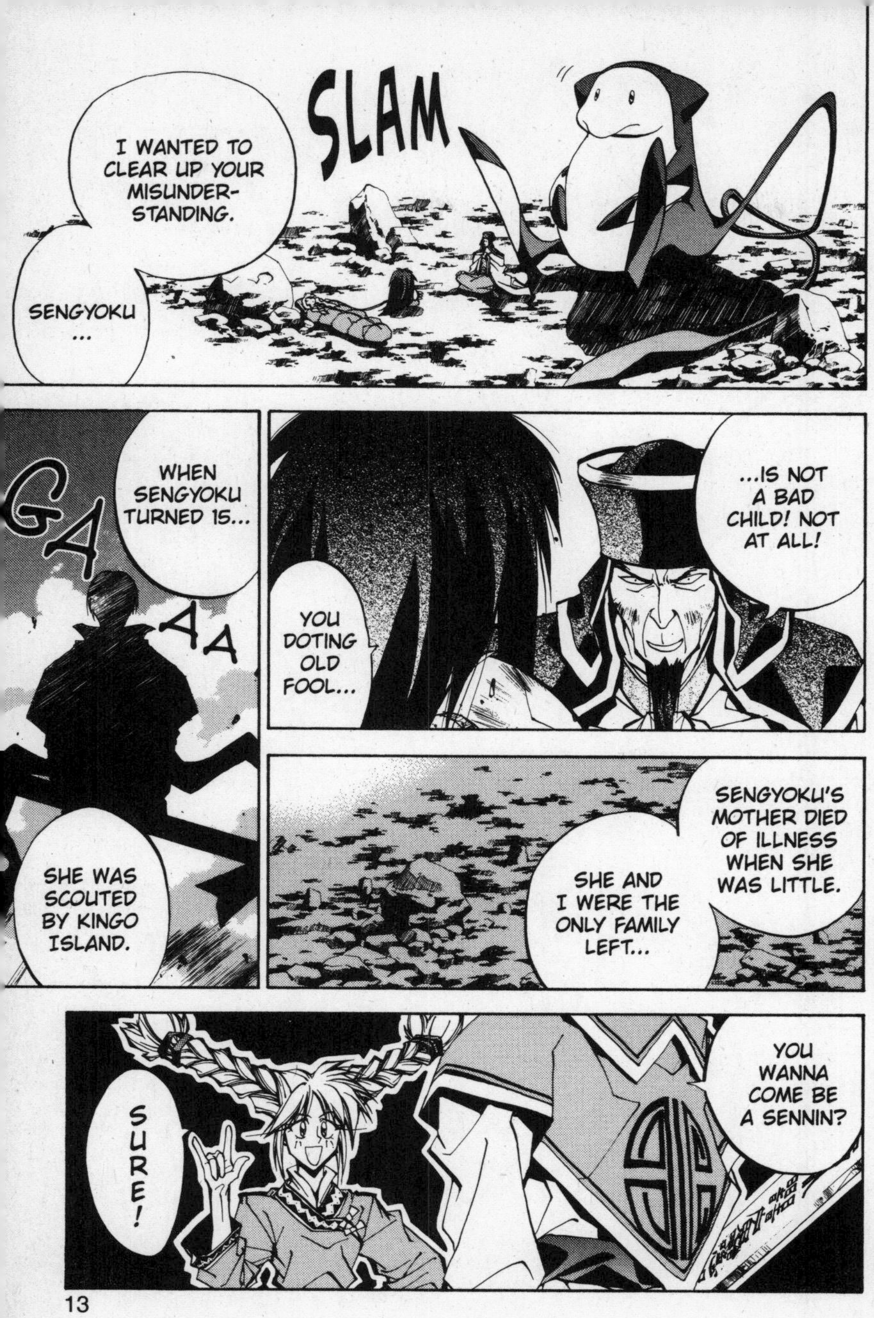
SLAM
I WANTED TO CLEAR UP YOUR MISUNDER-STANDING.
SENGYOKU ...
...IS NOT A BAD CHILD! NOT AT ALL!
YOU DOTING OLD FOOL...
SENGYOKU'S MOTHER DIED OF ILLNESS WHEN SHE WAS LITTLE.
SHE AND I WERE THE ONLY FAMILY LEFT...
GAAA
WHEN SENGYOKU TURNED 15...
SHE WAS SCOUTED BY KINGO ISLAND.
YOU WANNA COME BE A SENNIN?
SURE!

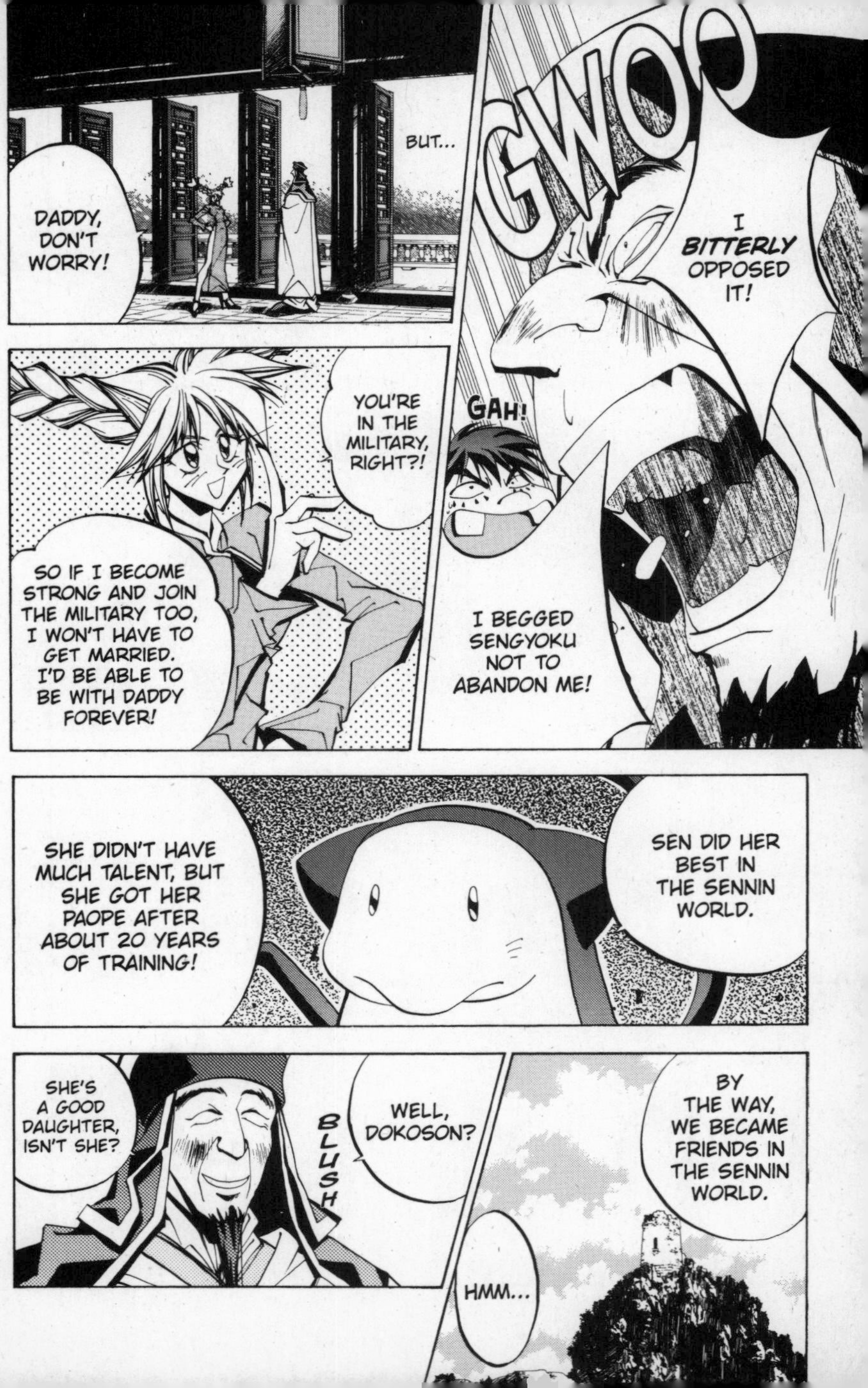
GWOO
I BITTERLY OPPOSED IT!
GAH!
I BEGGED SENGYOKU NOT TO ABANDON ME!
BUT...
DADDY, DON'T WORRY!
YOU'RE IN THE MILITARY, RIGHT?!
SO IF I BECOME STRONG AND JOIN THE MILITARY TOO, I WON'T HAVE TO GET MARRIED. I'D BE ABLE TO BE WITH DADDY FOREVER!
SEN DID HER BEST IN THE SENNIN WORLD.
SHE DIDN'T HAVE MUCH TALENT, BUT SHE GOT HER PAOPE AFTER ABOUT 20 YEARS OF TRAINING!
BY THE WAY, WE BECAME FRIENDS IN THE SENNIN WORLD.
HMM...
WELL, DOKOSON?
BLUSH
SHE'S A GOOD DAUGHTER, ISN'T SHE?

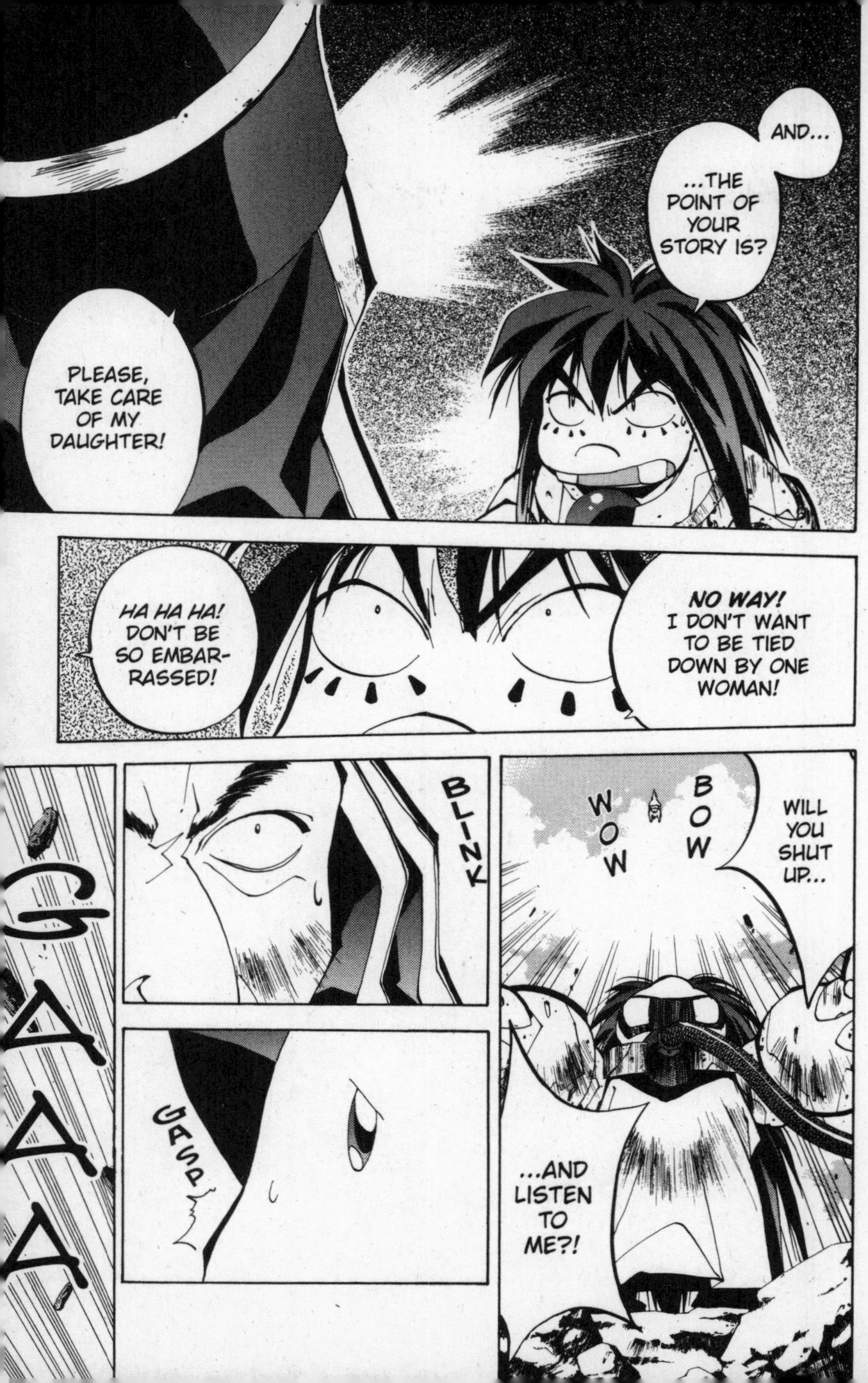
AND...
...THE POINT OF YOUR STORY IS?
PLEASE, TAKE CARE OF MY DAUGHTER!
NO WAY! I DON'T WANT TO BE TIED DOWN BY ONE WOMAN!
HA HA HA! DON'T BE SO EMBAR-RASSED!
BOW WOW
WILL YOU SHUT UP...
...AND LISTEN TO ME?!
BLINK
GASP

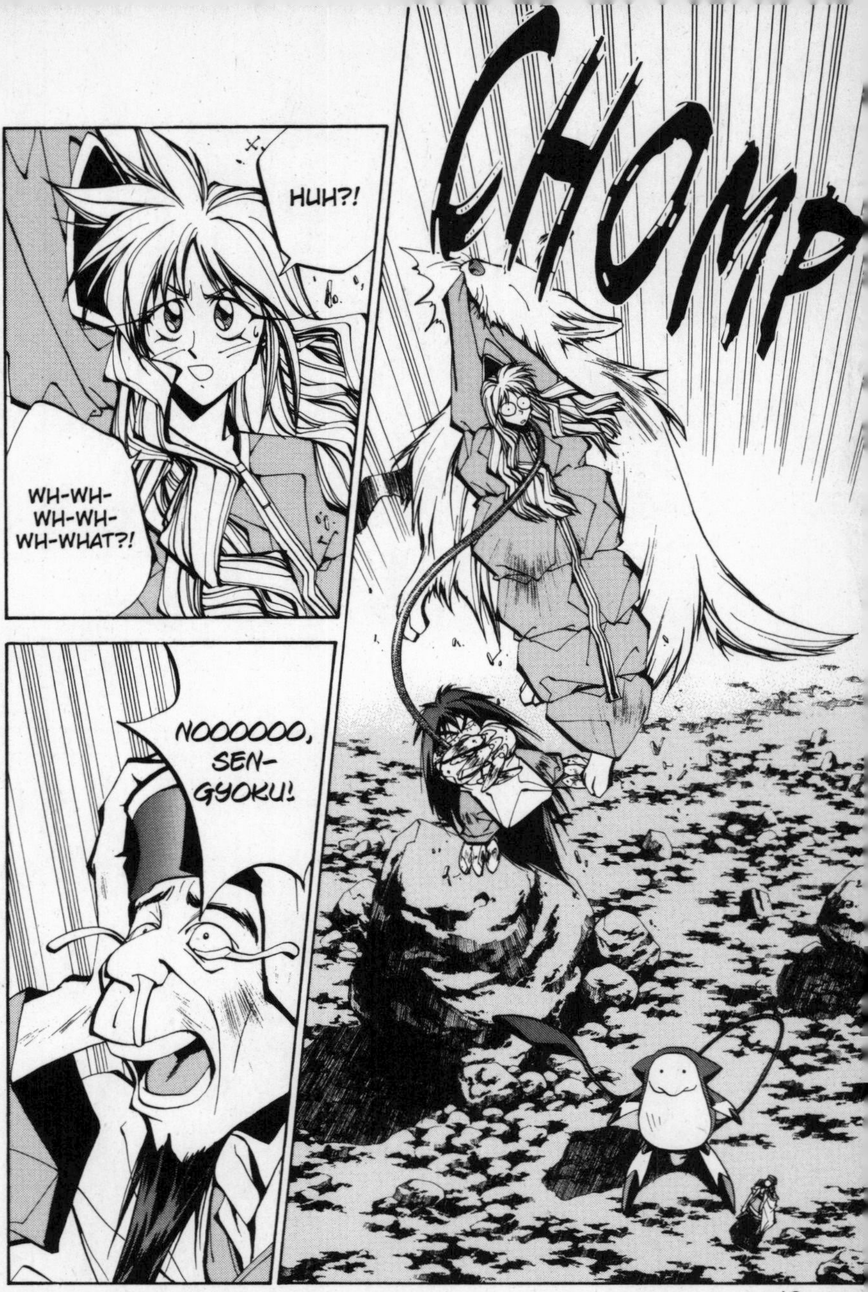
CHOMP
HUH?!
WH-WH-
WH-WH-
WH-WHAT?!
NOOOOOO, SEN-GYOKU!

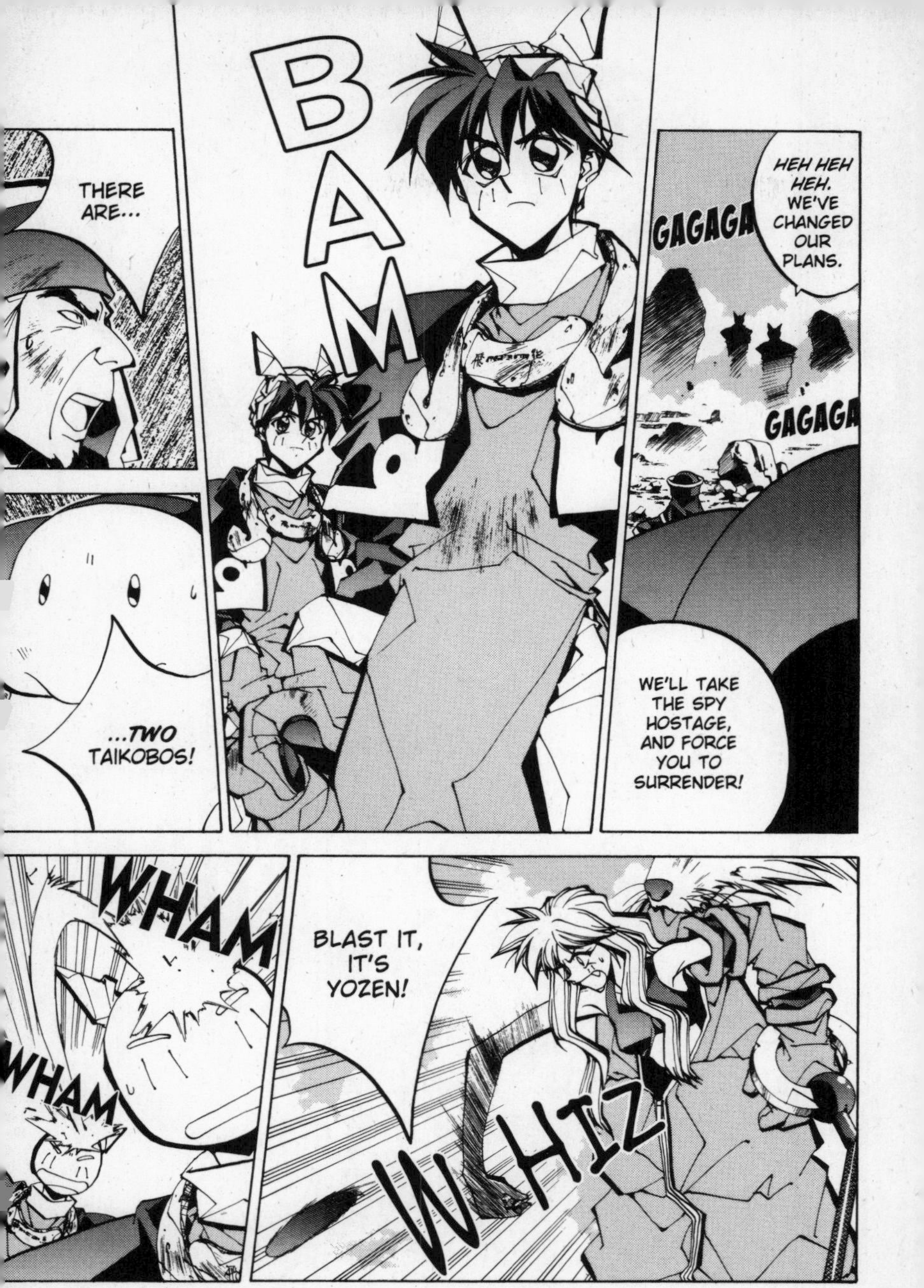
GAGAGA
HEH HEH HEH. WE'VE CHANGED OUR PLANS.
GAGAGA
WE'LL TAKE THE SPY HOSTAGE, AND FORCE YOU TO SURRENDER!
BAM
THERE ARE...
...TWO TAIKOBOS!
BLAST IT, IT'S YOZEN!
WHIZ
WHAM
WHAM

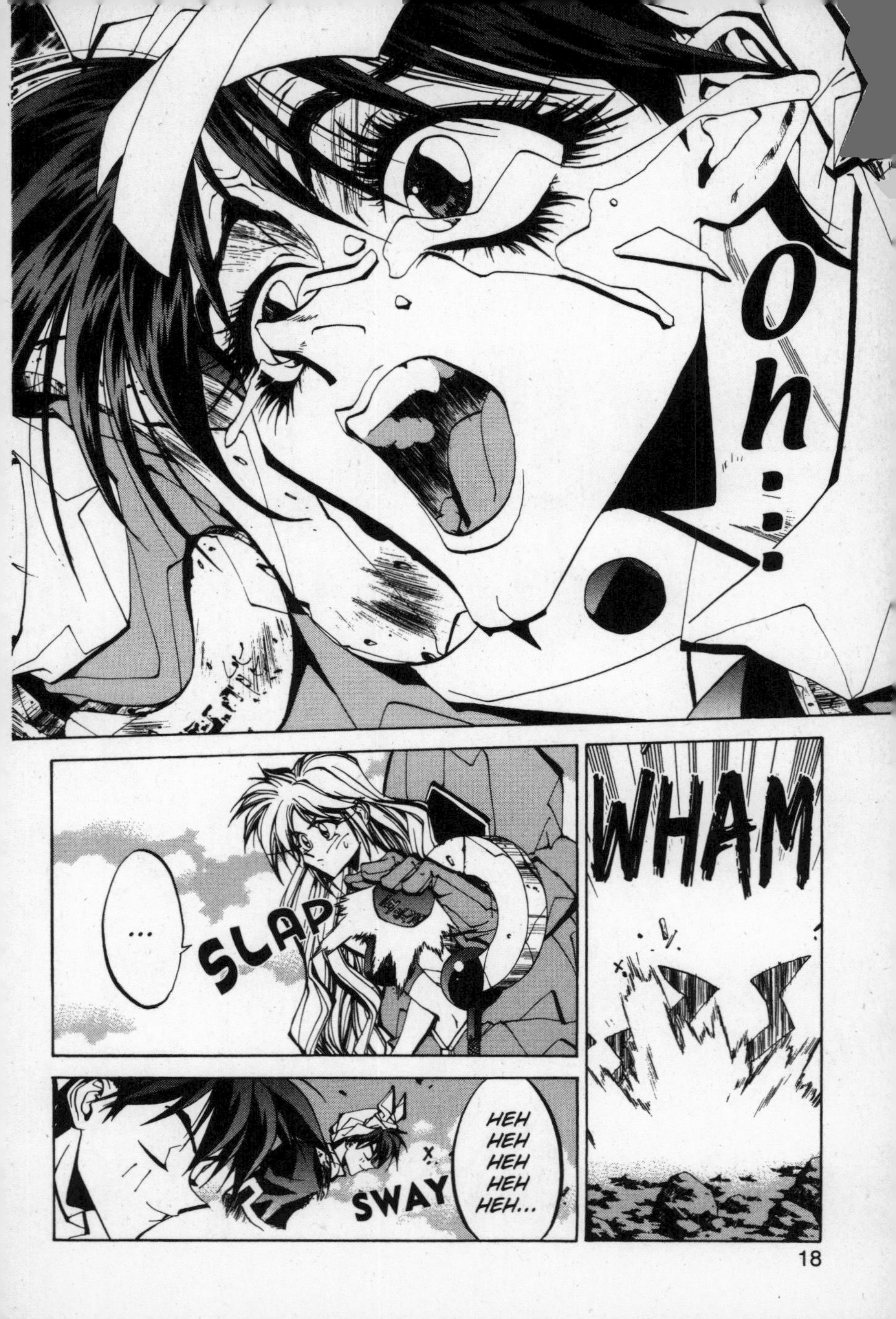
Oh...!
WHAM
SLAP
...
HEH HEH HEH HEH HEH...
SWAY

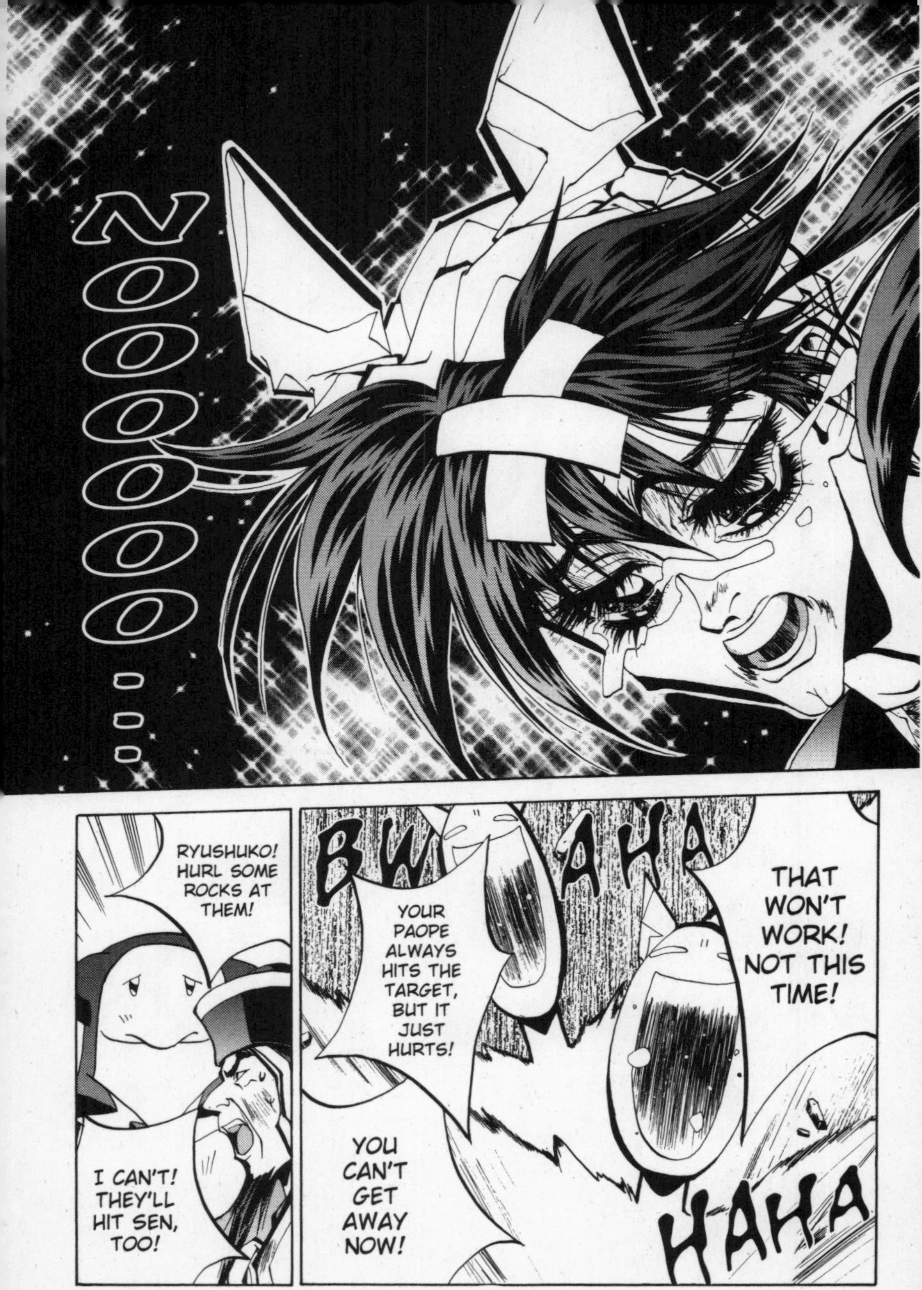
NOOOOOOO...
BWAHAHA
THAT WON'T WORK! NOT THIS TIME!
YOUR PAOPE ALWAYS HITS THE TARGET, BUT IT JUST HURTS!
YOU CAN'T GET AWAY NOW!
HAHA
RYUSHUKO! HURL SOME ROCKS AT THEM!
I CAN'T! THEY'LL HIT SEN, TOO!

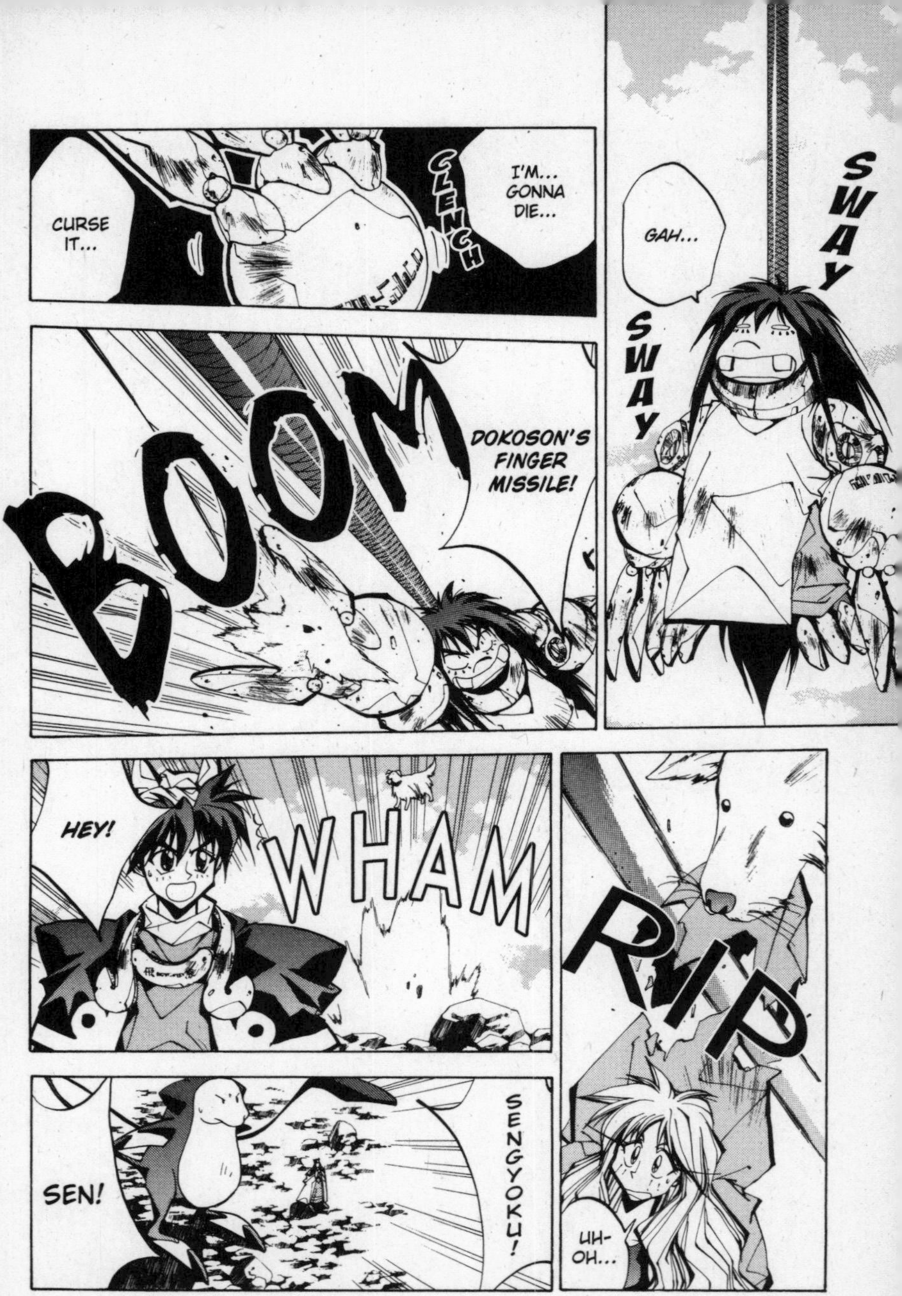
SWAY
GAH...
SWAY
I'M... GONNA DIE...
CLENCH
CURSE IT...
DOKOSON'S FINGER MISSILE!
BOOM
RIP
UH-OH...
WHAM
HEY!
SENGYOKU!
SEN!

READ THIS WAY

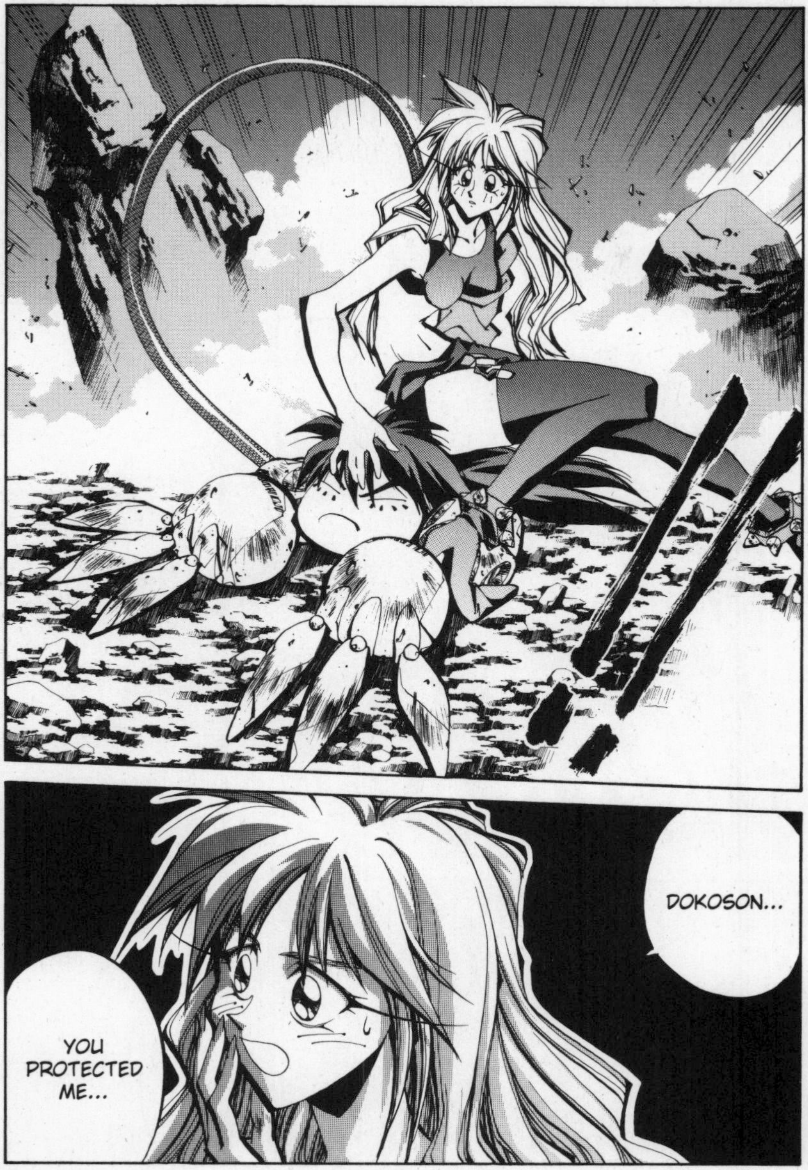
DOKOSON...
YOU PROTECTED ME...

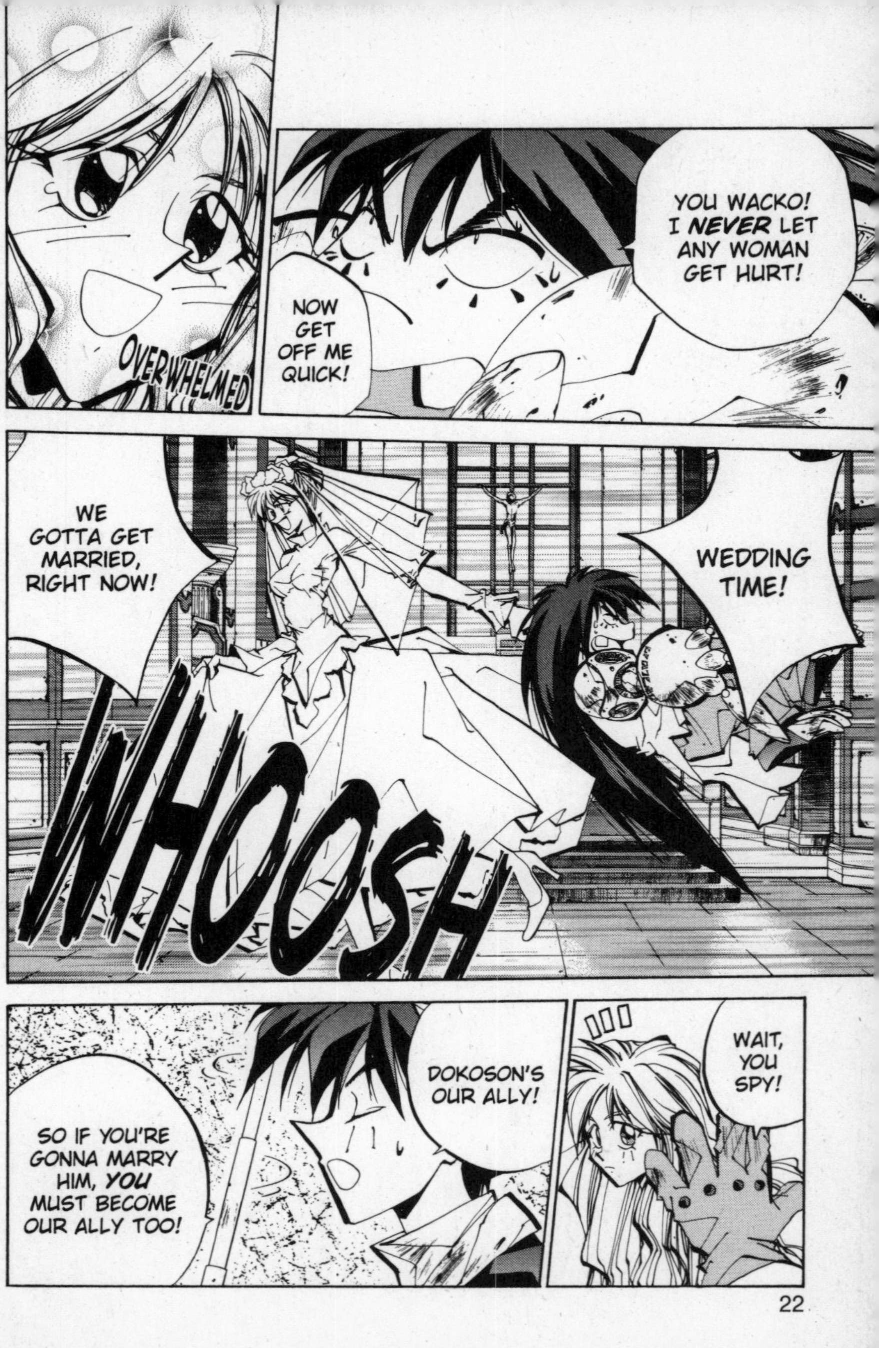
YOU WACKO! I NEVER LET ANY WOMAN GET HURT!
NOW GET OFF ME QUICK!
OVERWHELMED
WEDDING TIME!
WE GOTTA GET MARRIED, RIGHT NOW!
WHOOSH
WAIT, YOU SPY!
DOKOSON'S OUR ALLY!
SO IF YOU'RE GONNA MARRY HIM, YOU MUST BECOME OUR ALLY TOO!

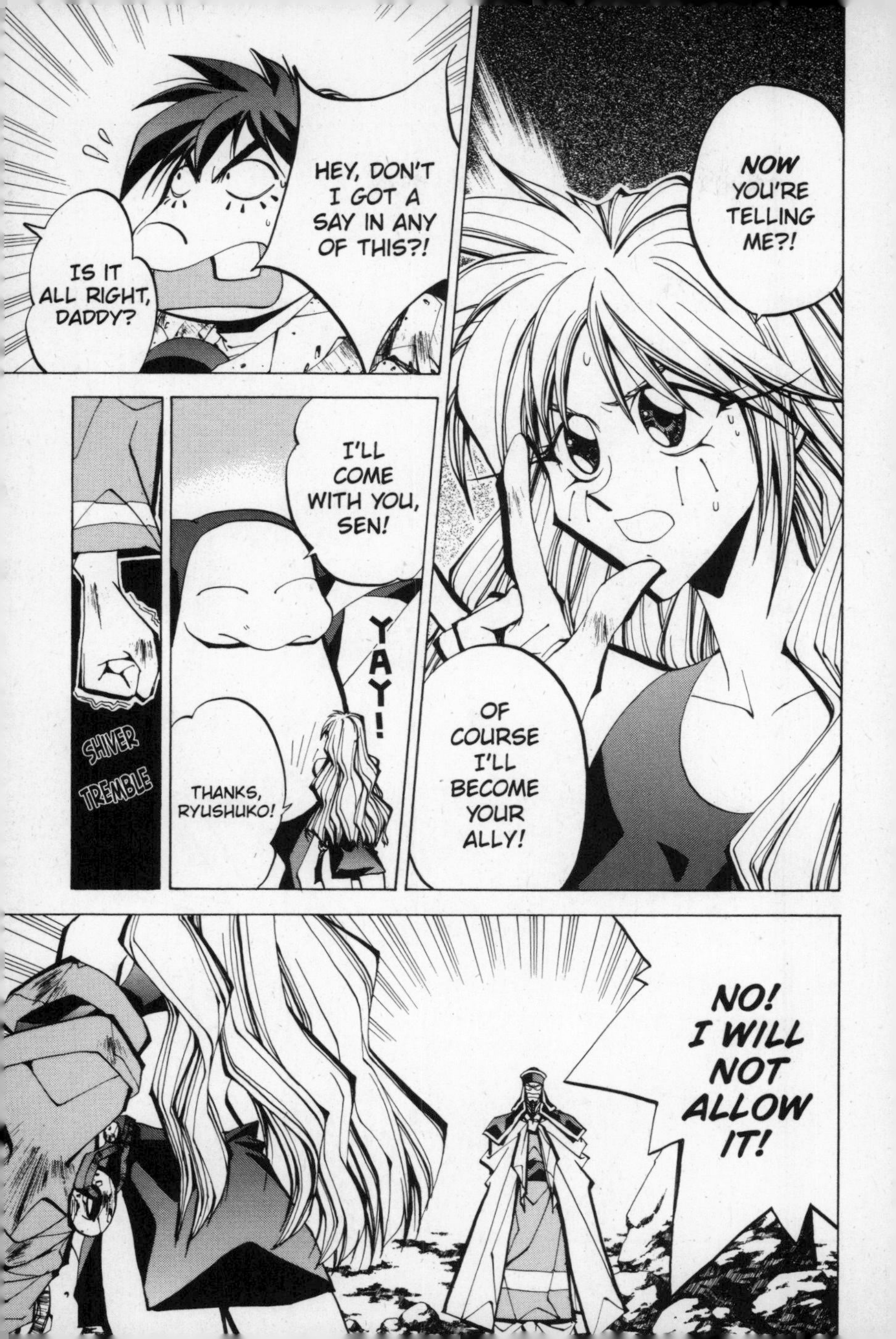
NOW YOU'RE TELLING ME?!
OF COURSE I'LL BECOME YOUR ALLY!
HEY, DON'T I GOT A SAY IN ANY OF THIS?!
IS IT ALL RIGHT, DADDY?
I'LL COME WITH YOU, SEN!
YAY!
THANKS, RYUSHUKO!
SHIVER
TREMBLE
NO! I WILL NOT ALLOW IT!

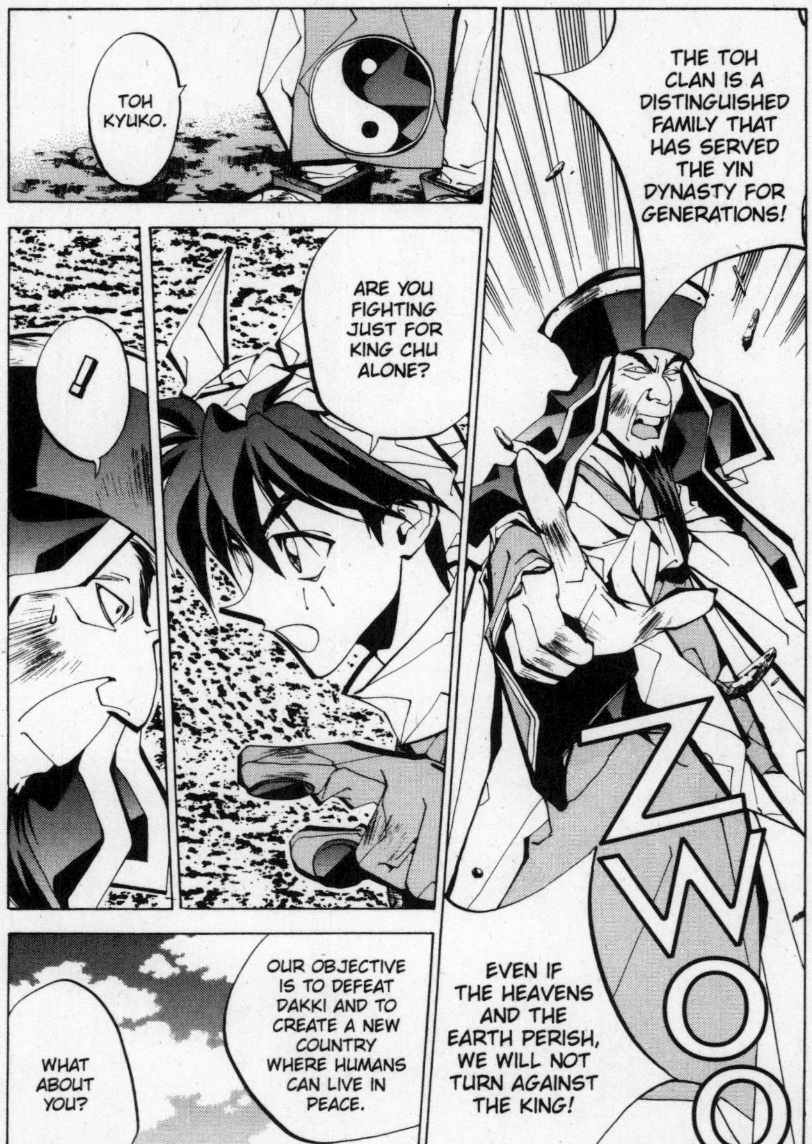
THE TOH CLAN IS A DISTINGUISHED FAMILY THAT HAS SERVED THE YIN DYNASTY FOR GENERATIONS!
EVEN IF THE HEAVENS AND THE EARTH PERISH, WE WILL NOT TURN AGAINST THE KING!
ZWOOO
TOH KYUKO.
ARE YOU FIGHTING JUST FOR KING CHU ALONE?
!
OUR OBJECTIVE IS TO DEFEAT DAKKI AND TO CREATE A NEW COUNTRY WHERE HUMANS CAN LIVE IN PEACE.
WHAT ABOUT YOU?

READ THIS WAY

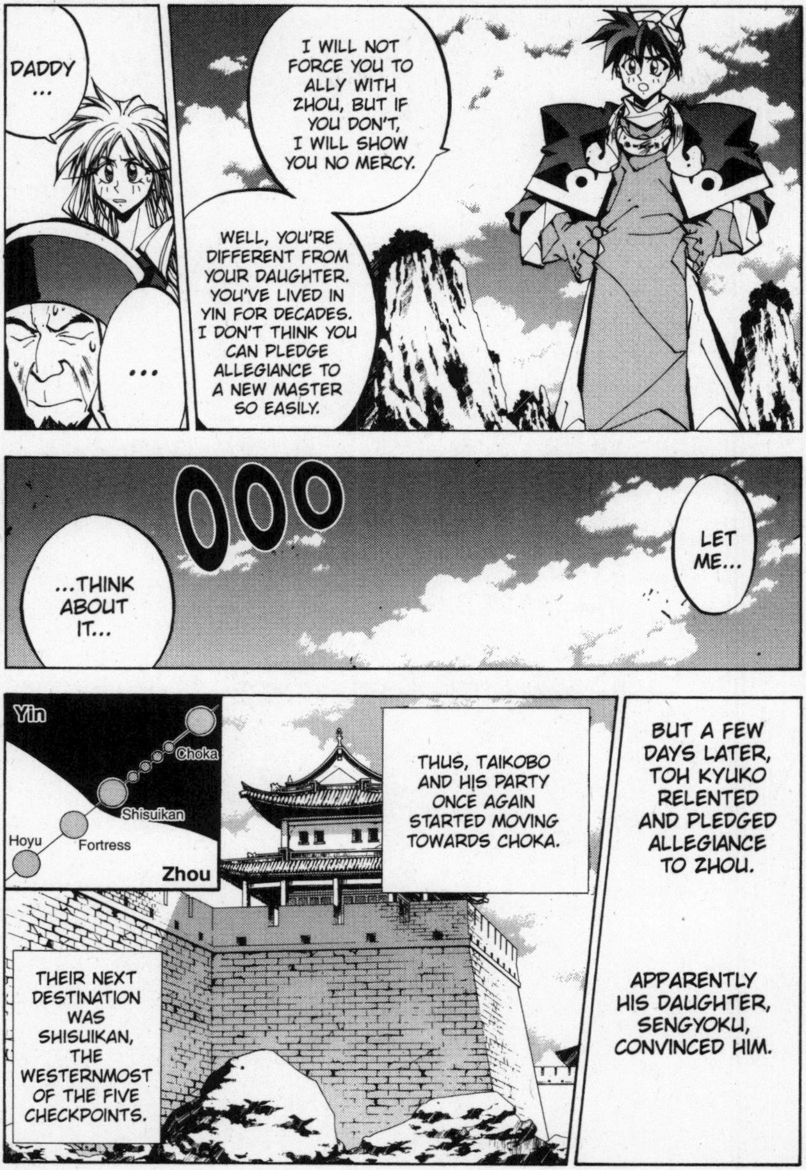
I WILL NOT FORCE YOU TO ALLY WITH ZHOU, BUT IF YOU DON'T, I WILL SHOW YOU NO MERCY.
WELL, YOU'RE DIFFERENT FROM YOUR DAUGHTER. YOU'VE LIVED IN YIN FOR DECADES. I DON'T THINK YOU CAN PLEDGE ALLEGIANCE TO A NEW MASTER SO EASILY.
DADDY ...
...
LET ME...
OOO
...THINK ABOUT IT...
BUT A FEW DAYS LATER, TOH KYUKO RELENTED AND PLEDGED ALLEGIANCE TO ZHOU.
APPARENTLY HIS DAUGHTER, SENGYOKU, CONVINCED HIM.
THUS, TAIKOBO AND HIS PARTY ONCE AGAIN STARTED MOVING TOWARDS CHOKA.
Yin
Choka
Shisuikan
Hoyu
Fortress
Zhou
THEIR NEXT DESTINATION WAS SHISUIKAN, THE WESTERNMOST OF THE FIVE CHECKPOINTS.

封神演義

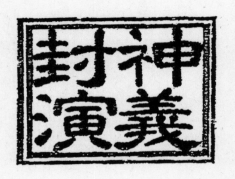

Chapter 71

THE LONELY WARRIOR

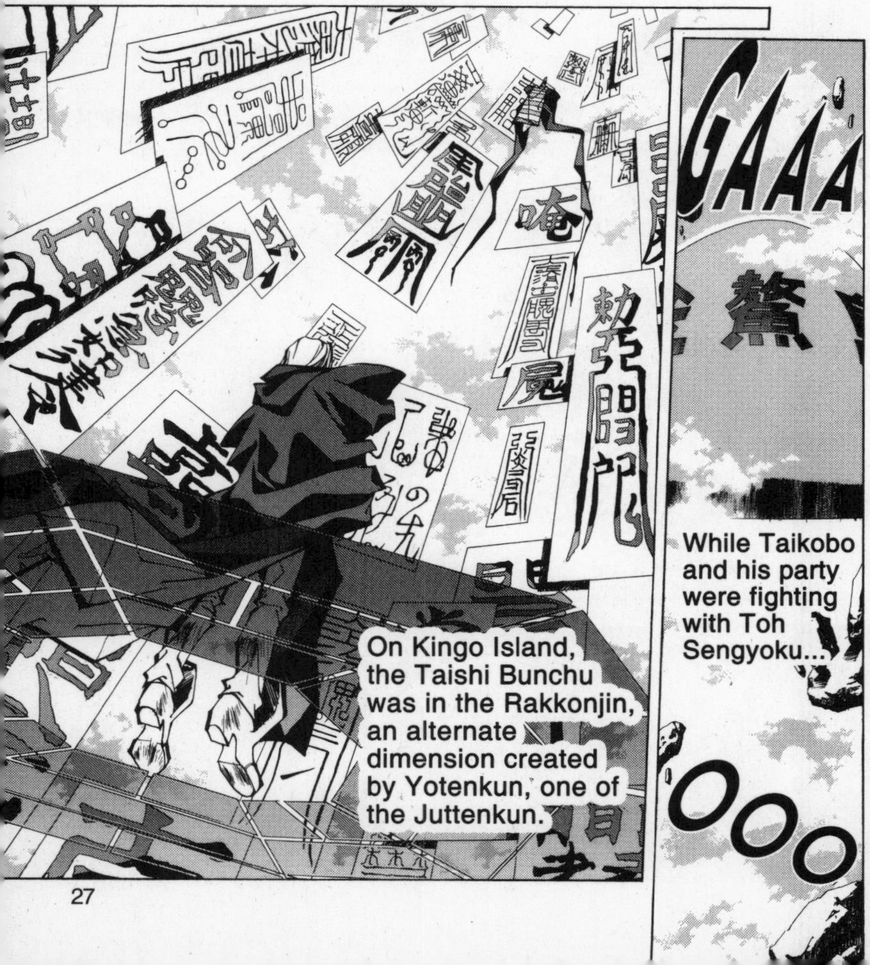
GAAAOOO
While Taikobo and his party were fighting with Toh Sengyoku...
On Kingo Island, the Taishi Bunchu was in the Rakkonjin, an alternate dimension created by Yotenkun, one of the Juttenkun.

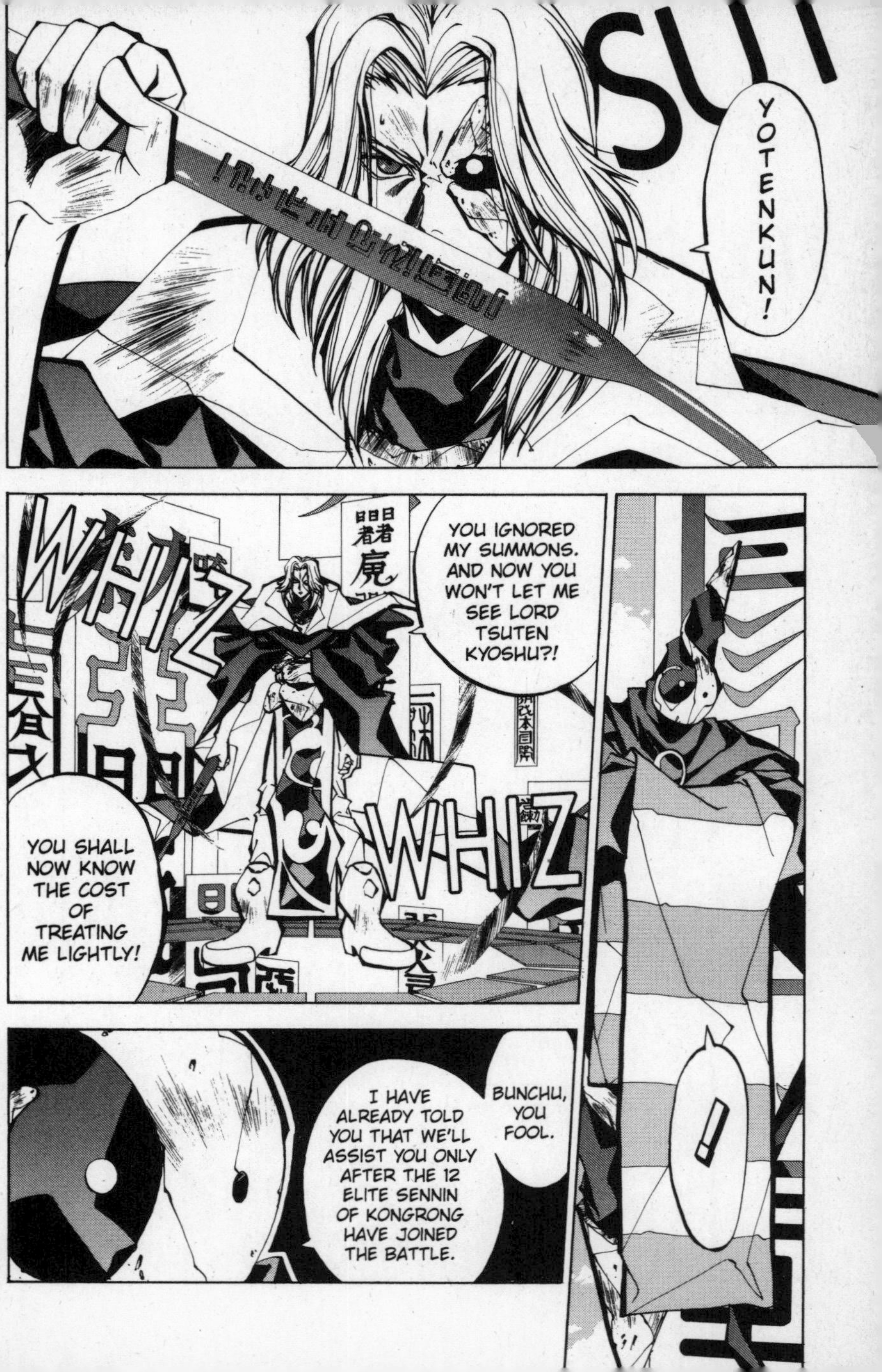
SUI
YOTENKUN!
!
WHIZ
YOU IGNORED MY SUMMONS. AND NOW YOU WON'T LET ME SEE LORD TSUTEN KYOSHU?!
WHIZ
YOU SHALL NOW KNOW THE COST OF TREATING ME LIGHTLY!
BUNCHU, YOU FOOL.
I HAVE ALREADY TOLD YOU THAT WE'LL ASSIST YOU ONLY AFTER THE 12 ELITE SENNIN OF KONGRONG HAVE JOINED THE BATTLE.

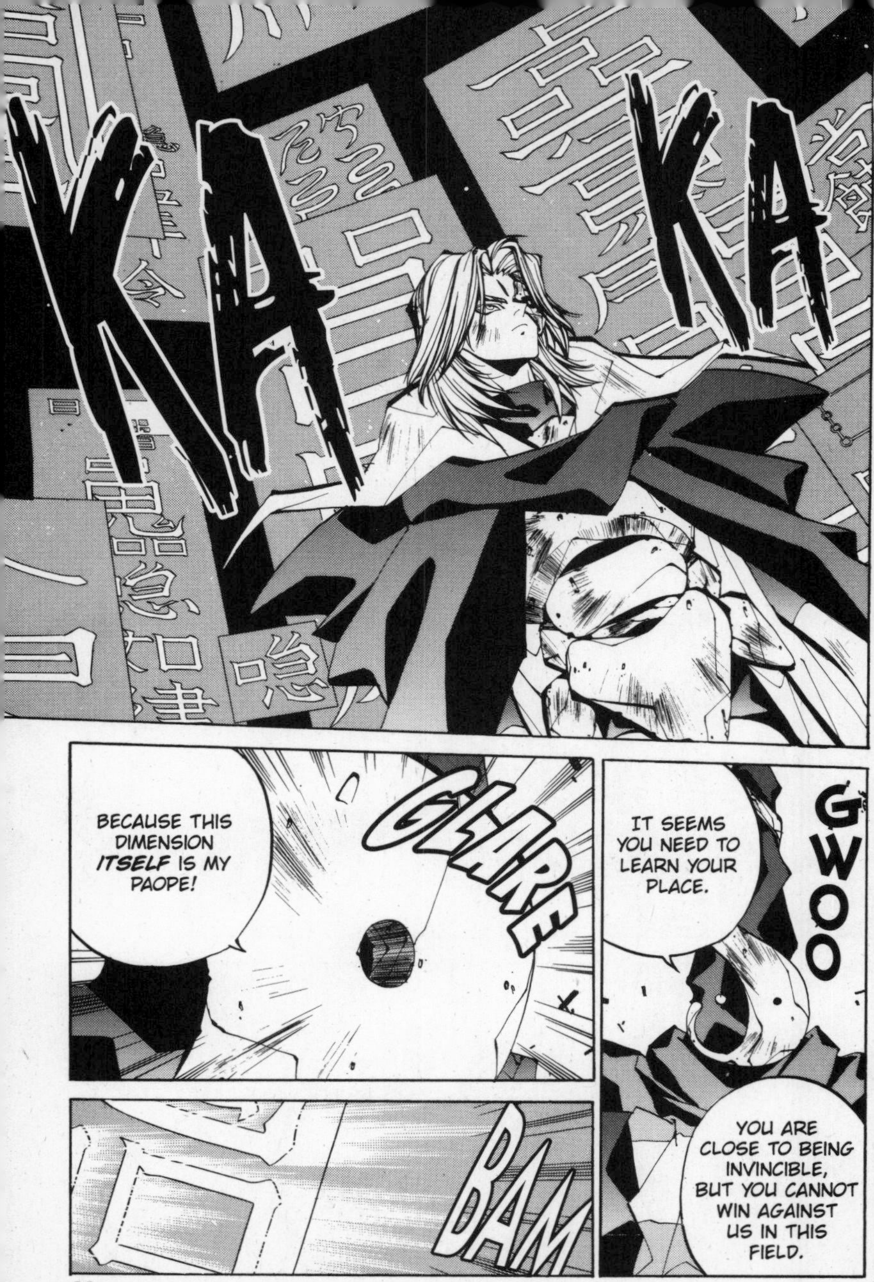
KA
KA
IT SEEMS YOU NEED TO LEARN YOUR PLACE.
GWOO
YOU ARE CLOSE TO BEING INVINCIBLE, BUT YOU CANNOT WIN AGAINST US IN THIS FIELD.
BECAUSE THIS DIMENSION *ITSELF* IS MY PAOPE!
GLARE
BAM

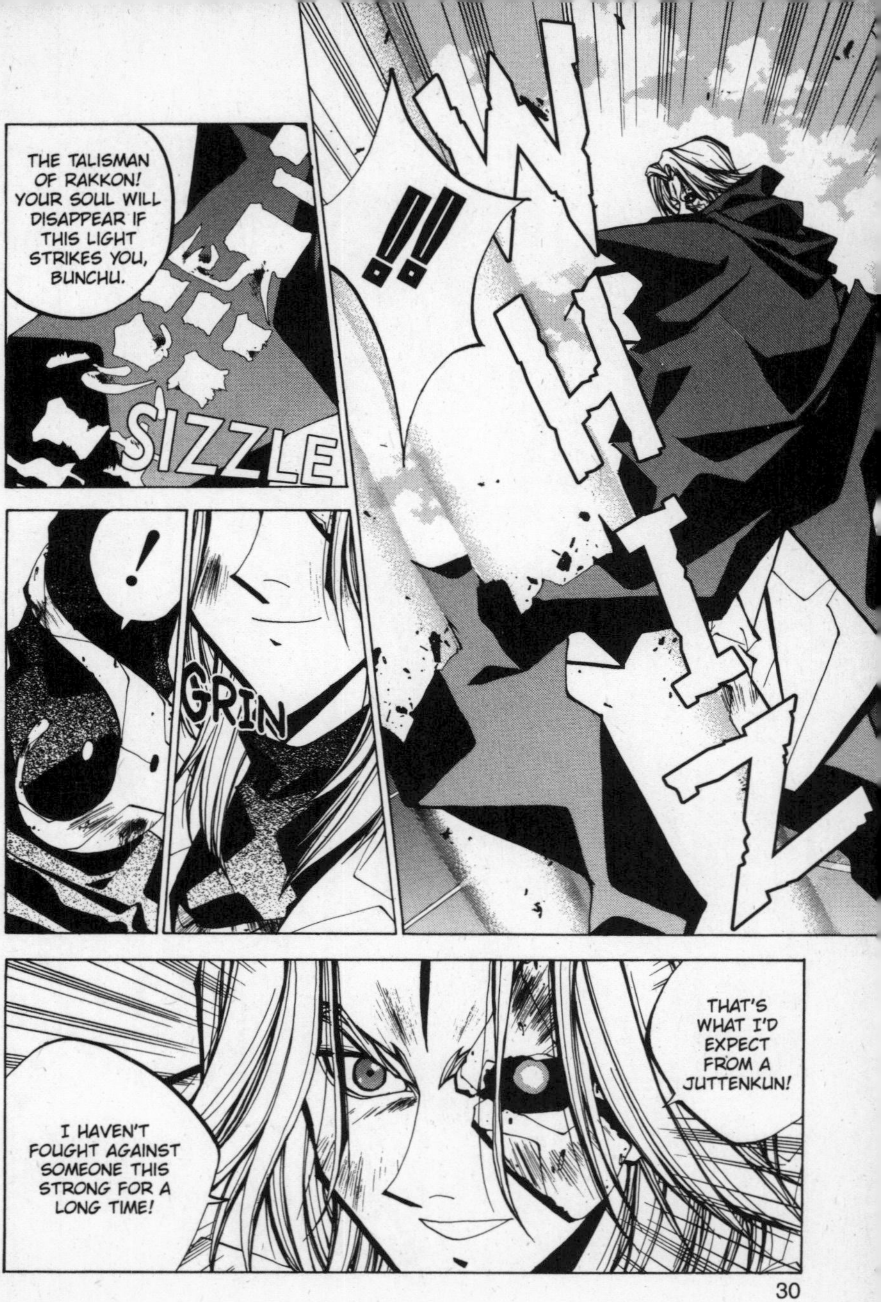
WHIZ
!!
THE TALISMAN OF RAKKON! YOUR SOUL WILL DISAPPEAR IF THIS LIGHT STRIKES YOU, BUNCHU.
SIZZLE
GRIN
!
THAT'S WHAT I'D EXPECT FROM A JUTTENKUN!
I HAVEN'T FOUGHT AGAINST SOMEONE THIS STRONG FOR A LONG TIME!

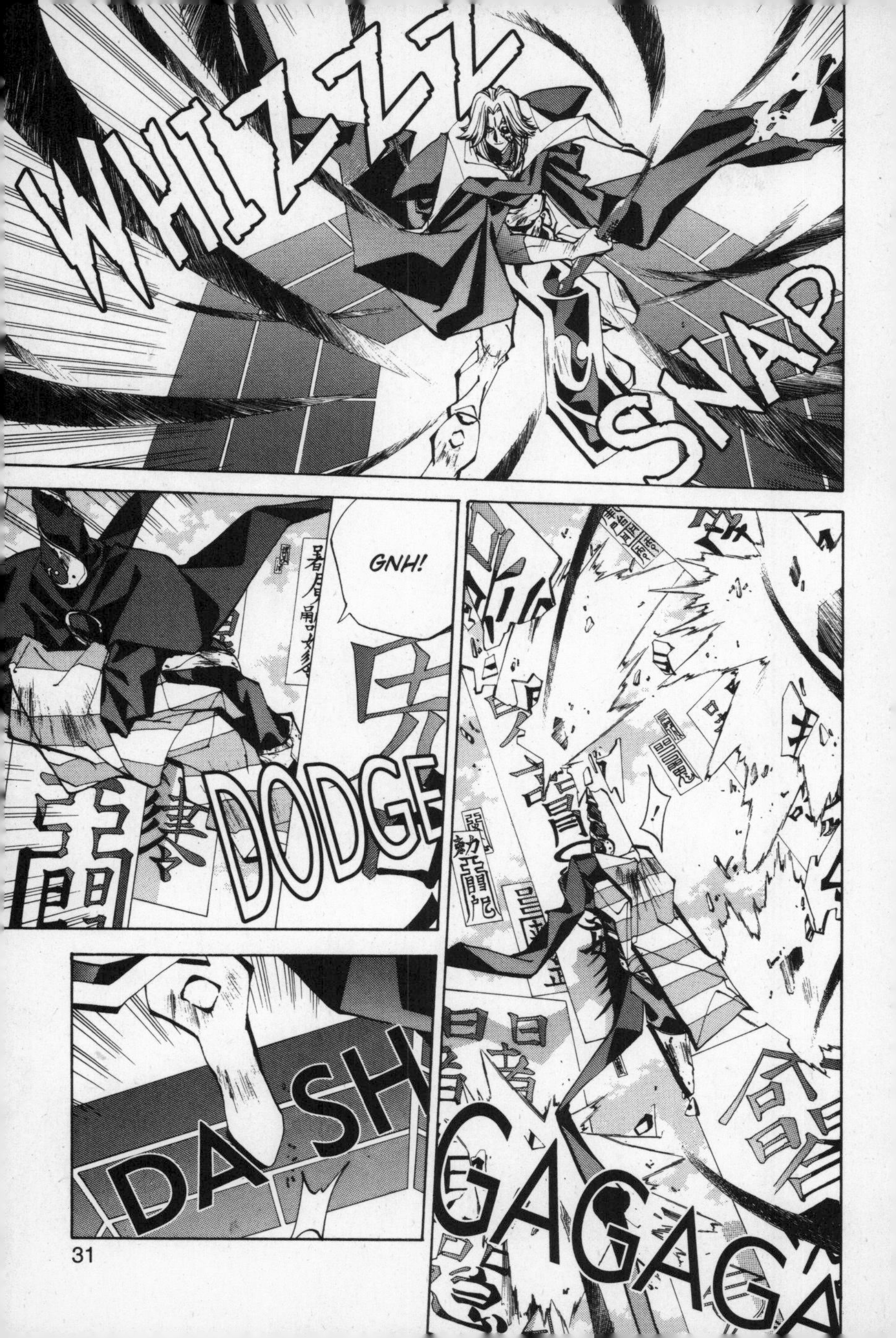
WHIZZZZ
SNAP
GAGAGA
GNH!
DODGE
DASH

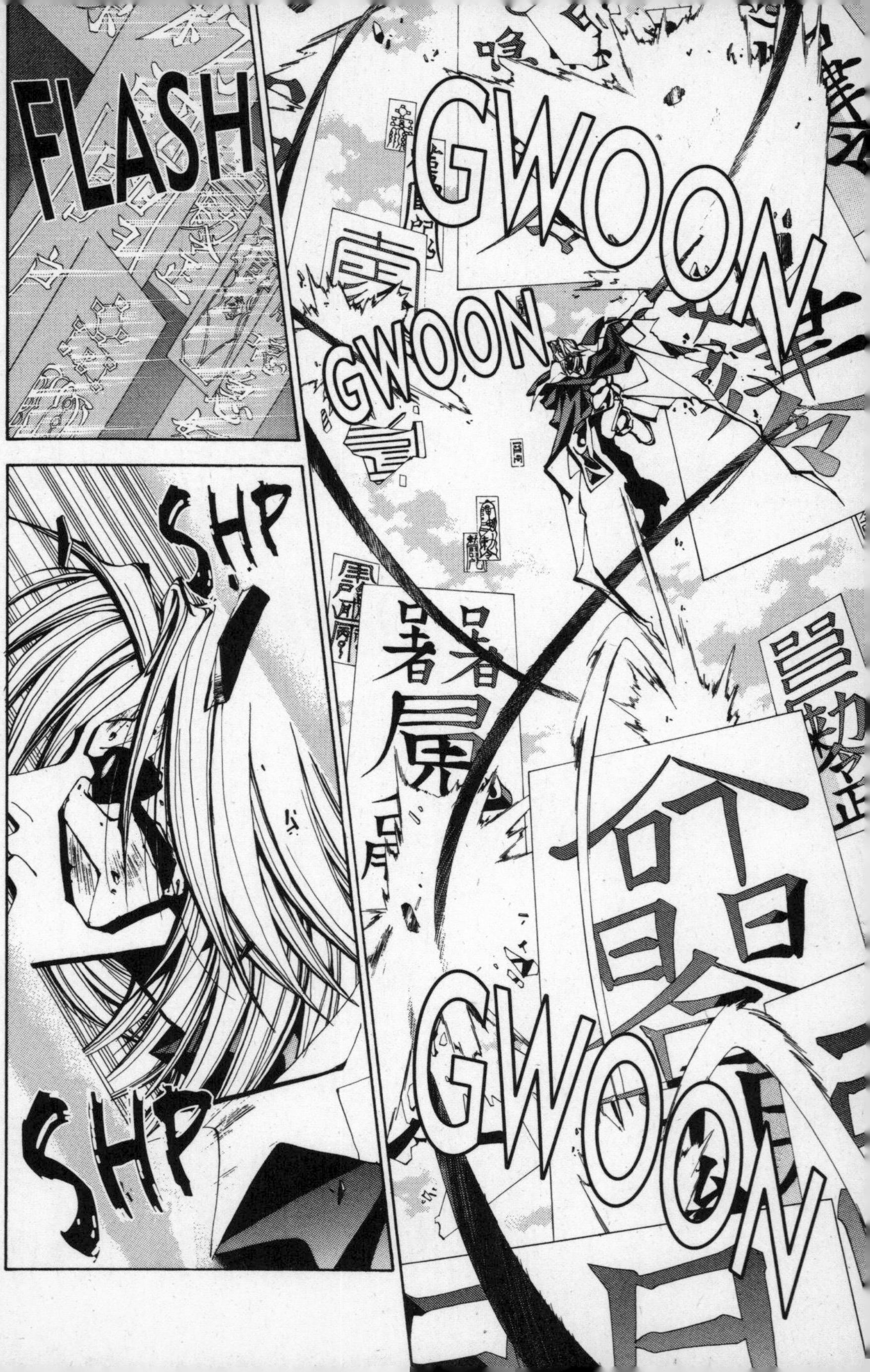
GWOON
GWOON
GWOON
FLASH
SHP
SHP

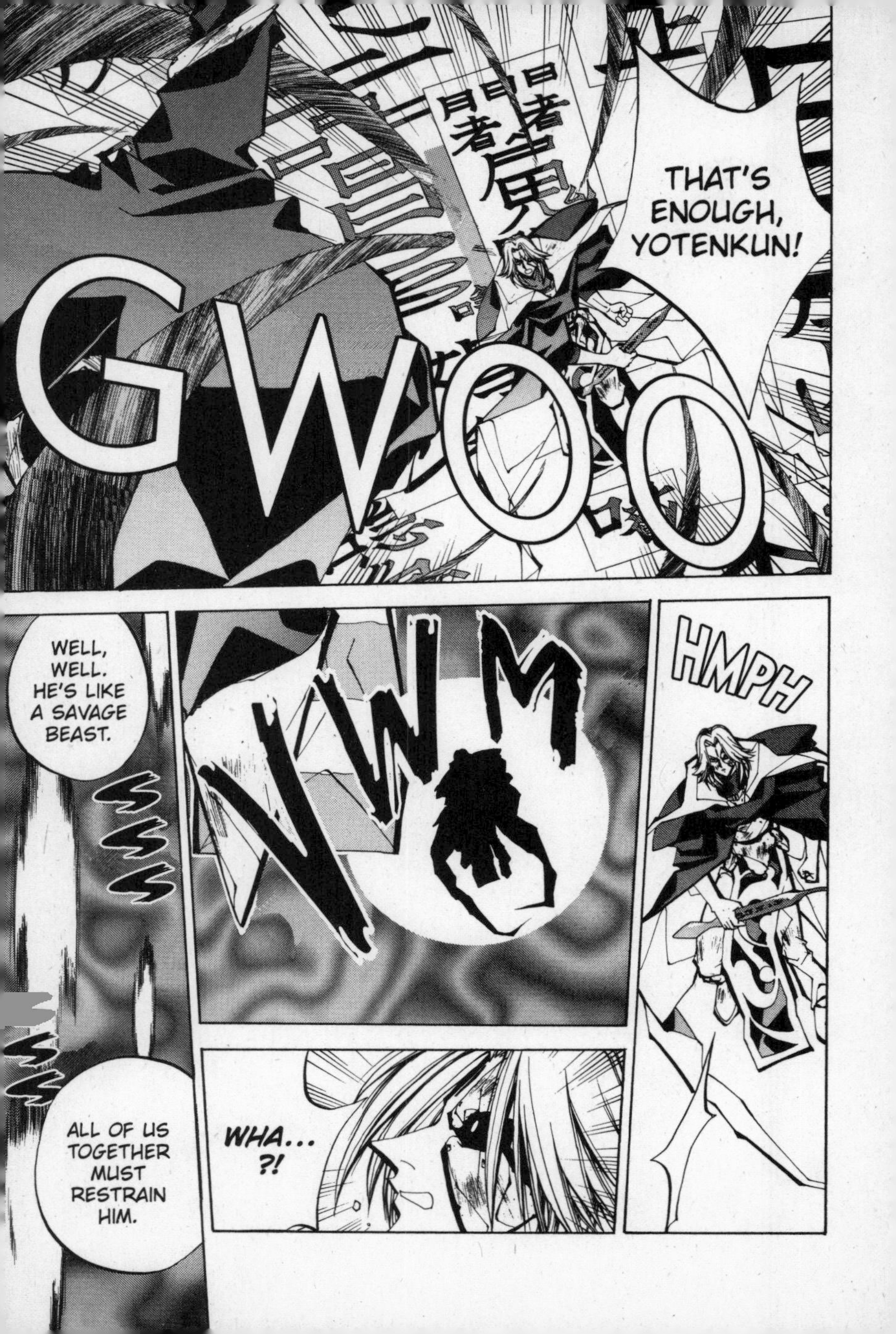
THAT'S ENOUGH, YOTENKUN!
GWOOO
HMPH
VWM
WELL, WELL. HE'S LIKE A SAVAGE BEAST.
SSS
WHA... ?!
ALL OF US TOGETHER MUST RESTRAIN HIM.

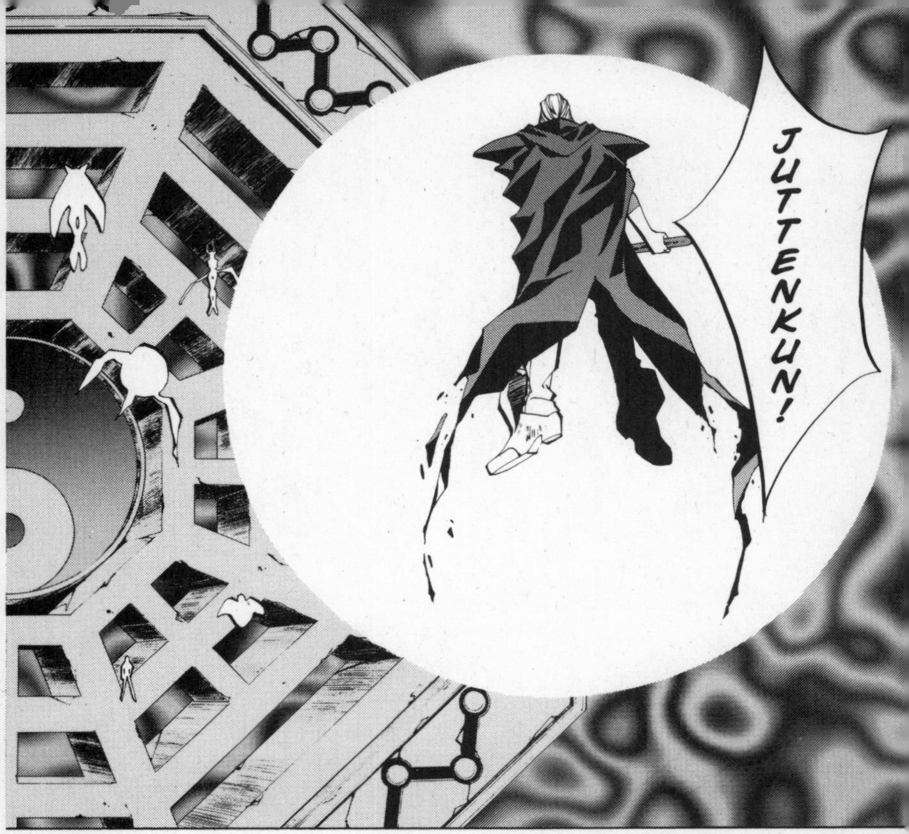
JUTTENKUN!

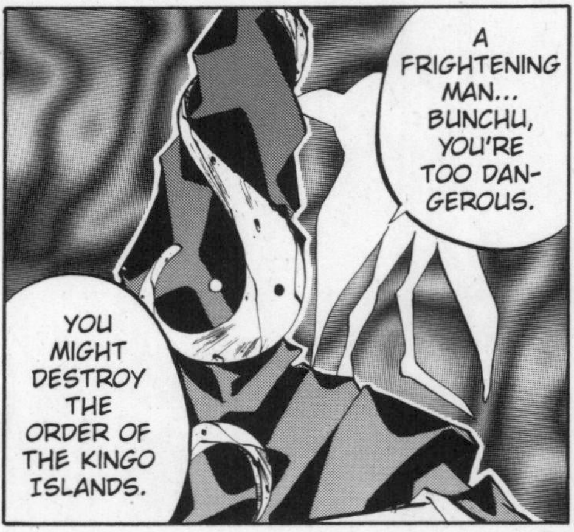
A FRIGHTENING MAN... BUNCHU, YOU'RE TOO DAN-GEROUS.
YOU MIGHT DESTROY THE ORDER OF THE KINGO ISLANDS.

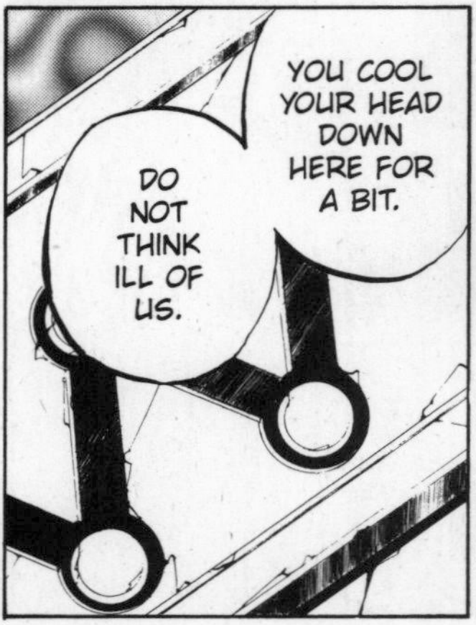
YOU COOL YOUR HEAD DOWN HERE FOR A BIT.
DO NOT THINK ILL OF US.

READ THIS WAY

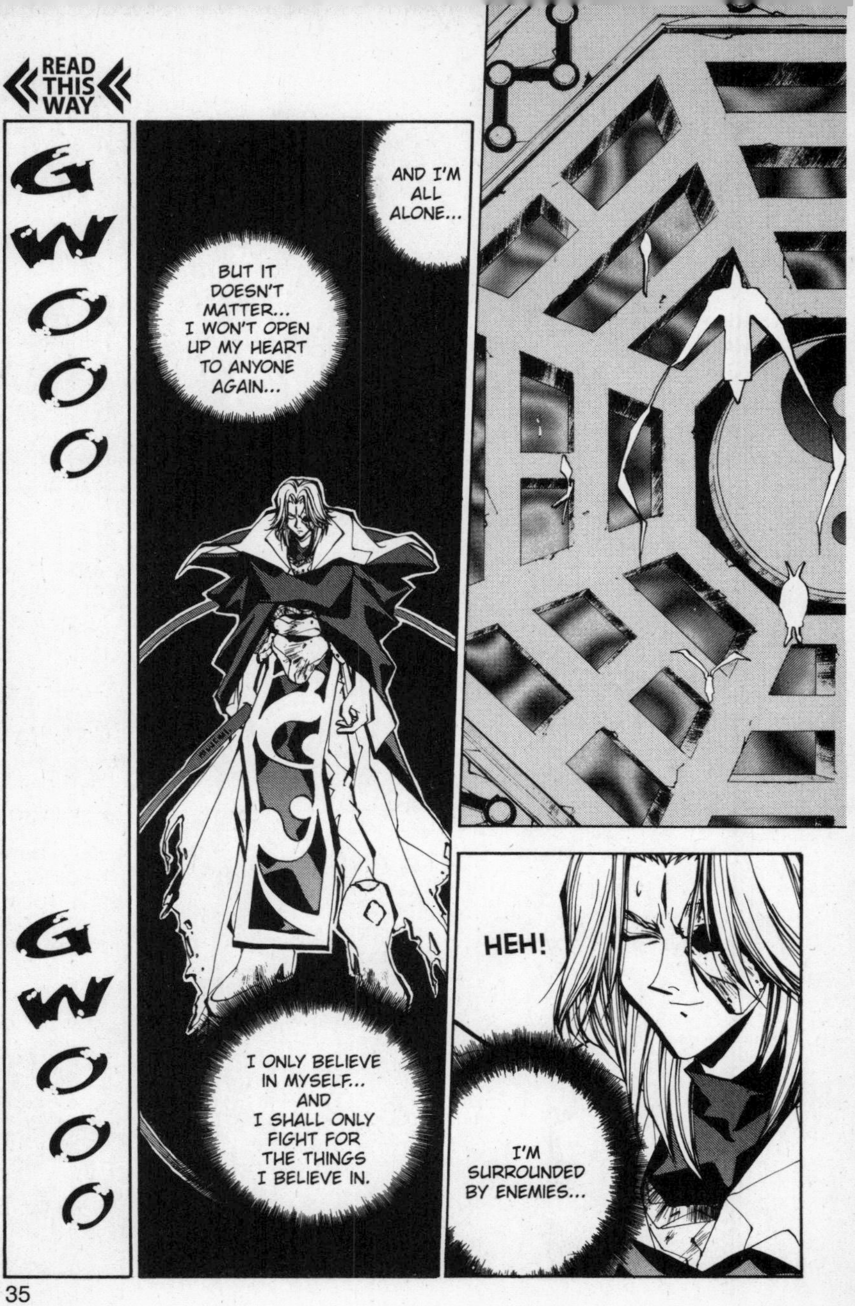

HEH!
I'M SURROUNDED BY ENEMIES...
AND I'M ALL ALONE...
BUT IT DOESN'T MATTER... I WON'T OPEN UP MY HEART TO ANYONE AGAIN...
I ONLY BELIEVE IN MYSELF... AND I SHALL ONLY FIGHT FOR THE THINGS I BELIEVE IN.
GWOOO
GWOOO

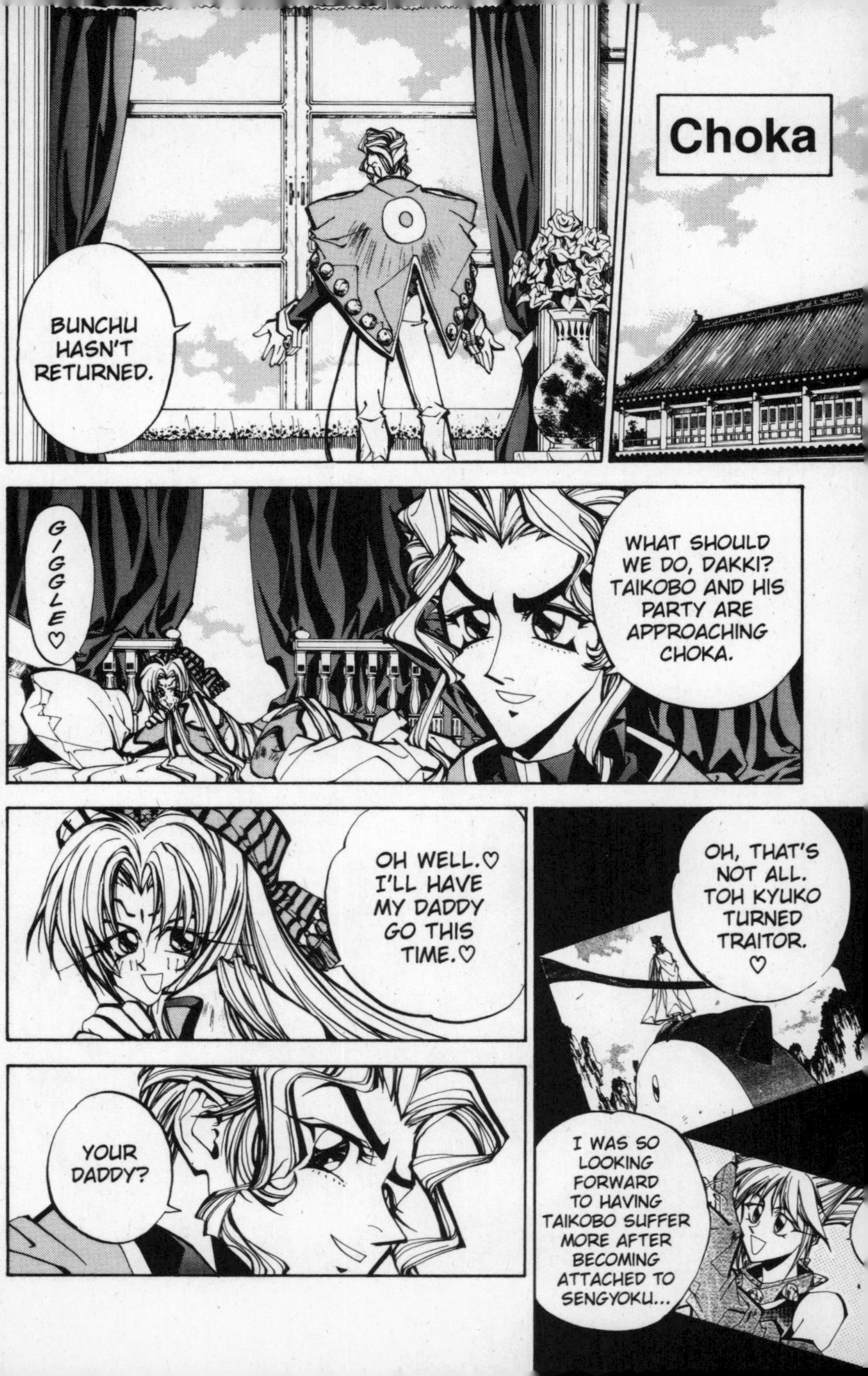
Choka
BUNCHU HASN'T RETURNED.
WHAT SHOULD WE DO, DAKKI? TAIKOBO AND HIS PARTY ARE APPROACHING CHOKA.
GIGGLE♡
OH, THAT'S NOT ALL. TOH KYUKO TURNED TRAITOR. ♡
I WAS SO LOOKING FORWARD TO HAVING TAIKOBO SUFFER MORE AFTER BECOMING ATTACHED TO SENGYOKU...
OH WELL.♡ I'LL HAVE MY DADDY GO THIS TIME.♡
YOUR DADDY?

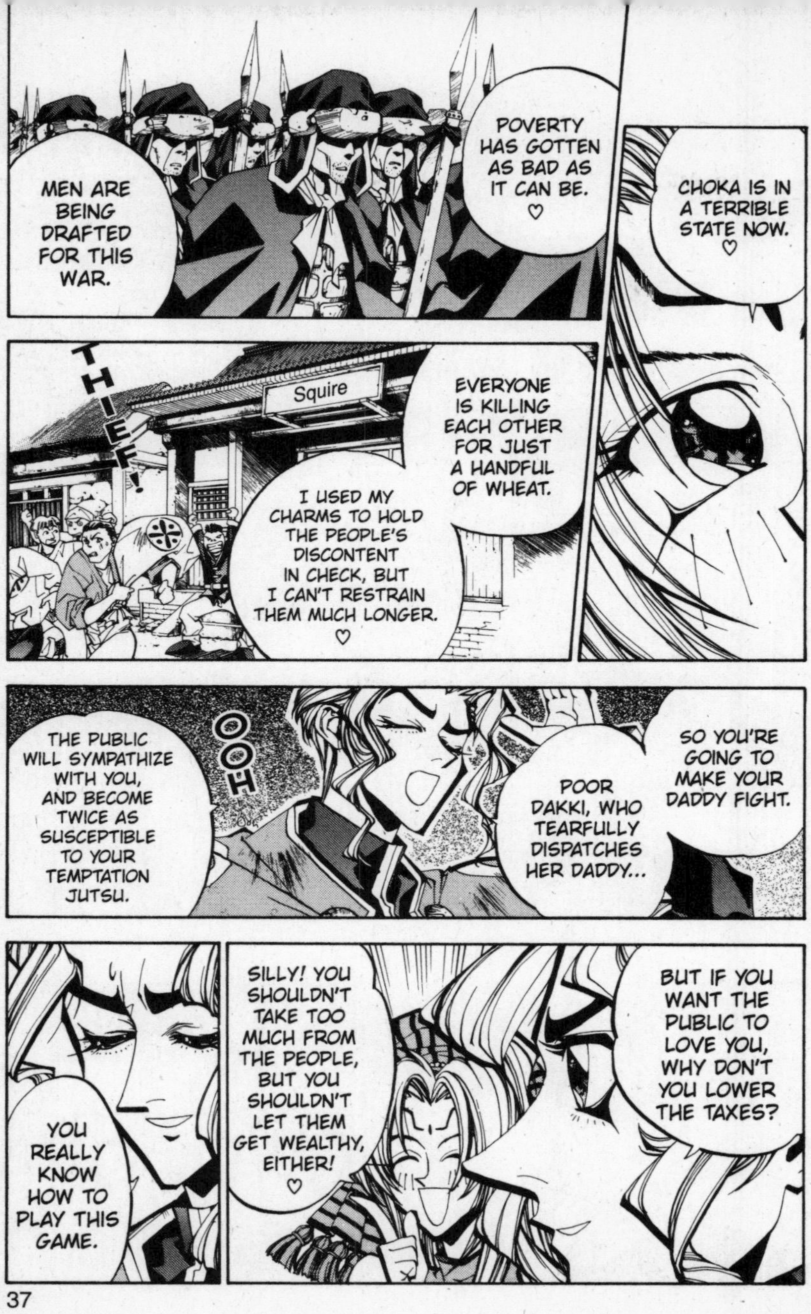
CHOKA IS IN A TERRIBLE STATE NOW. ♡
POVERTY HAS GOTTEN AS BAD AS IT CAN BE. ♡
MEN ARE BEING DRAFTED FOR THIS WAR.
EVERYONE IS KILLING EACH OTHER FOR JUST A HANDFUL OF WHEAT.
I USED MY CHARMS TO HOLD THE PEOPLE'S DISCONTENT IN CHECK, BUT I CAN'T RESTRAIN THEM MUCH LONGER. ♡
Squire
THIEF!
SO YOU'RE GOING TO MAKE YOUR DADDY FIGHT.
POOR DAKKI, WHO TEARFULLY DISPATCHES HER DADDY...
OOOH
THE PUBLIC WILL SYMPATHIZE WITH YOU, AND BECOME TWICE AS SUSCEPTIBLE TO YOUR TEMPTATION JUTSU.
BUT IF YOU WANT THE PUBLIC TO LOVE YOU, WHY DON'T YOU LOWER THE TAXES?
SILLY! YOU SHOULDN'T TAKE TOO MUCH FROM THE PEOPLE, BUT YOU SHOULDN'T LET THEM GET WEALTHY, EITHER! ♡
YOU REALLY KNOW HOW TO PLAY THIS GAME.

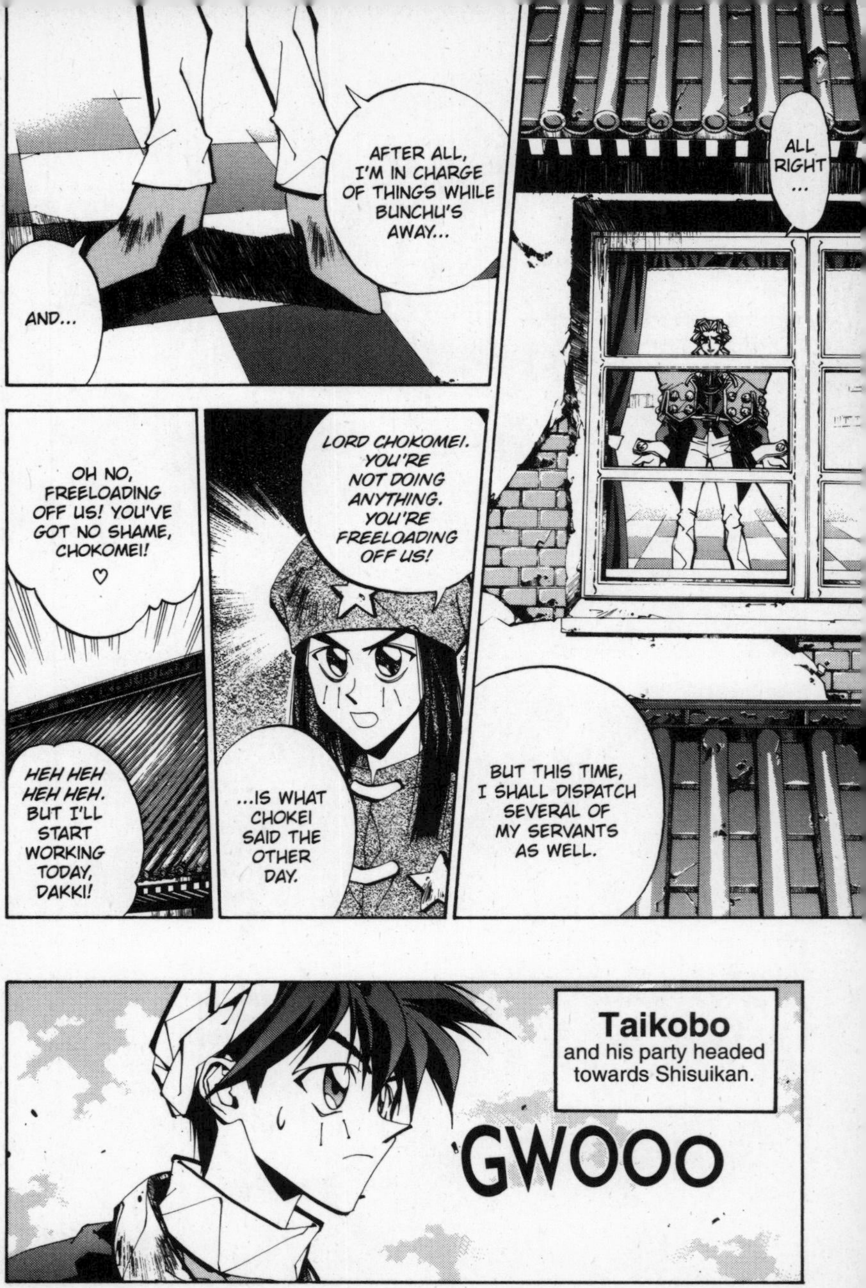
ALL RIGHT ...
BUT THIS TIME, I SHALL DISPATCH SEVERAL OF MY SERVANTS AS WELL.
AFTER ALL, I'M IN CHARGE OF THINGS WHILE BUNCHU'S AWAY...
AND...
LORD CHOKOMEI. YOU'RE NOT DOING ANYTHING. YOU'RE FREELOADING OFF US!
...IS WHAT CHOKEI SAID THE OTHER DAY.
OH NO, FREELOADING OFF US! YOU'VE GOT NO SHAME, CHOKOMEI! ♡
HEH HEH HEH HEH. BUT I'LL START WORKING TODAY, DAKKI!
Taikobo and his party headed towards Shisuikan.
GWOOO

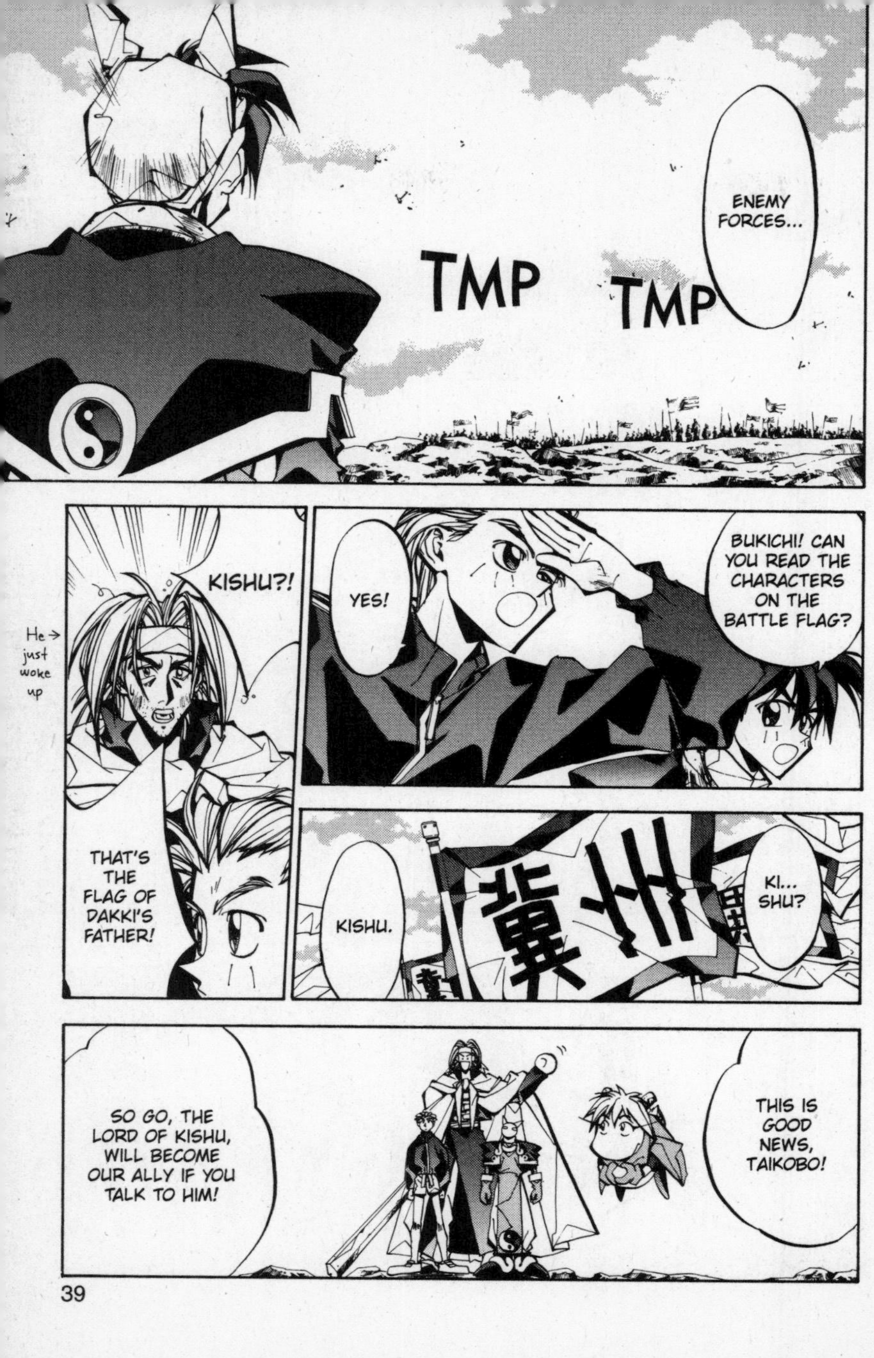
ENEMY FORCES...
TMP
TMP
BUKICHI! CAN YOU READ THE CHARACTERS ON THE BATTLE FLAG?
YES!
KI... SHU?
冀州
KISHU.
KISHU?!
He just woke up
THAT'S THE FLAG OF DAKKI'S FATHER!
THIS IS GOOD NEWS, TAIKOBO!
SO GO, THE LORD OF KISHU, WILL BECOME OUR ALLY IF YOU TALK TO HIM!

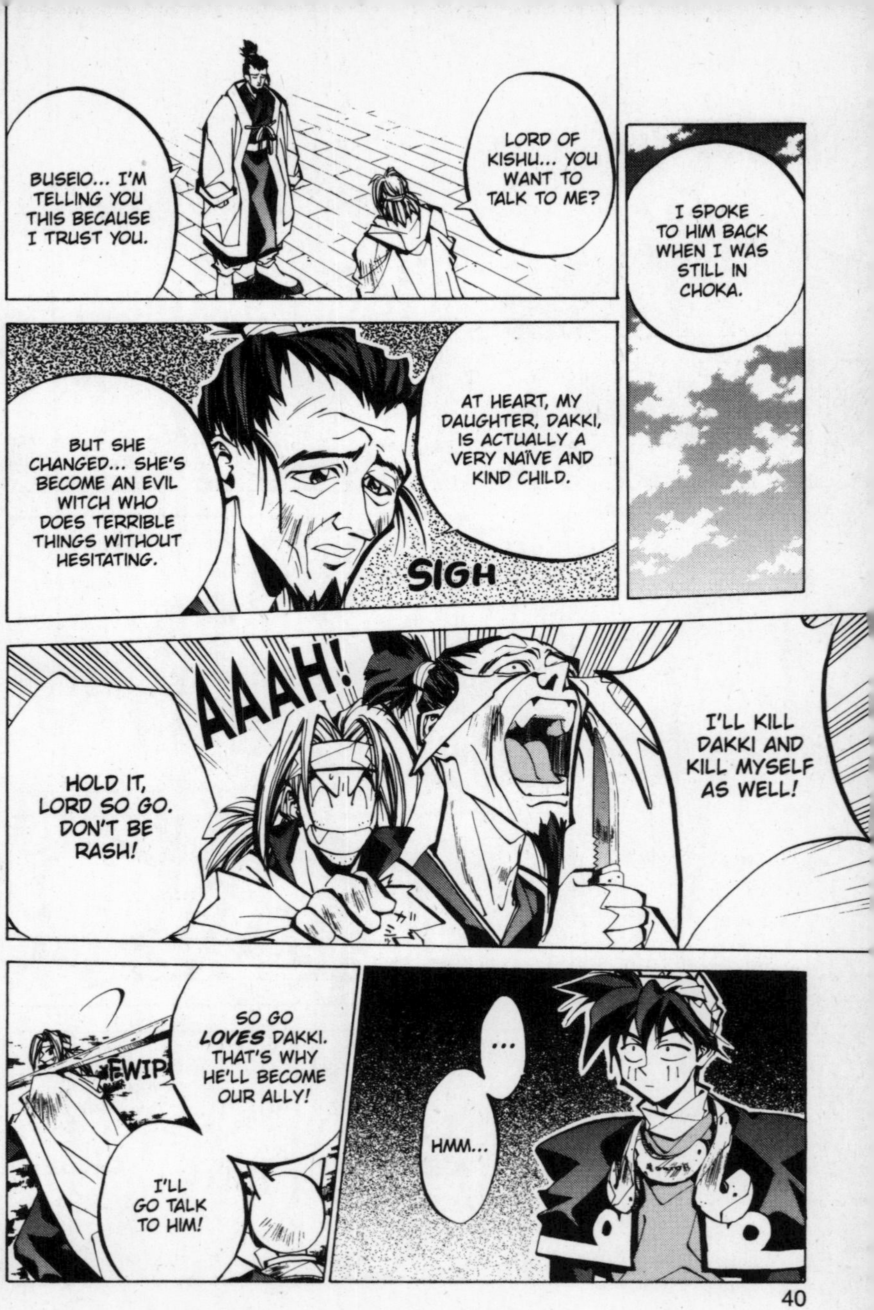
I SPOKE TO HIM BACK WHEN I WAS STILL IN CHOKA.
LORD OF KISHU... YOU WANT TO TALK TO ME?
BUSEIO... I'M TELLING YOU THIS BECAUSE I TRUST YOU.
AT HEART, MY DAUGHTER, DAKKI, IS ACTUALLY A VERY NAÏVE AND KIND CHILD.
SIGH
BUT SHE CHANGED... SHE'S BECOME AN EVIL WITCH WHO DOES TERRIBLE THINGS WITHOUT HESITATING.
I'LL KILL DAKKI AND KILL MYSELF AS WELL!
AAAH!
HOLD IT, LORD SO GO. DON'T BE RASH!
...
HMM...
SO GO *LOVES* DAKKI. THAT'S WHY HE'LL BECOME OUR ALLY!
FWIP
I'LL GO TALK TO HIM!

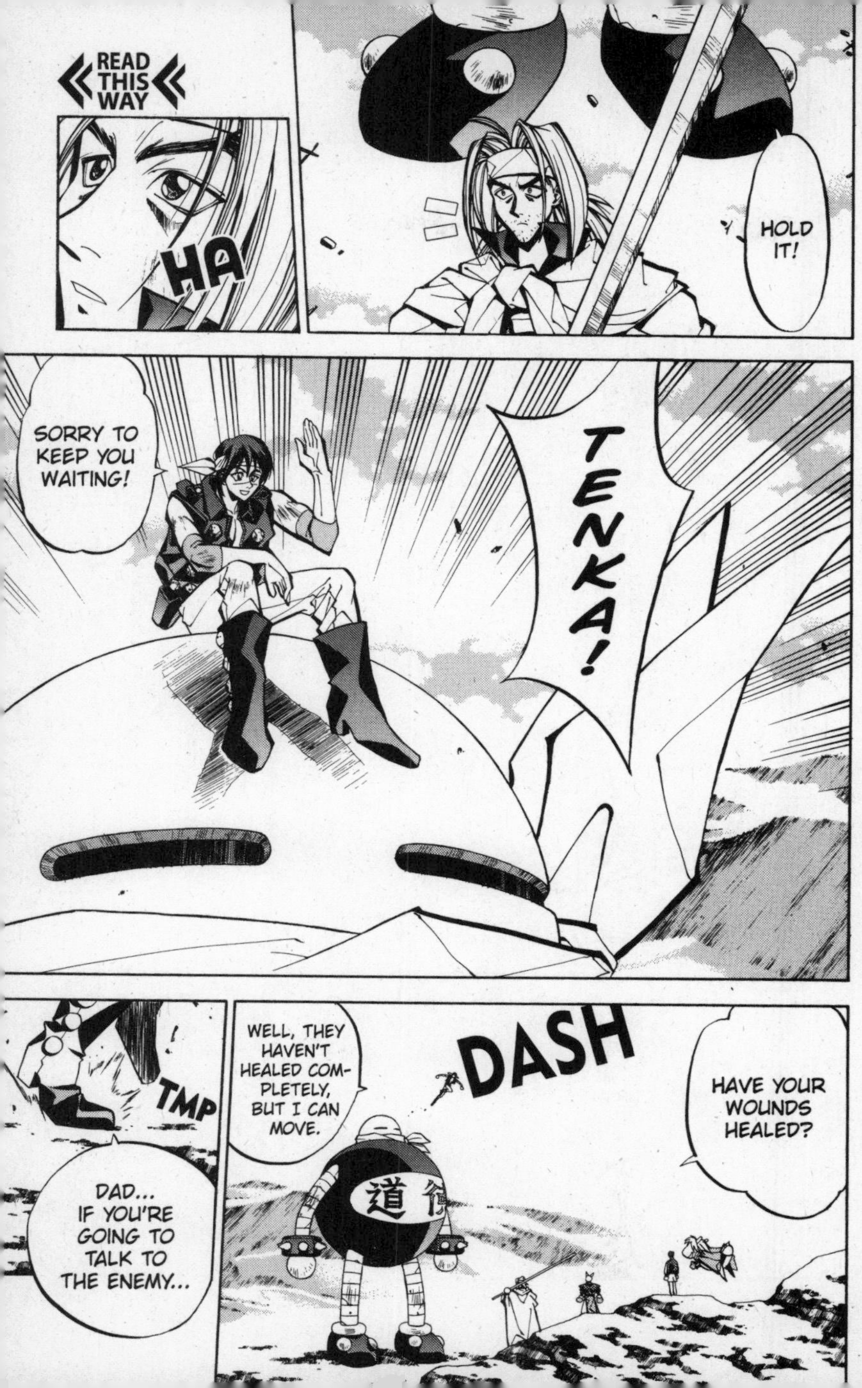
READ THIS WAY
HOLD IT!
HA
TENKA!
SORRY TO KEEP YOU WAITING!
HAVE YOUR WOUNDS HEALED?
DASH
WELL, THEY HAVEN'T HEALED COM-PLETELY, BUT I CAN MOVE.
TMP
DAD... IF YOU'RE GOING TO TALK TO THE ENEMY...

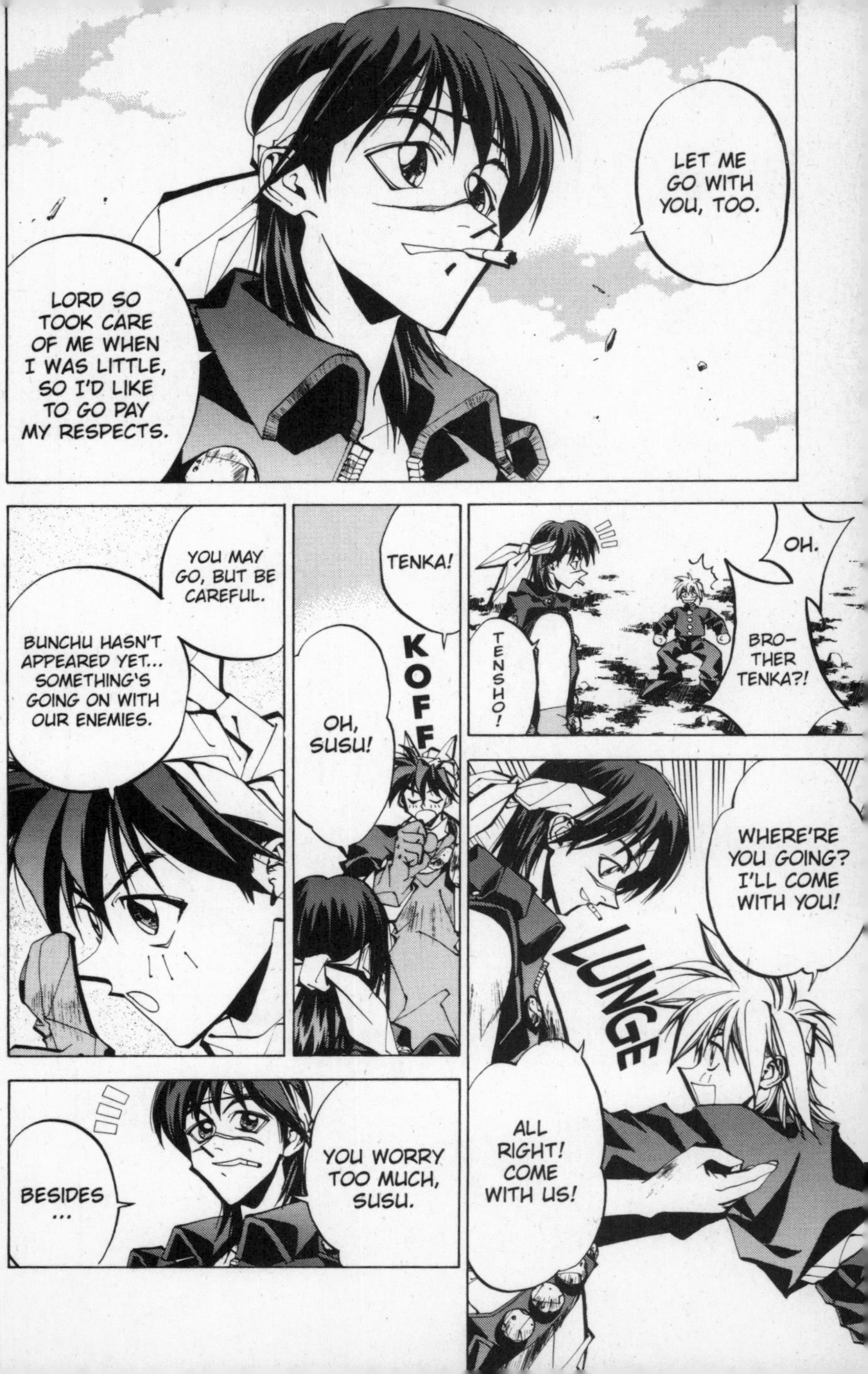
LET ME GO WITH YOU, TOO.
LORD SO TOOK CARE OF ME WHEN I WAS LITTLE, SO I'D LIKE TO GO PAY MY RESPECTS.
TENKA!
KOFF
OH, SUSU!
YOU MAY GO, BUT BE CAREFUL.
BUNCHU HASN'T APPEARED YET... SOMETHING'S GOING ON WITH OUR ENEMIES.
YOU WORRY TOO MUCH, SUSU.
BESIDES ...
OH.
BRO- THER TENKA?!
TENSHO!
WHERE'RE YOU GOING? I'LL COME WITH YOU!
LUNGE
ALL RIGHT! COME WITH US!

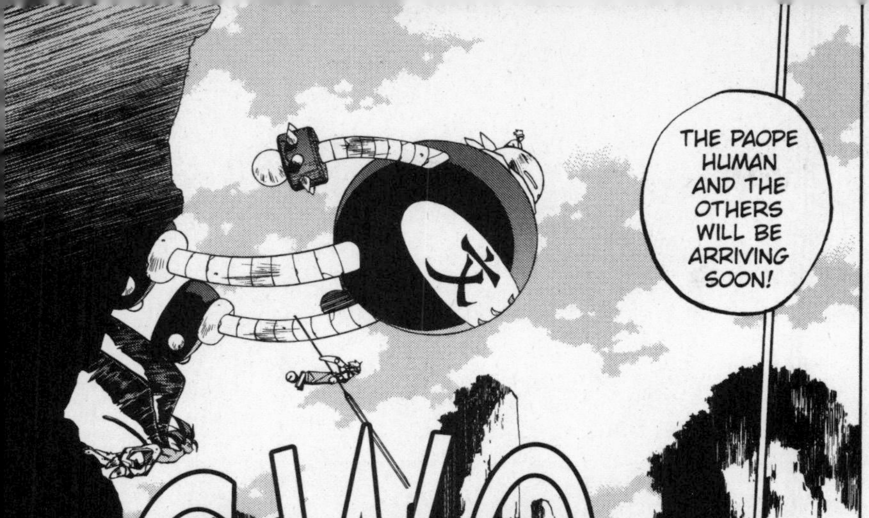
THE PAOPE HUMAN AND THE OTHERS WILL BE ARRIVING SOON!
GWOOOO
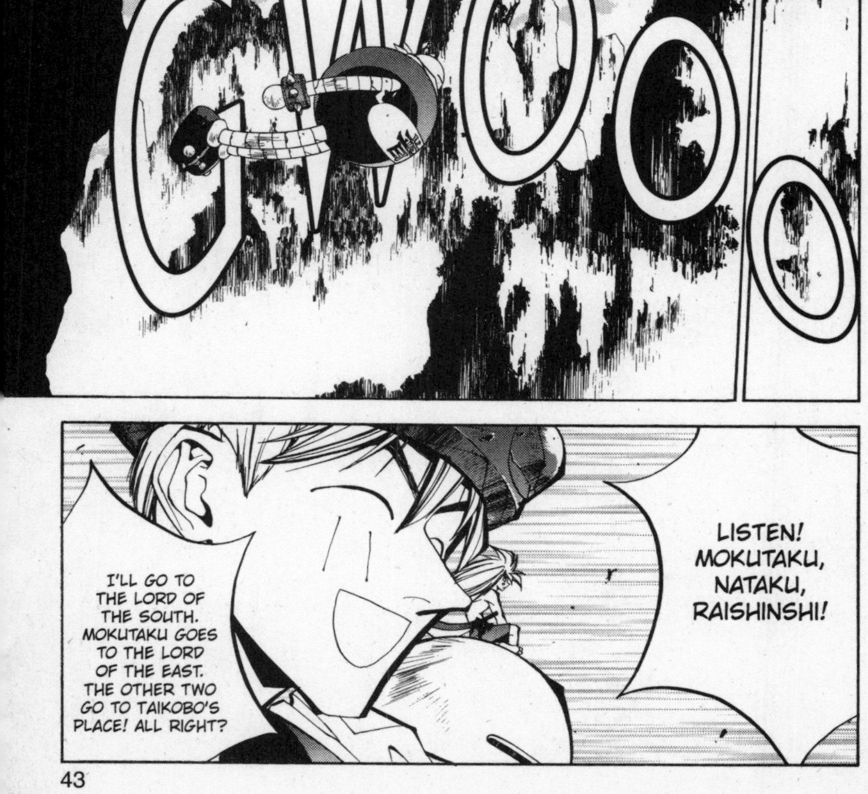
LISTEN! MOKUTAKU, NATAKU, RAISHINSHI!
I'LL GO TO THE LORD OF THE SOUTH. MOKUTAKU GOES TO THE LORD OF THE EAST. THE OTHER TWO GO TO TAIKOBO'S PLACE! ALL RIGHT?

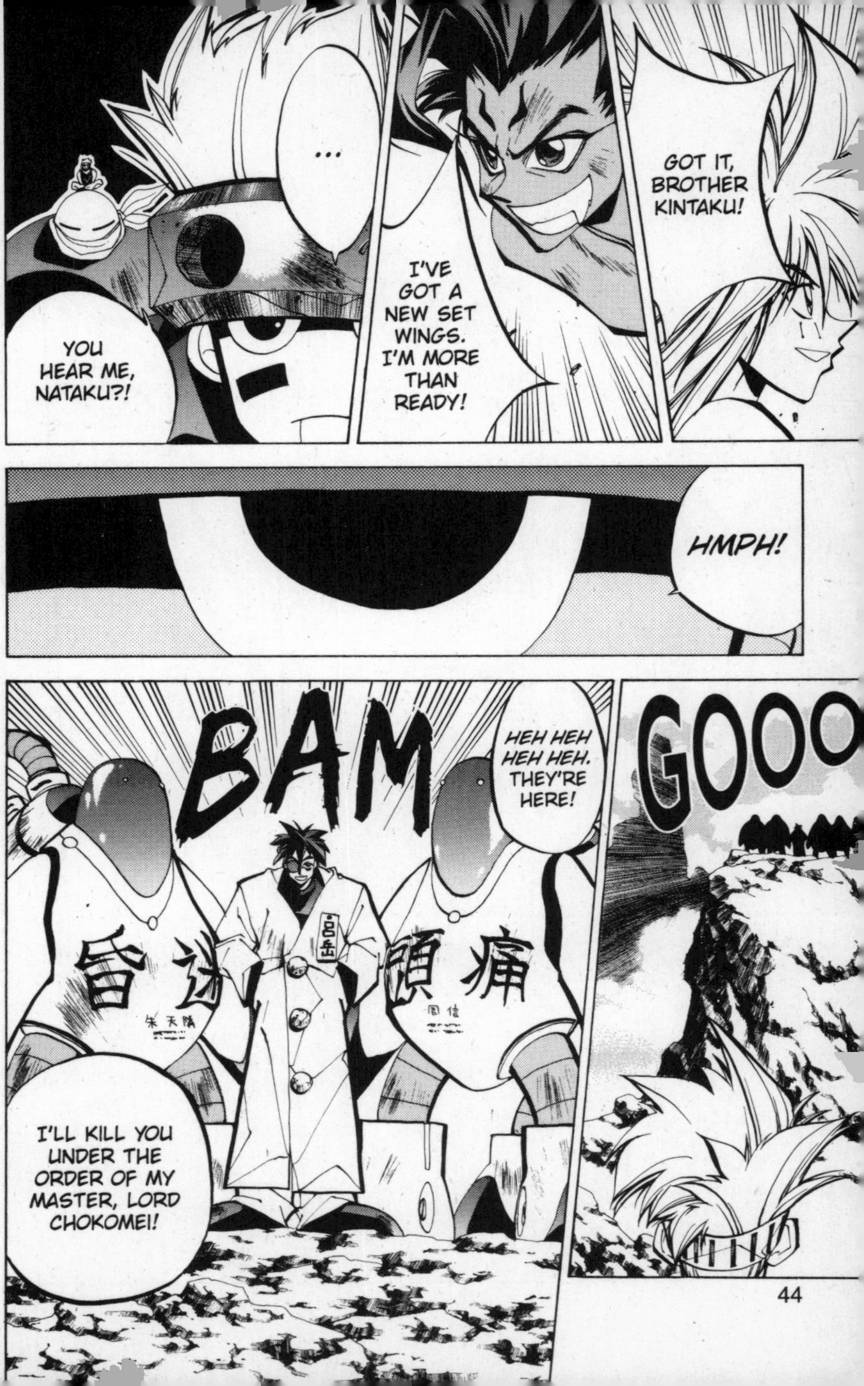
GOT IT, BROTHER KINTAKU!
I'VE GOT A NEW SET WINGS. I'M MORE THAN READY!
...
YOU HEAR ME, NATAKU?!
HMPH!
GOOO
HEH HEH HEH HEH. THEY'RE HERE!
BAM
頭痛
昏迷
I'LL KILL YOU UNDER THE ORDER OF MY MASTER, LORD CHOKOMEI!

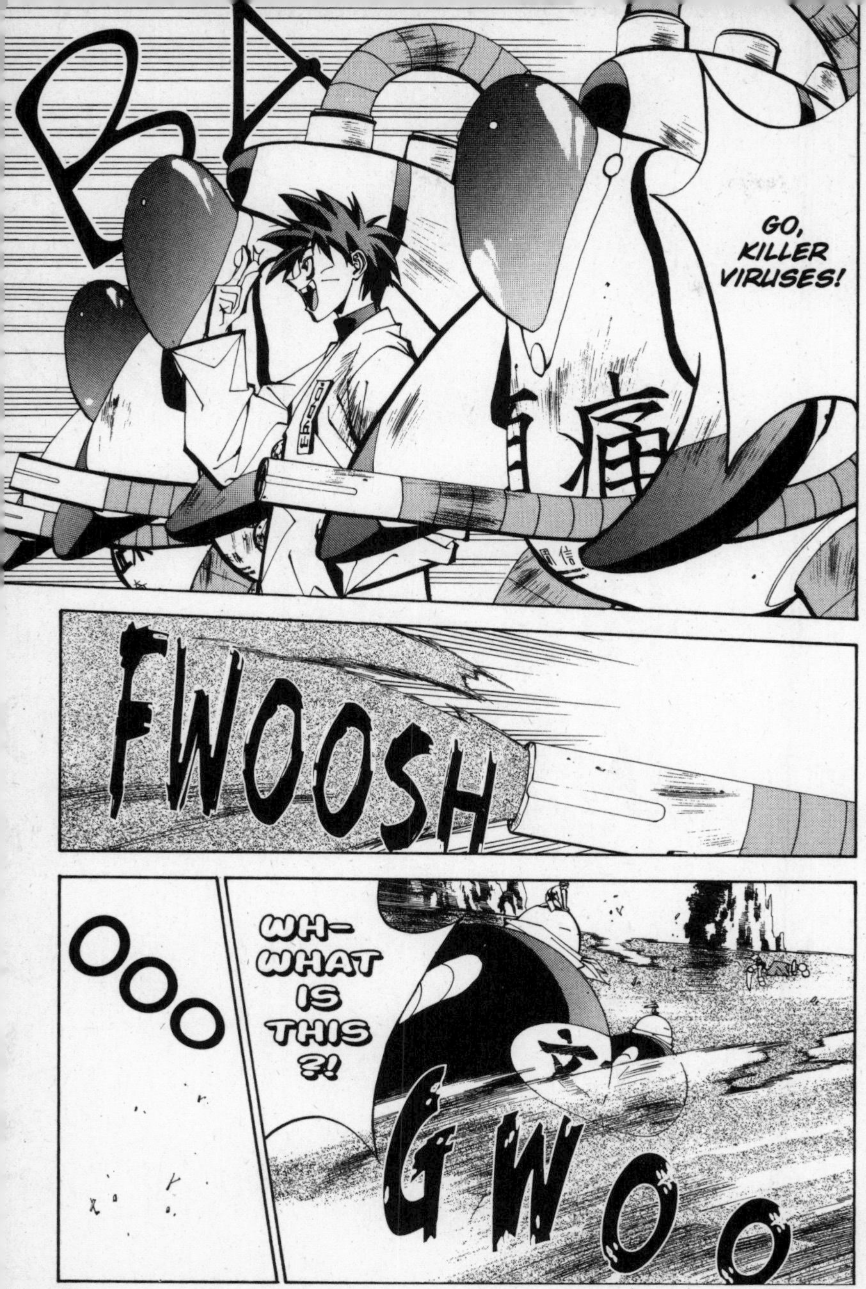
GO, KILLER VIRUSES!
BAM
FWOOSH
WH-WHAT IS THIS?!
GWOOO
OOO

封神演義

Chapter 72

VIRUS

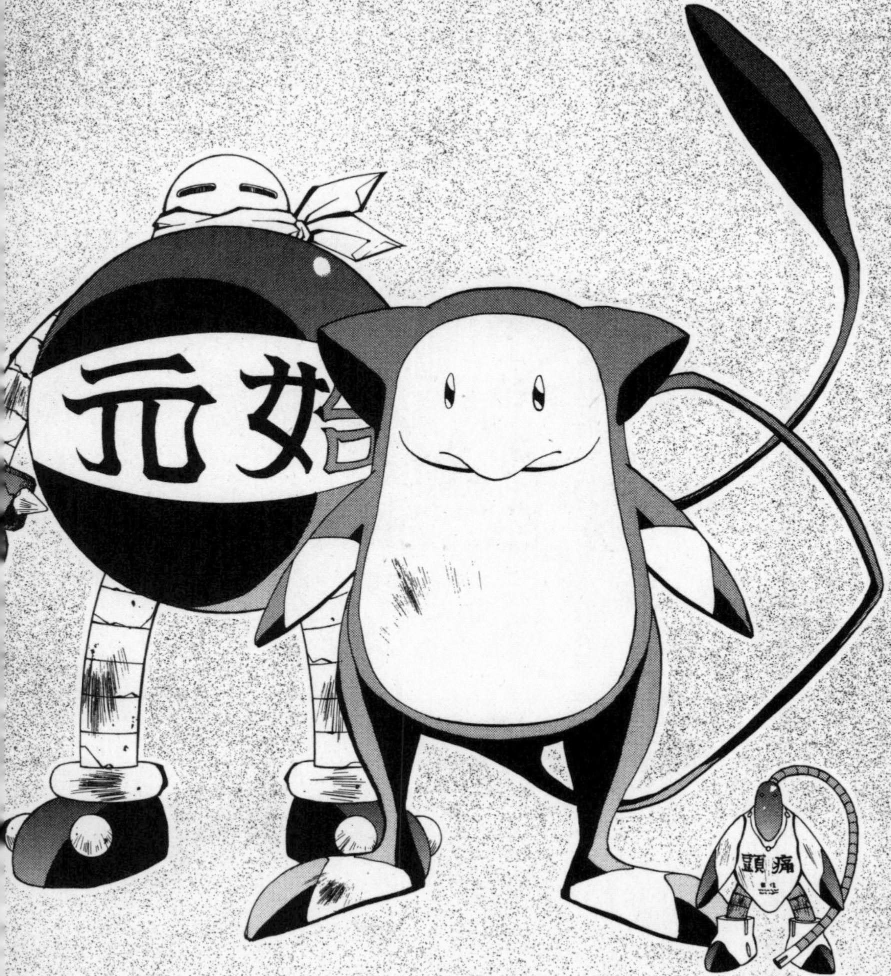
頭痛

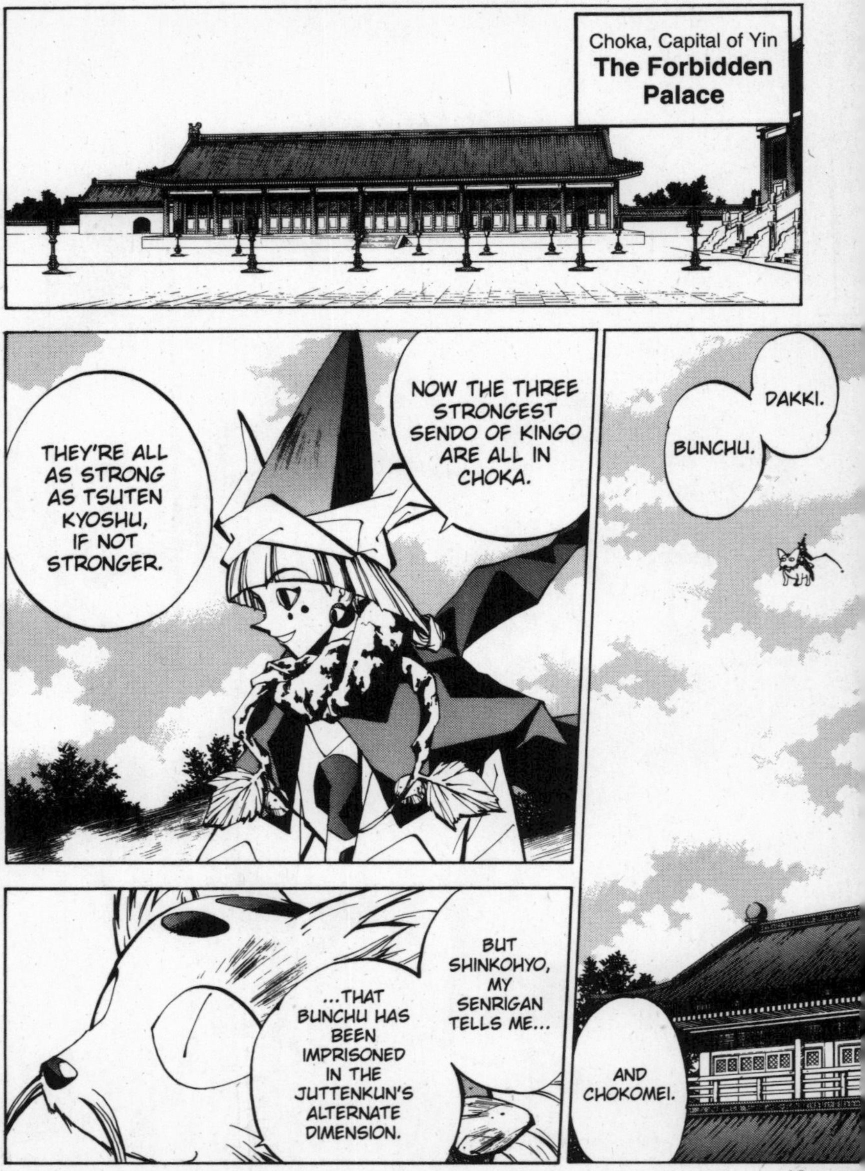
Choka, Capital of Yin
The Forbidden Palace
DAKKI.
BUNCHU.
AND CHOKOMEI.
NOW THE THREE STRONGEST SENDO OF KINGO ARE ALL IN CHOKA.
THEY'RE ALL AS STRONG AS TSUTEN KYOSHU, IF NOT STRONGER.
BUT SHINKOHYO, MY SENRIGAN TELLS ME...
...THAT BUNCHU HAS BEEN IMPRISONED IN THE JUTTENKUN'S ALTERNATE DIMENSION.

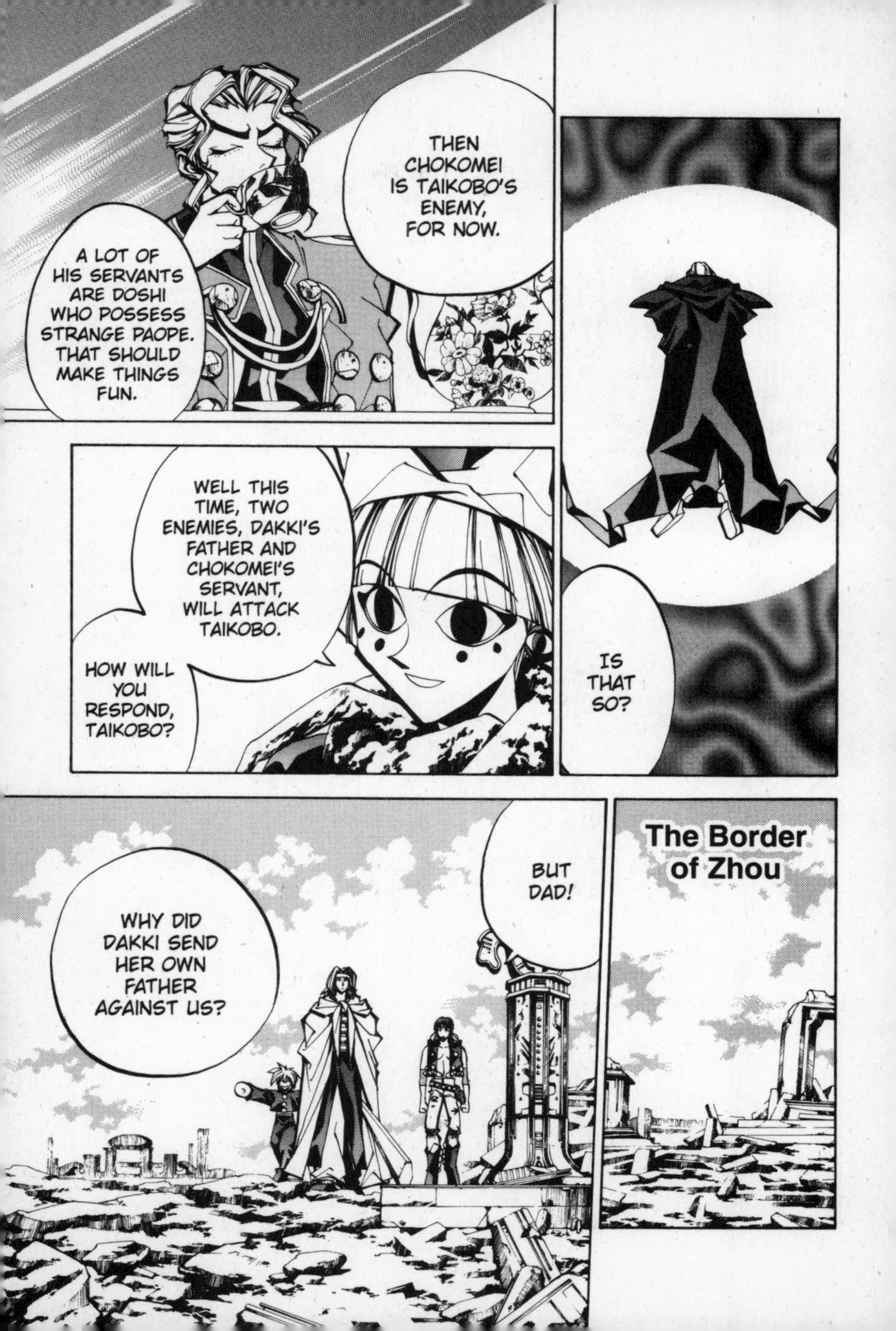
THEN CHOKOMEI IS TAIKOBO'S ENEMY, FOR NOW.
A LOT OF HIS SERVANTS ARE DOSHI WHO POSSESS STRANGE PAOPE. THAT SHOULD MAKE THINGS FUN.
WELL THIS TIME, TWO ENEMIES, DAKKI'S FATHER AND CHOKOMEI'S SERVANT, WILL ATTACK TAIKOBO.
HOW WILL YOU RESPOND, TAIKOBO?
IS THAT SO?
The Border of Zhou
BUT DAD!
WHY DID DAKKI SEND HER OWN FATHER AGAINST US?

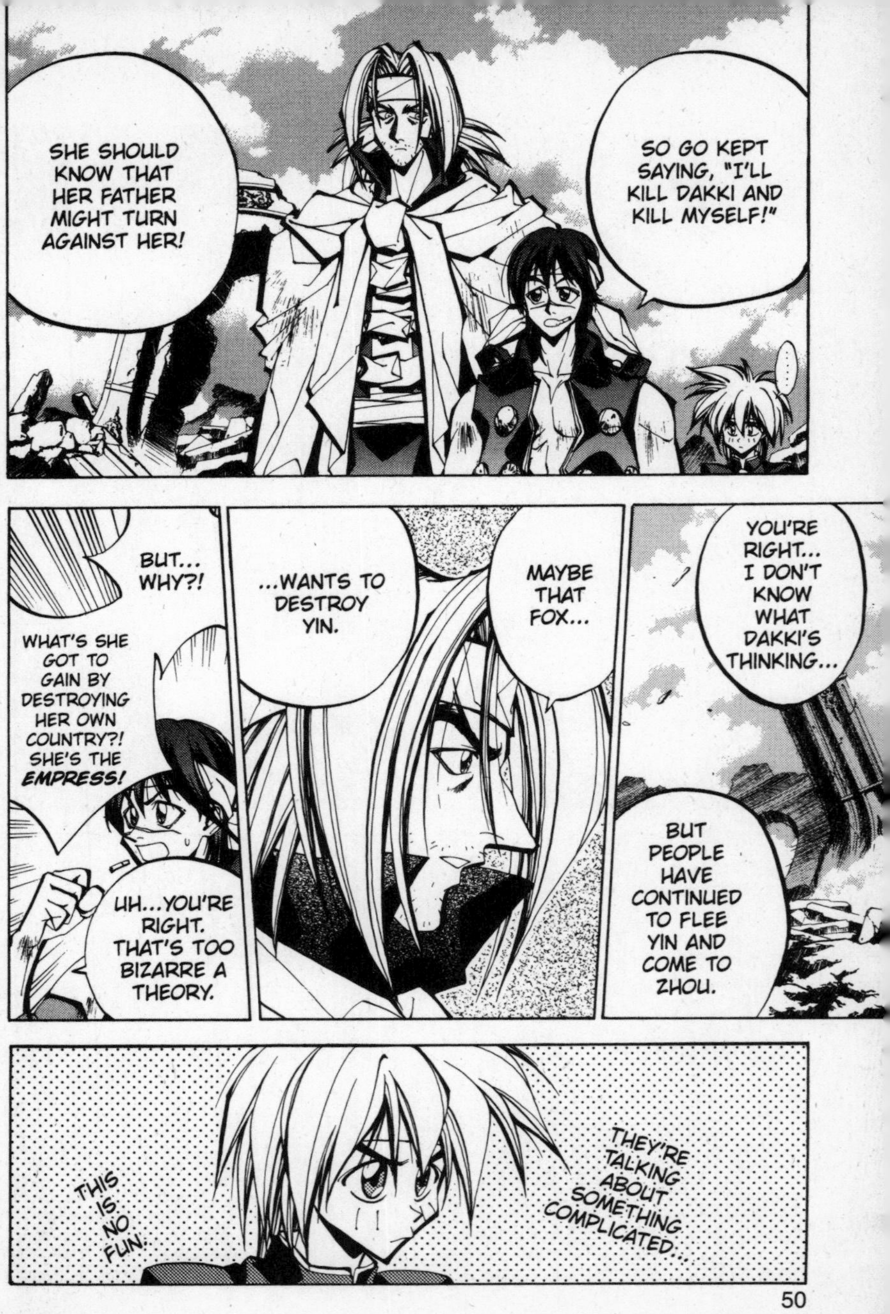
SO GO KEPT SAYING, "I'LL KILL DAKKI AND KILL MYSELF!"
SHE SHOULD KNOW THAT HER FATHER MIGHT TURN AGAINST HER!
...
YOU'RE RIGHT... I DON'T KNOW WHAT DAKKI'S THINKING...
BUT PEOPLE HAVE CONTINUED TO FLEE YIN AND COME TO ZHOU.
MAYBE THAT FOX...
...WANTS TO DESTROY YIN.
BUT... WHY?!
WHAT'S SHE GOT TO GAIN BY DESTROYING HER OWN COUNTRY?! SHE'S THE ***EMPRESS!***
UH...YOU'RE RIGHT. THAT'S TOO BIZARRE A THEORY.
THEY'RE TALKING ABOUT SOMETHING COMPLICATED...
THIS IS NO FUN.

READ THIS WAY

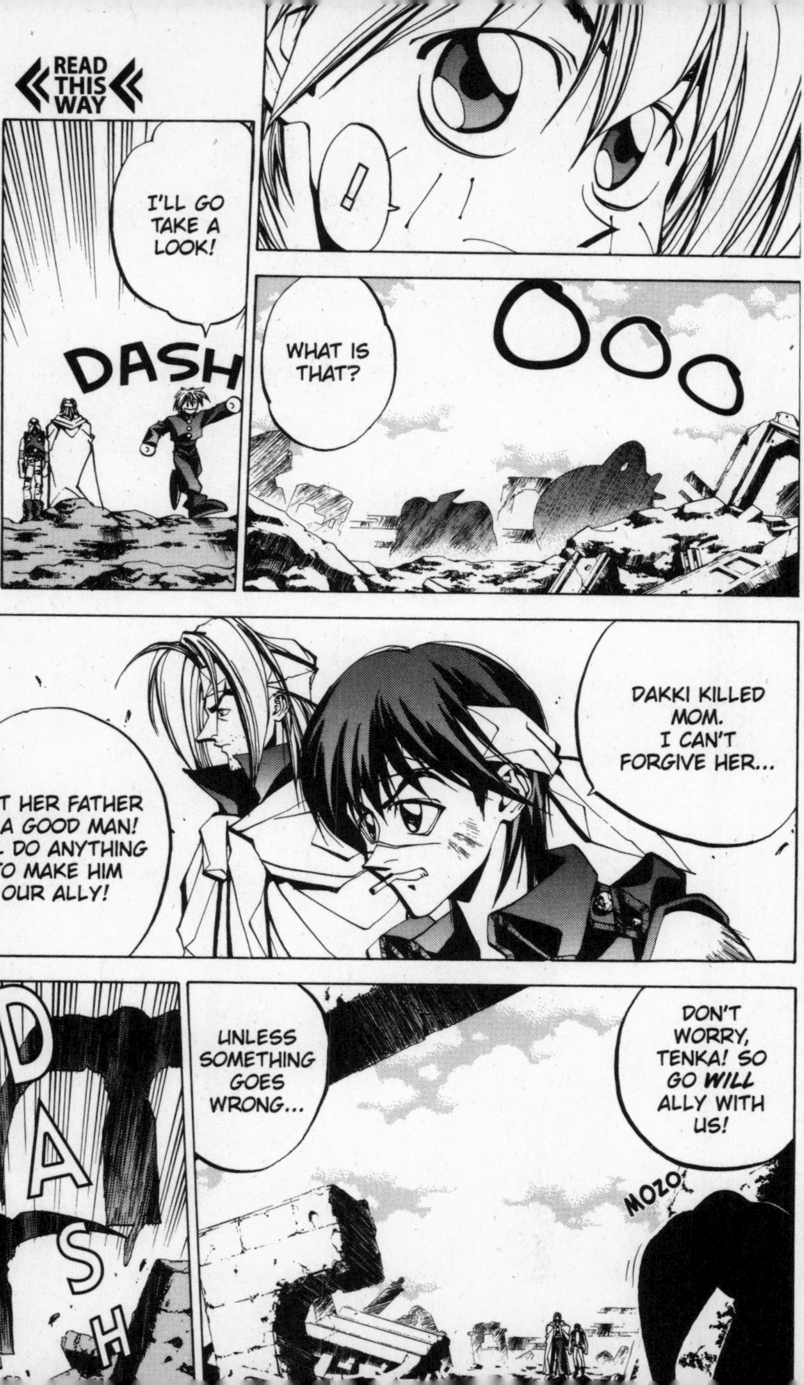
!
OOO
WHAT IS THAT?
I'LL GO TAKE A LOOK!
DASH
DAKKI KILLED MOM. I CAN'T FORGIVE HER...
BUT HER FATHER IS A GOOD MAN! I'LL DO ANYTHING TO MAKE HIM OUR ALLY!
DON'T WORRY, TENKA! SO GO *WILL* ALLY WITH US!
UNLESS SOMETHING GOES WRONG...
MOZO
DASH

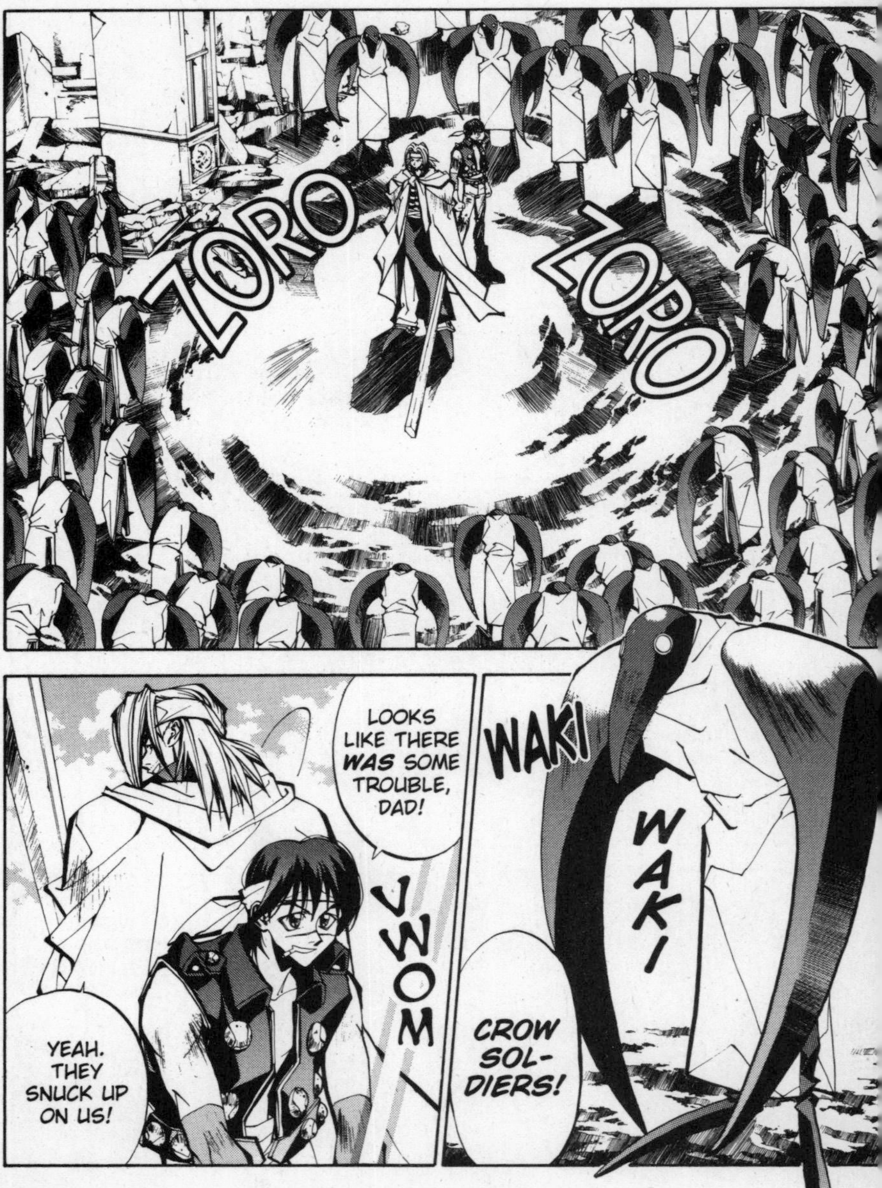
ZORO
ZORO
WAKI
WAKI
CROW SOL-DIERS!
LOOKS LIKE THERE **WAS** SOME TROUBLE, DAD!
JWOM
YEAH. THEY SNUCK UP ON US!

READ THIS WAY

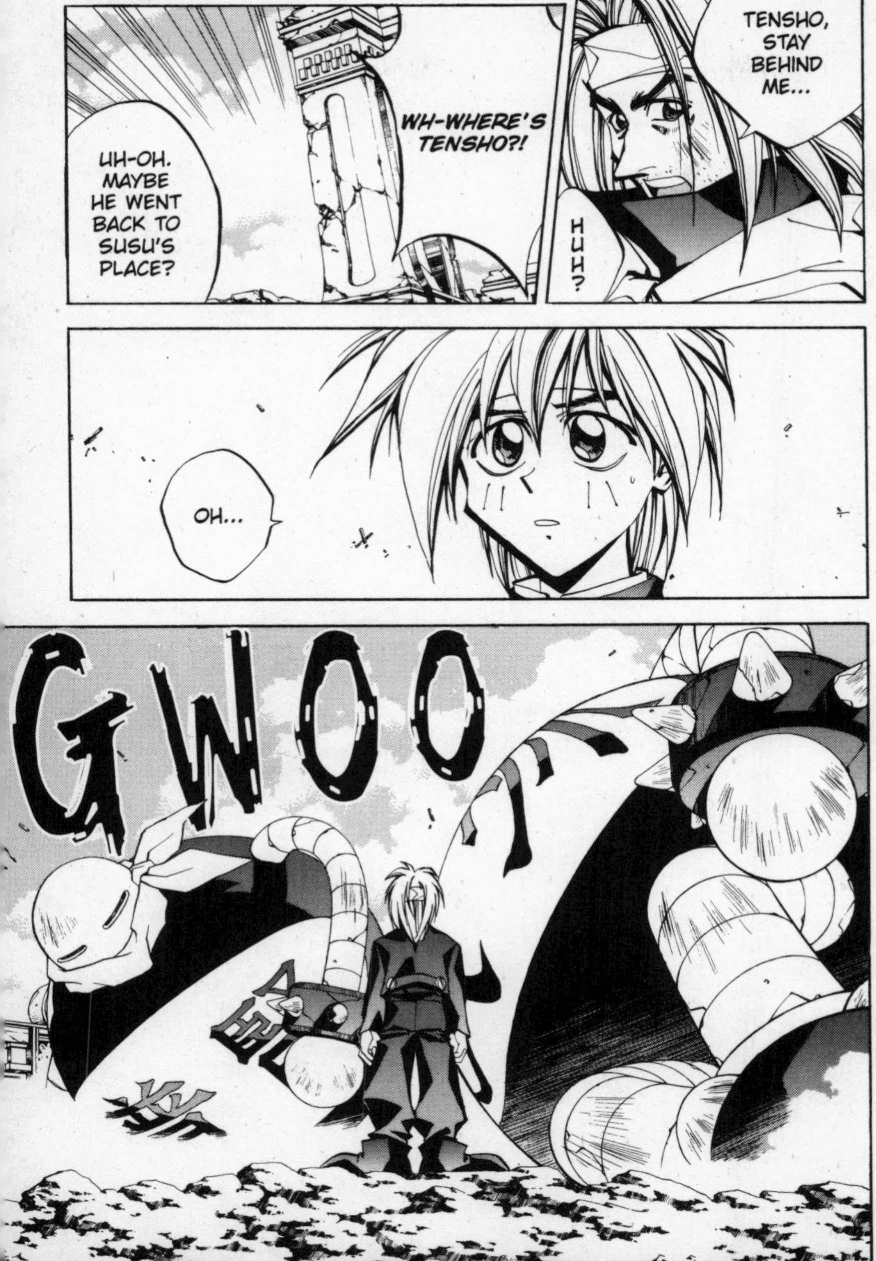
TENSHO, STAY BEHIND ME...
HUH?
WH-WHERE'S TENSHO?!
UH-OH. MAYBE HE WENT BACK TO SUSU'S PLACE?
OH...
GWOO

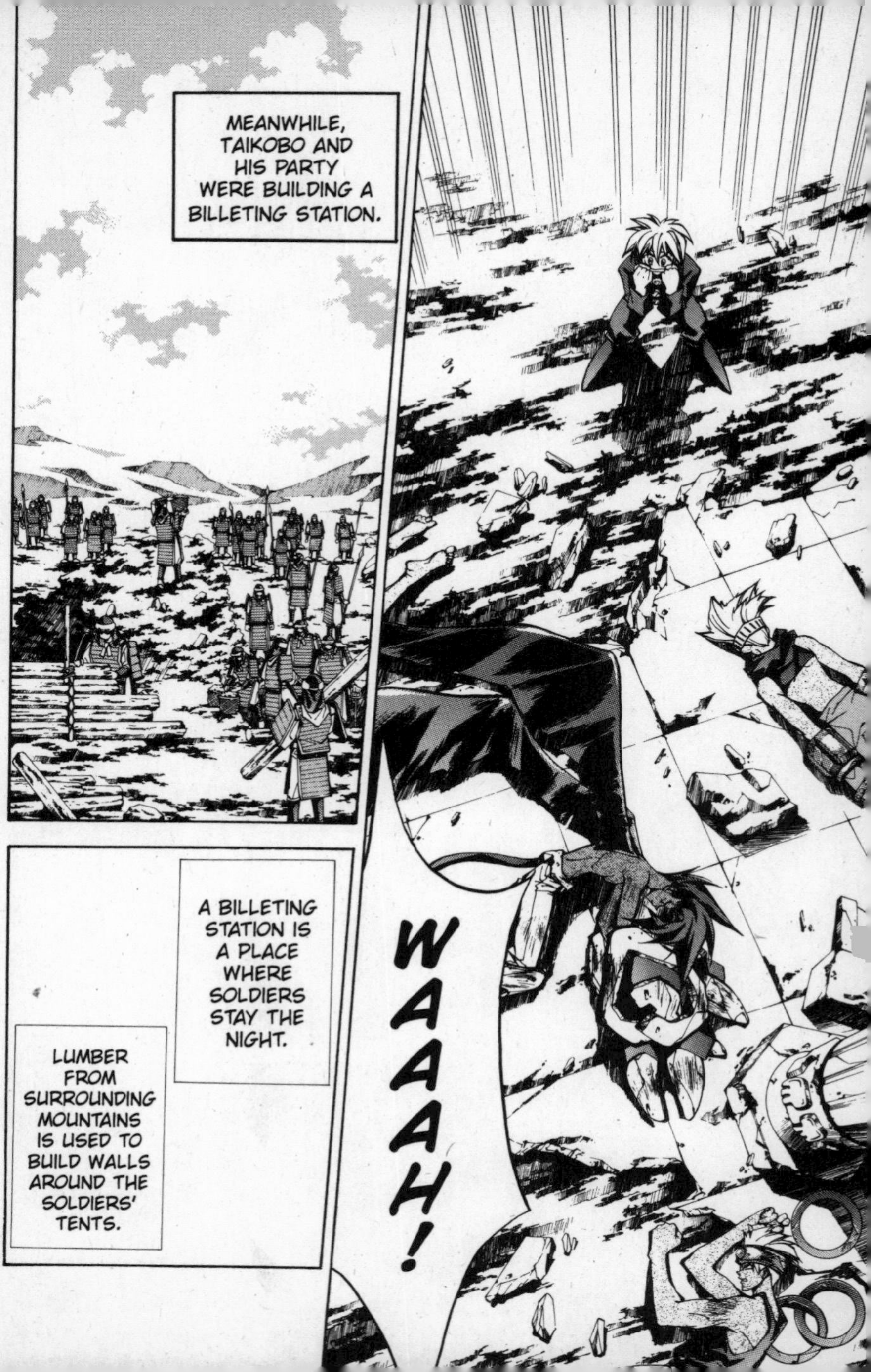
WAAAH!
MEANWHILE, TAIKOBO AND HIS PARTY WERE BUILDING A BILLETING STATION.
A BILLETING STATION IS A PLACE WHERE SOLDIERS STAY THE NIGHT.
LUMBER FROM SURROUNDING MOUNTAINS IS USED TO BUILD WALLS AROUND THE SOLDIERS' TENTS.

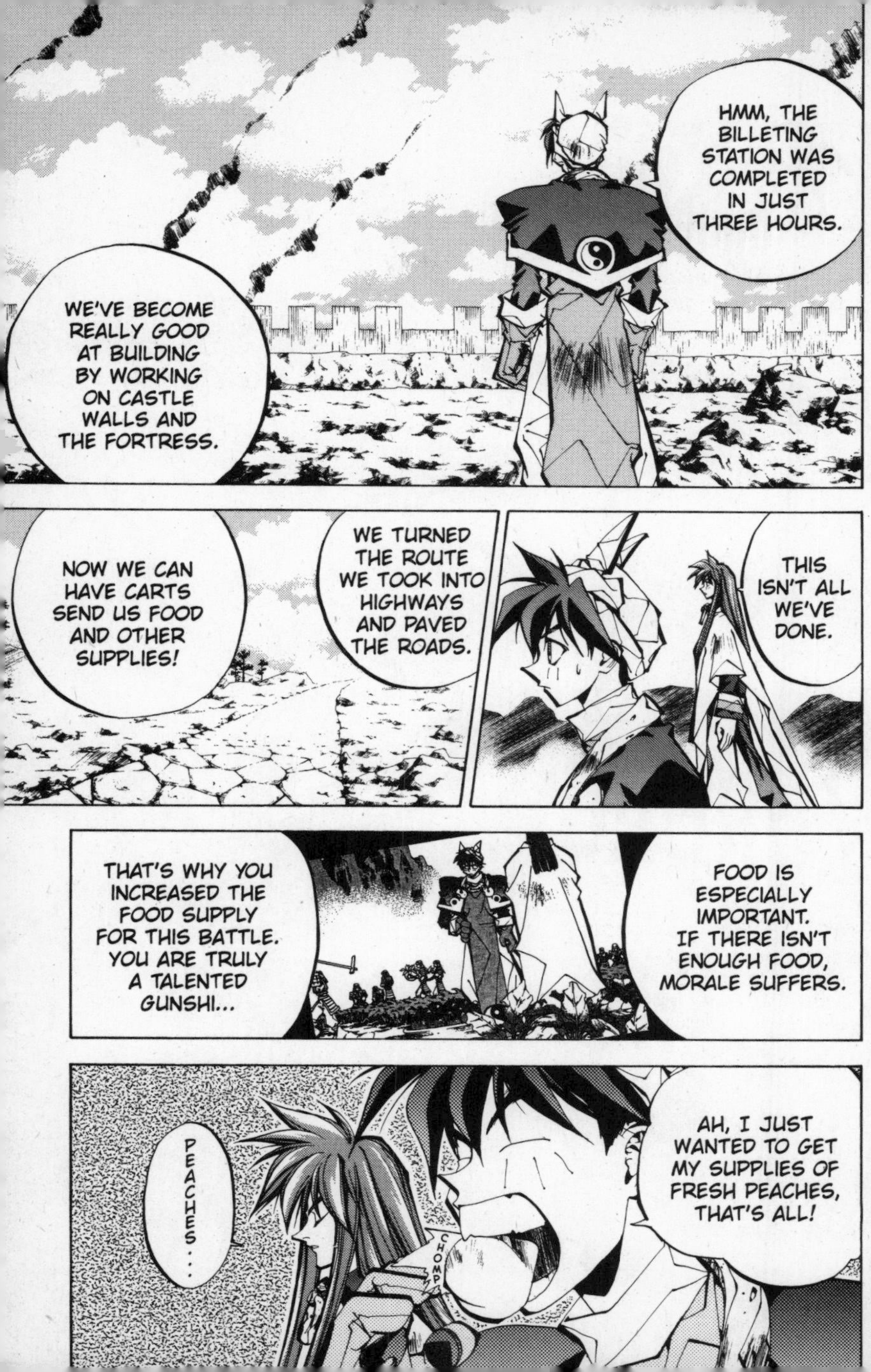
HMM, THE BILLETING STATION WAS COMPLETED IN JUST THREE HOURS.
WE'VE BECOME REALLY GOOD AT BUILDING BY WORKING ON CASTLE WALLS AND THE FORTRESS.
THIS ISN'T ALL WE'VE DONE.
WE TURNED THE ROUTE WE TOOK INTO HIGHWAYS AND PAVED THE ROADS.
NOW WE CAN HAVE CARTS SEND US FOOD AND OTHER SUPPLIES!
FOOD IS ESPECIALLY IMPORTANT. IF THERE ISN'T ENOUGH FOOD, MORALE SUFFERS.
THAT'S WHY YOU INCREASED THE FOOD SUPPLY FOR THIS BATTLE. YOU ARE TRULY A TALENTED GUNSHI...
AH, I JUST WANTED TO GET MY SUPPLIES OF FRESH PEACHES, THAT'S ALL!
CHOMP
PEACHES...

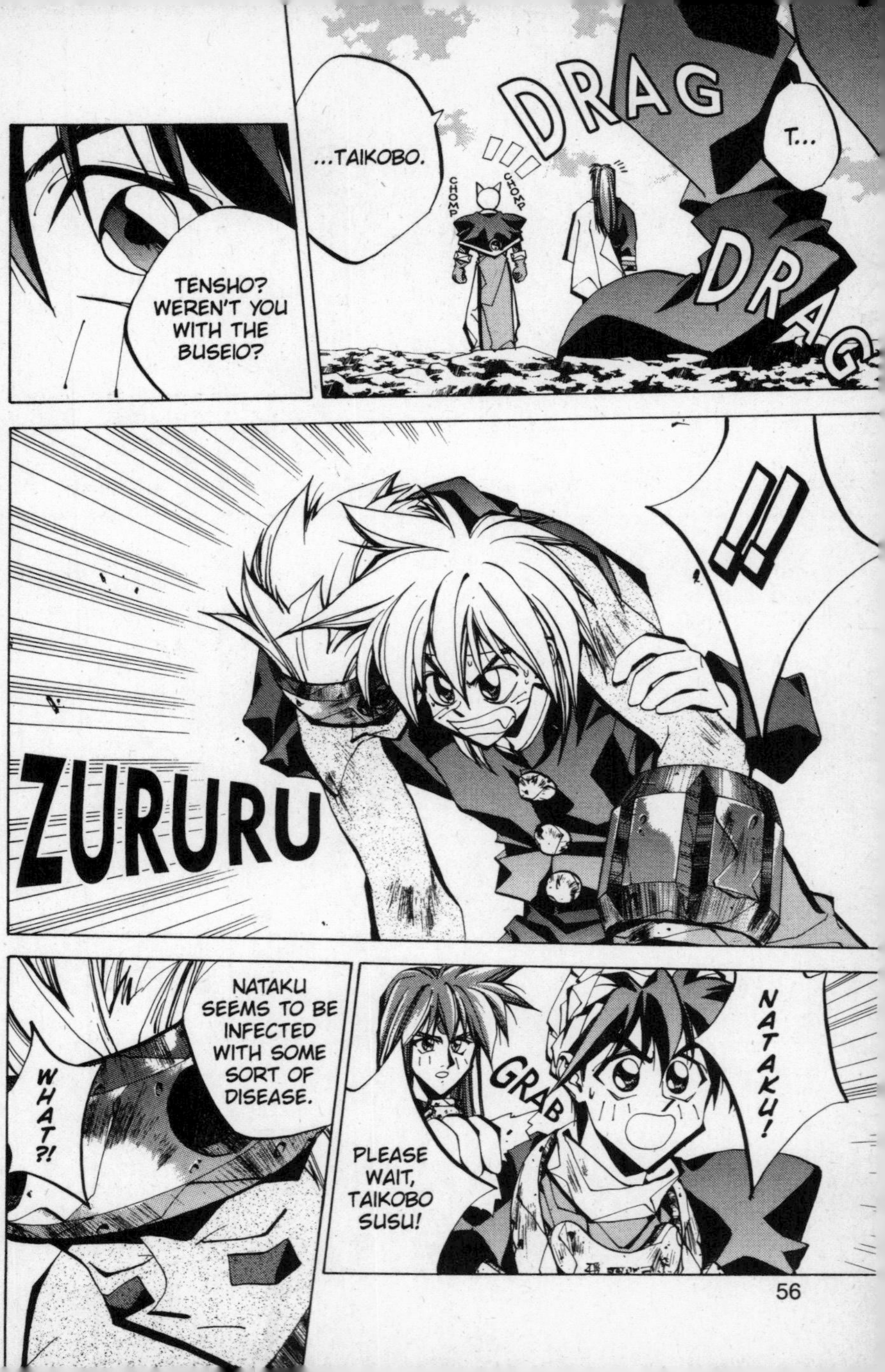

T...
DRAG
...TAIKOBO.
CHOMP
CHOMP
DRAG
TENSHO? WEREN'T YOU WITH THE BUSEIO?
!!
ZURURU
NATAKU!
GRAB
PLEASE WAIT, TAIKOBO SUSU!
NATAKU SEEMS TO BE INFECTED WITH SOME SORT OF DISEASE.
WHAT?!

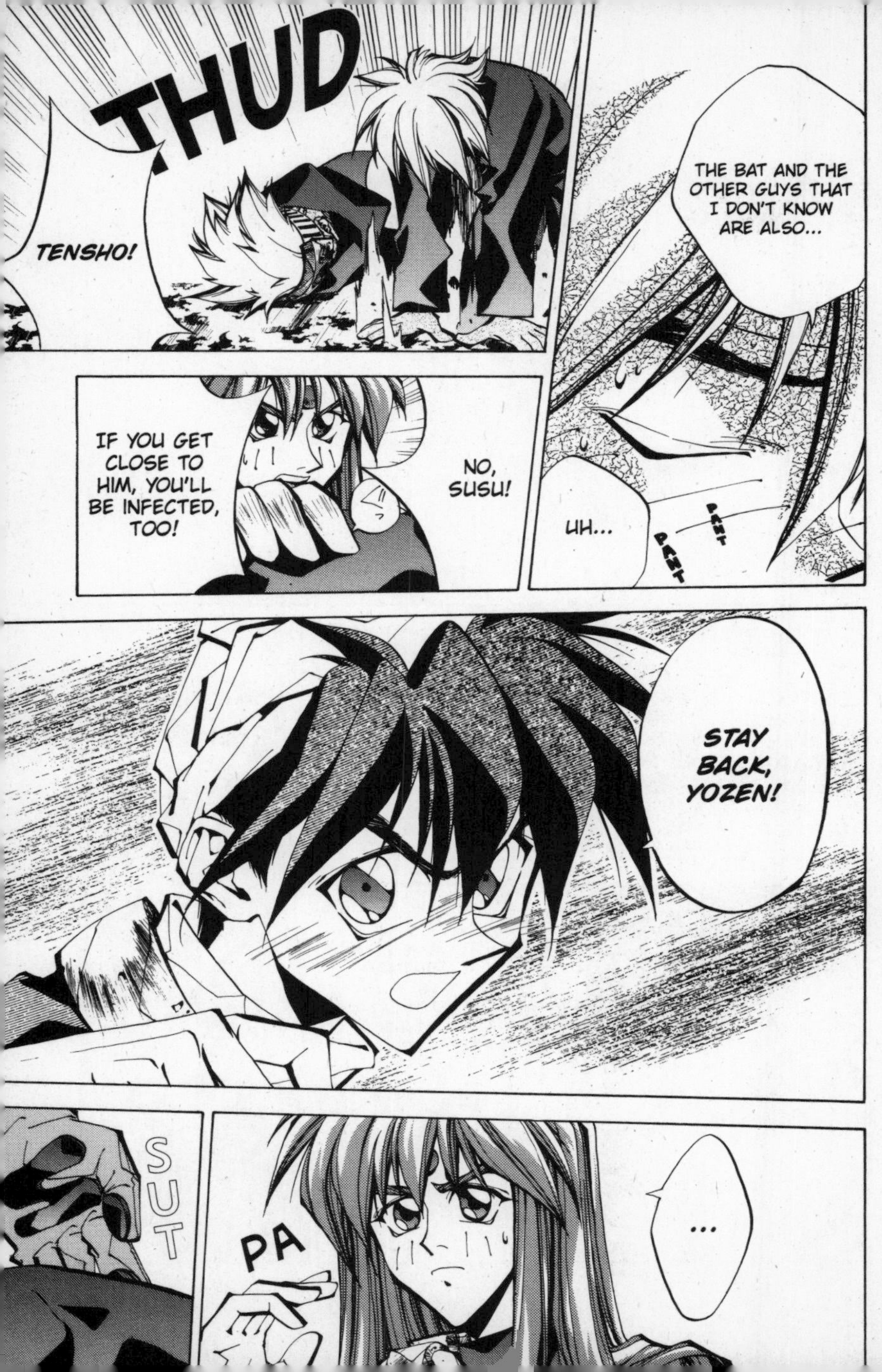

THE BAT AND THE OTHER GUYS THAT I DON'T KNOW ARE ALSO...
UH...
PANT
PANT
THUD
TENSHO!
NO, SUSU!
IF YOU GET CLOSE TO HIM, YOU'LL BE INFECTED, TOO!
STAY BACK, YOZEN!
...
PA
SUT

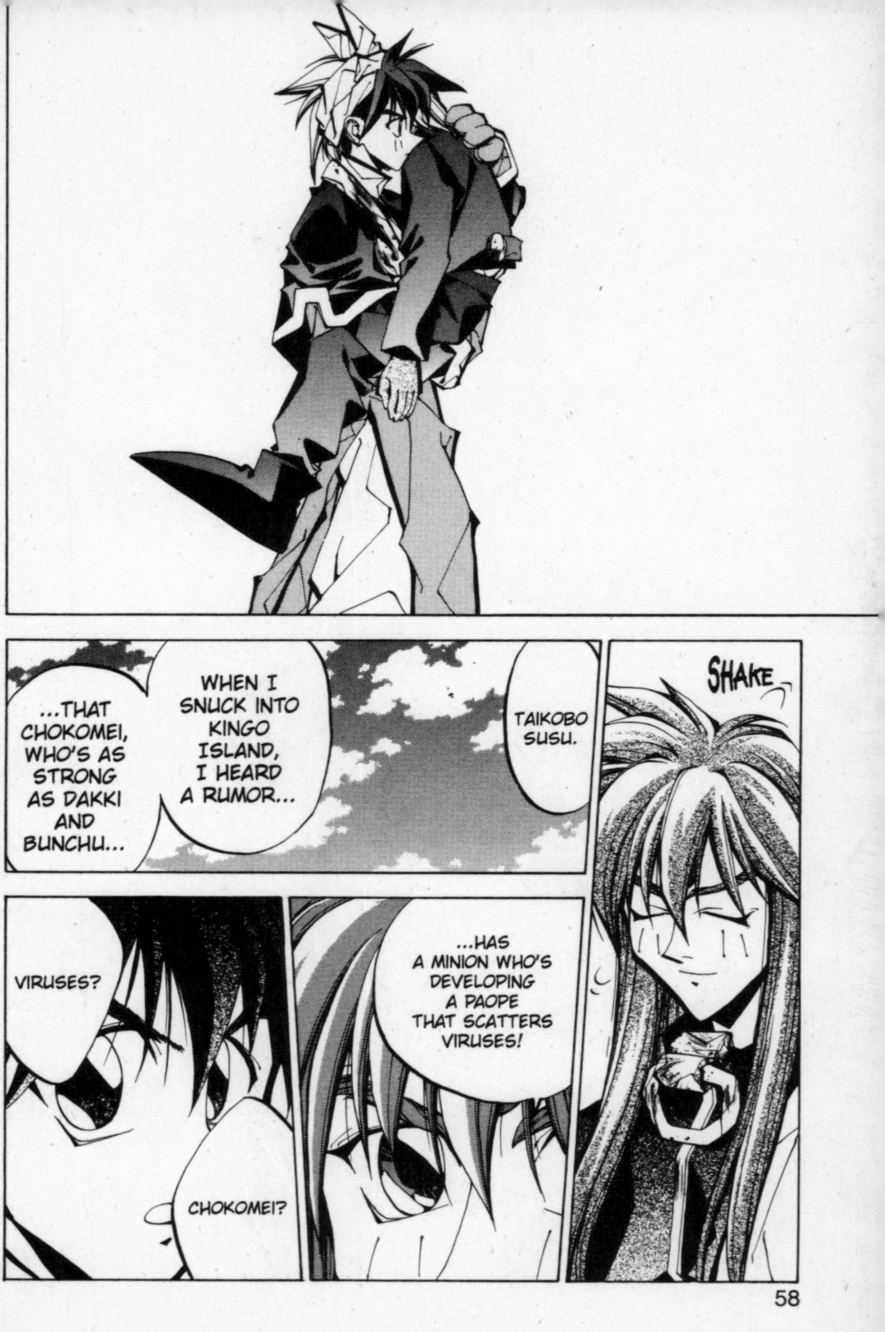
SHAKE
TAIKOBO SUSU.
WHEN I SNUCK INTO KINGO ISLAND, I HEARD A RUMOR...
...THAT CHOKOMEI, WHO'S AS STRONG AS DAKKI AND BUNCHU...
...HAS A MINION WHO'S DEVELOPING A PAOPE THAT SCATTERS VIRUSES!
VIRUSES?
CHOKOMEI?

READ THIS WAY

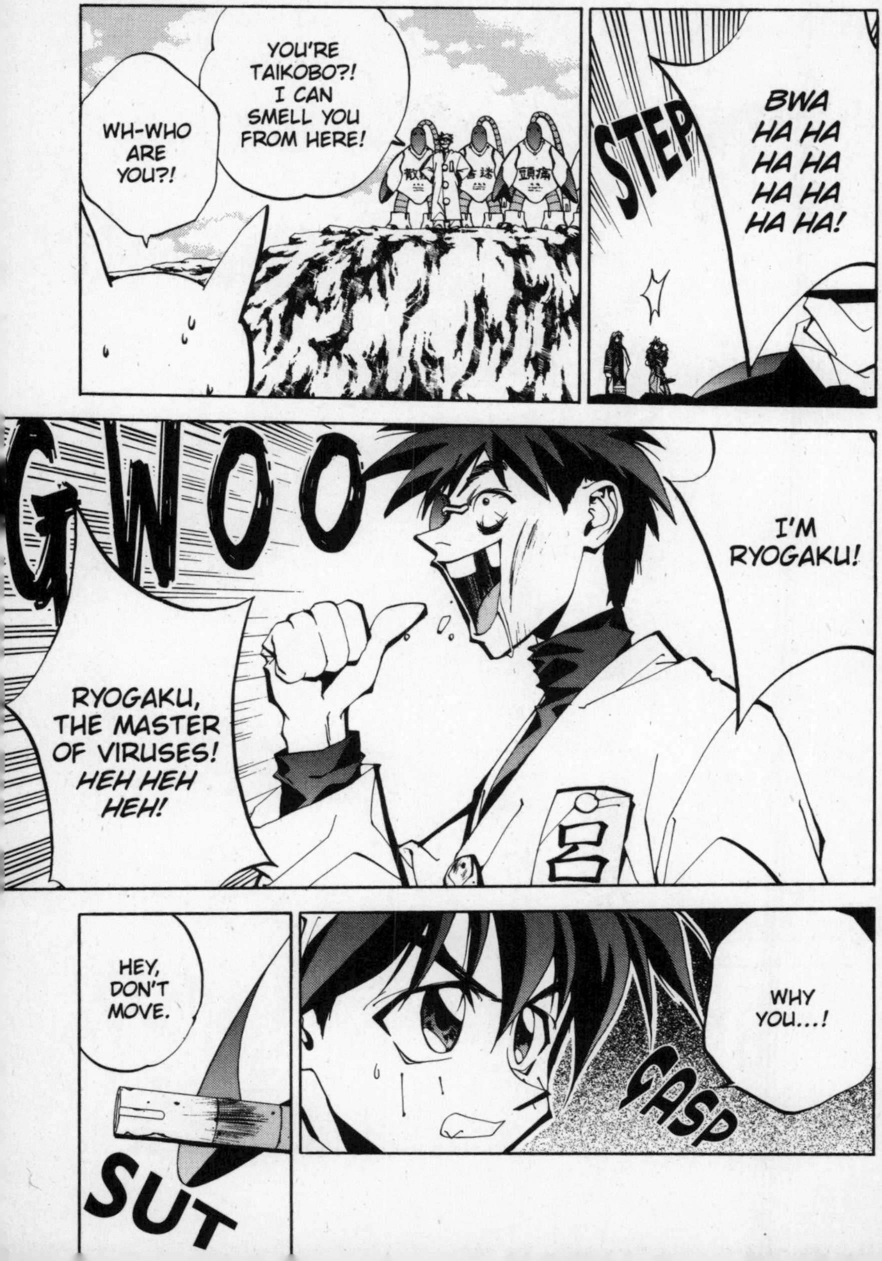

STEP
BWA HA HA HA HA HA HA HA HA!
YOU'RE TAIKOBO?! I CAN SMELL YOU FROM HERE!
WH-WHO ARE YOU?!
GWOOO
I'M RYOGAKU!
RYOGAKU, THE MASTER OF VIRUSES! HEH HEH HEH!
WHY YOU...!
GASP
HEY, DON'T MOVE.
SUT

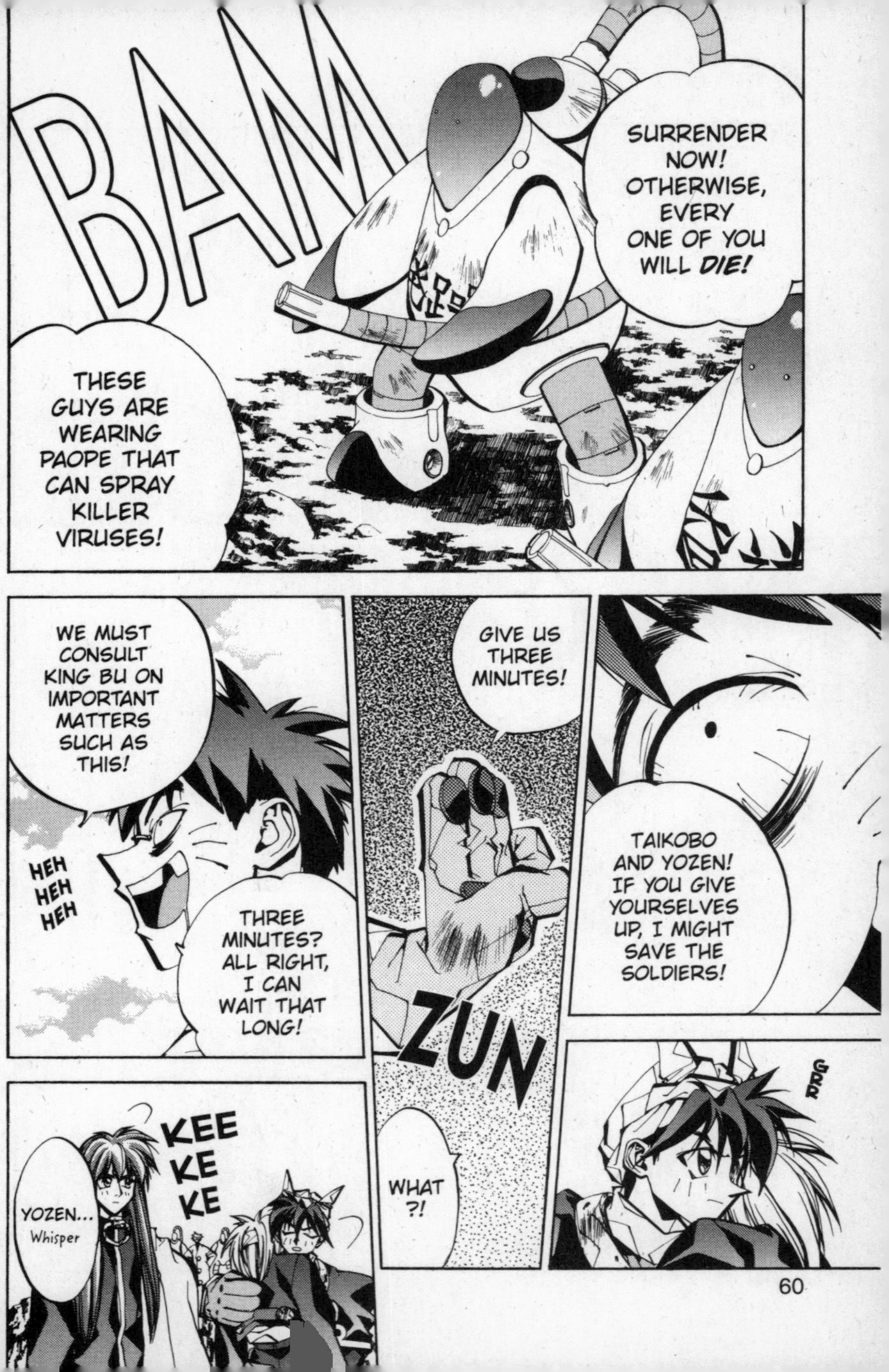
BAM
SURRENDER NOW! OTHERWISE, EVERY ONE OF YOU WILL ***DIE!***
THESE GUYS ARE WEARING PAOPE THAT CAN SPRAY KILLER VIRUSES!
TAIKOBO AND YOZEN! IF YOU GIVE YOURSELVES UP, I MIGHT SAVE THE SOLDIERS!
GRR
GIVE US THREE MINUTES!
ZUN
WHAT ?!
WE MUST CONSULT KING BU ON IMPORTANT MATTERS SUCH AS THIS!
HEH HEH HEH
THREE MINUTES? ALL RIGHT, I CAN WAIT THAT LONG!
KEE KE KE
YOZEN...
Whisper

READ THIS WAY

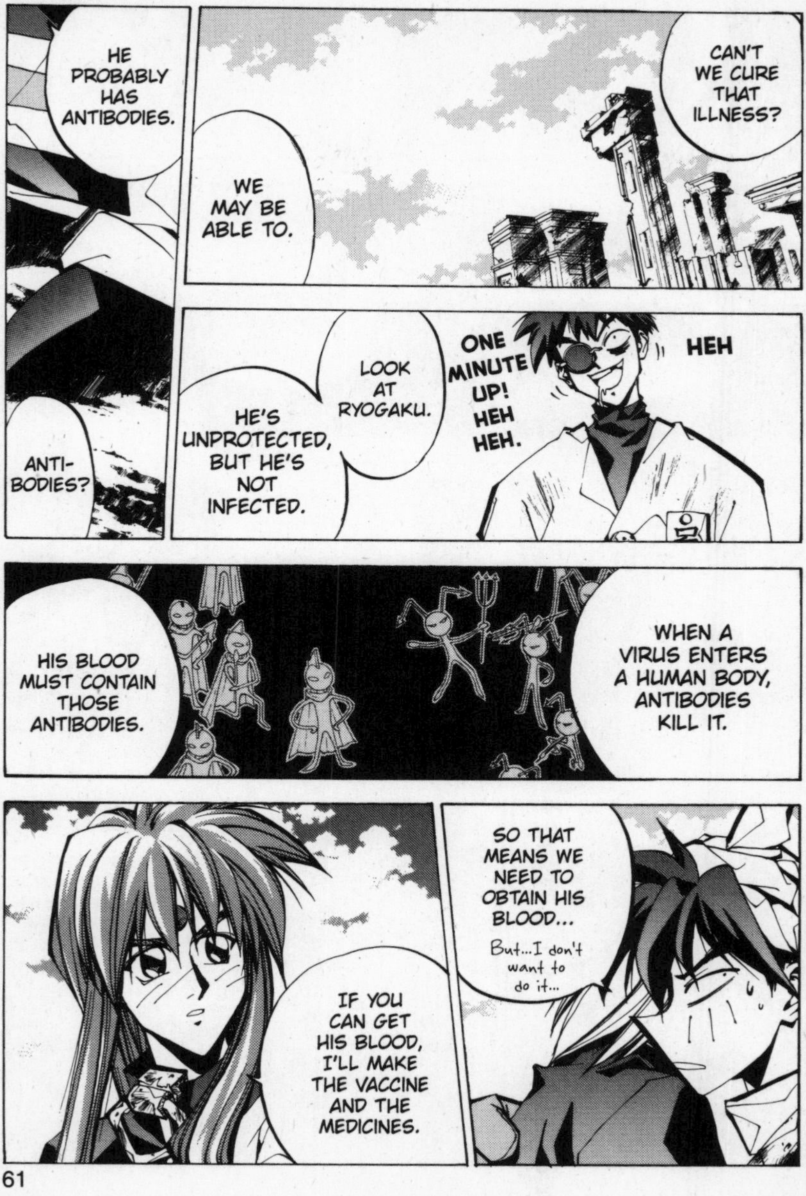
CAN'T WE CURE THAT ILLNESS?
WE MAY BE ABLE TO.
HEH
ONE MINUTE UP! HEH HEH.
LOOK AT RYOGAKU.
HE'S UNPROTECTED, BUT HE'S NOT INFECTED.
HE PROBABLY HAS ANTIBODIES.
ANTI-BODIES?
WHEN A VIRUS ENTERS A HUMAN BODY, ANTIBODIES KILL IT.
HIS BLOOD MUST CONTAIN THOSE ANTIBODIES.
SO THAT MEANS WE NEED TO OBTAIN HIS BLOOD...
But...I don't want to do it...
IF YOU CAN GET HIS BLOOD, I'LL MAKE THE VACCINE AND THE MEDICINES.

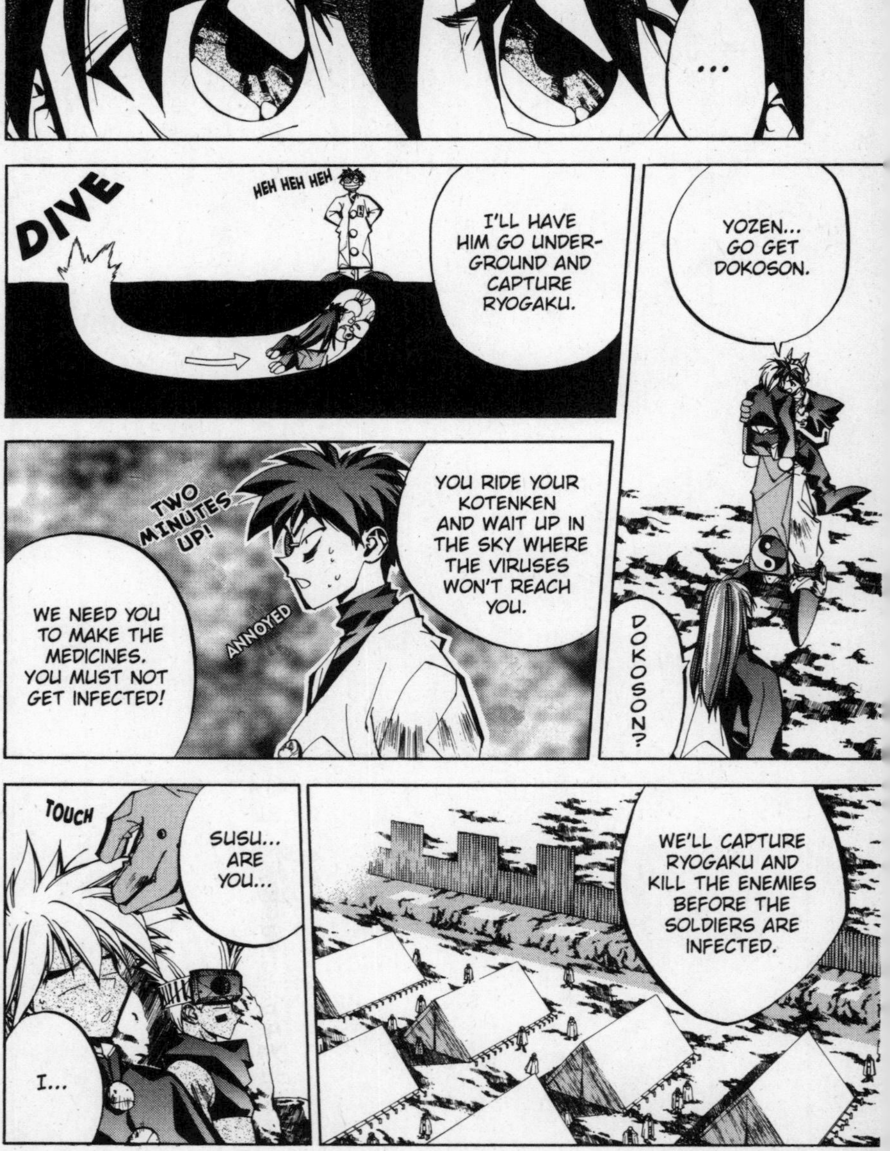

...
YOZEN... GO GET DOKOSON.
DOKOSON?
I'LL HAVE HIM GO UNDER-GROUND AND CAPTURE RYOGAKU.
HEH HEH HEH
DIVE
YOU RIDE YOUR KOTENKEN AND WAIT UP IN THE SKY WHERE THE VIRUSES WON'T REACH YOU.
TWO MINUTES UP!
ANNOYED
WE NEED YOU TO MAKE THE MEDICINES. YOU MUST NOT GET INFECTED!
WE'LL CAPTURE RYOGAKU AND KILL THE ENEMIES BEFORE THE SOLDIERS ARE INFECTED.
SUSU... ARE YOU...
TOUCH
I...

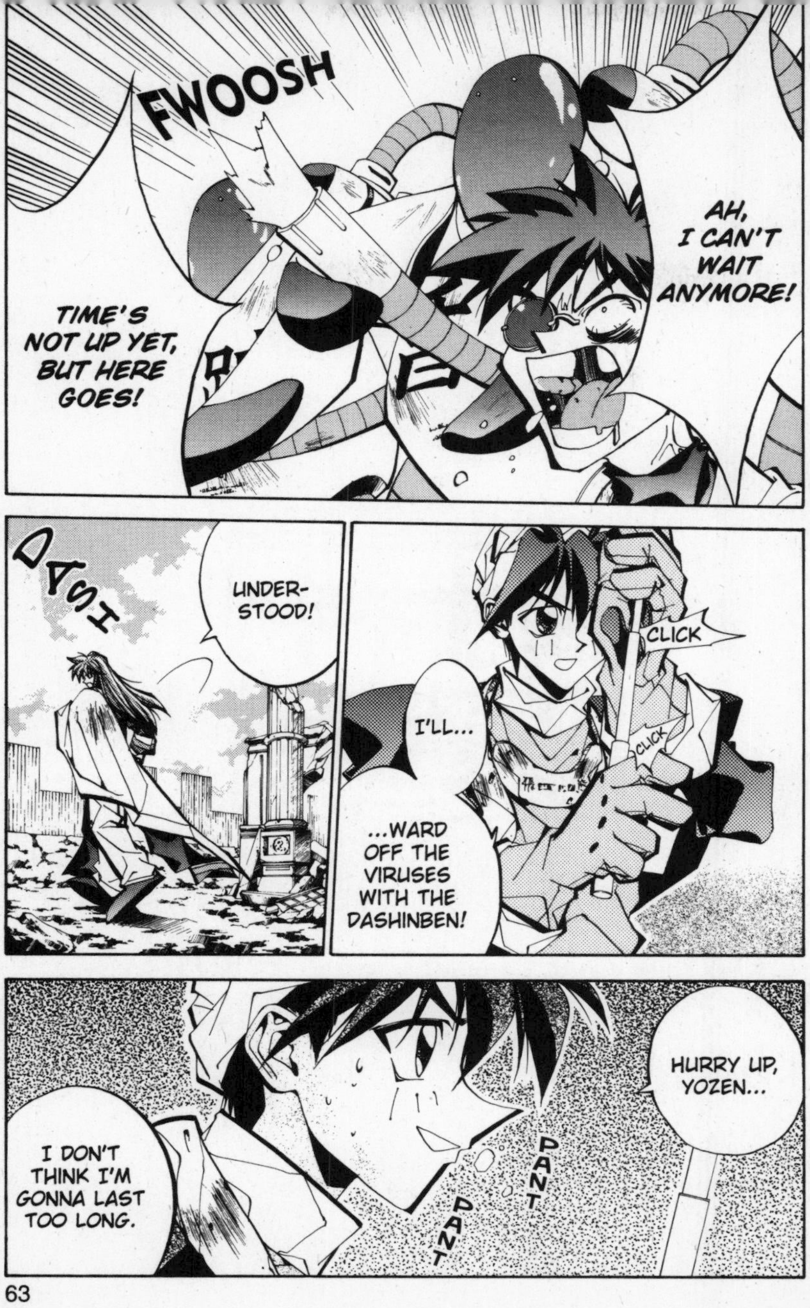
FWOOSH
AH, I CAN'T WAIT ANYMORE!
TIME'S NOT UP YET, BUT HERE GOES!
CLICK
I'LL...
CLICK
...WARD OFF THE VIRUSES WITH THE DASHINBEN!
UNDER-STOOD!
DASH
HURRY UP, YOZEN...
PANT
PANT
PANT
I DON'T THINK I'M GONNA LAST TOO LONG.

封神演義

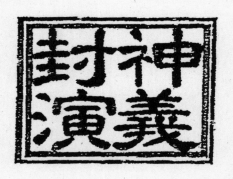

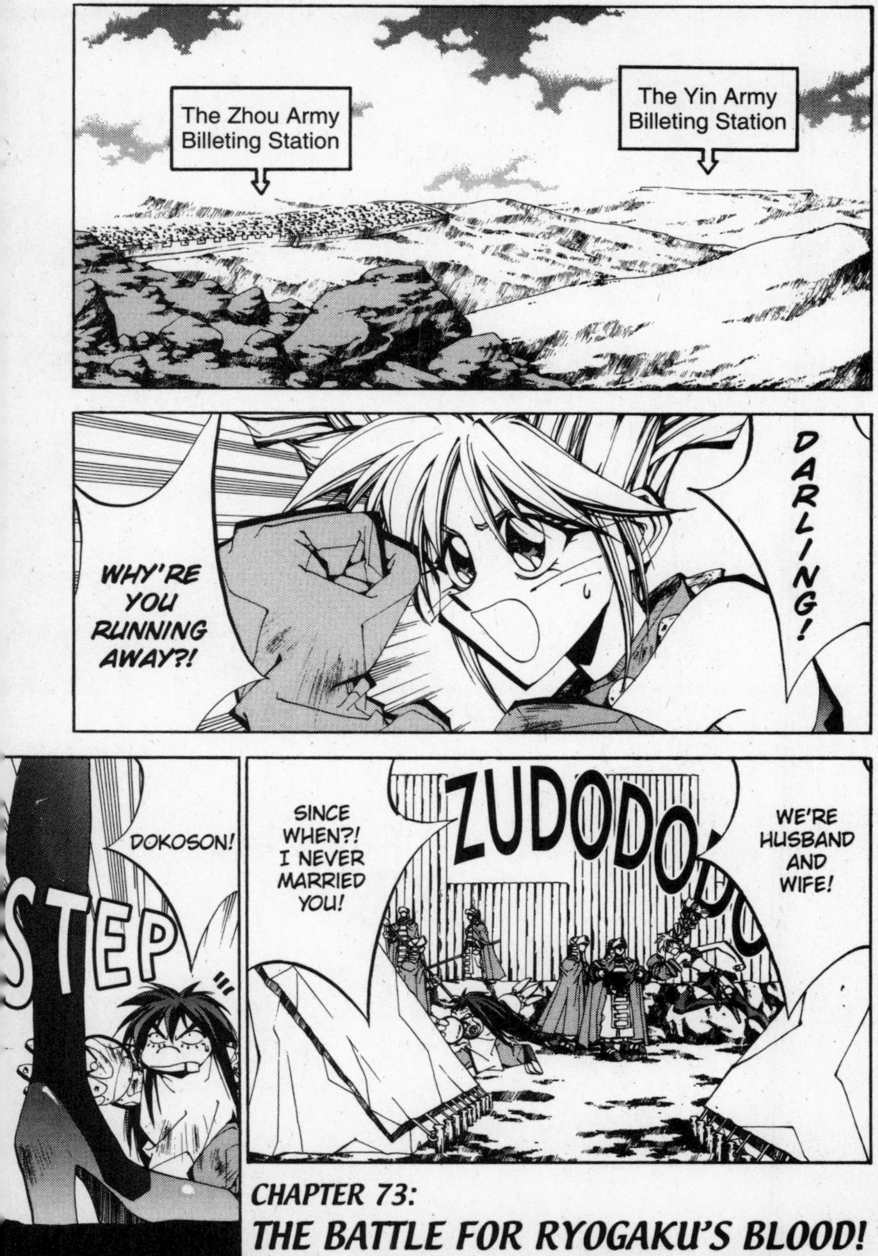
The Yin Army Billeting Station
The Zhou Army Billeting Station
DARLING!
WHY'RE YOU RUNNING AWAY?!
WE'RE HUSBAND AND WIFE!
ZUDODODO
SINCE WHEN?! I NEVER MARRIED YOU!
DOKOSON!
STEP

CHAPTER 73:
THE BATTLE FOR RYOGAKU'S BLOOD!

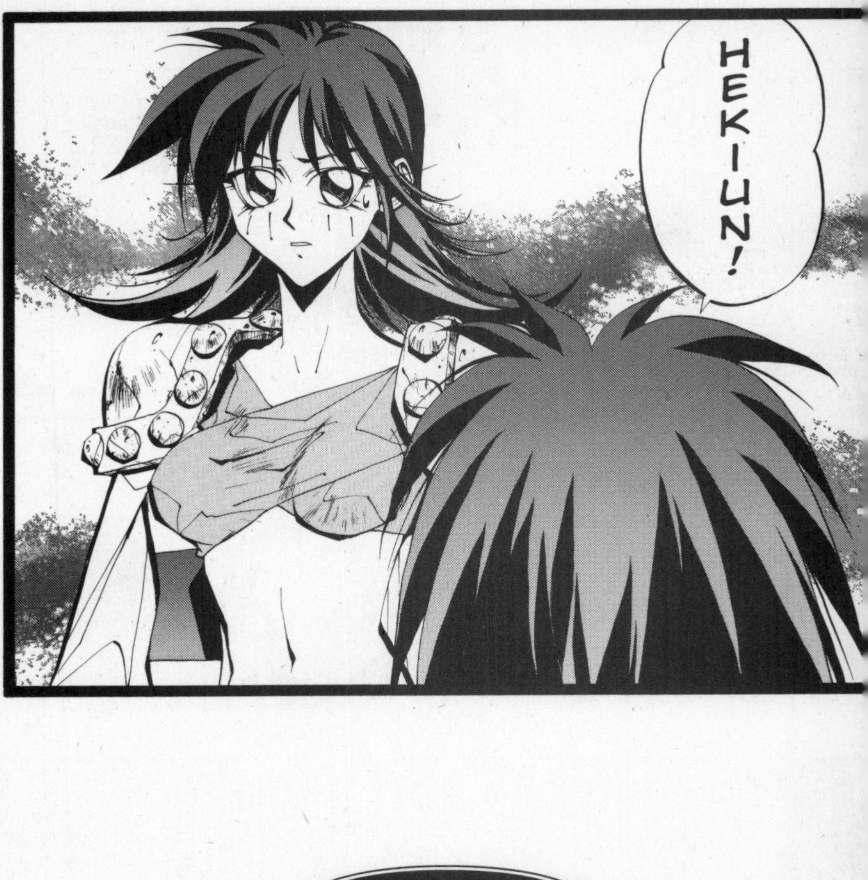
HEKIUN!

Chapter 73

THE BATTLE FOR RYOGAKU'S BLOOD!

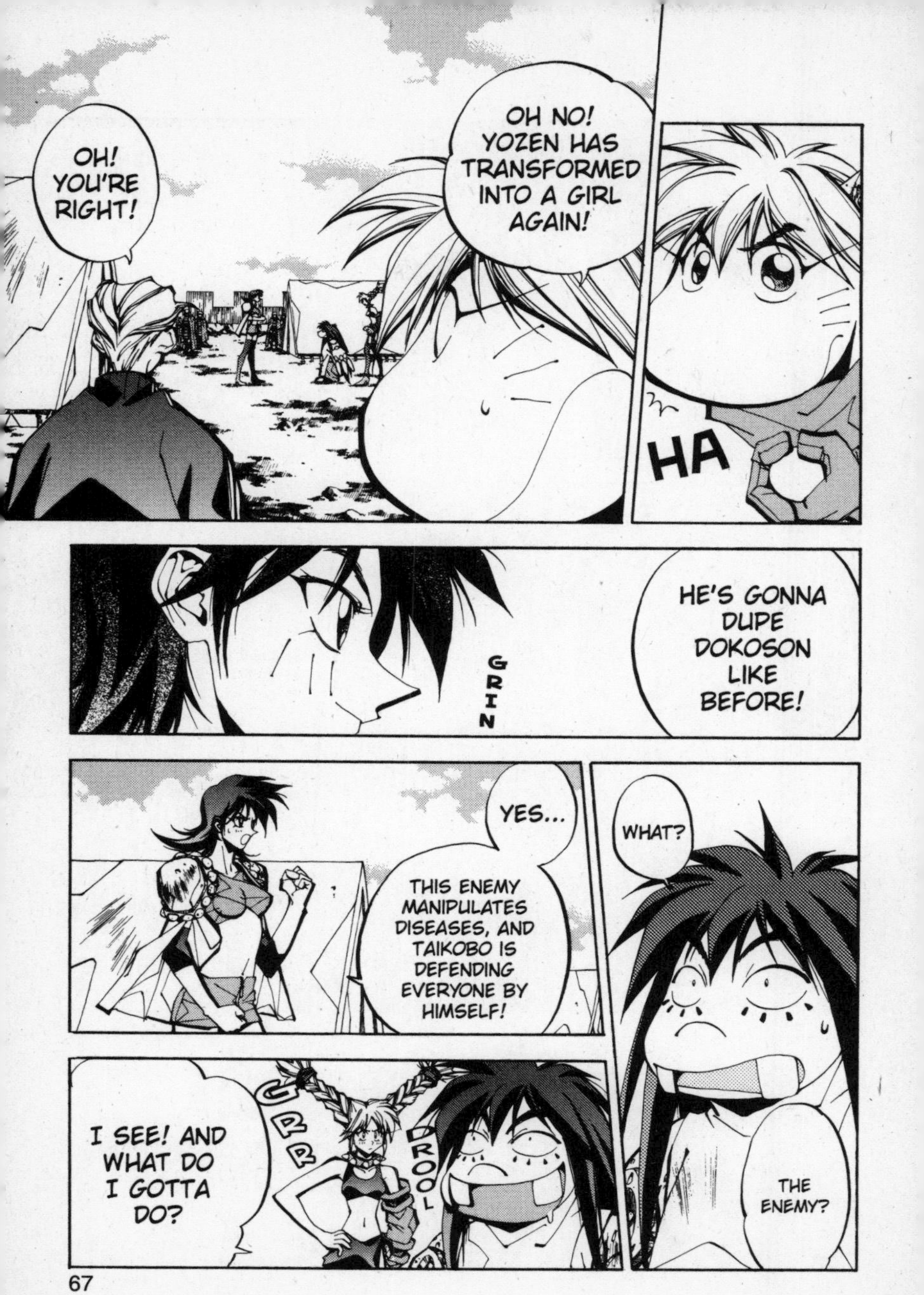
HA
OH NO! YOZEN HAS TRANSFORMED INTO A GIRL AGAIN!
OH! YOU'RE RIGHT!
HE'S GONNA DUPE DOKOSON LIKE BEFORE!
GRIN
WHAT?
THE ENEMY?
YES...
THIS ENEMY MANIPULATES DISEASES, AND TAIKOBO IS DEFENDING EVERYONE BY HIMSELF!
DROOL
GRR
I SEE! AND WHAT DO I GOTTA DO?

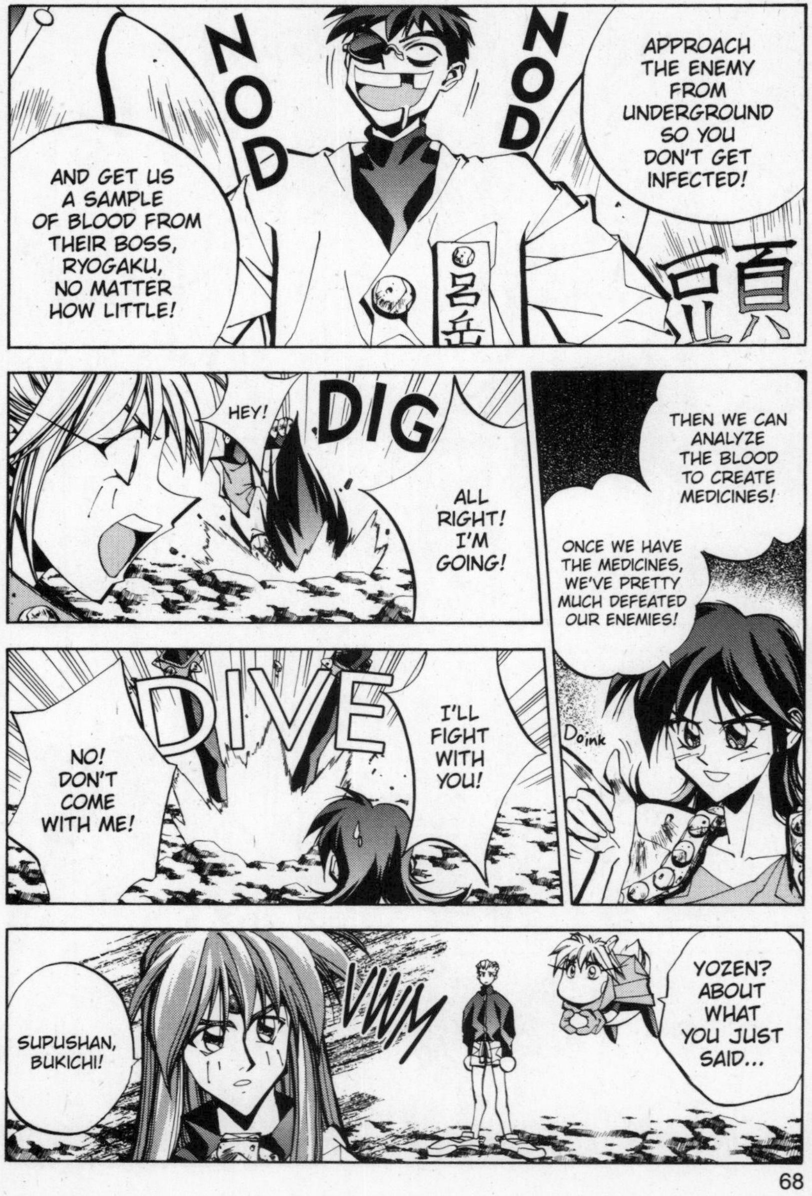
APPROACH THE ENEMY FROM UNDERGROUND SO YOU DON'T GET INFECTED!
NOD
NOD
AND GET US A SAMPLE OF BLOOD FROM THEIR BOSS, RYOGAKU, NO MATTER HOW LITTLE!
頷
呂岳
THEN WE CAN ANALYZE THE BLOOD TO CREATE MEDICINES!
ONCE WE HAVE THE MEDICINES, WE'VE PRETTY MUCH DEFEATED OUR ENEMIES!
Doink
ALL RIGHT! I'M GOING!
DIG
HEY!
I'LL FIGHT WITH YOU!
DIVE
NO! DON'T COME WITH ME!
YOZEN? ABOUT WHAT YOU JUST SAID...
VWM
SUPUSHAN, BUKICHI!

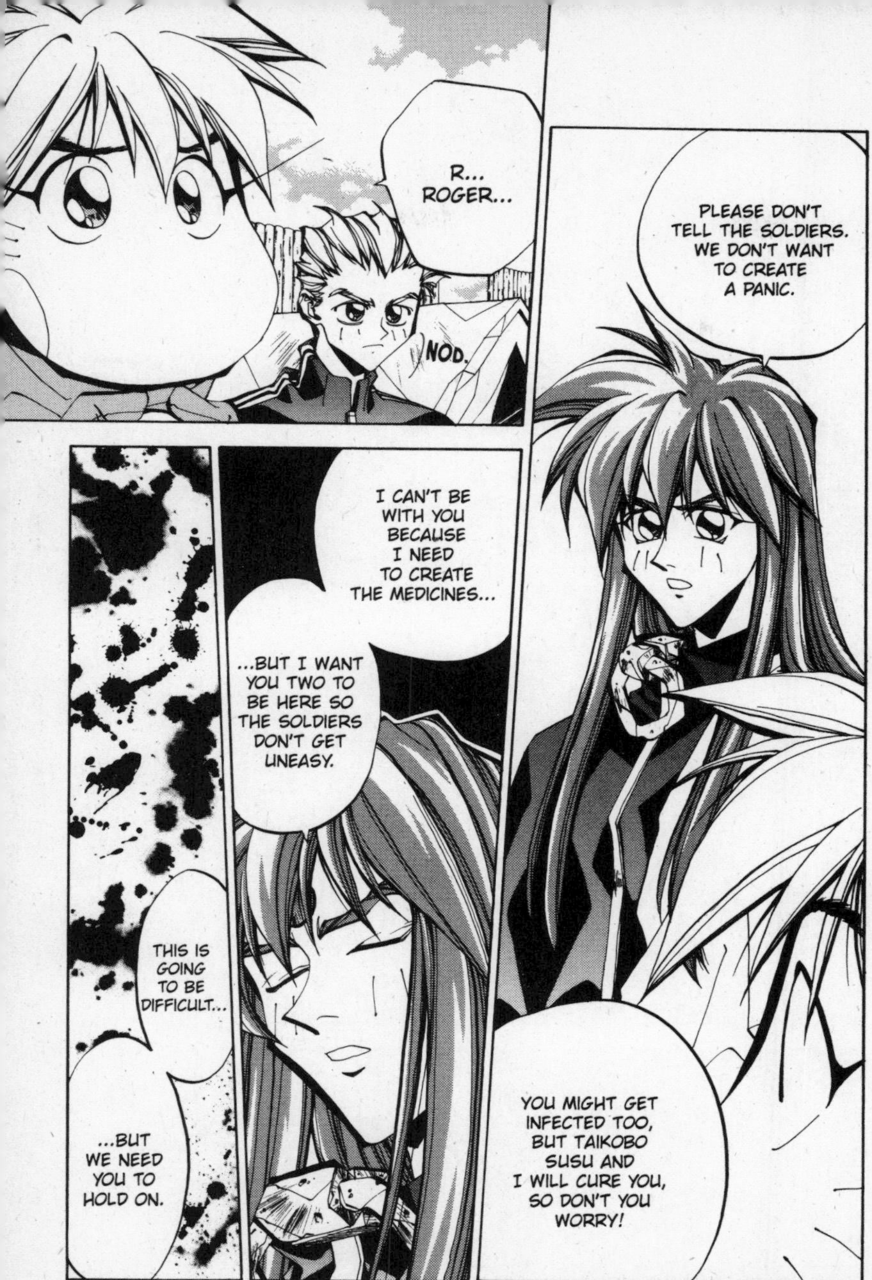

R... ROGER...
NOD.
PLEASE DON'T TELL THE SOLDIERS. WE DON'T WANT TO CREATE A PANIC.
YOU MIGHT GET INFECTED TOO, BUT TAIKOBO SUSU AND I WILL CURE YOU, SO DON'T YOU WORRY!
I CAN'T BE WITH YOU BECAUSE I NEED TO CREATE THE MEDICINES...
...BUT I WANT YOU TWO TO BE HERE SO THE SOLDIERS DON'T GET UNEASY.
THIS IS GOING TO BE DIFFICULT...
...BUT WE NEED YOU TO HOLD ON.

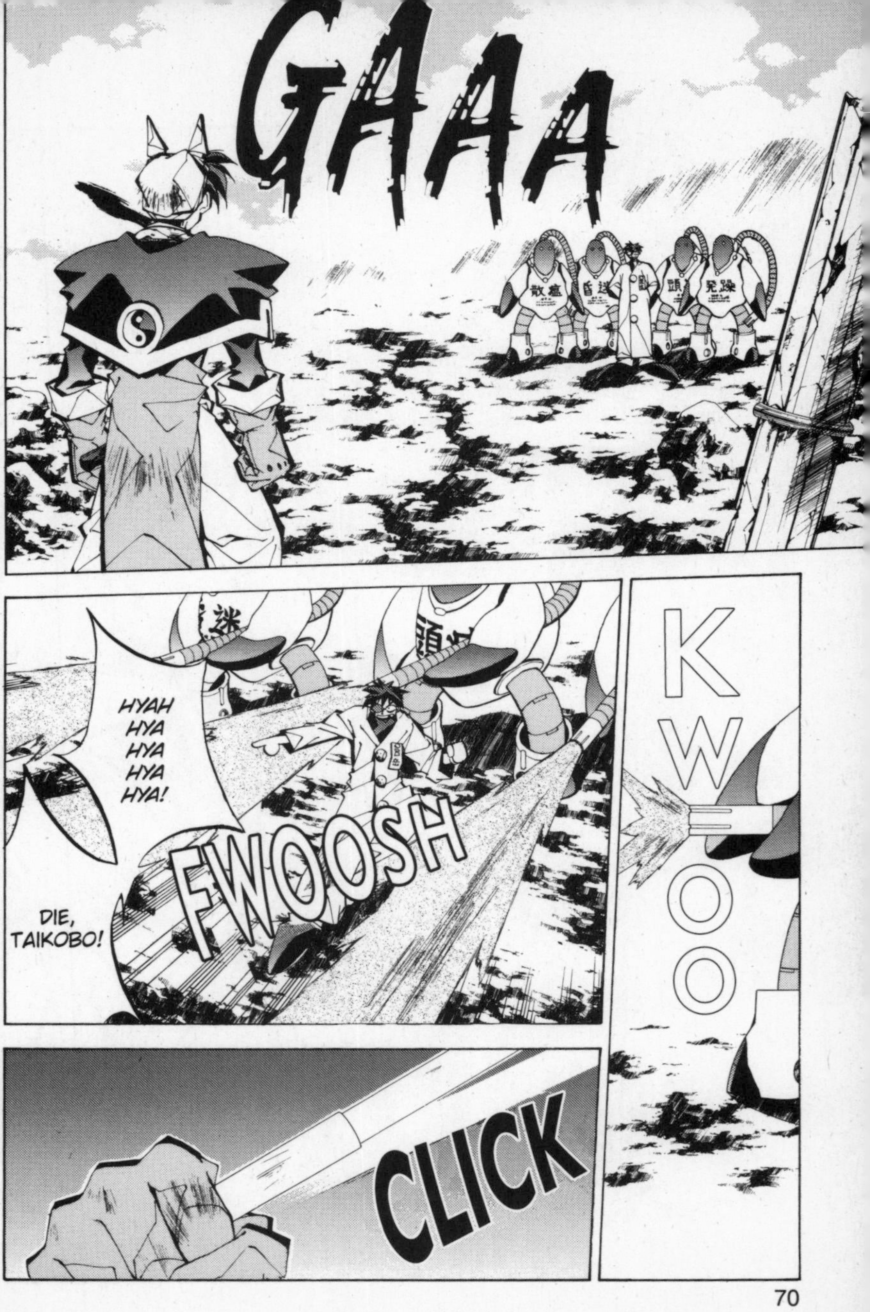
GAAA
KWOO
HYAH HYA HYA HYA HYA!
FWOOSH
DIE, TAIKOBO!
CLICK

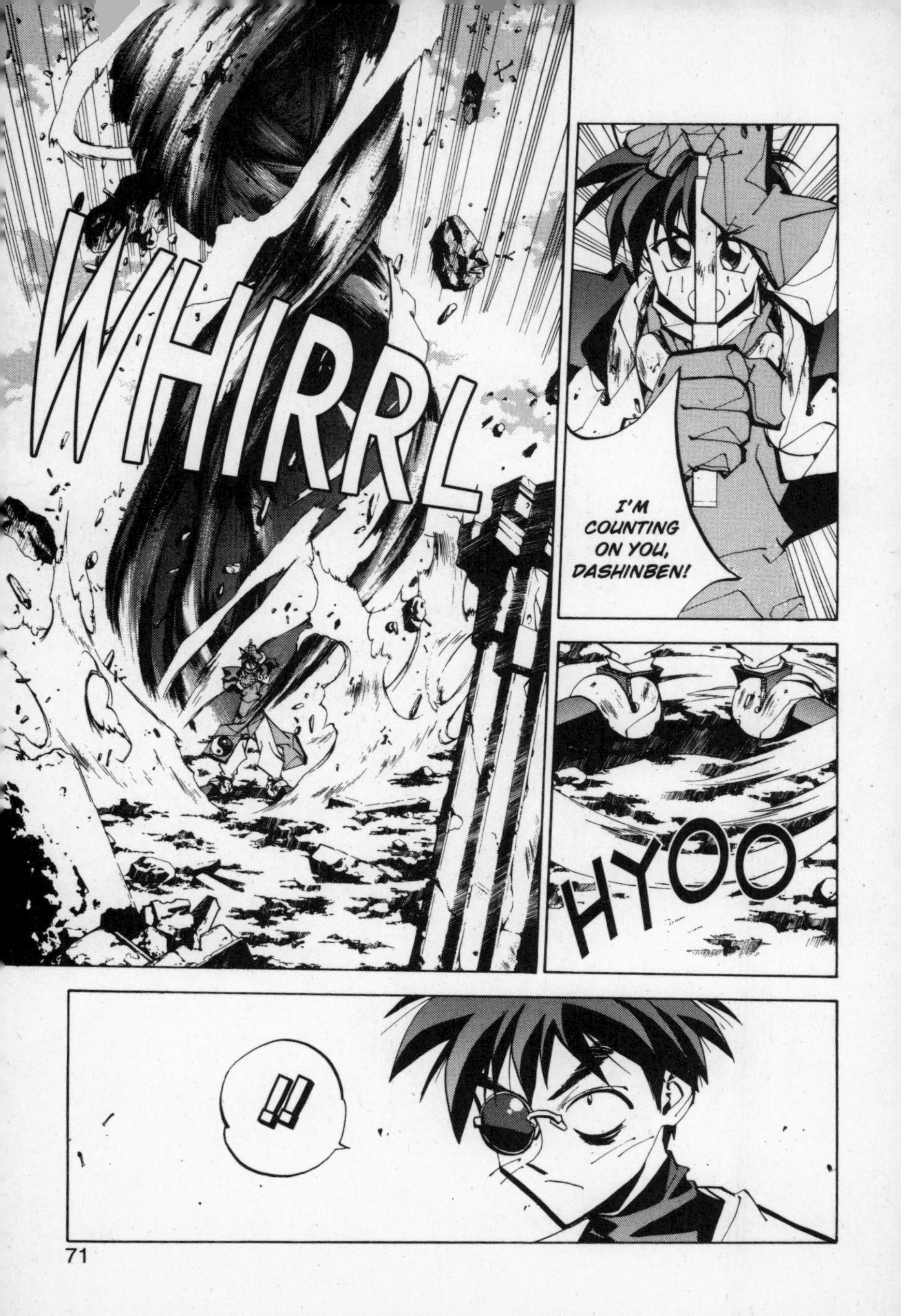

I'M COUNTING ON YOU, DASHINBEN!
HYOO
WHIRRL
!!

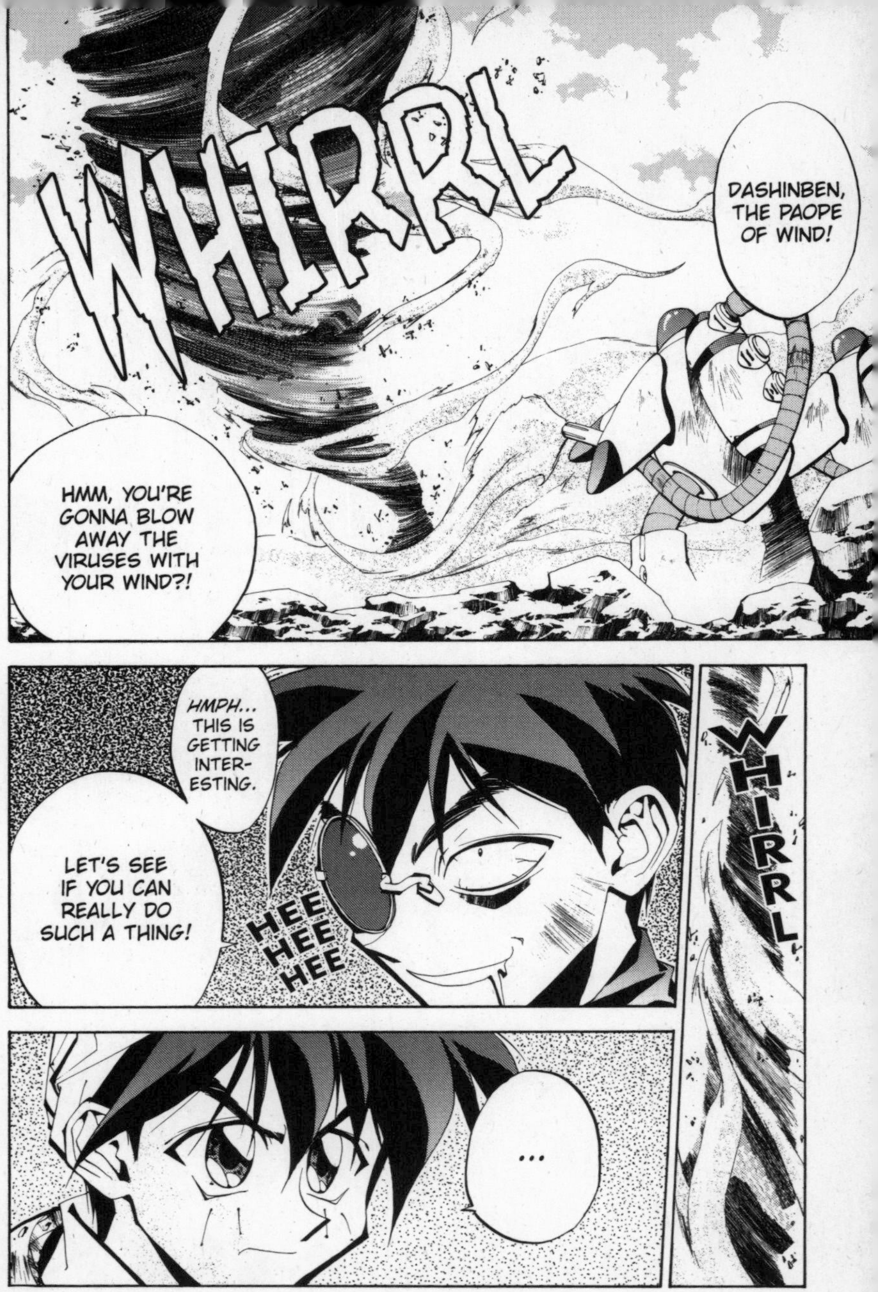
DASHINBEN, THE PAOPE OF WIND!
WHIRRL
HMM, YOU'RE GONNA BLOW AWAY THE VIRUSES WITH YOUR WIND?!
WHIRRL
HMPH... THIS IS GETTING INTER-ESTING.
LET'S SEE IF YOU CAN REALLY DO SUCH A THING!
HEE HEE HEE
...

READ THIS WAY

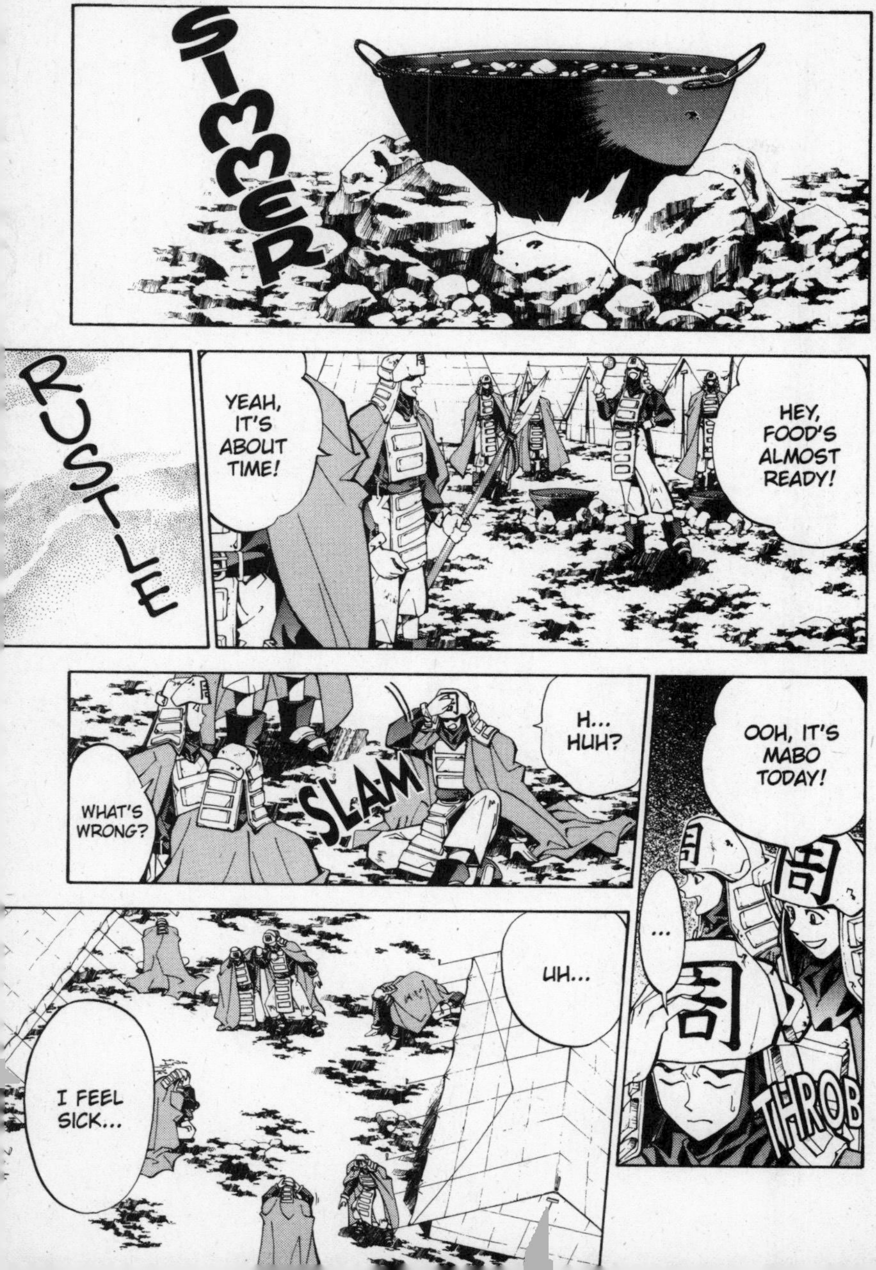
SIMMER
HEY, FOOD'S ALMOST READY!
YEAH, IT'S ABOUT TIME!
RUSTLE
OOH, IT'S MABO TODAY!
...
THROB
H... HUH?
SLAM
WHAT'S WRONG?
UH...
I FEEL SICK...

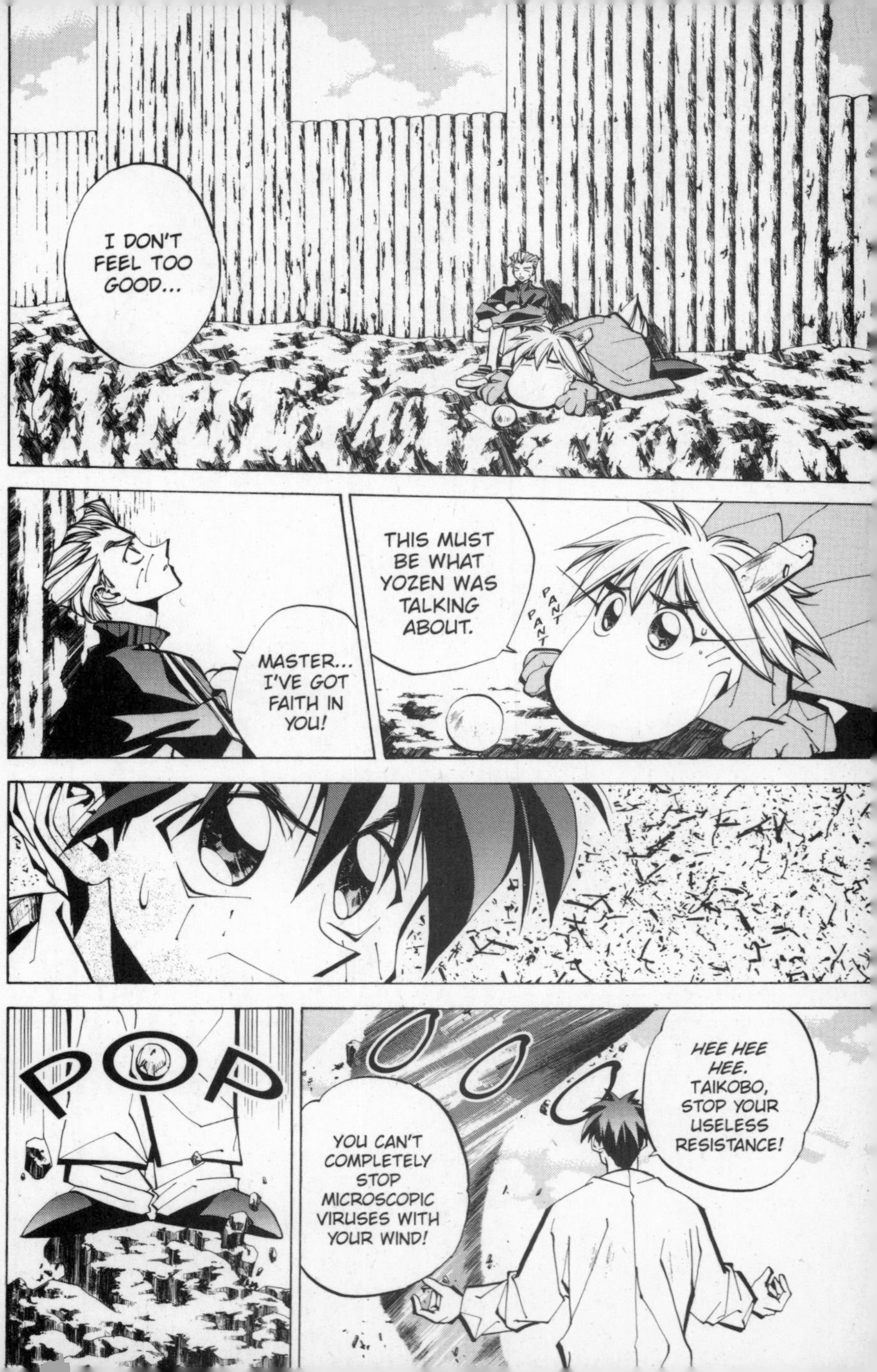
I DON'T FEEL TOO GOOD...
THIS MUST BE WHAT YOZEN WAS TALKING ABOUT.
PANT PANT
MASTER... I'VE GOT FAITH IN YOU!
HEE HEE HEE. TAIKOBO, STOP YOUR USELESS RESISTANCE!
YOU CAN'T COMPLETELY STOP MICROSCOPIC VIRUSES WITH YOUR WIND!
POP

READ THIS WAY

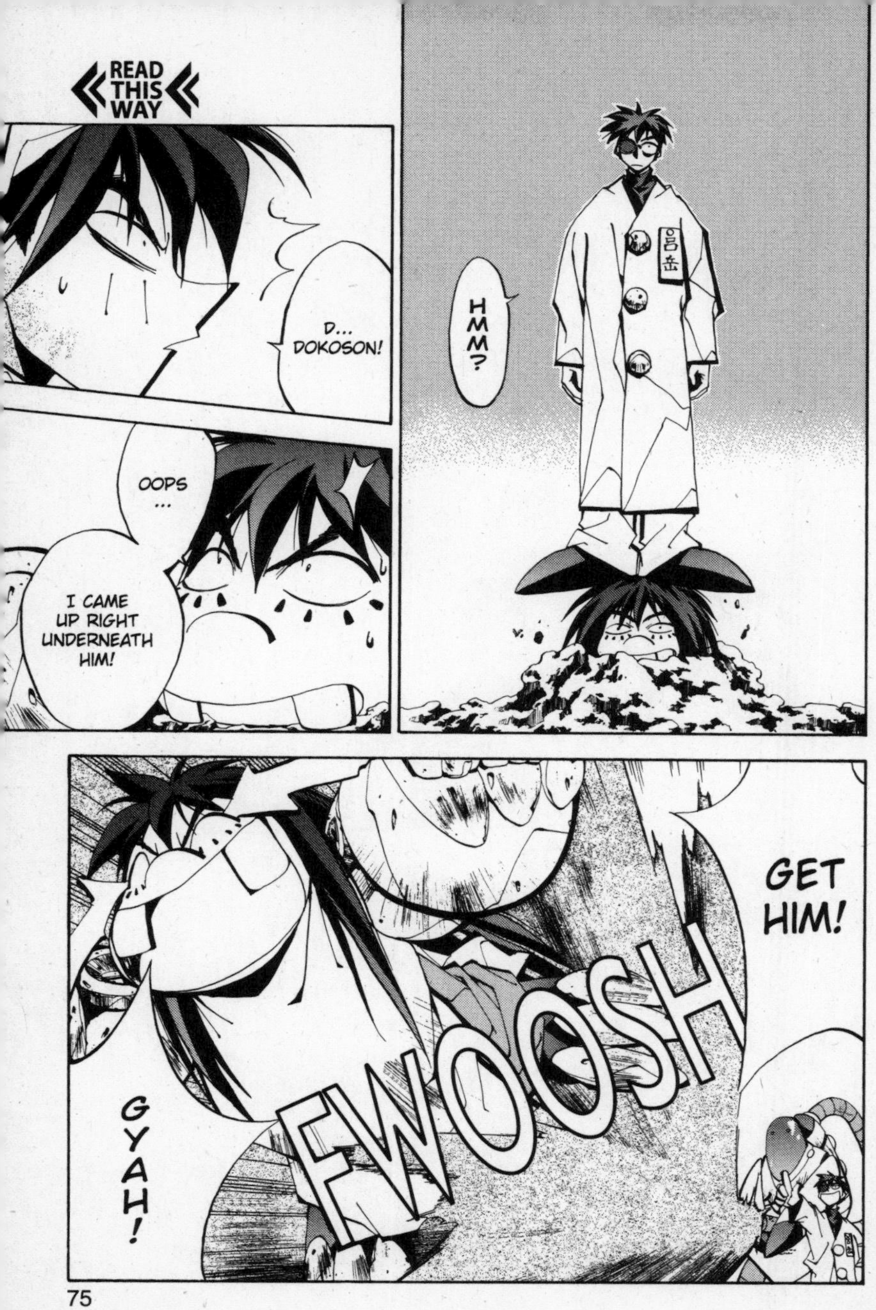

呂岳
HMM?
D... DOKOSON!
OOPS ...
I CAME UP RIGHT UNDERNEATH HIM!
GET HIM!
FWOOSH
GYAH!

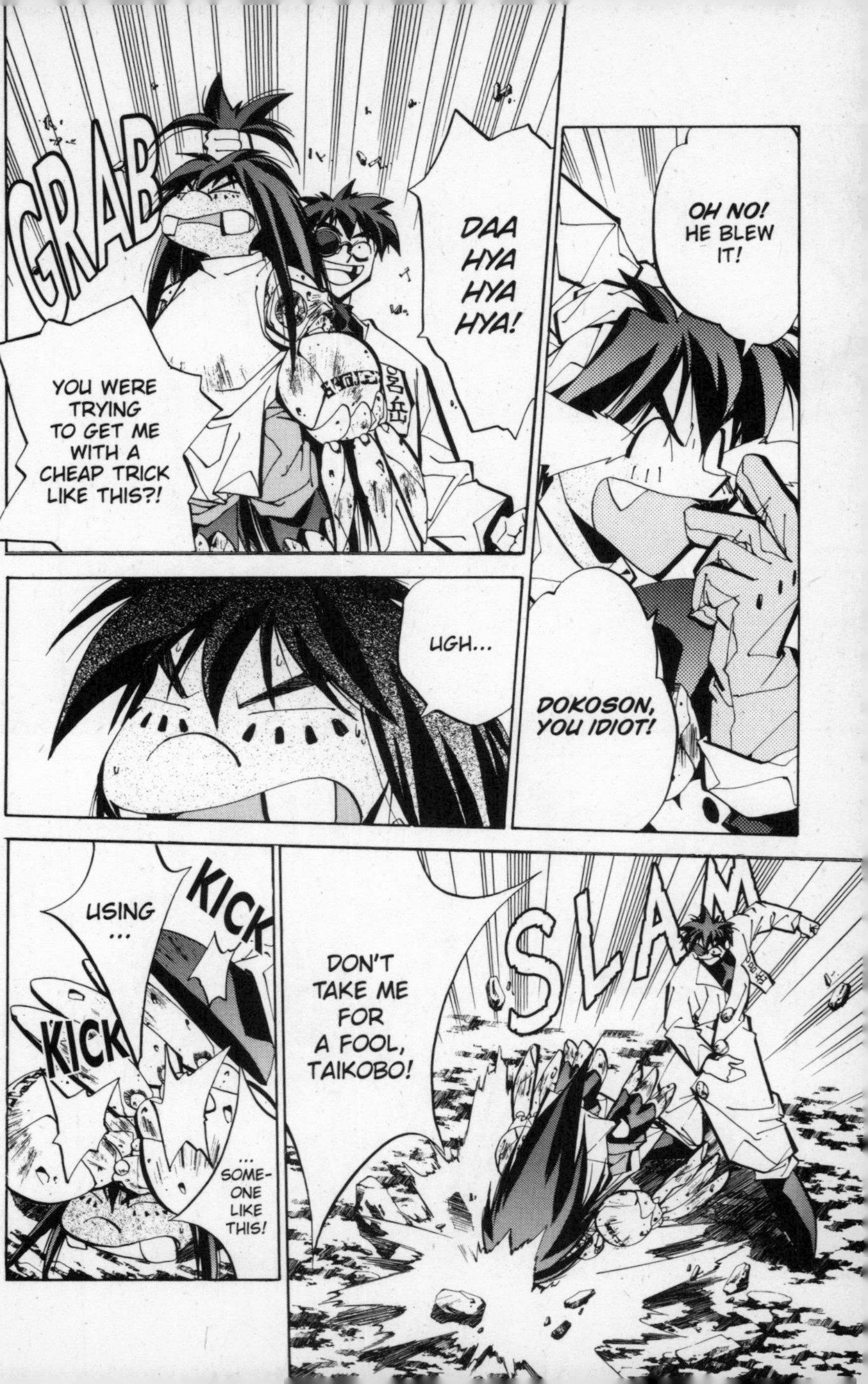
GRAB
DAA HYA HYA HYA!
YOU WERE TRYING TO GET ME WITH A CHEAP TRICK LIKE THIS?!
OH NO! HE BLEW IT!
UGH...
DOKOSON, YOU IDIOT!
SLAM
DON'T TAKE ME FOR A FOOL, TAIKOBO!
USING ...
KICK
KICK
... SOME-ONE LIKE THIS!

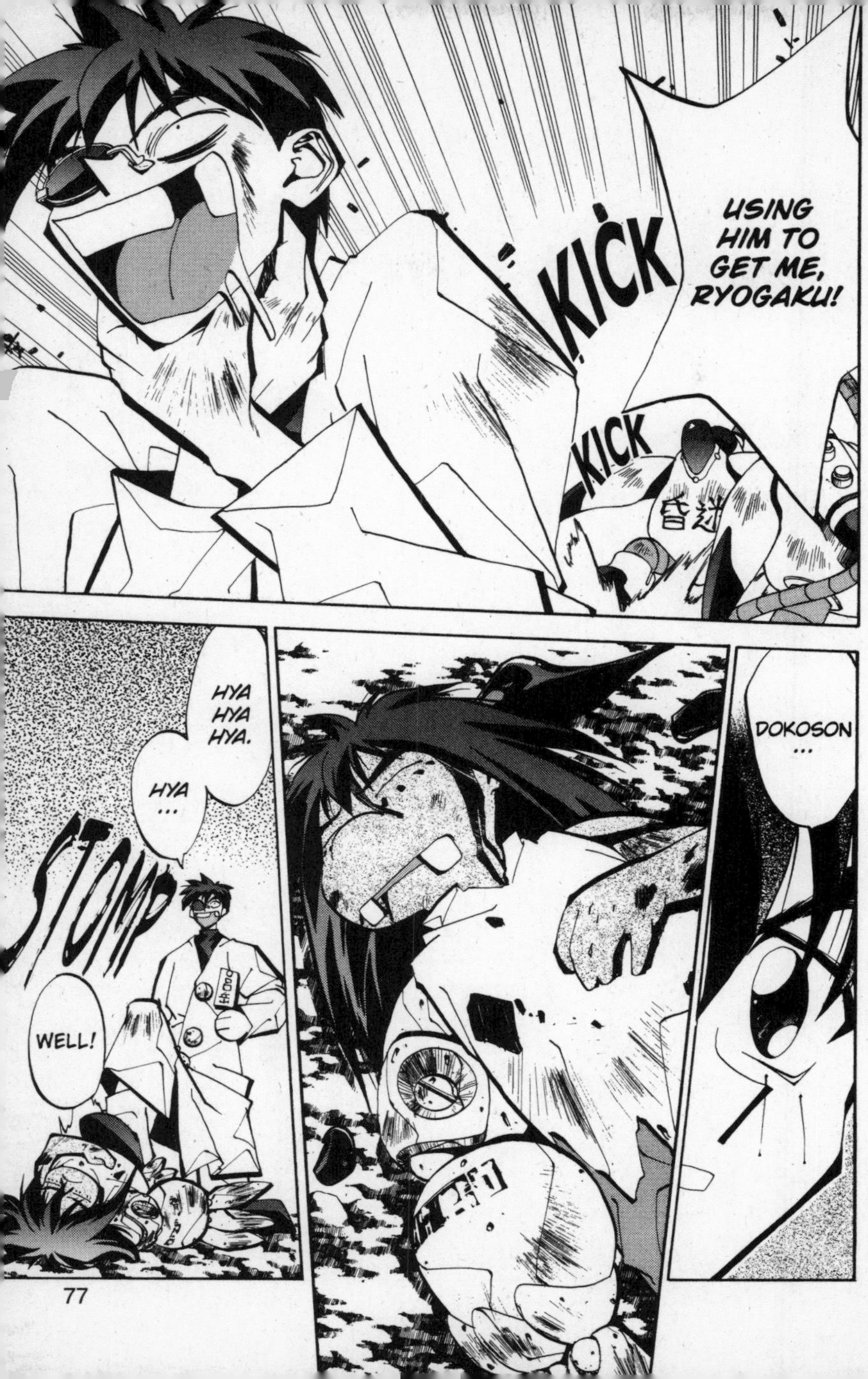
USING HIM TO GET ME, RYOGAKU!
KICK
KICK
DOKOSON ...
HYA HYA HYA.
HYA ...
STOMP
WELL!

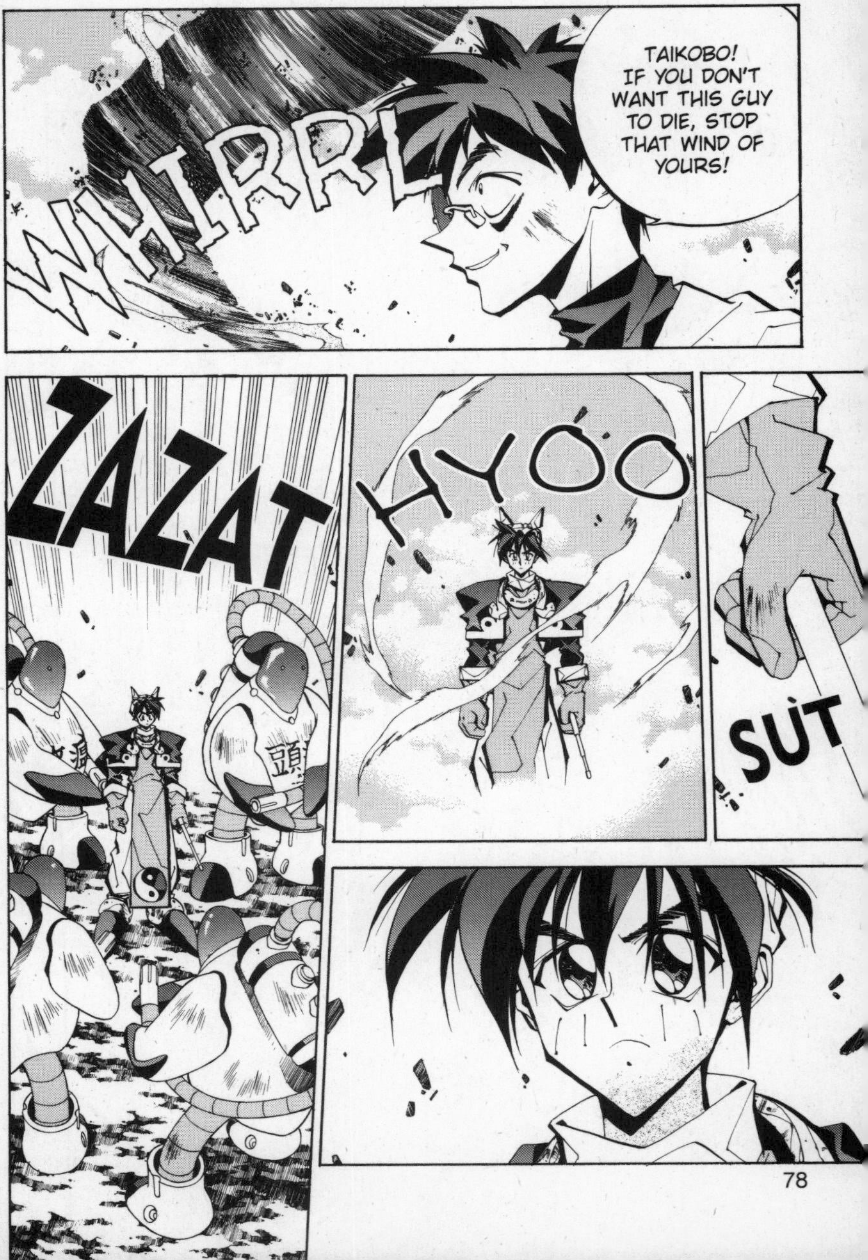
TAIKOBO! IF YOU DON'T WANT THIS GUY TO DIE, STOP THAT WIND OF YOURS!
WHIRRL
SUT
HYOO
ZAZAT

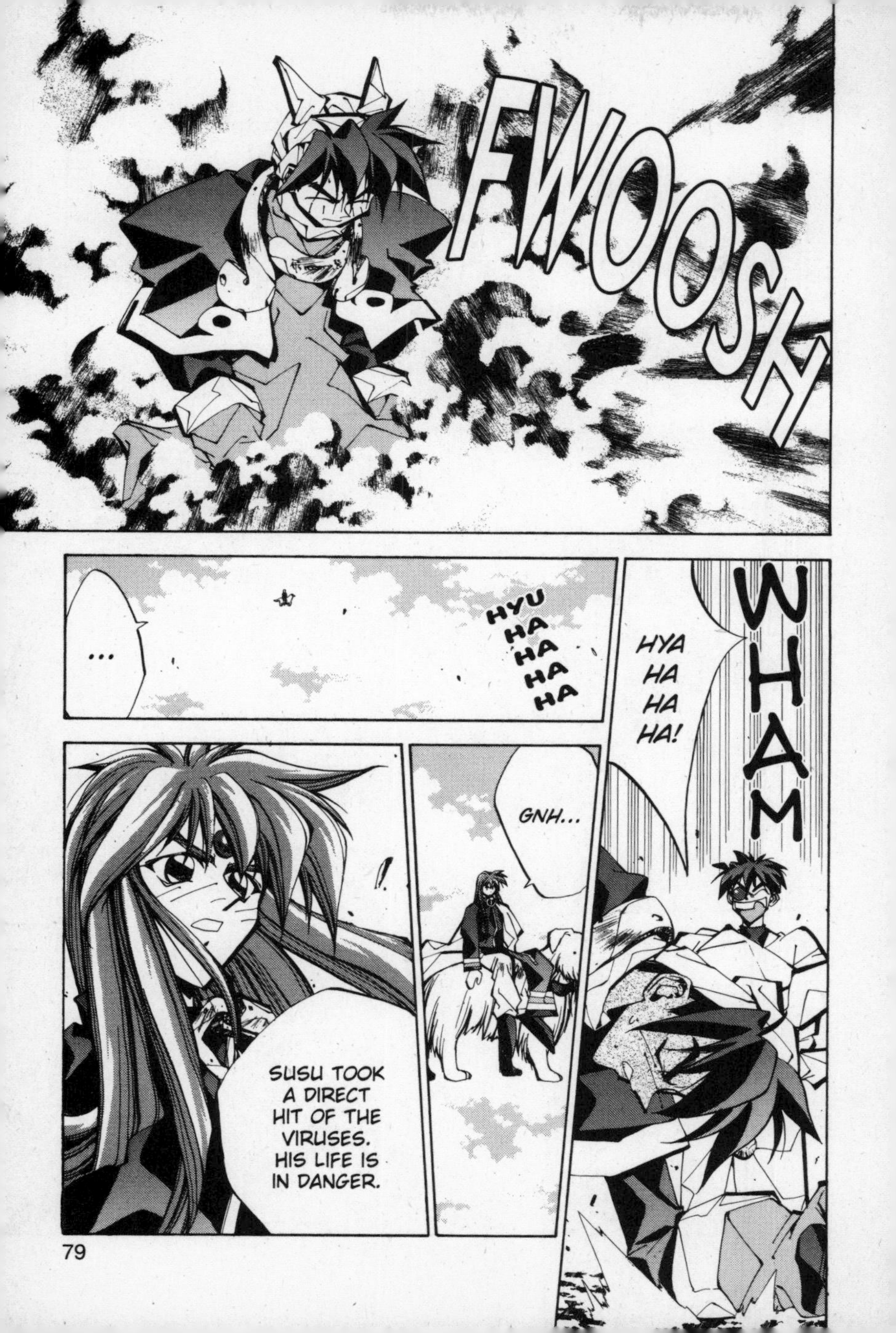
FWOOSH
WHAM
HYA HA HA HA!
HYU HA HA HA HA
...
GNH...
SUSU TOOK A DIRECT HIT OF THE VIRUSES. HIS LIFE IS IN DANGER.

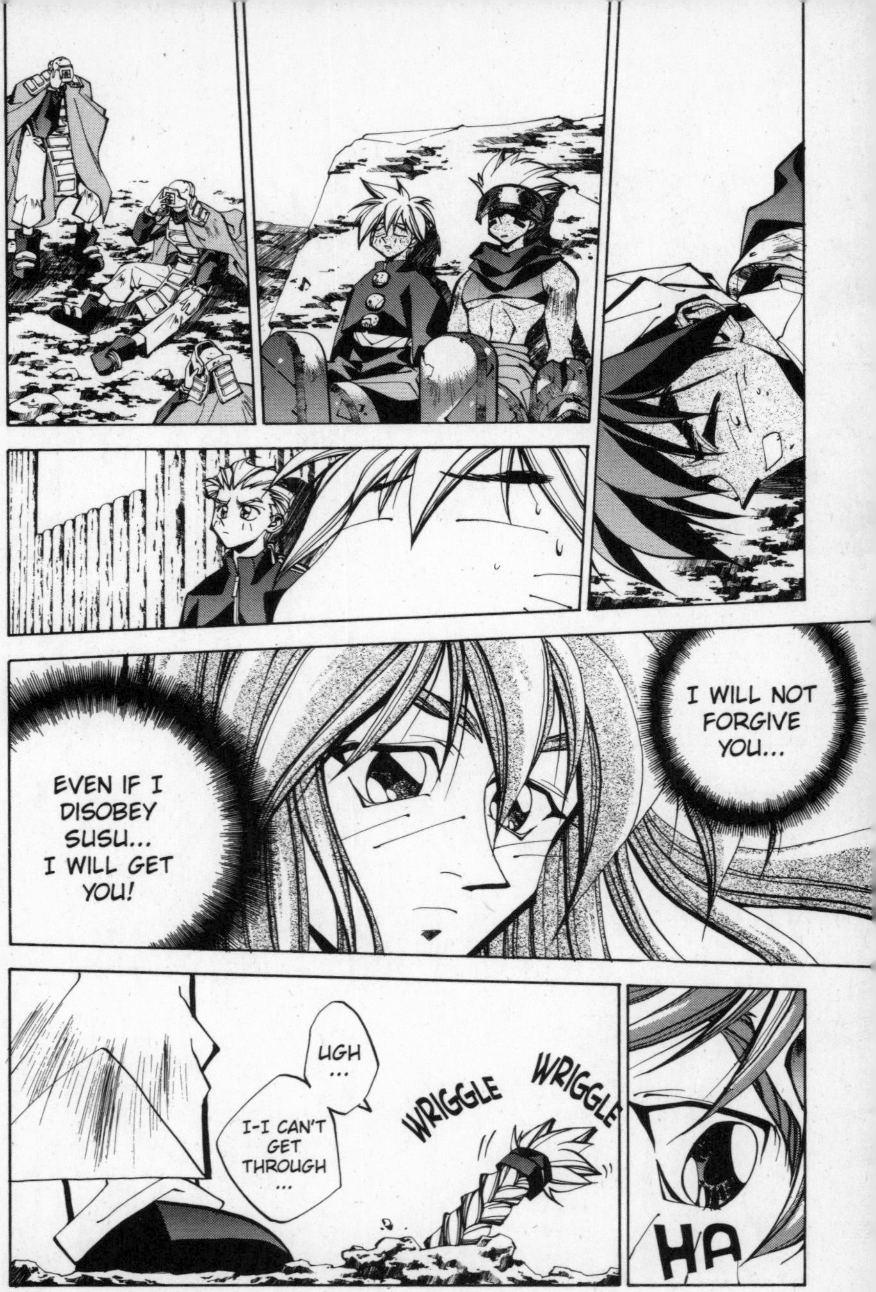
I WILL NOT FORGIVE YOU...
EVEN IF I DISOBEY SUSU... I WILL GET YOU!
HA
WRIGGLE
WRIGGLE
UGH ...
I-I CAN'T GET THROUGH ...

READ THIS WAY

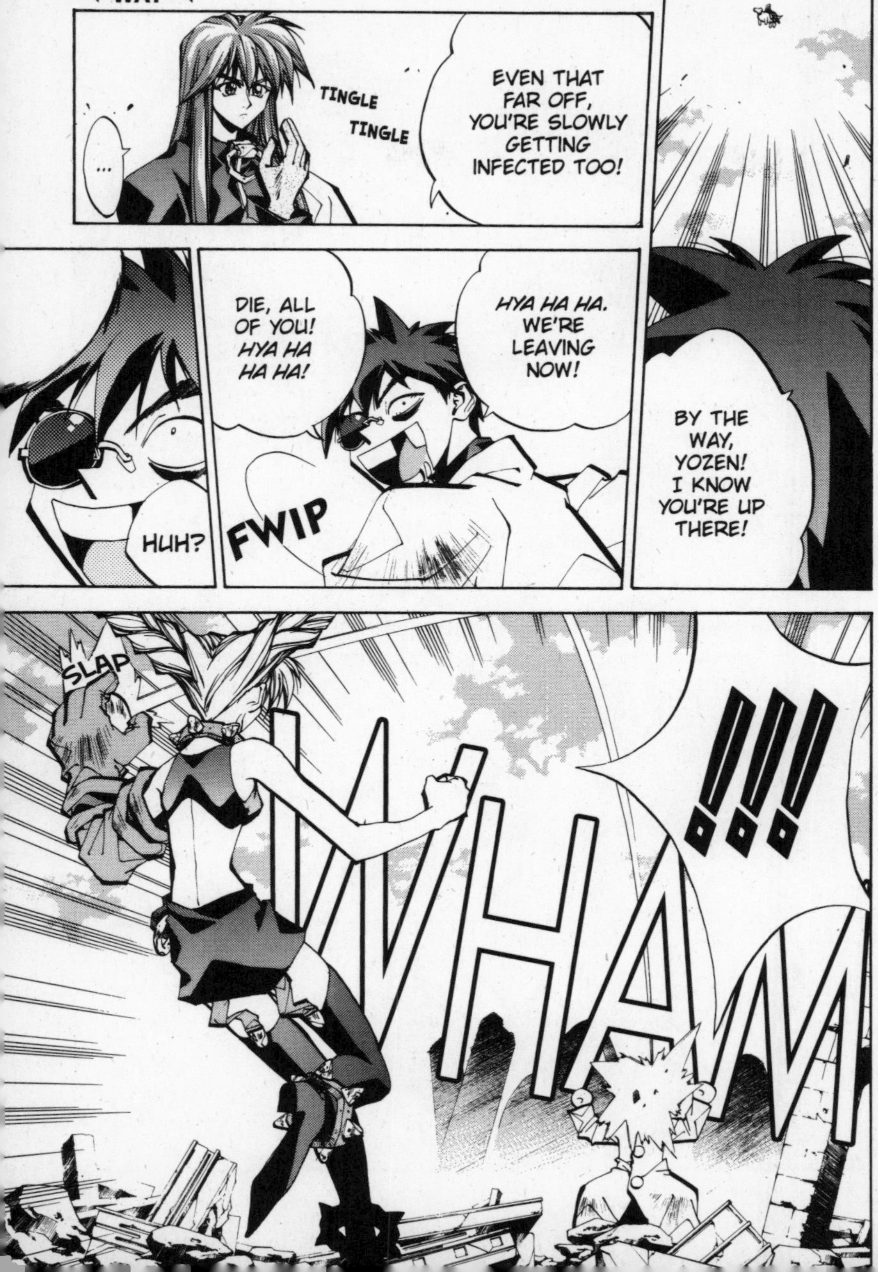
EVEN THAT FAR OFF, YOU'RE SLOWLY GETTING INFECTED TOO!
TINGLE
TINGLE
...
BY THE WAY, YOZEN! I KNOW YOU'RE UP THERE!
HYA HA HA. WE'RE LEAVING NOW!
DIE, ALL OF YOU! HYA HA HA HA!
FWIP
HUH?
WHAM!!!
SLAP

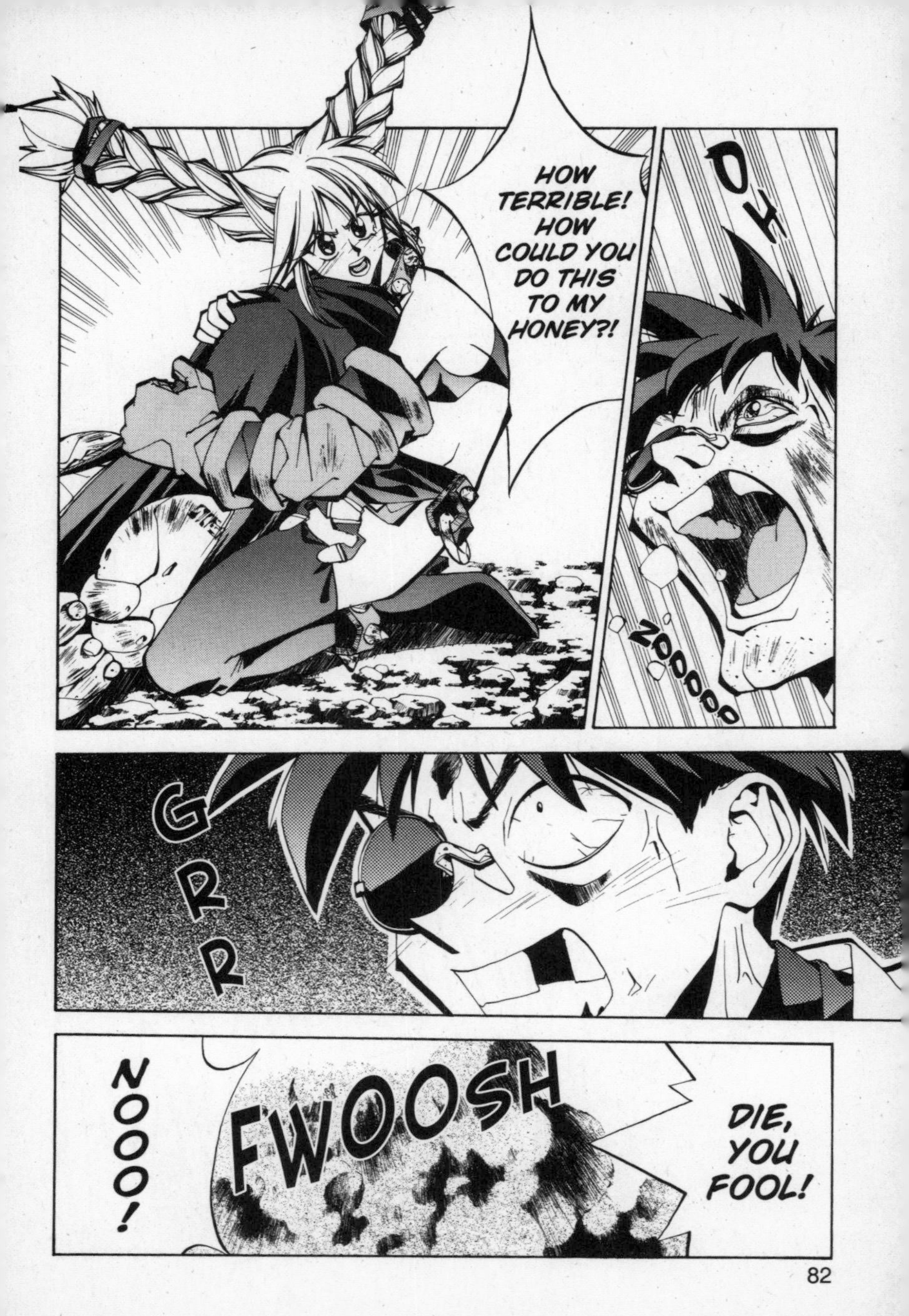
OH
ZOOOOOO
HOW TERRIBLE! HOW COULD YOU DO THIS TO MY HONEY?!
GRR
DIE, YOU FOOL!
FWOOSH
NOOOO!

READ THIS WAY

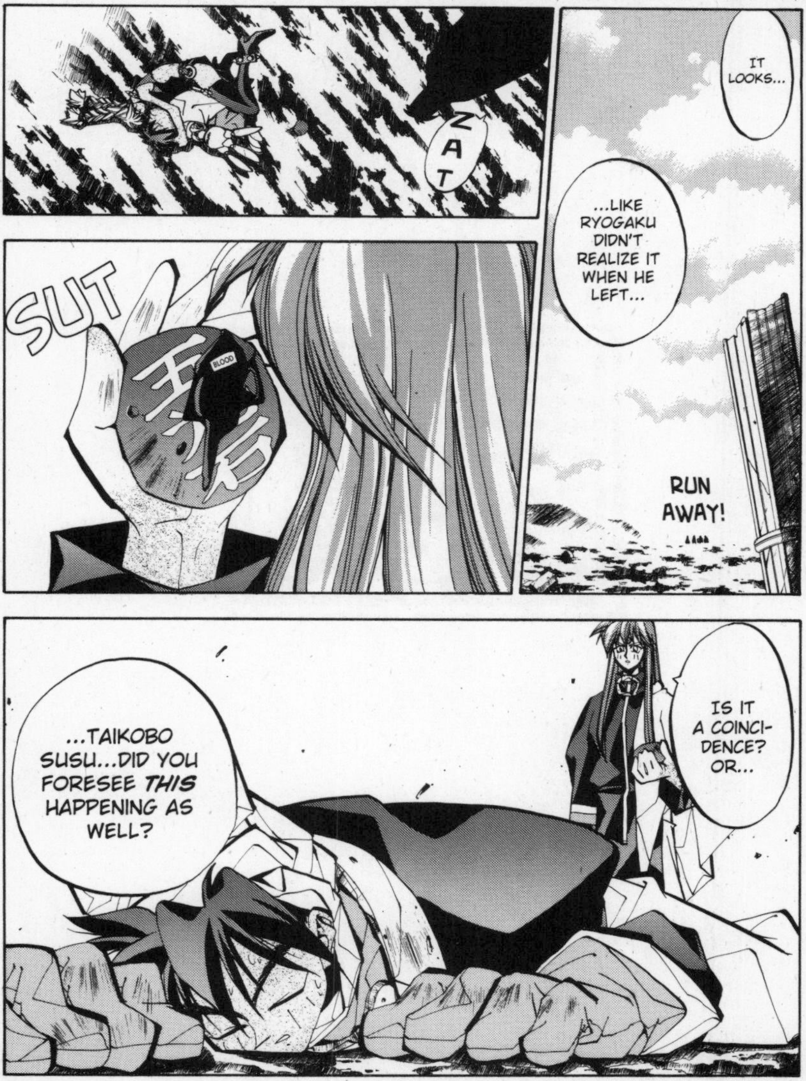
IT LOOKS...
...LIKE RYOGAKU DIDN'T REALIZE IT WHEN HE LEFT...
RUN AWAY!
ZAT
SUT
BLOOD
IS IT A COINCIDENCE? OR...
...TAIKOBO SUSU...DID YOU FORESEE *THIS* HAPPENING AS WELL?

封神演義

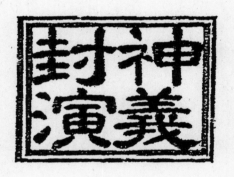

Chapter 74

THE SO FAMILY'S STATE OF AFFAIRS

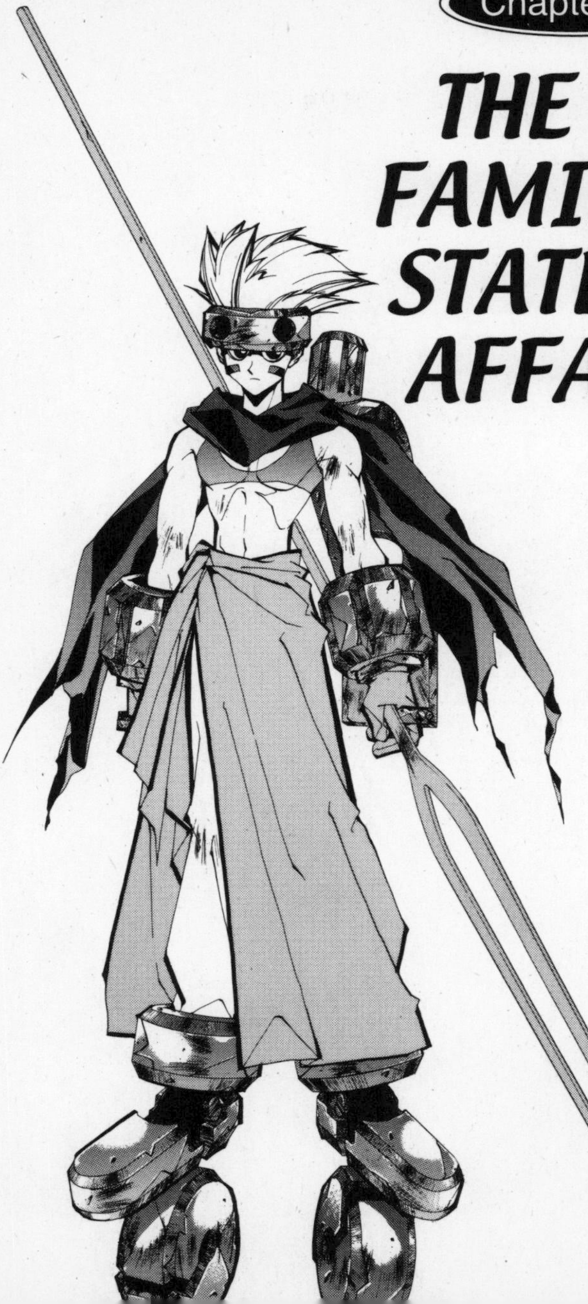

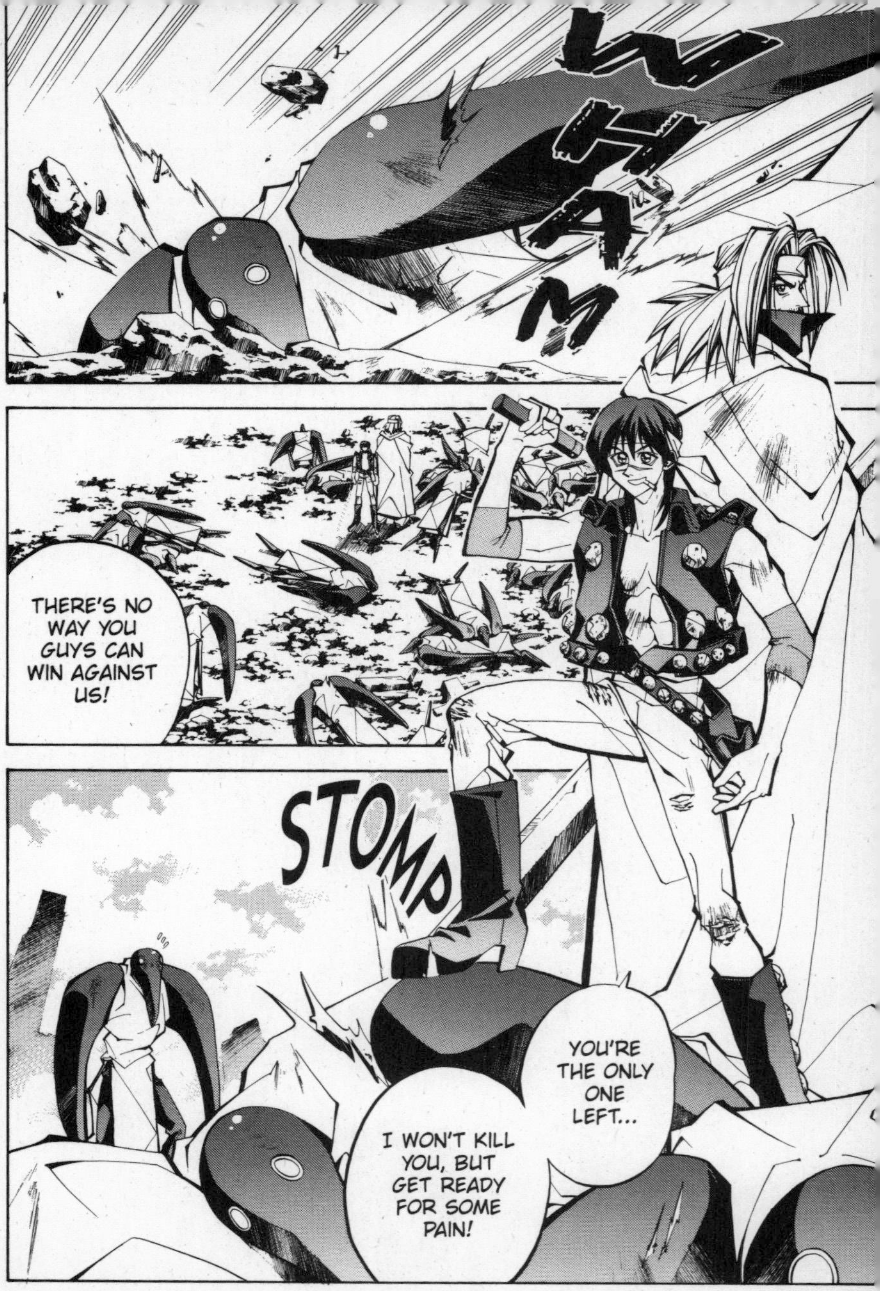
WHAM
THERE'S NO WAY YOU GUYS CAN WIN AGAINST US!
STOMP
YOU'RE THE ONLY ONE LEFT...
I WON'T KILL YOU, BUT GET READY FOR SOME PAIN!

READ THIS WAY

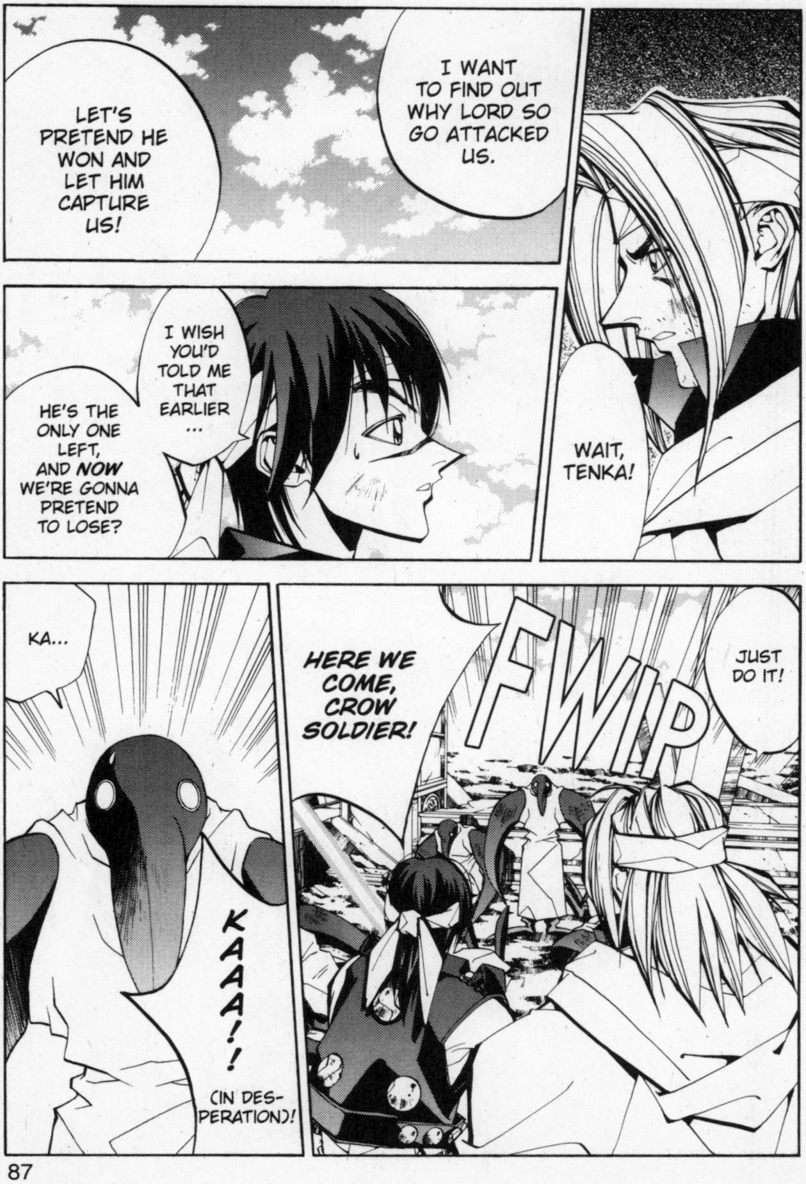

WAIT, TENKA!
I WANT TO FIND OUT WHY LORD SO GO ATTACKED US.
LET'S PRETEND HE WON AND LET HIM CAPTURE US!
I WISH YOU'D TOLD ME THAT EARLIER ...
HE'S THE ONLY ONE LEFT, AND *NOW* WE'RE GONNA PRETEND TO LOSE?
JUST DO IT!
FWIP
HERE WE COME, CROW SOLDIER!
KA...
KAAAA!!
(IN DESPERATION)!

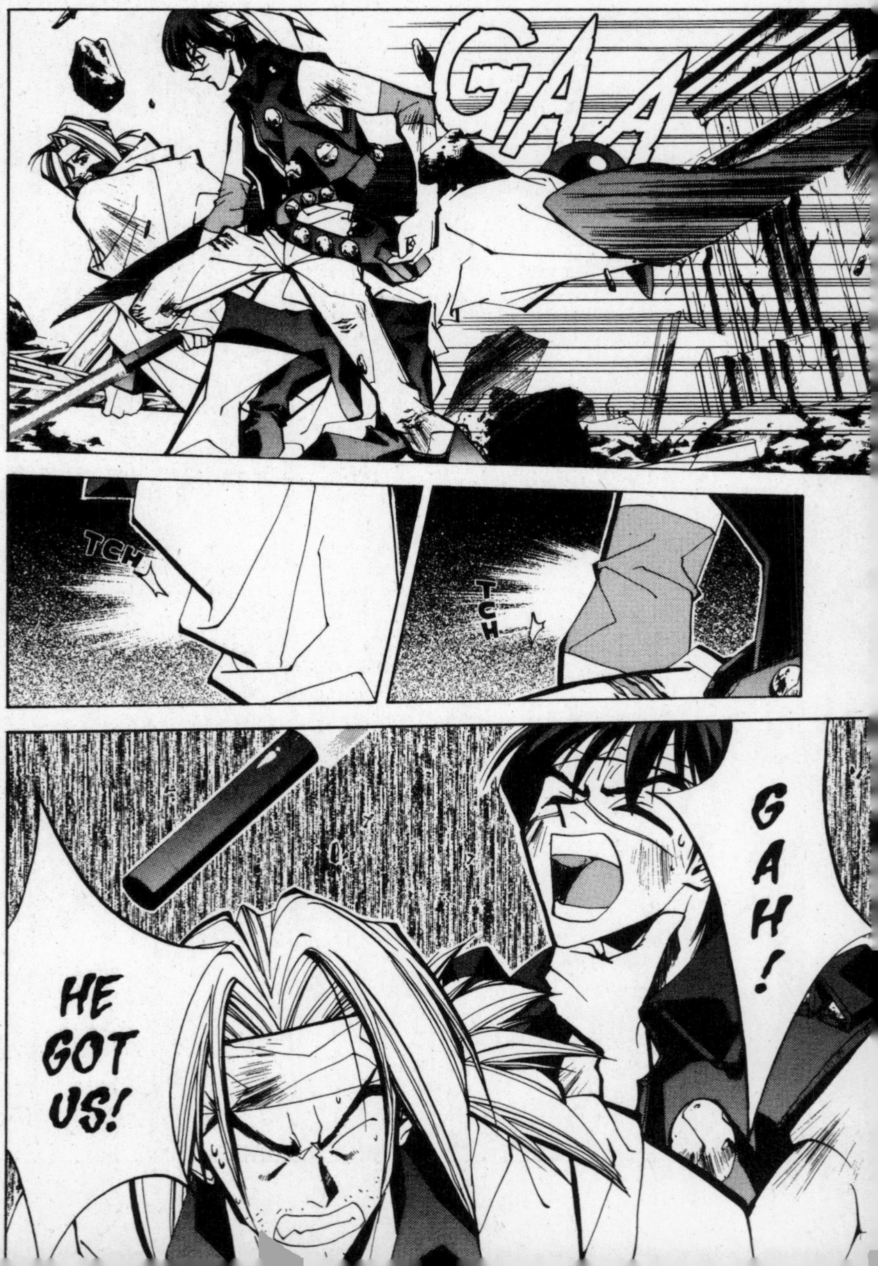
GA A
TCH
TCH
GAH!
HE GOT US!

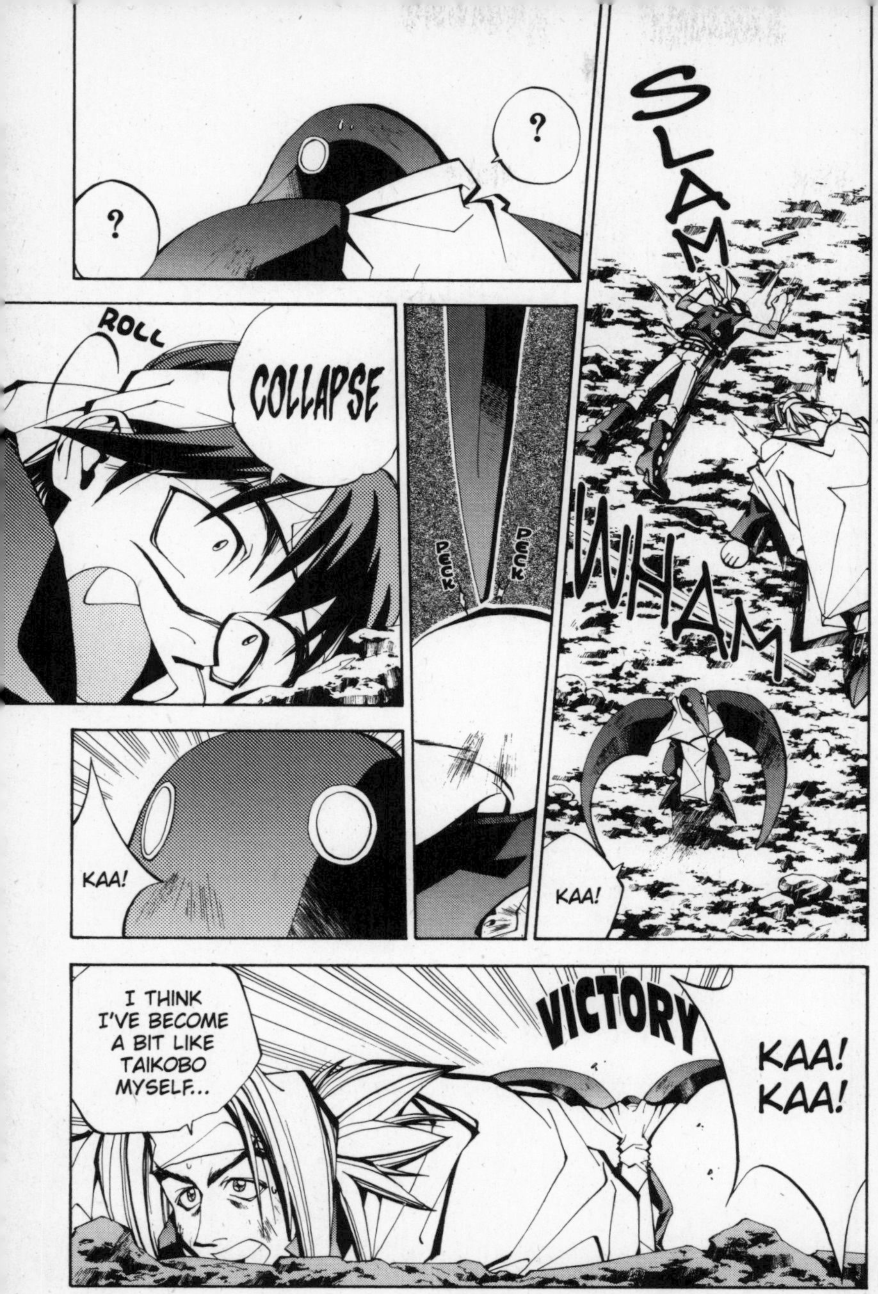
SLAM
WHAM
KAA!
?
?
PECK
PECK
COLLAPSE
ROLL
KAA!
KAA! KAA!
VICTORY
I THINK I'VE BECOME A BIT LIKE TAIKOBO MYSELF...

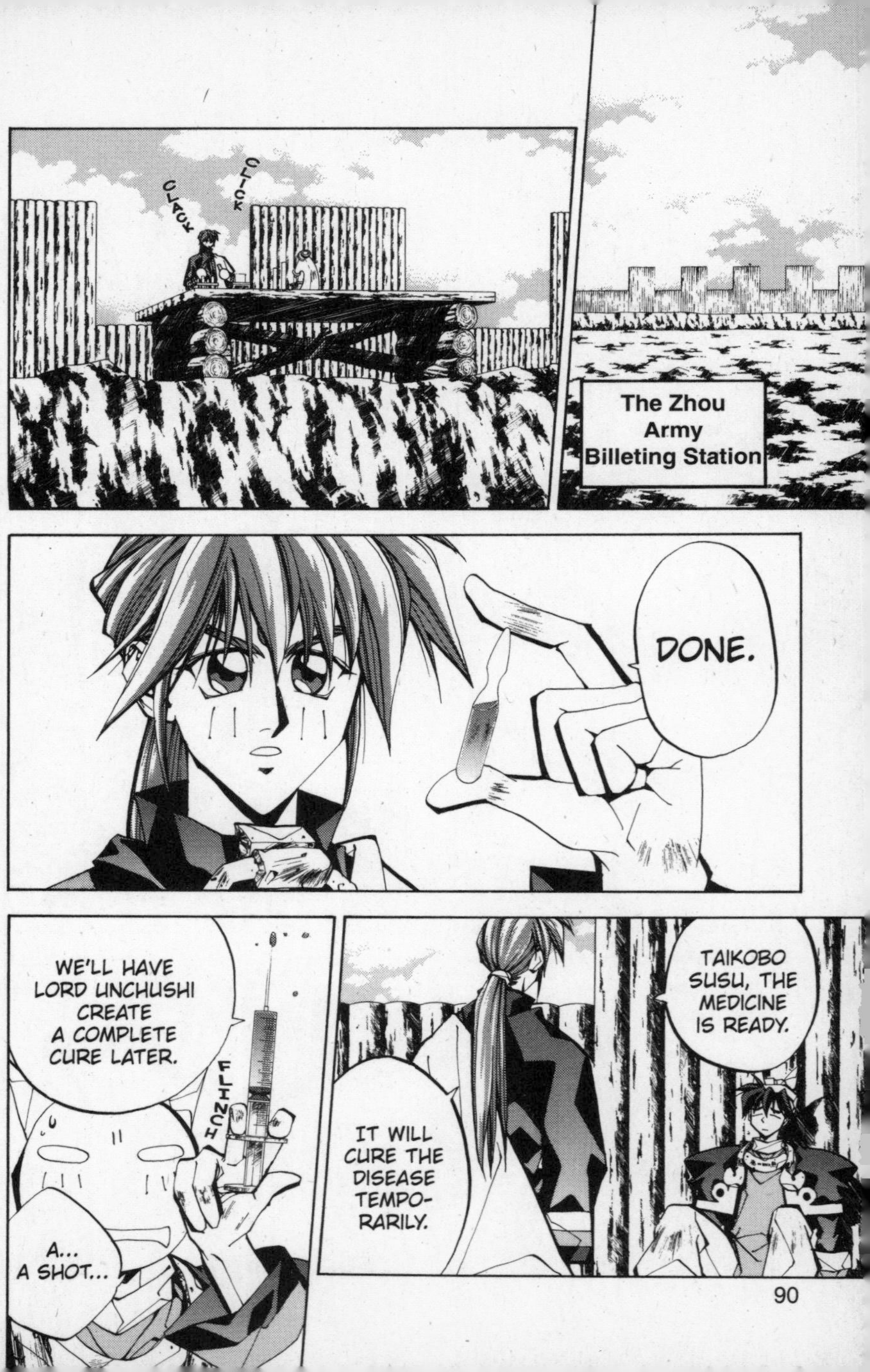
The Zhou Army Billeting Station
CLACK
CLICK
DONE.
TAIKOBO SUSU, THE MEDICINE IS READY.
IT WILL CURE THE DISEASE TEMPO-RARILY.
WE'LL HAVE LORD UNCHUSHI CREATE A COMPLETE CURE LATER.
FLINCH
A... A SHOT...

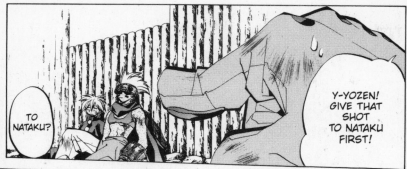

READ THIS WAY

Y-YOZEN! GIVE THAT SHOT TO NATAKU FIRST!
TO NATAKU?
YOU'VE ONLY MADE A LITTLE OF THAT MEDICINE.
HEAL NATAKU FIRST AND HAVE HIM DEFEAT RYOGAKU!
YOU'RE RIGHT.
I ONLY NEED A LITTLE OF IT.
OH! YOU'RE AWAKE.
THIS KID'S GONNA DIE SOON.
I'M STRONG. EVEN IF MY BODY DIES, MY CORE WON'T DIE.

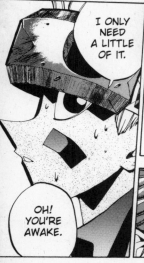

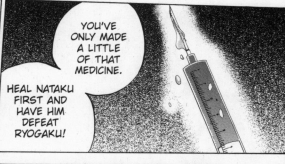

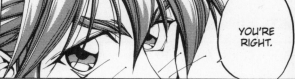

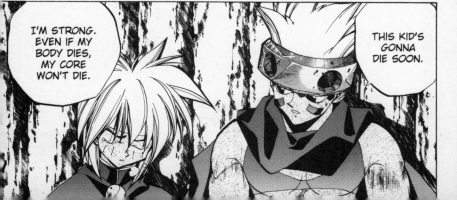

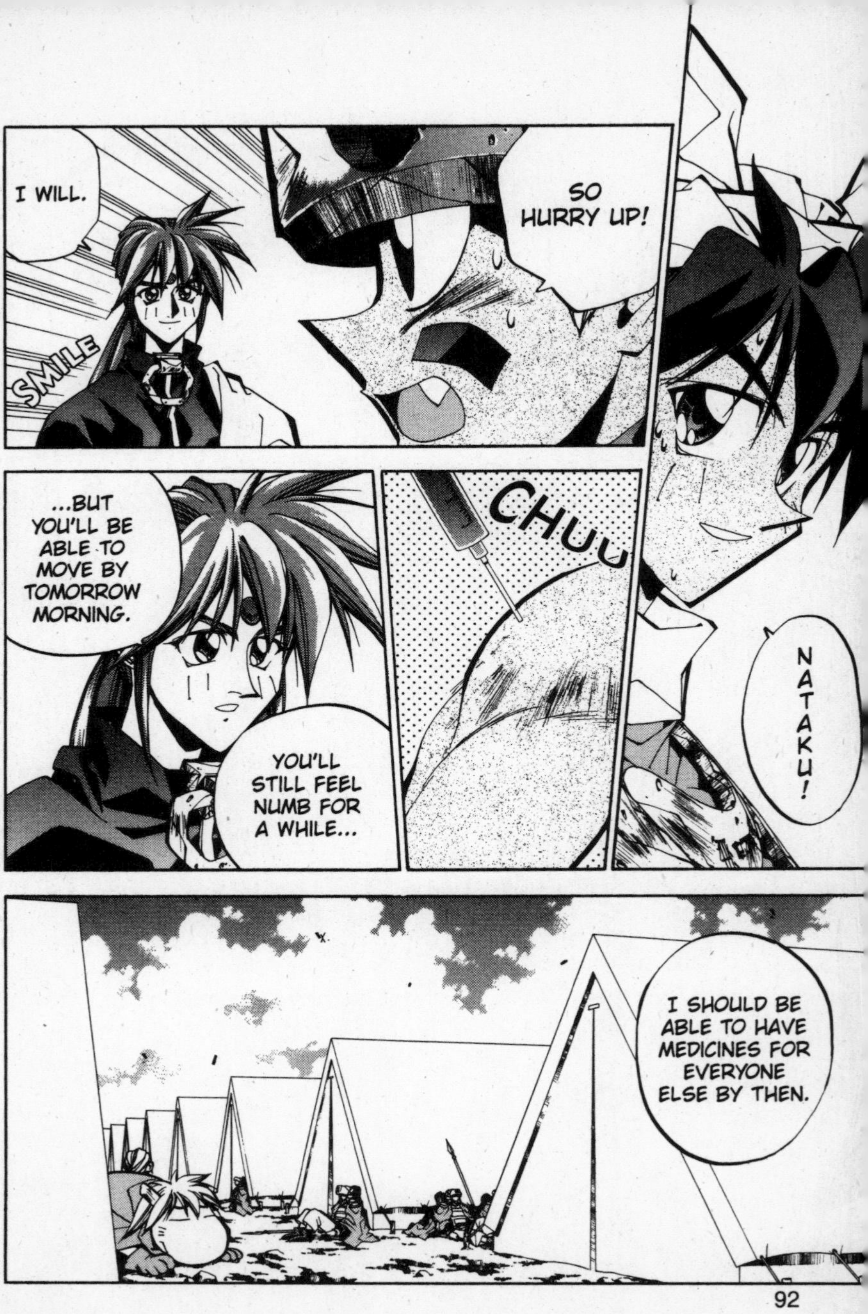
NATAKU!
SO HURRY UP!
I WILL.
SMILE
CHUU
YOU'LL STILL FEEL NUMB FOR A WHILE...
...BUT YOU'LL BE ABLE TO MOVE BY TOMORROW MORNING.
I SHOULD BE ABLE TO HAVE MEDICINES FOR EVERYONE ELSE BY THEN.

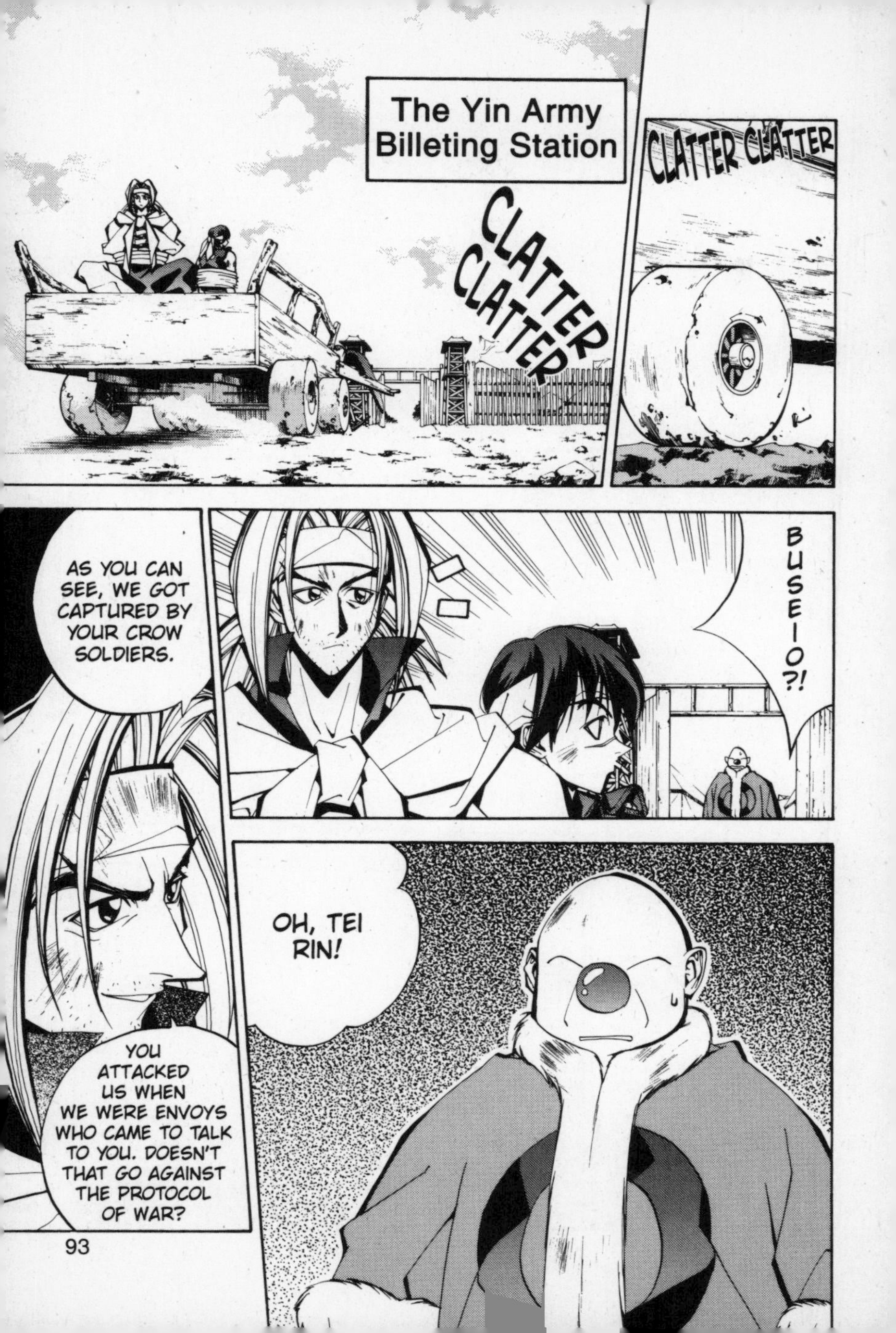
CLATTER CLATTER
The Yin Army Billeting Station
CLATTER CLATTER
BUSEI-O?!
AS YOU CAN SEE, WE GOT CAPTURED BY YOUR CROW SOLDIERS.
OH, TEI RIN!
YOU ATTACKED US WHEN WE WERE ENVOYS WHO CAME TO TALK TO YOU. DOESN'T THAT GO AGAINST THE PROTOCOL OF WAR?

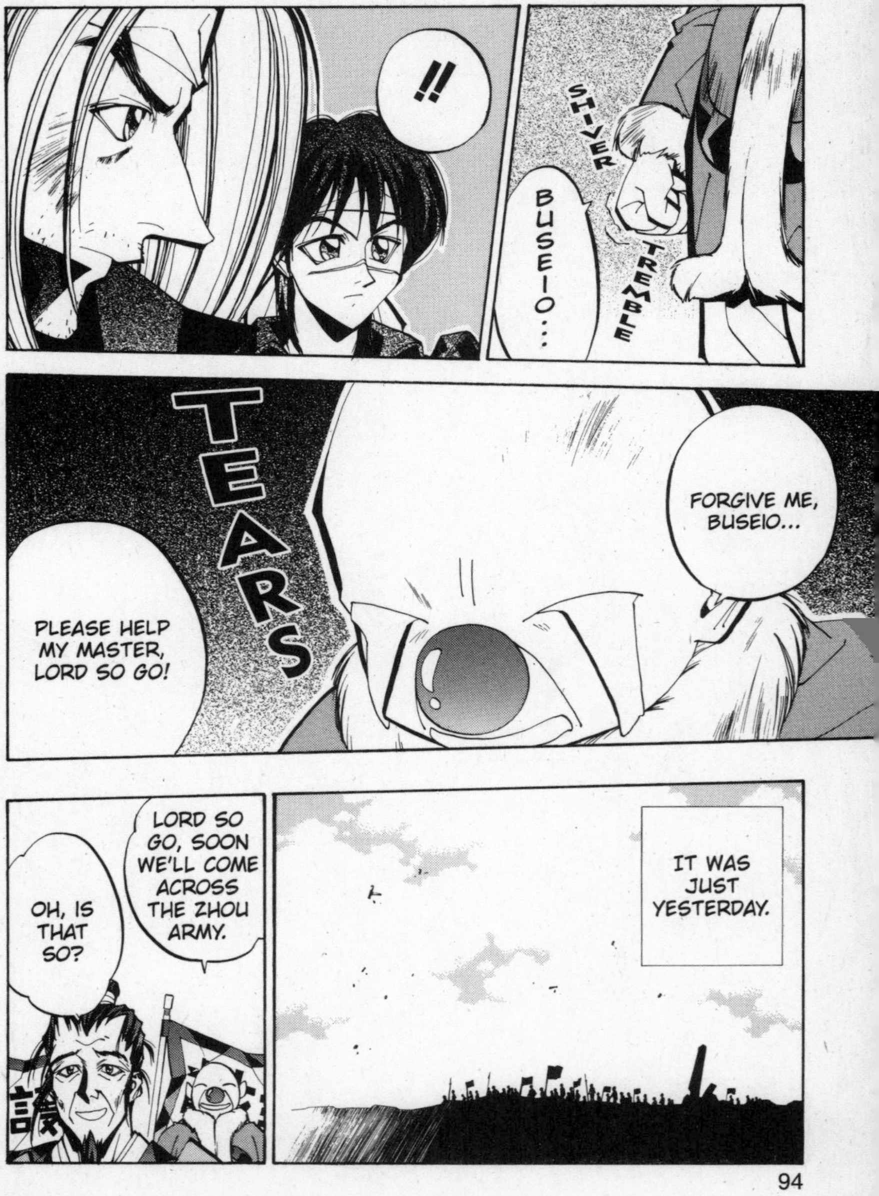
SHIVER
TREMBLE
BUSEIO...
!!
FORGIVE ME, BUSEIO...
TEARS
PLEASE HELP MY MASTER, LORD SO GO!
IT WAS JUST YESTERDAY.
LORD SO GO, SOON WE'LL COME ACROSS THE ZHOU ARMY.
OH, IS THAT SO?

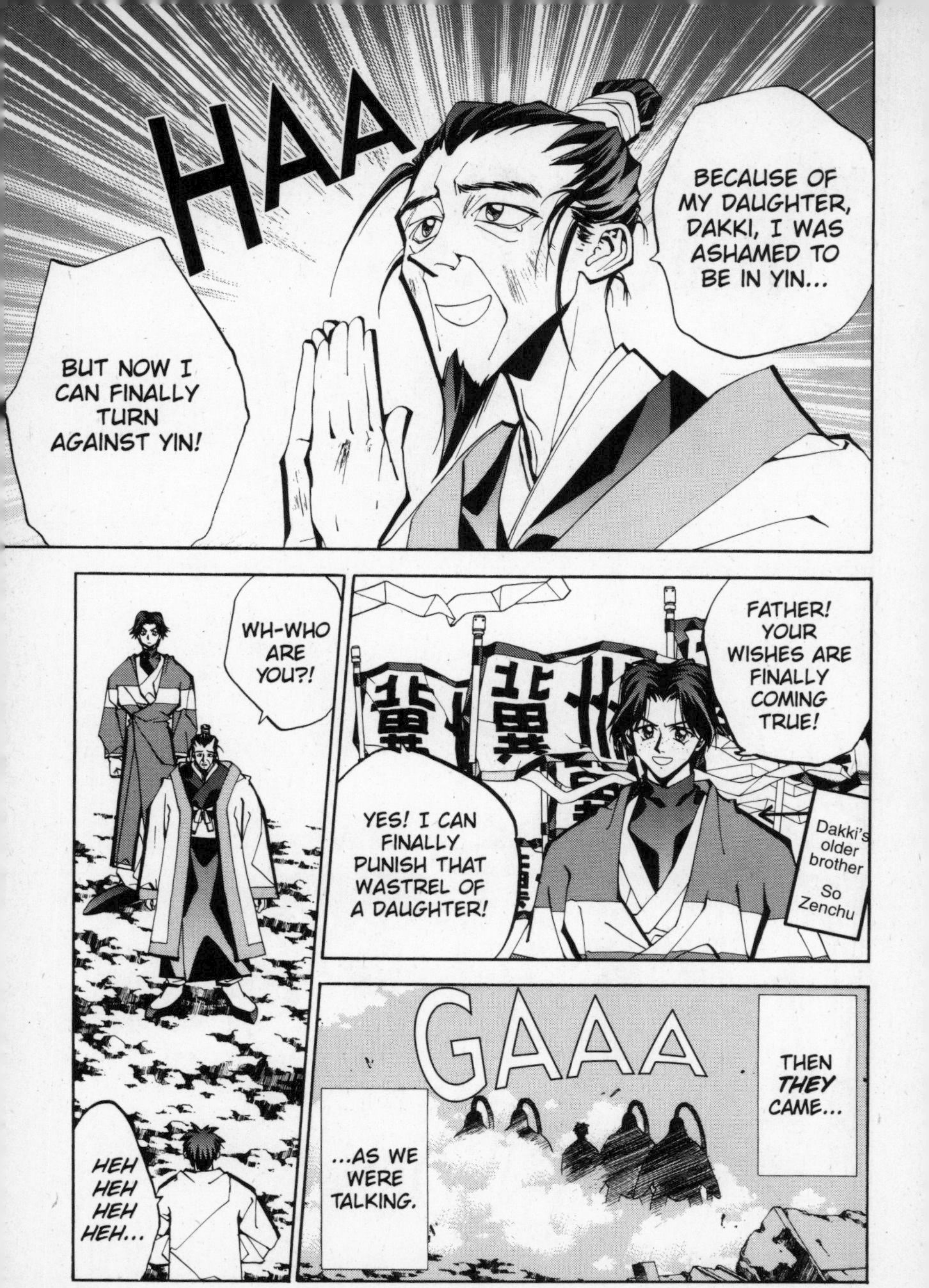
BECAUSE OF MY DAUGHTER, DAKKI, I WAS ASHAMED TO BE IN YIN...
HAA
BUT NOW I CAN FINALLY TURN AGAINST YIN!
FATHER! YOUR WISHES ARE FINALLY COMING TRUE!
Dakki's older brother So Zenchu
YES! I CAN FINALLY PUNISH THAT WASTREL OF A DAUGHTER!
THEN *THEY* CAME...
GAAA
...AS WE WERE TALKING.
WH-WHO ARE YOU?!
HEH HEH HEH HEH...

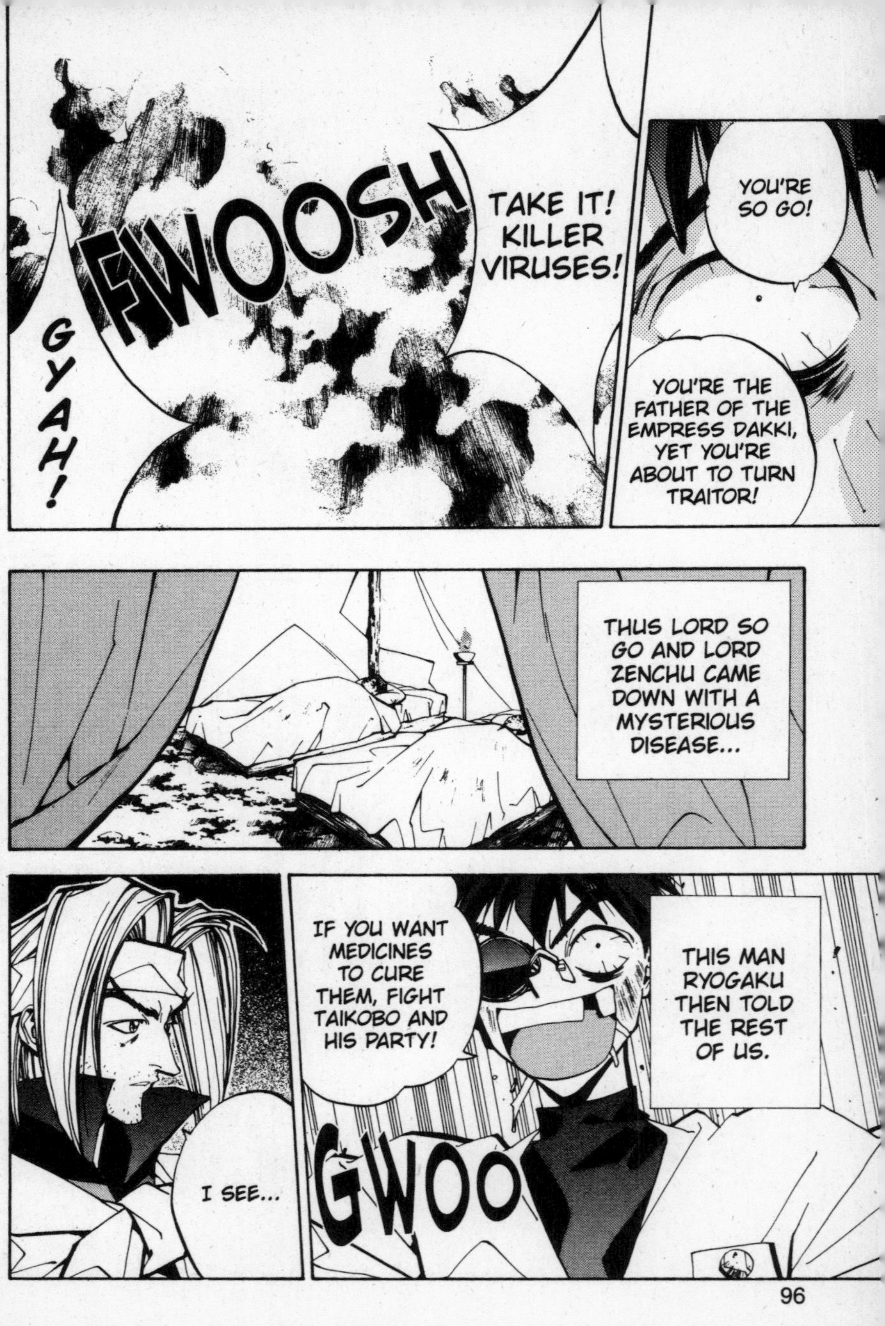
YOU'RE SO GO!
YOU'RE THE FATHER OF THE EMPRESS DAKKI, YET YOU'RE ABOUT TO TURN TRAITOR!
TAKE IT! KILLER VIRUSES!
FWOOSH
GYAH!
THUS LORD SO GO AND LORD ZENCHU CAME DOWN WITH A MYSTERIOUS DISEASE...
THIS MAN RYOGAKU THEN TOLD THE REST OF US.
IF YOU WANT MEDICINES TO CURE THEM, FIGHT TAIKOBO AND HIS PARTY!
GWOO
I SEE...

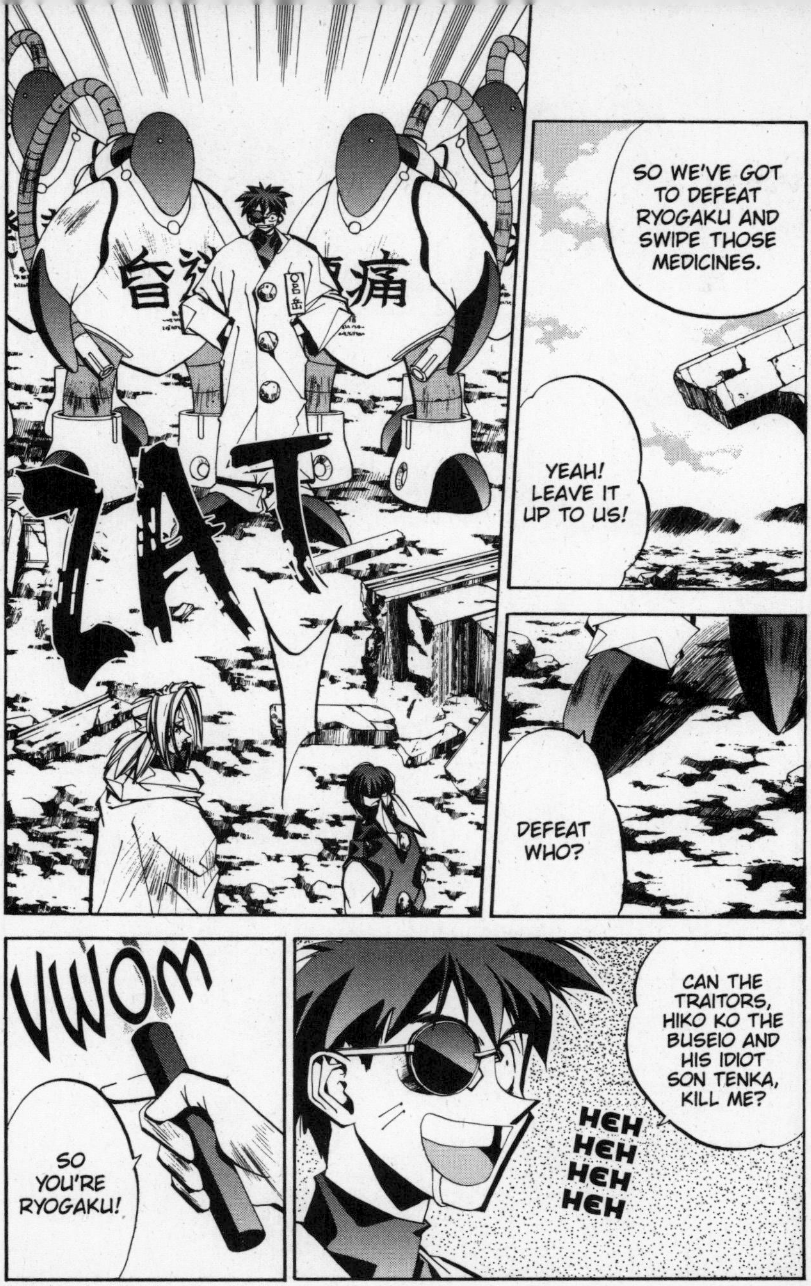
SO WE'VE GOT TO DEFEAT RYOGAKU AND SWIPE THOSE MEDICINES.
YEAH! LEAVE IT UP TO US!
DEFEAT WHO?
ZAT
CAN THE TRAITORS, HIKO KO THE BUSEIO AND HIS IDIOT SON TENKA, KILL ME?
HEH HEH HEH HEH
VWOM
SO YOU'RE RYOGAKU!

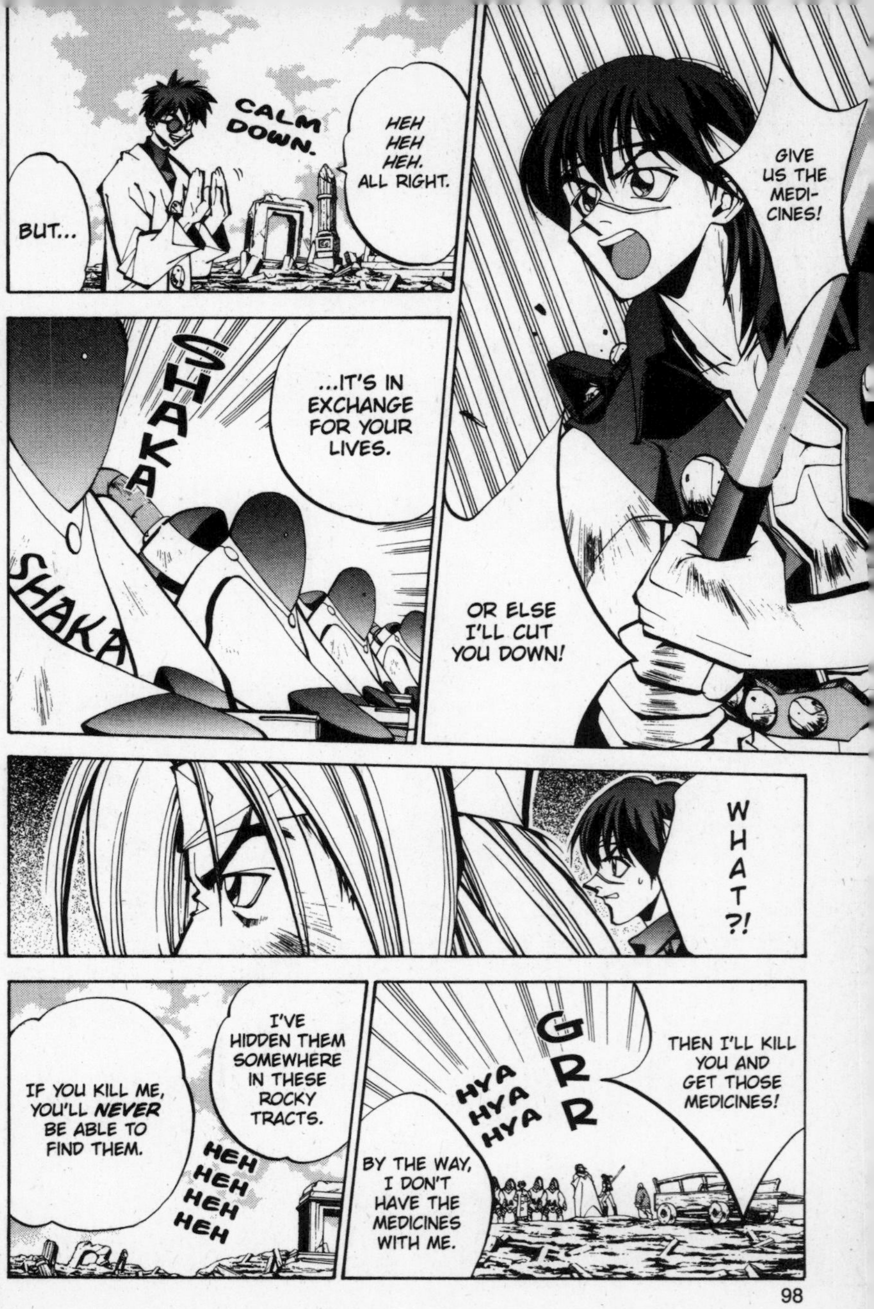
GIVE US THE MEDICINES!
OR ELSE I'LL CUT YOU DOWN!
HEH HEH HEH. ALL RIGHT.
CALM DOWN.
BUT...
...IT'S IN EXCHANGE FOR YOUR LIVES.
SHAKA
SHAKA
WHAT?!
THEN I'LL KILL YOU AND GET THOSE MEDICINES!
GRR
HYA HYA HYA
BY THE WAY, I DON'T HAVE THE MEDICINES WITH ME.
I'VE HIDDEN THEM SOMEWHERE IN THESE ROCKY TRACTS.
HEH HEH HEH HEH
IF YOU KILL ME, YOU'LL *NEVER* BE ABLE TO FIND THEM.

READ THIS WAY

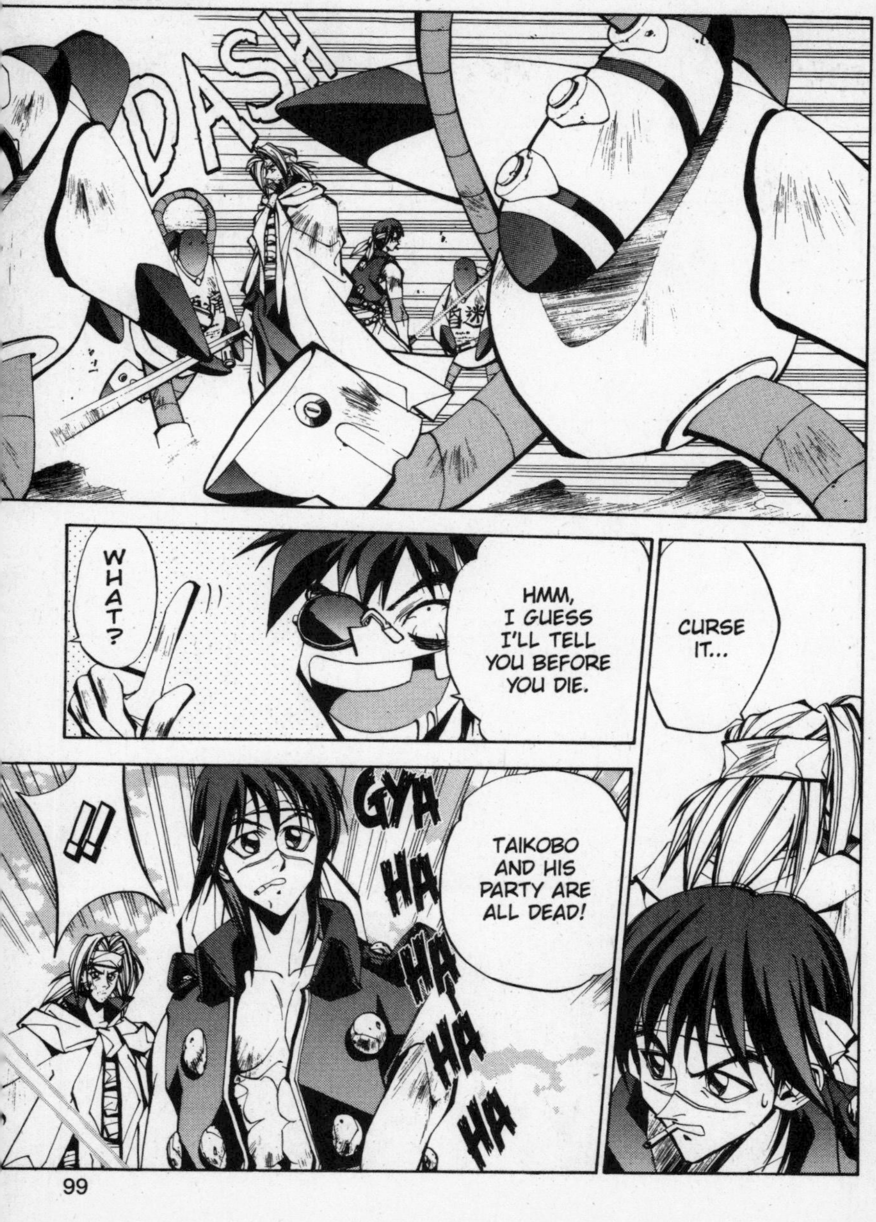
DASH
CURSE IT...
HMM, I GUESS I'LL TELL YOU BEFORE YOU DIE.
WHAT?
TAIKOBO AND HIS PARTY ARE ALL DEAD!
GYA HA HA HA HA HA
!!

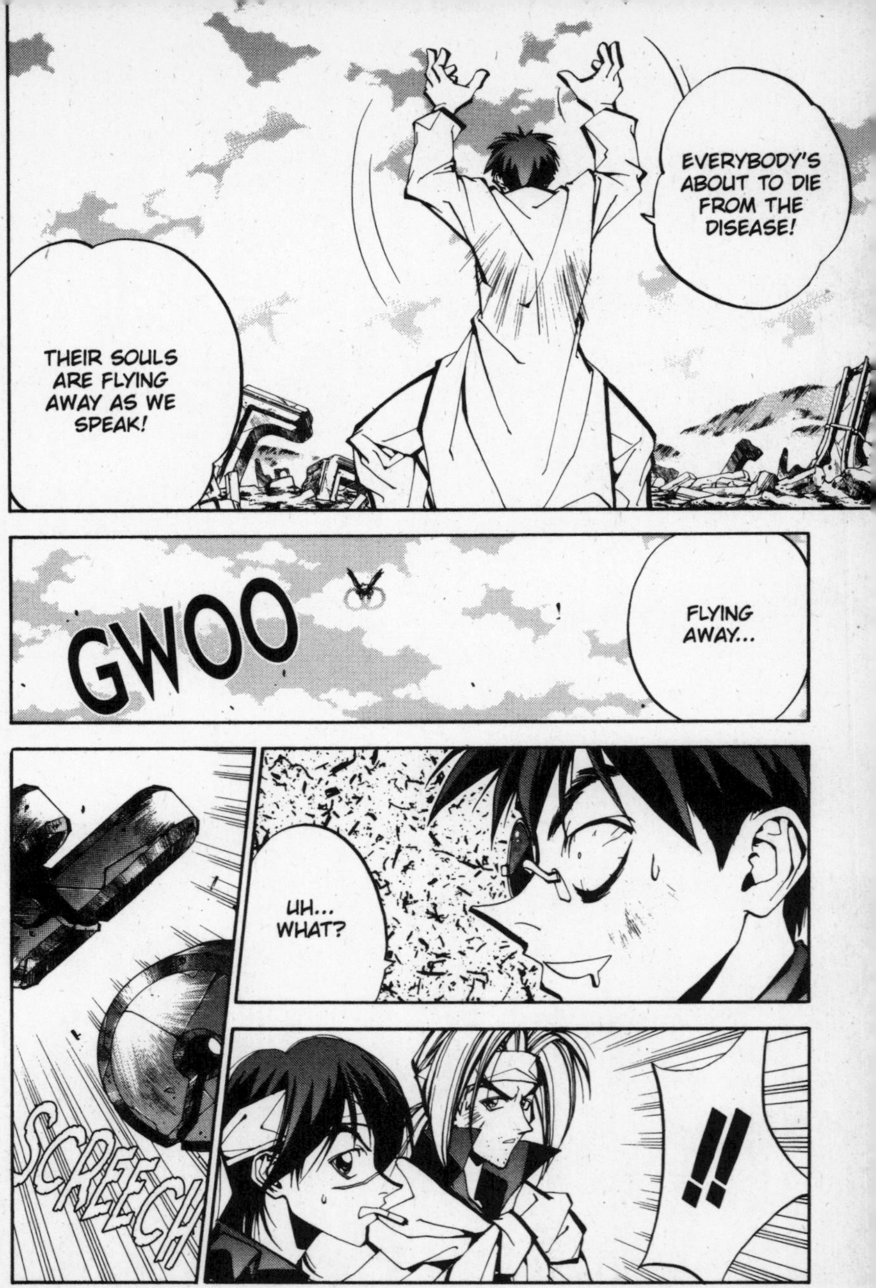
EVERYBODY'S ABOUT TO DIE FROM THE DISEASE!
THEIR SOULS ARE FLYING AWAY AS WE SPEAK!
FLYING AWAY...
GWOO
UH... WHAT?
!!
SCREECH

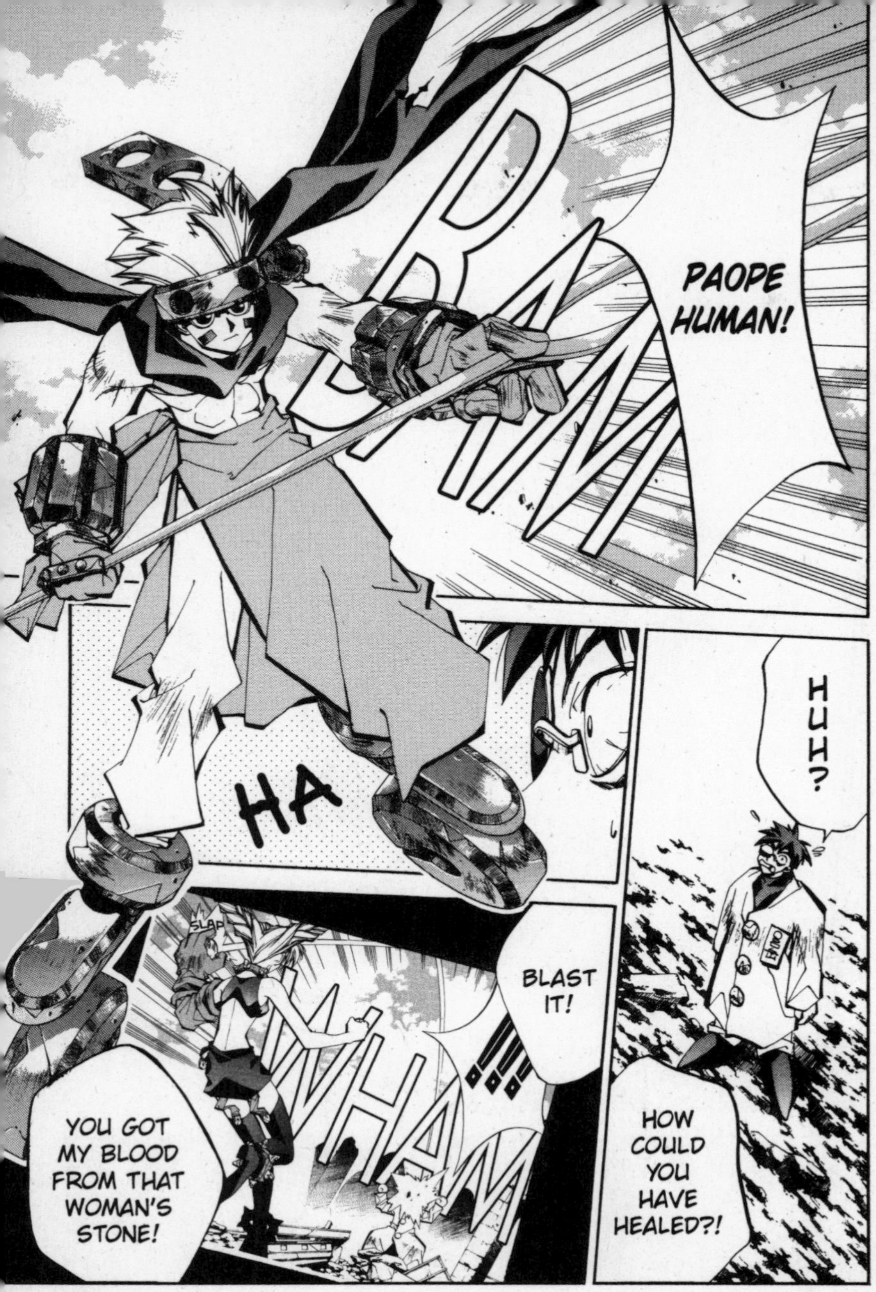
PAOPE HUMAN!
RAM
HUH?
HA
HOW COULD YOU HAVE HEALED?!
BLAST IT!
SLAP
WHAM
YOU GOT MY BLOOD FROM THAT WOMAN'S STONE!

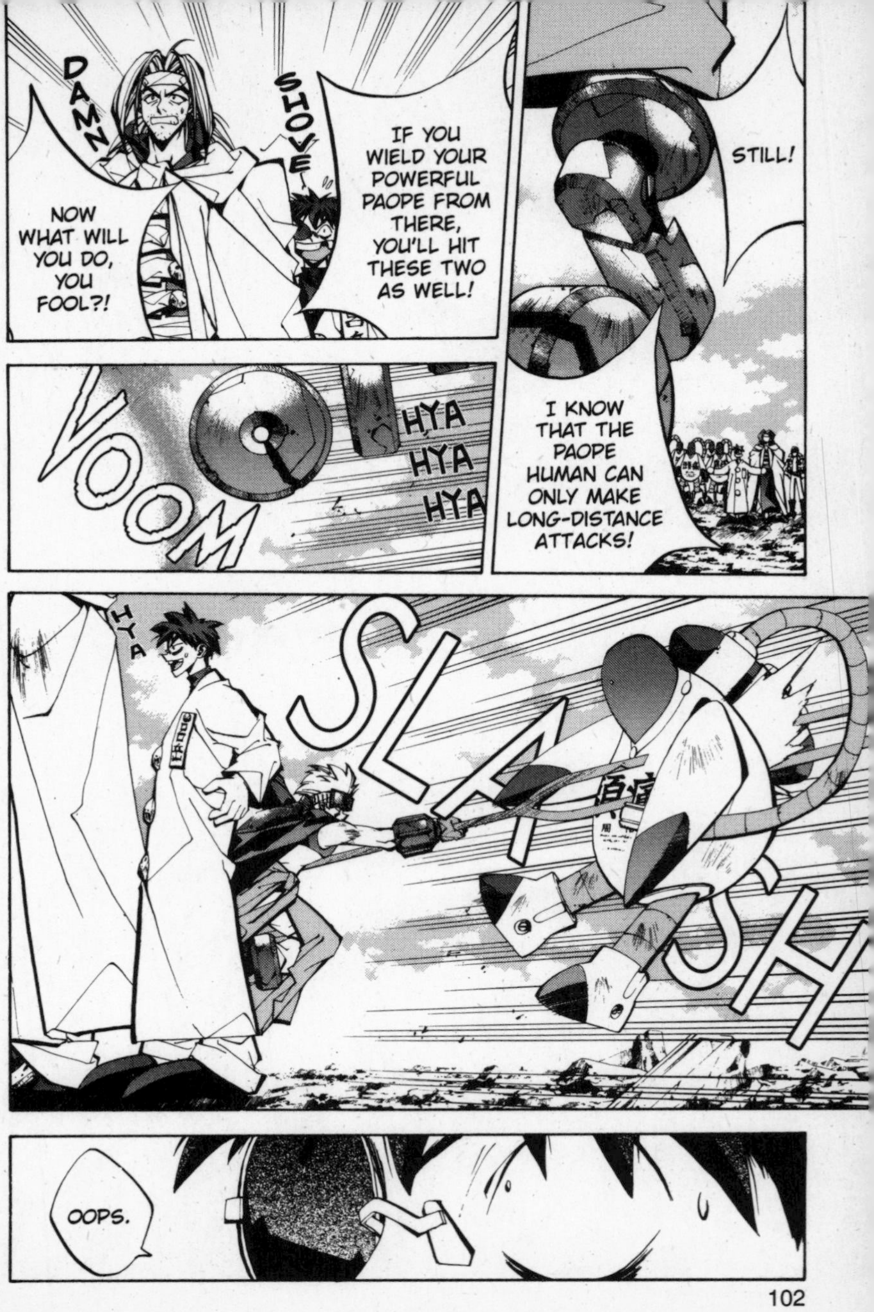
STILL!
I KNOW THAT THE PAOPE HUMAN CAN ONLY MAKE LONG-DISTANCE ATTACKS!
SHOVE
IF YOU WIELD YOUR POWERFUL PAOPE FROM THERE, YOU'LL HIT THESE TWO AS WELL!
DAMN
NOW WHAT WILL YOU DO, YOU FOOL?!
HYA HYA HYA
VOOM
SLASH
HYA
OOPS.

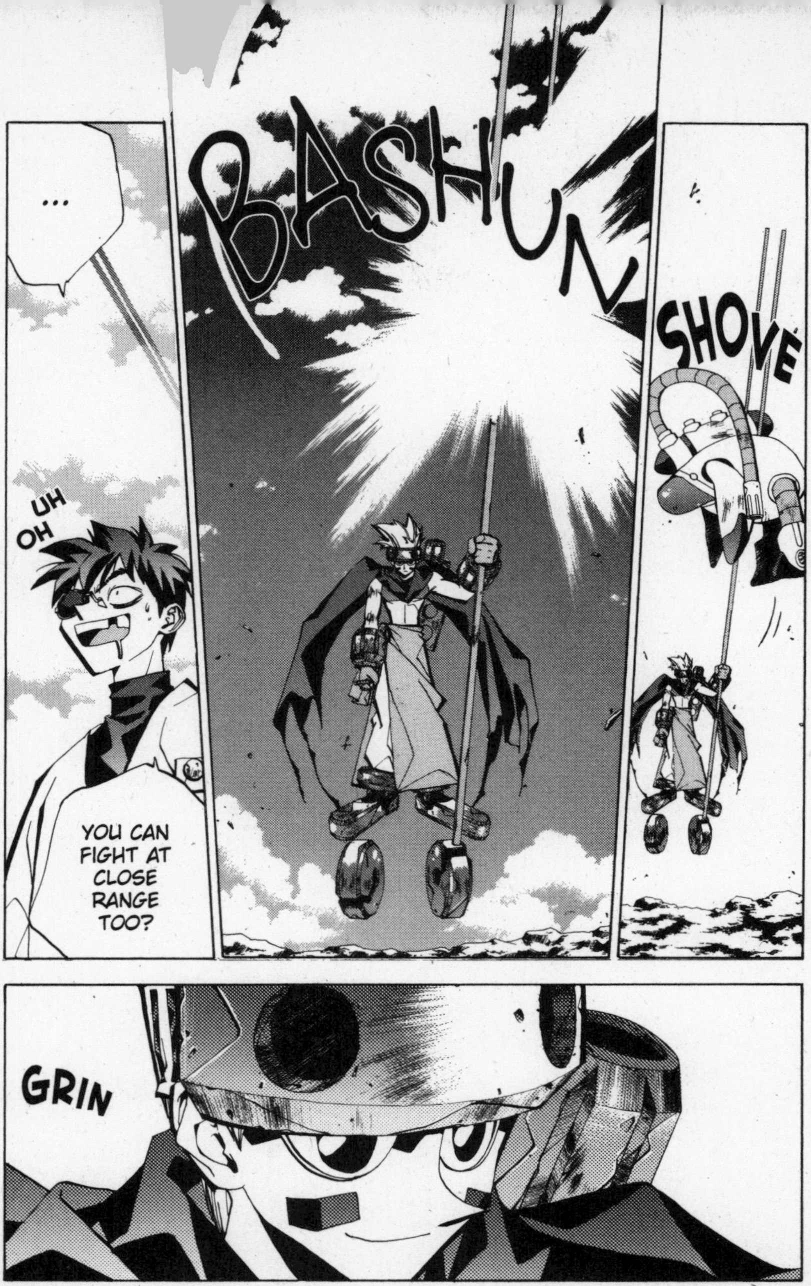
SHOVE
BASHUN
...
UH OH
YOU CAN FIGHT AT CLOSE RANGE TOO?
GRIN

封神演義

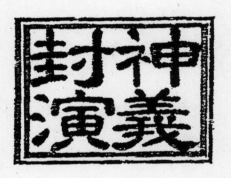

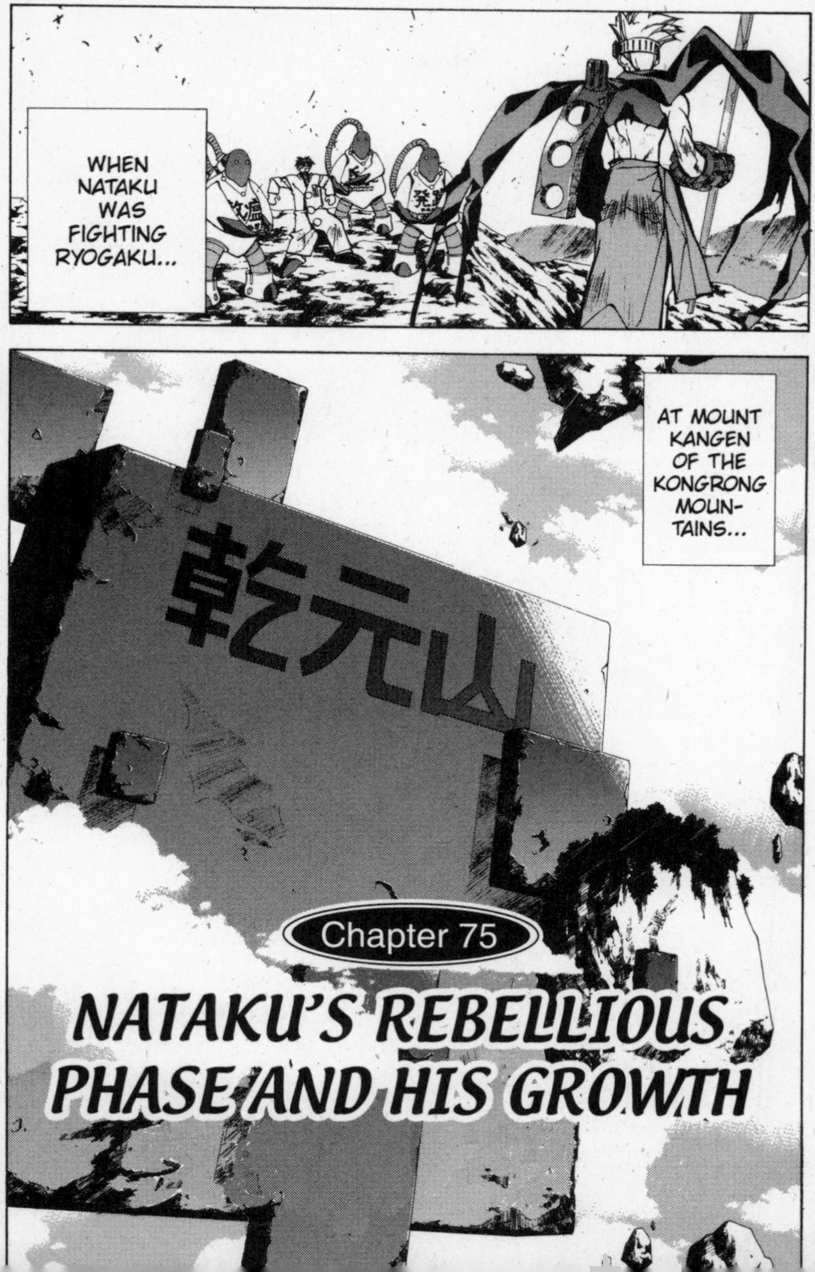
WHEN NATAKU WAS FIGHTING RYOGAKU...
AT MOUNT KANGEN OF THE KONGRONG MOUN-TAINS...
乾元山
Chapter 75
NATAKU'S REBELLIOUS PHASE AND HIS GROWTH

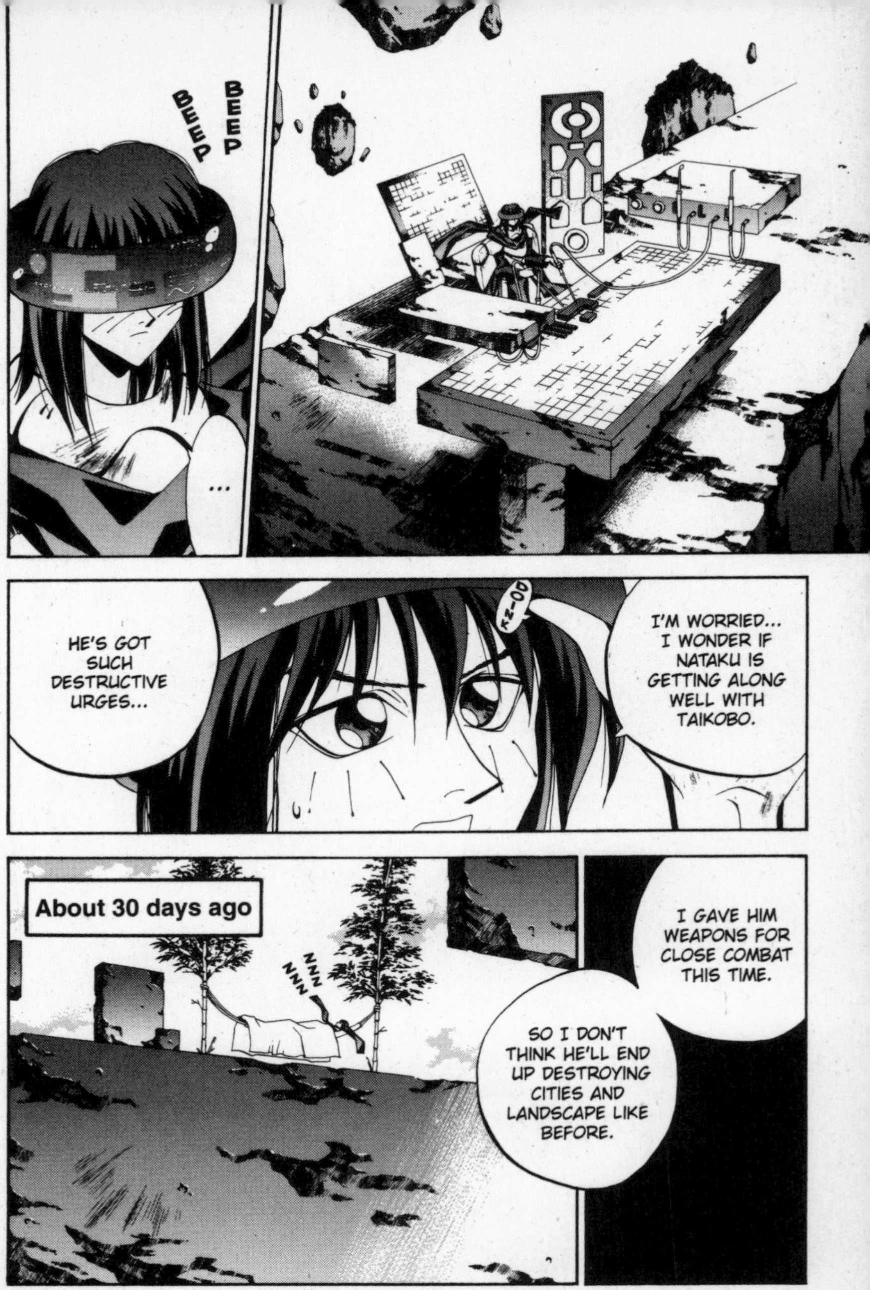
BEEP BEEP
...
DOINK
I'M WORRIED... I WONDER IF NATAKU IS GETTING ALONG WELL WITH TAIKOBO.
HE'S GOT SUCH DESTRUCTIVE URGES...
I GAVE HIM WEAPONS FOR CLOSE COMBAT THIS TIME.
SO I DON'T THINK HE'LL END UP DESTROYING CITIES AND LANDSCAPE LIKE BEFORE.
About 30 days ago
ZZZ ZZZ

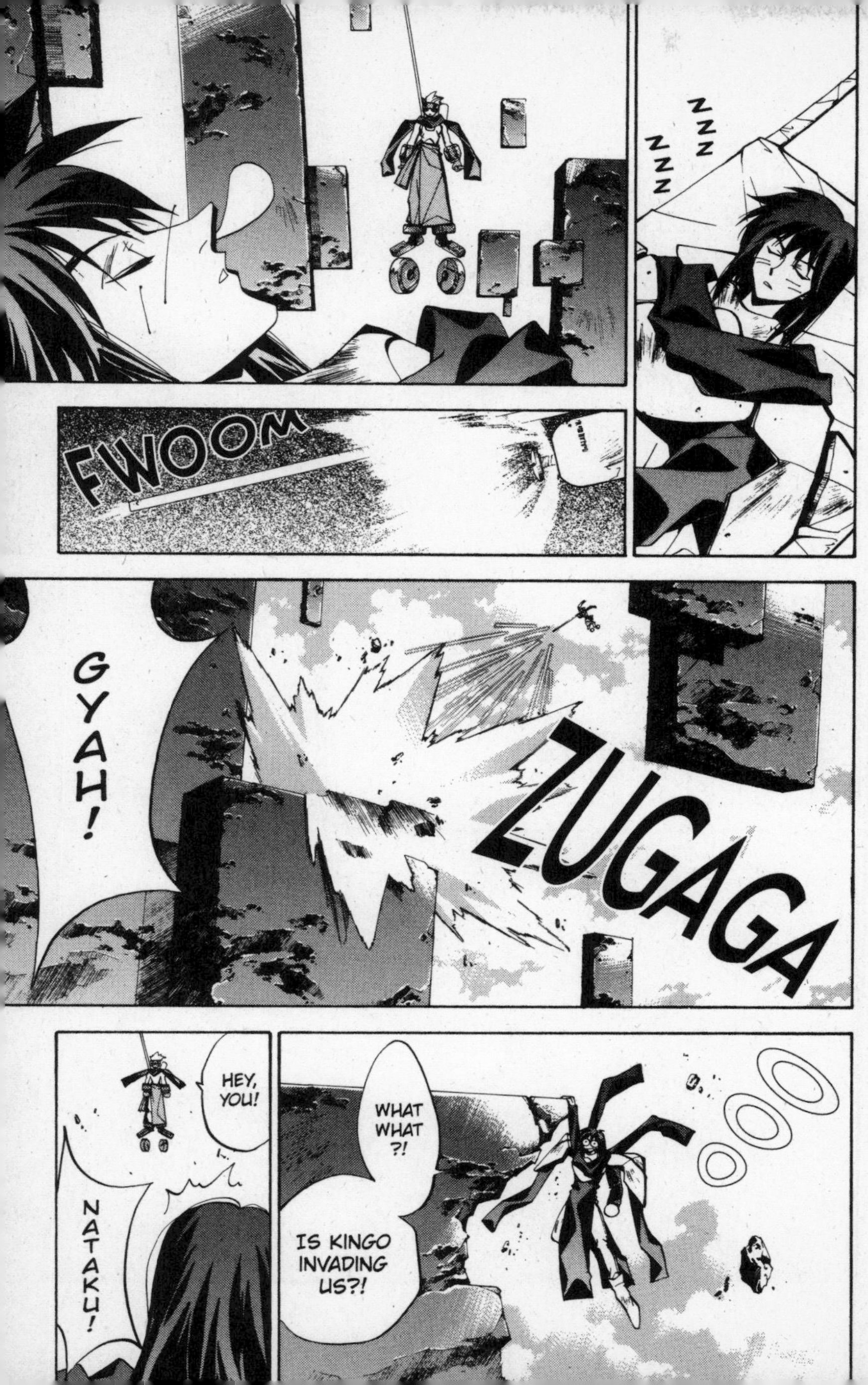
ZZZ
ZZZ
FWOOM
ZUGAGA
GYAH!
WHAT WHAT ?!
IS KINGO INVADING US?!
HEY, YOU!
NATAKU!

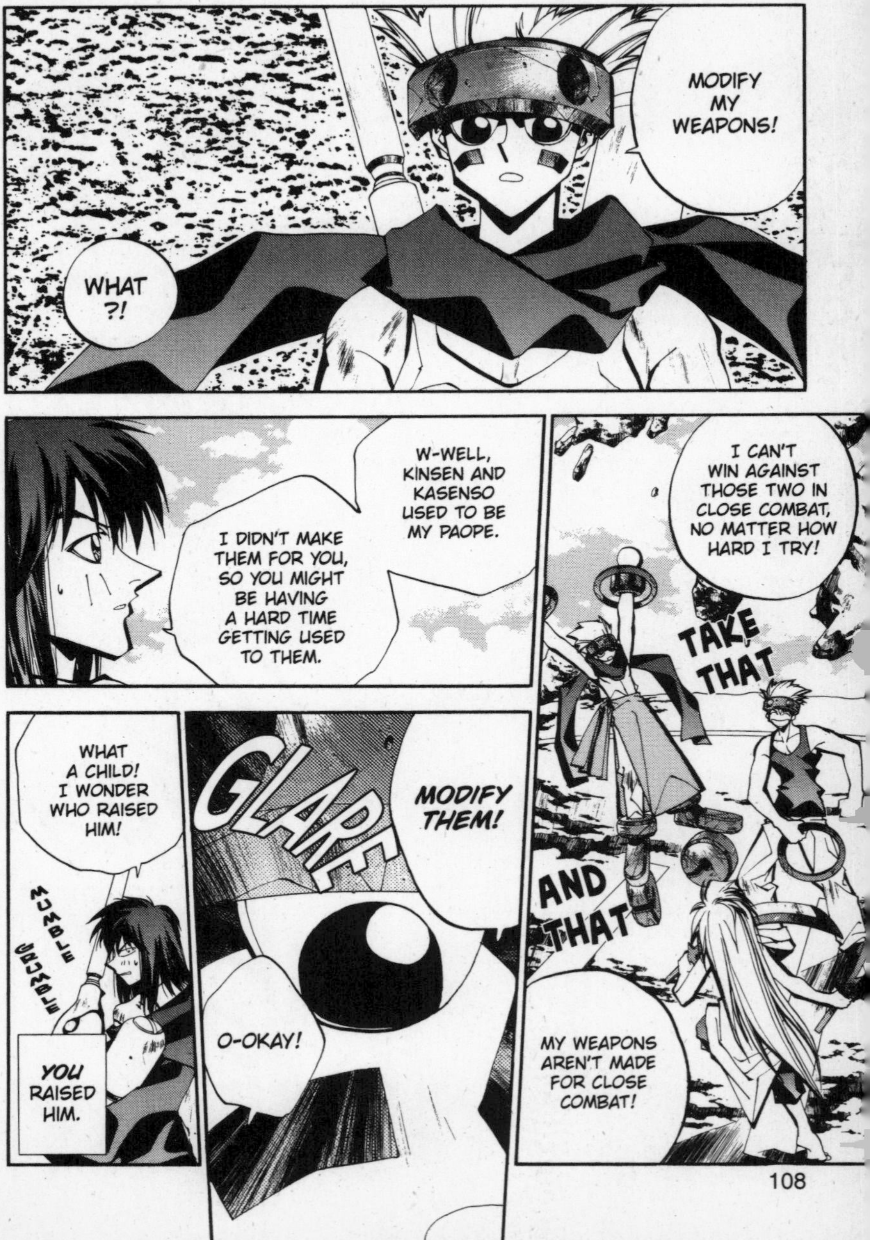
MODIFY MY WEAPONS!
WHAT ?!
I CAN'T WIN AGAINST THOSE TWO IN CLOSE COMBAT, NO MATTER HOW HARD I TRY!
TAKE THAT
AND THAT
MY WEAPONS AREN'T MADE FOR CLOSE COMBAT!
W-WELL, KINSEN AND KASENSO USED TO BE MY PAOPE.
I DIDN'T MAKE THEM FOR YOU, SO YOU MIGHT BE HAVING A HARD TIME GETTING USED TO THEM.
MODIFY THEM!
GLARE
O-OKAY!
WHAT A CHILD! I WONDER WHO RAISED HIM!
MUMBLE
GRUMBLE
YOU RAISED HIM.

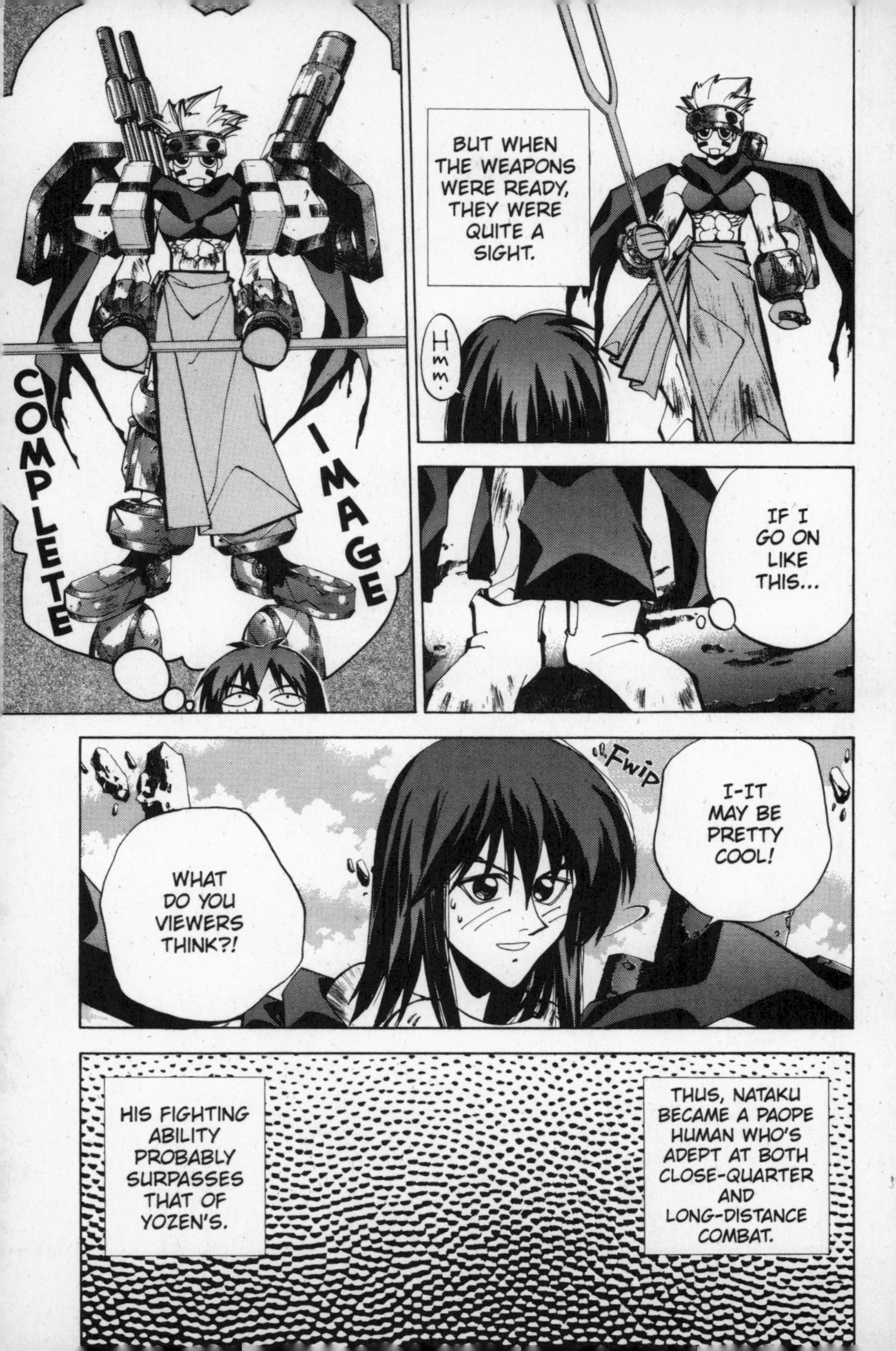

BUT WHEN THE WEAPONS WERE READY, THEY WERE QUITE A SIGHT.
Hmm.
IF I GO ON LIKE THIS...
COMPLETE IMAGE
Fwip
I-IT MAY BE PRETTY COOL!
WHAT DO YOU VIEWERS THINK?!
THUS, NATAKU BECAME A PAOPE HUMAN WHO'S ADEPT AT BOTH CLOSE-QUARTER AND LONG-DISTANCE COMBAT.
HIS FIGHTING ABILITY PROBABLY SURPASSES THAT OF YOZEN'S.

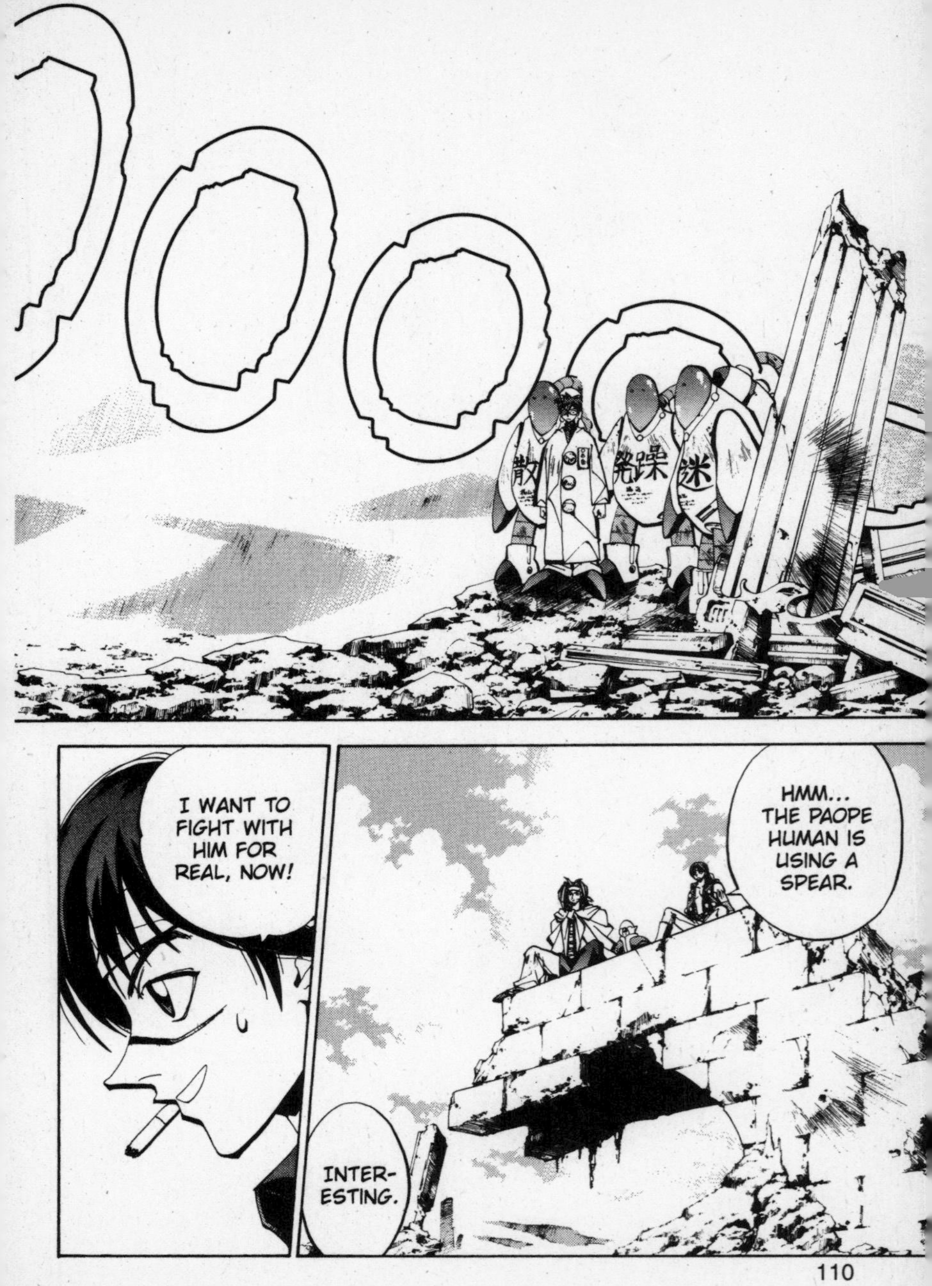
HMM... THE PAOPE HUMAN IS USING A SPEAR.
INTER-ESTING.
I WANT TO FIGHT WITH HIM FOR REAL, NOW!

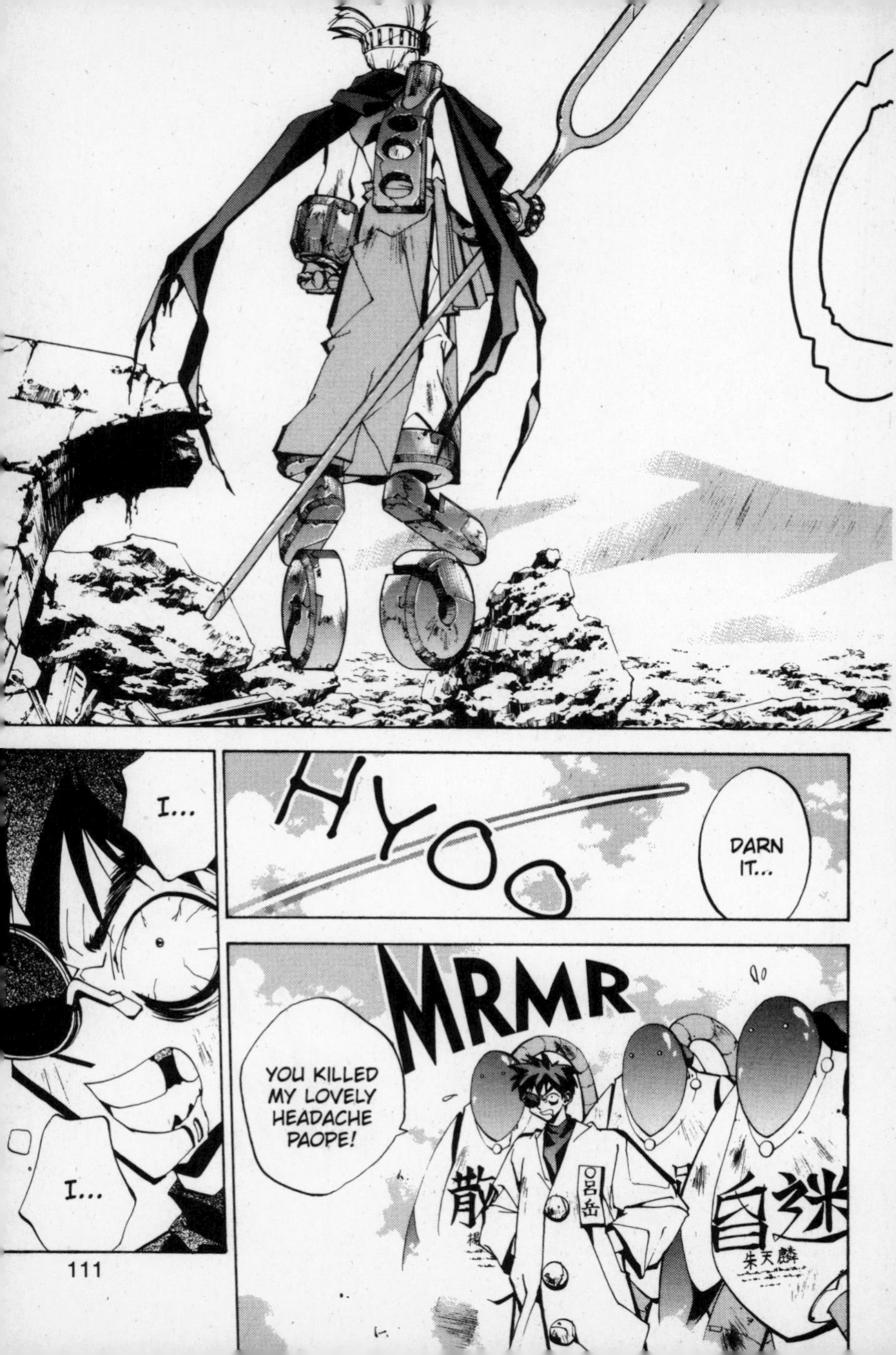
DARN IT...
HYOO
MRMR
YOU KILLED MY LOVELY HEADACHE PAOPE!
I...
I...

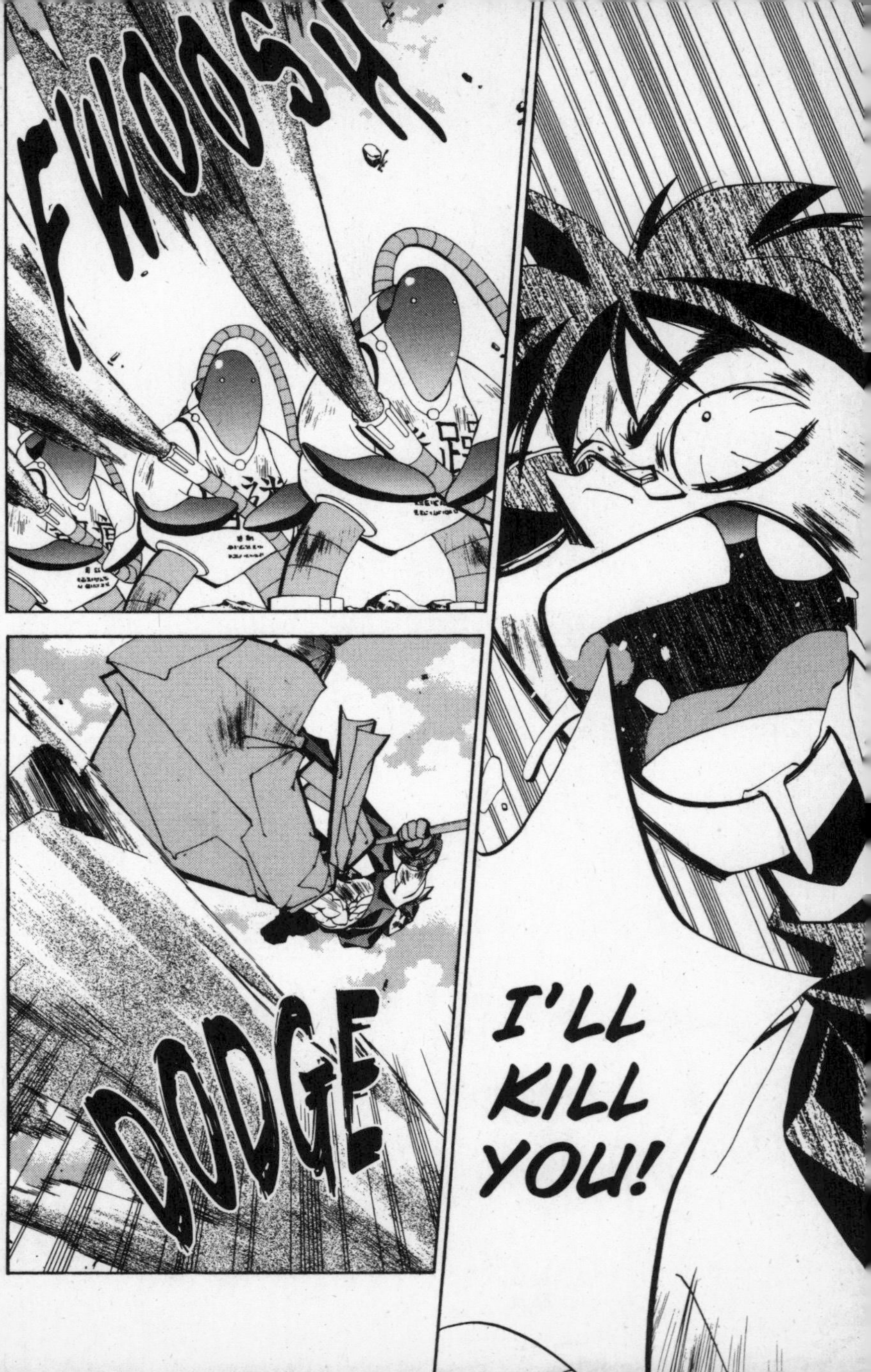
I'LL KILL YOU!
FWOOSH
DODGE

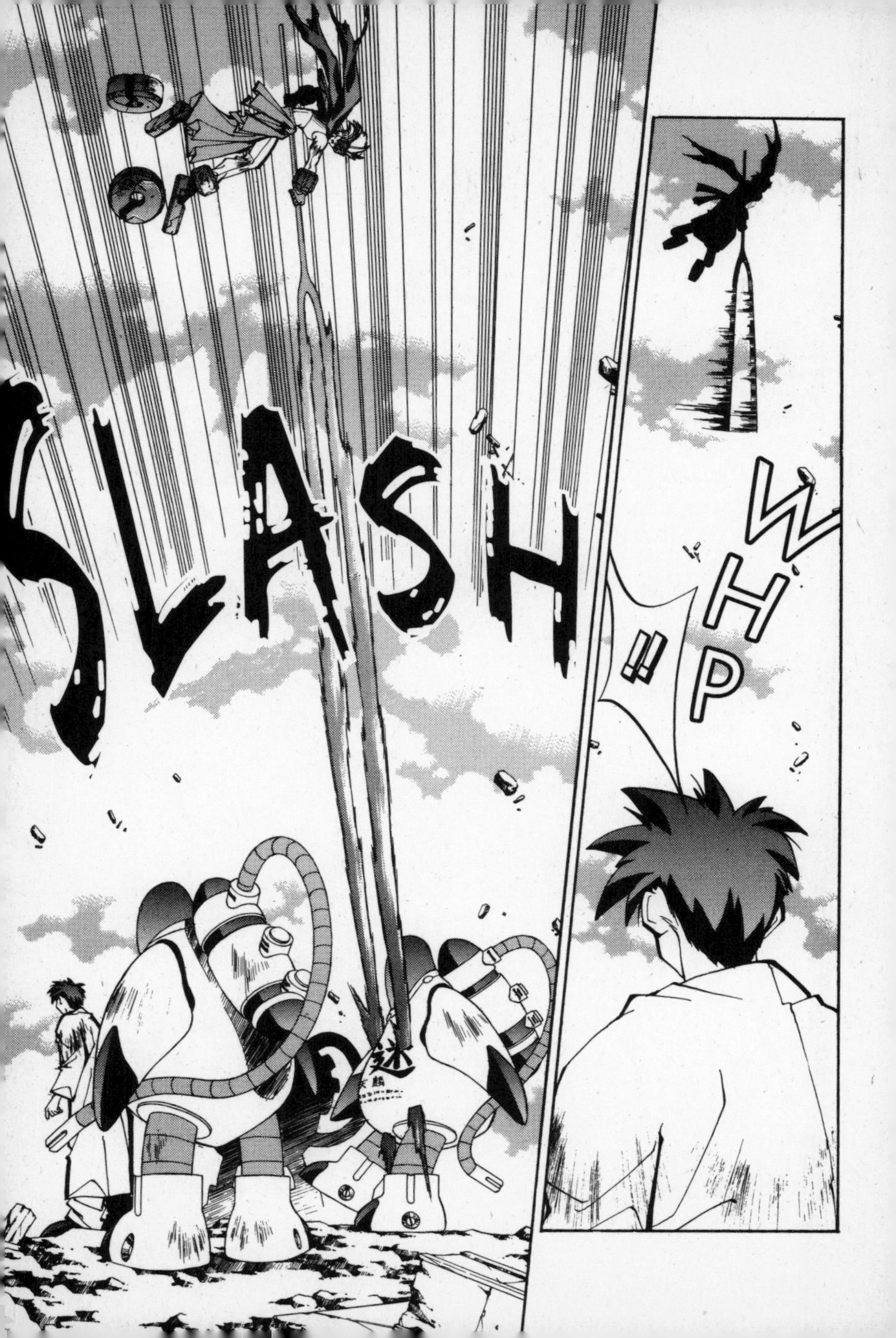
WHIP!!
SLASH

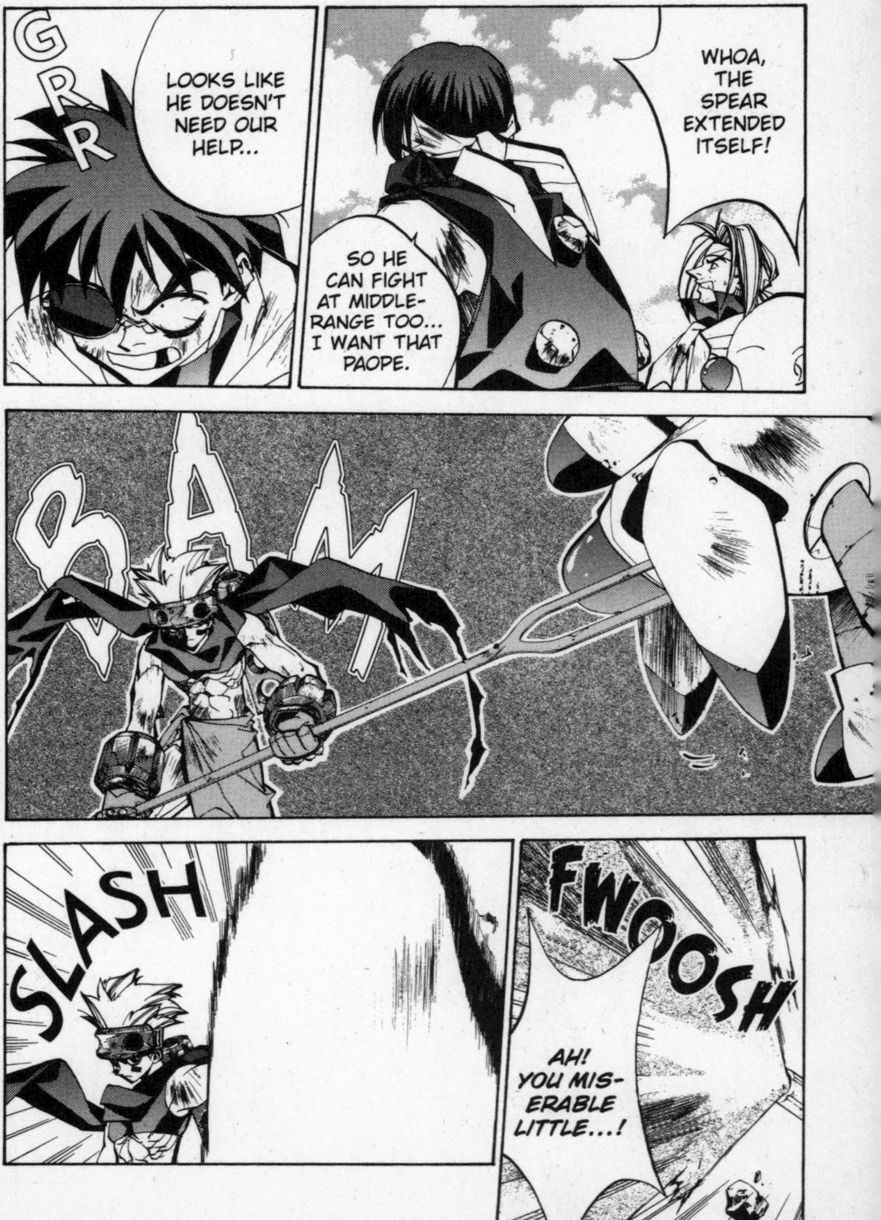
WHOA, THE SPEAR EXTENDED ITSELF!
SO HE CAN FIGHT AT MIDDLE-RANGE TOO... I WANT THAT PAOPE.
LOOKS LIKE HE DOESN'T NEED OUR HELP...
GRR
BAM
FWOOSH
AH! YOU MIS-ERABLE LITTLE...!
SLASH

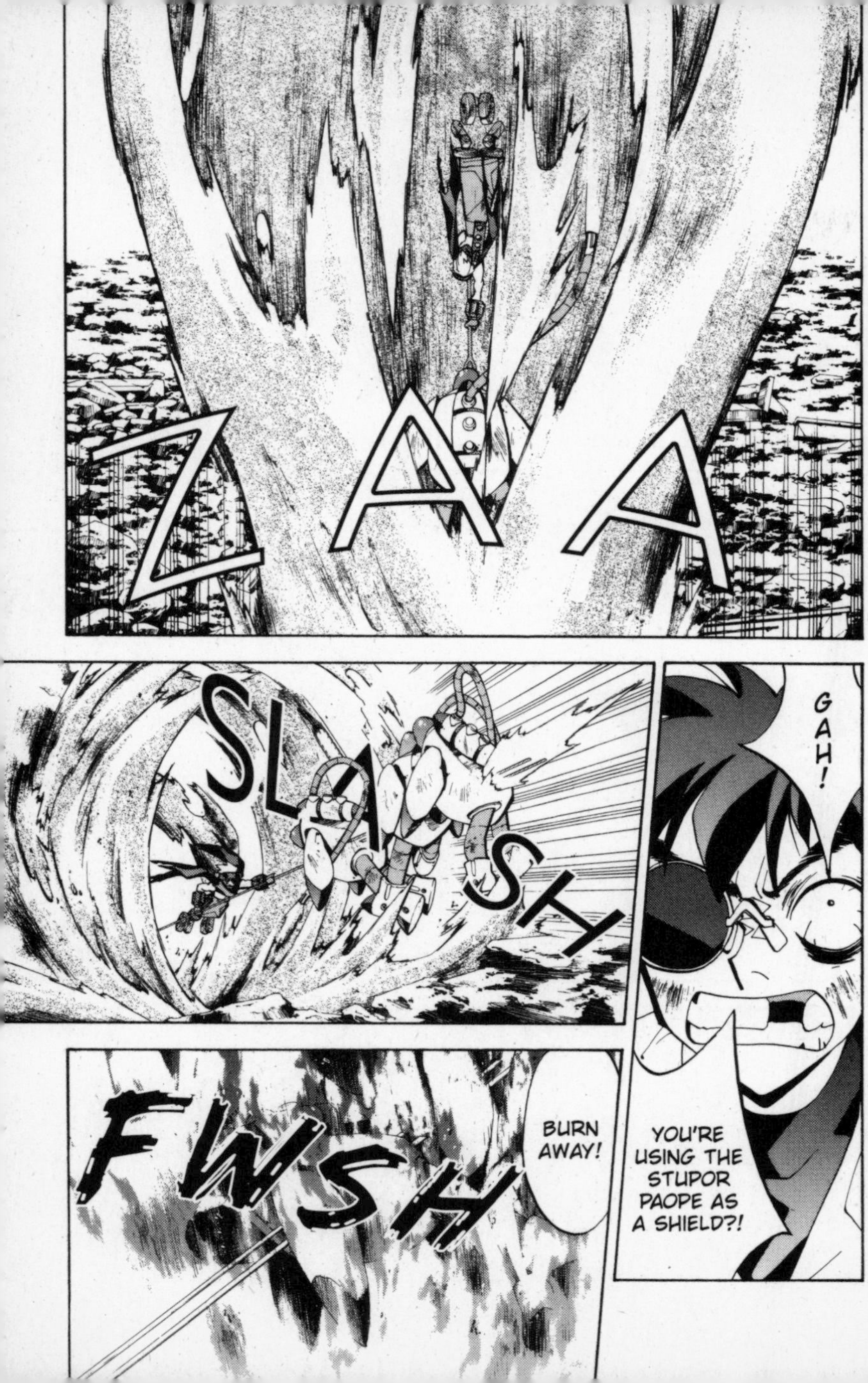
ZAA
GAH!
YOU'RE USING THE STUPOR PAOPE AS A SHIELD?!
SLASH
BURN AWAY!
FWSH

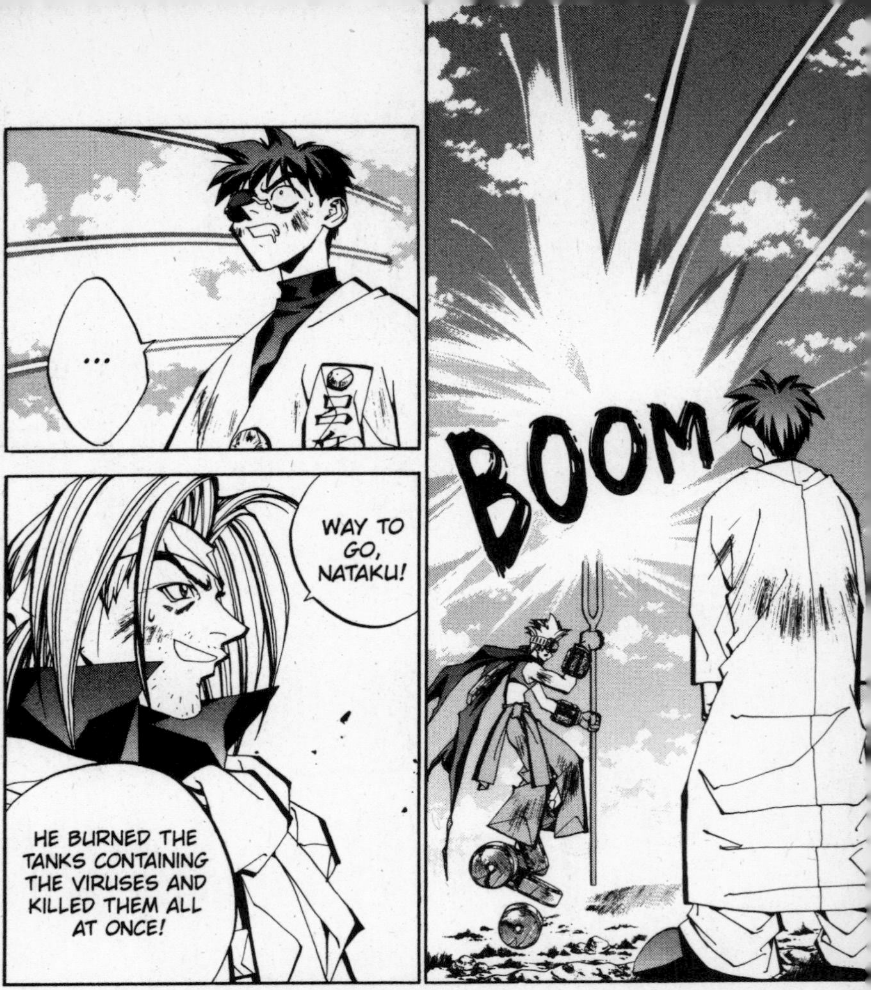
BOOM
...
WAY TO GO, NATAKU!
HE BURNED THE TANKS CONTAINING THE VIRUSES AND KILLED THEM ALL AT ONCE!
GNH...
FUMBLE
IF THAT'S HOW IT IS...

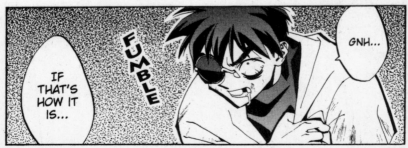

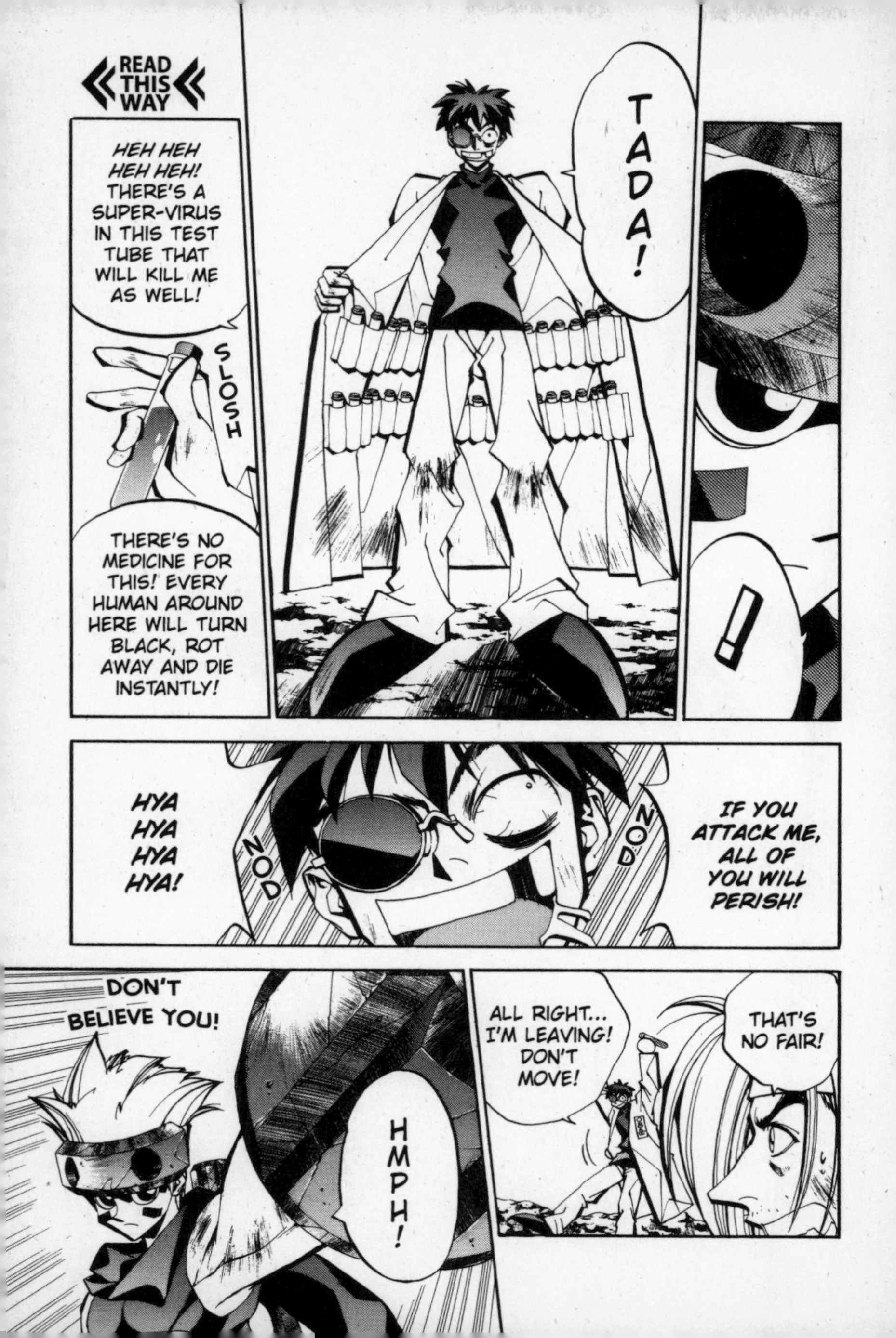
READ THIS WAY
!
TADA!
HEH HEH HEH HEH! THERE'S A SUPER-VIRUS IN THIS TEST TUBE THAT WILL KILL ME AS WELL!
SLOSH
THERE'S NO MEDICINE FOR THIS! EVERY HUMAN AROUND HERE WILL TURN BLACK, ROT AWAY AND DIE INSTANTLY!
IF YOU ATTACK ME, ALL OF YOU WILL PERISH!
NOD
NOD
HYA HYA HYA HYA!
THAT'S NO FAIR!
ALL RIGHT... I'M LEAVING! DON'T MOVE!
HMPH!
DON'T BELIEVE YOU!

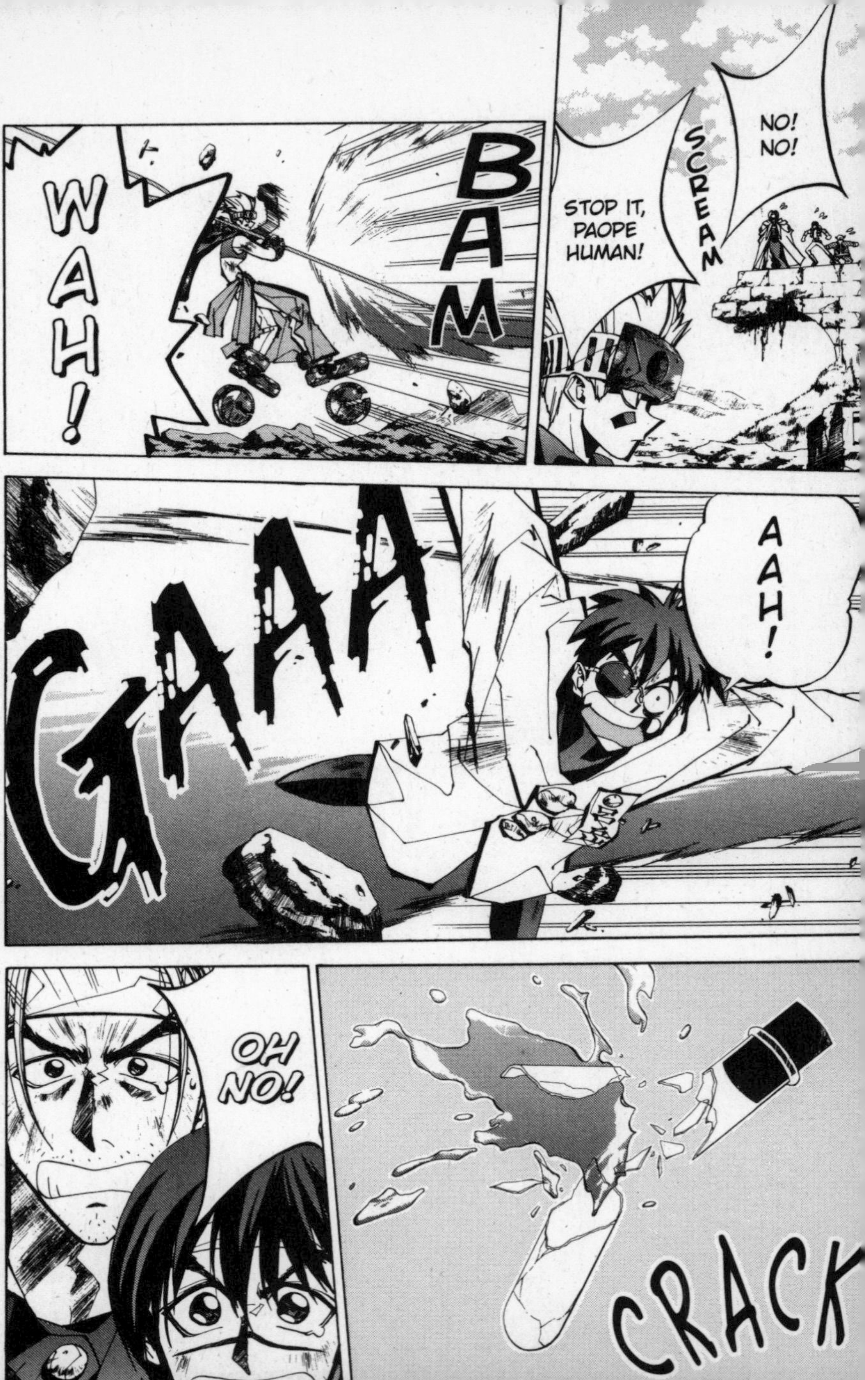
NO! NO!
SCREAM
STOP IT, PAOPE HUMAN!
BAM
WAH!
AAH!
GAAA
CRACK
OH NO!

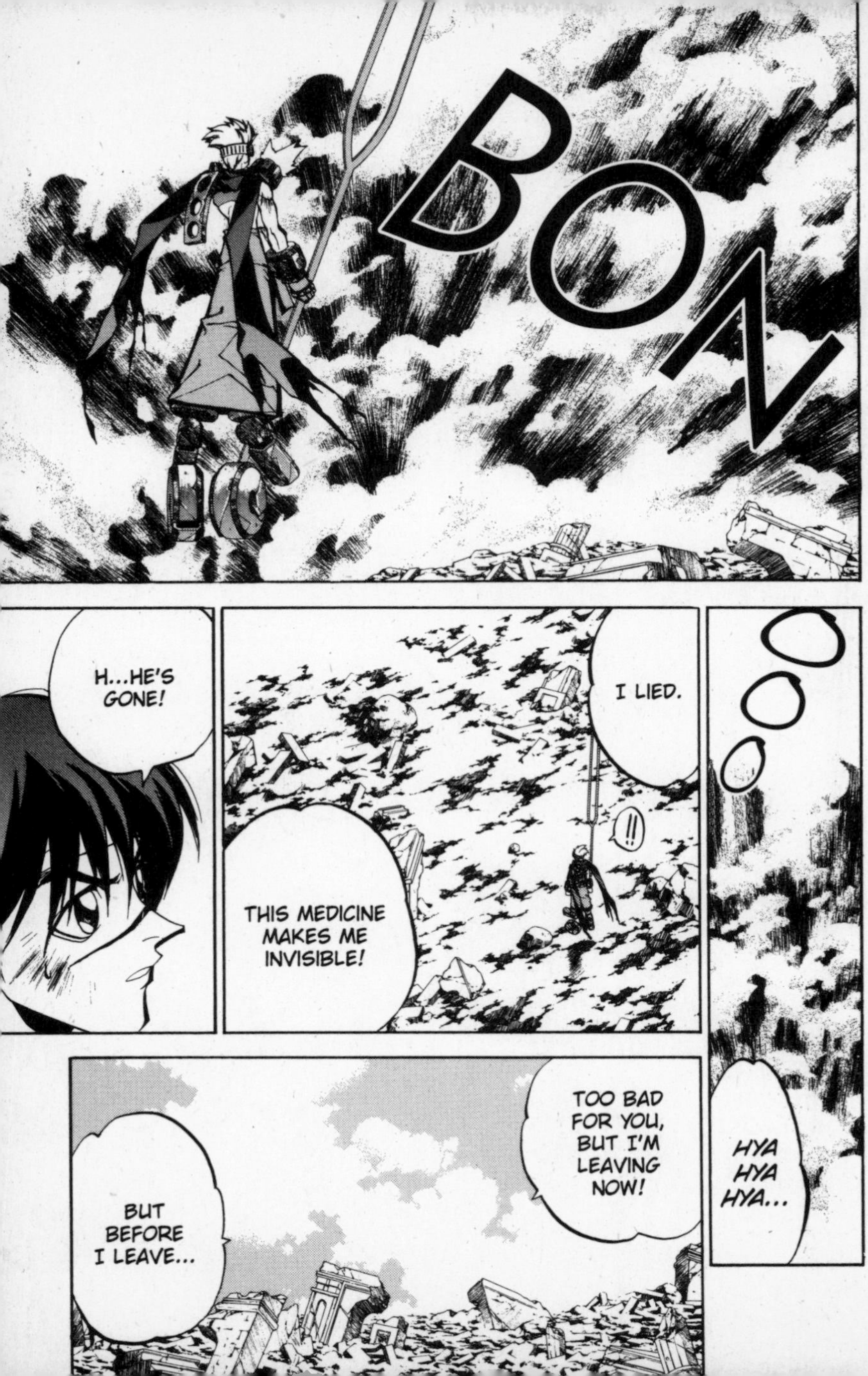
BON
HYA HYA HYA...
I LIED.
!!
THIS MEDICINE MAKES ME INVISIBLE!
H...HE'S GONE!
TOO BAD FOR YOU, BUT I'M LEAVING NOW!
BUT BEFORE I LEAVE...

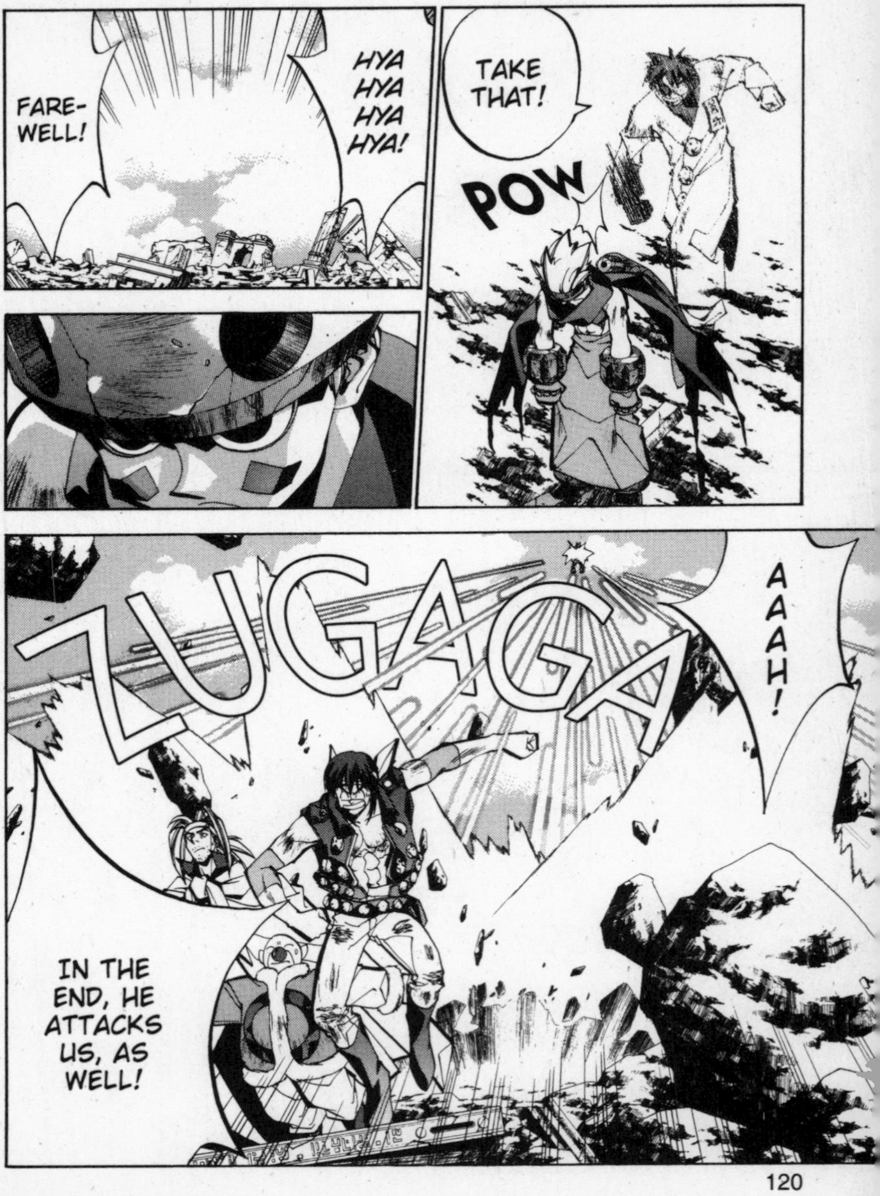
TAKE THAT!
POW
HYA HYA HYA HYA!
FARE-WELL!
ZUGAGA
AAAAH!
IN THE END, HE ATTACKS US, AS WELL!

READ THIS WAY

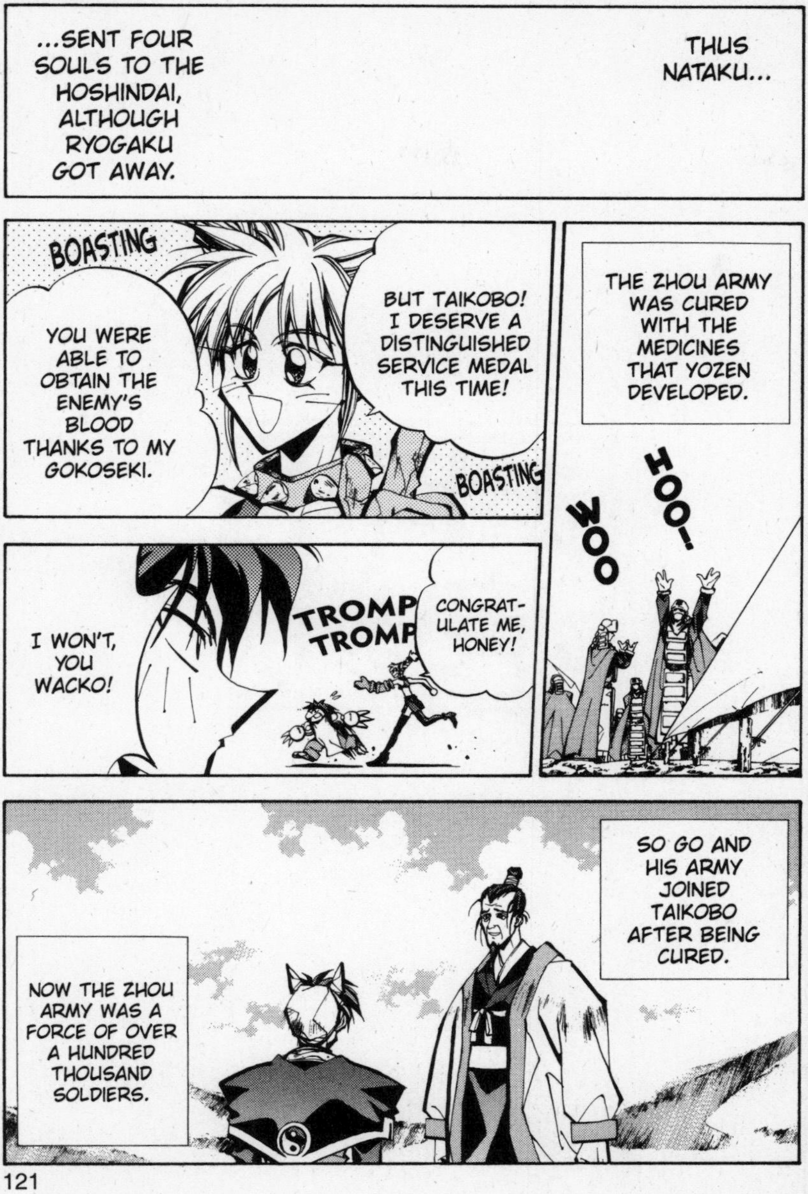
THUS NATAKU...
...SENT FOUR SOULS TO THE HOSHINDAI, ALTHOUGH RYOGAKU GOT AWAY.
THE ZHOU ARMY WAS CURED WITH THE MEDICINES THAT YOZEN DEVELOPED.
WOO HOO!
BOASTING
BUT TAIKOBO! I DESERVE A DISTINGUISHED SERVICE MEDAL THIS TIME!
YOU WERE ABLE TO OBTAIN THE ENEMY'S BLOOD THANKS TO MY GOKOSEKI.
BOASTING
CONGRAT-ULATE ME, HONEY!
TROMP TROMP
I WON'T, YOU WACKO!
SO GO AND HIS ARMY JOINED TAIKOBO AFTER BEING CURED.
NOW THE ZHOU ARMY WAS A FORCE OF OVER A HUNDRED THOUSAND SOLDIERS.

封神演義

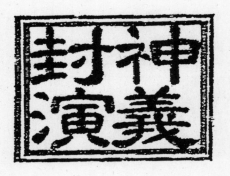

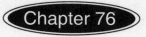

Chapter 76

THE TWO PRINCES RETURN FROM KONGRONG

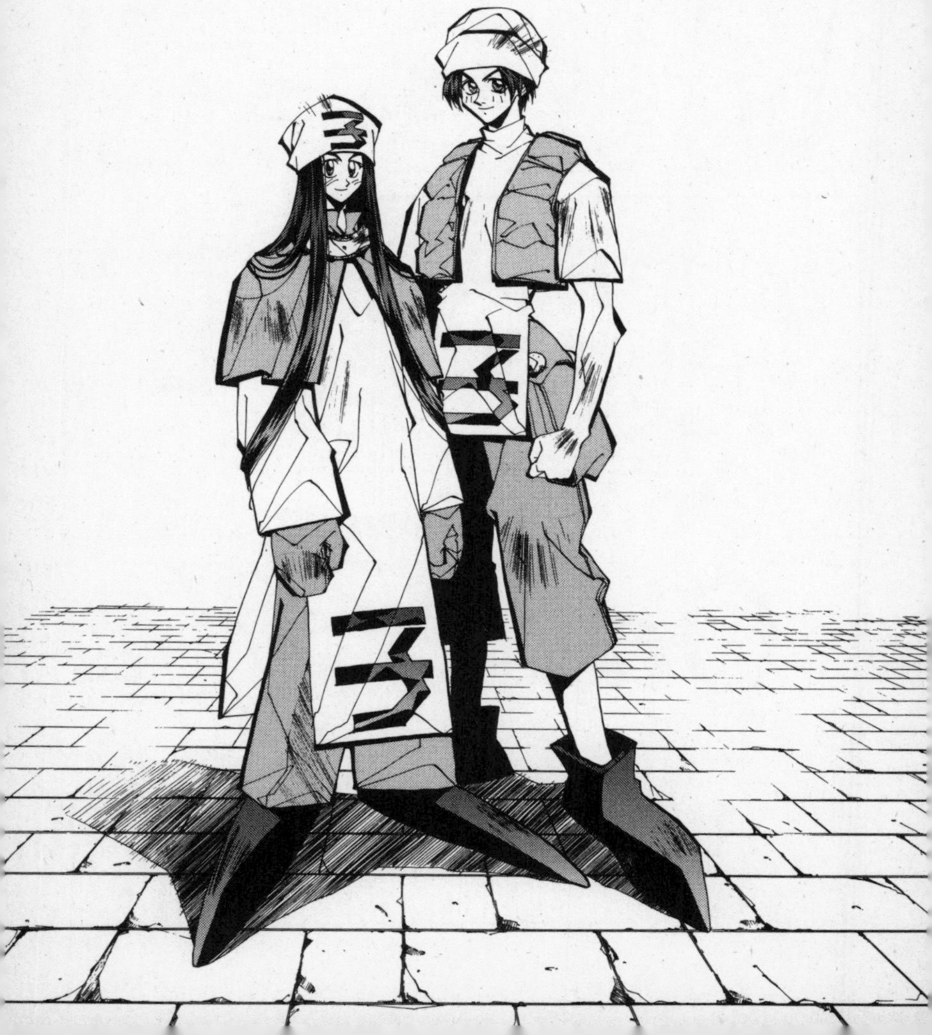

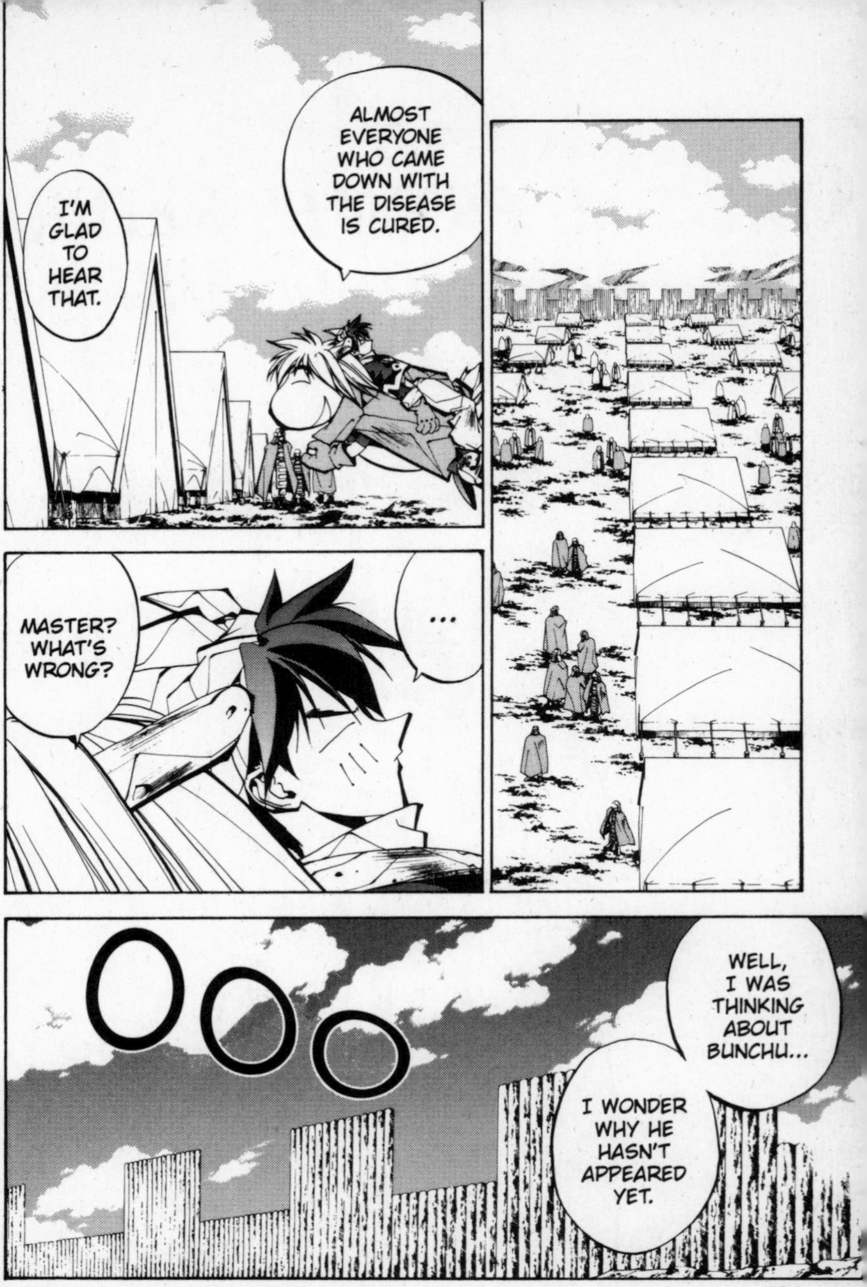
ALMOST EVERYONE WHO CAME DOWN WITH THE DISEASE IS CURED.
I'M GLAD TO HEAR THAT.
...
MASTER? WHAT'S WRONG?
WELL, I WAS THINKING ABOUT BUNCHU...
I WONDER WHY HE HASN'T APPEARED YET.

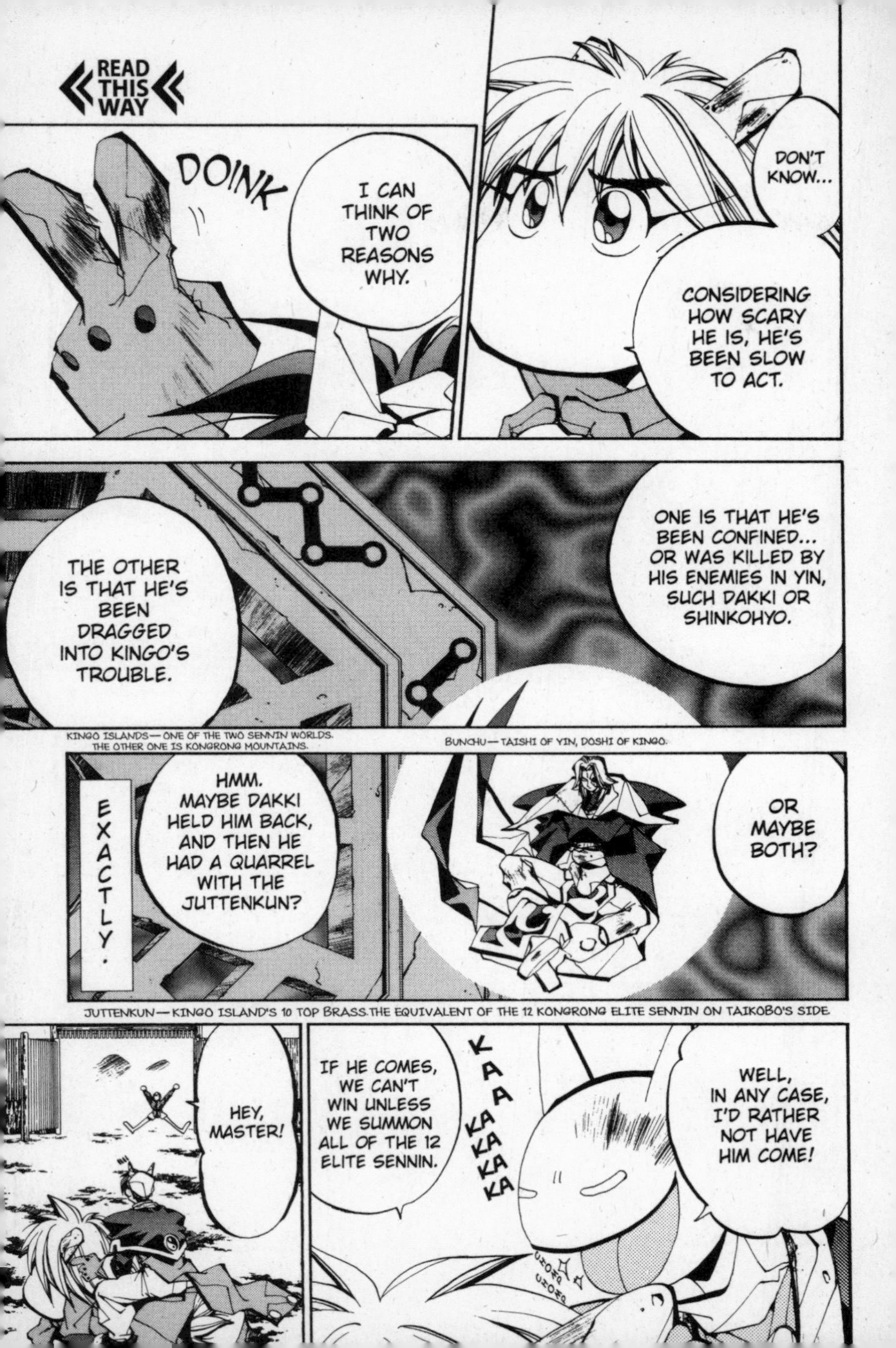
READ THIS WAY
DON'T KNOW...
CONSIDERING HOW SCARY HE IS, HE'S BEEN SLOW TO ACT.
DOINK
I CAN THINK OF TWO REASONS WHY.
ONE IS THAT HE'S BEEN CONFINED... OR WAS KILLED BY HIS ENEMIES IN YIN, SUCH DAKKI OR SHINKOHYO.
THE OTHER IS THAT HE'S BEEN DRAGGED INTO KINGO'S TROUBLE.
BUNCHU—TAISHI OF YIN, DOSHI OF KINGO.
KINGO ISLANDS—ONE OF THE TWO SENNIN WORLDS. THE OTHER ONE IS KONGRONG MOUNTAINS.
OR MAYBE BOTH?
HMM. MAYBE DAKKI HELD HIM BACK, AND THEN HE HAD A QUARREL WITH THE JUTTENKUN?
EXACTLY.
JUTTENKUN—KINGO ISLAND'S 10 TOP BRASS. THE EQUIVALENT OF THE 12 KONGRONG ELITE SENNIN ON TAIKOBO'S SIDE
WELL, IN ANY CASE, I'D RATHER NOT HAVE HIM COME!
KAA KAKAKAKA
IF HE COMES, WE CAN'T WIN UNLESS WE SUMMON ALL OF THE 12 ELITE SENNIN.
HEY, MASTER!

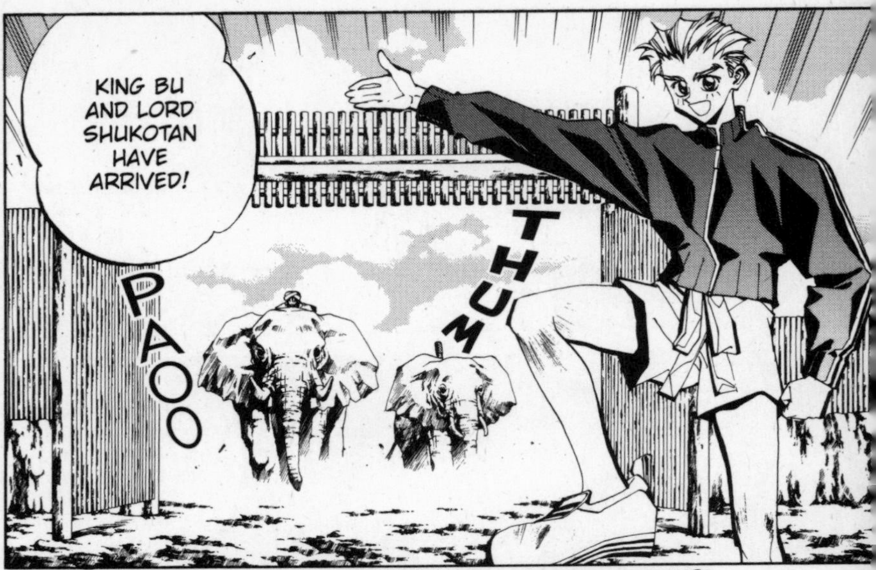
KING BU AND LORD SHUKOTAN HAVE ARRIVED!
THUM
PAOO
BUKICHI—(SELF-PROCLAIMED) DISCIPLE OF TAIKOBO.

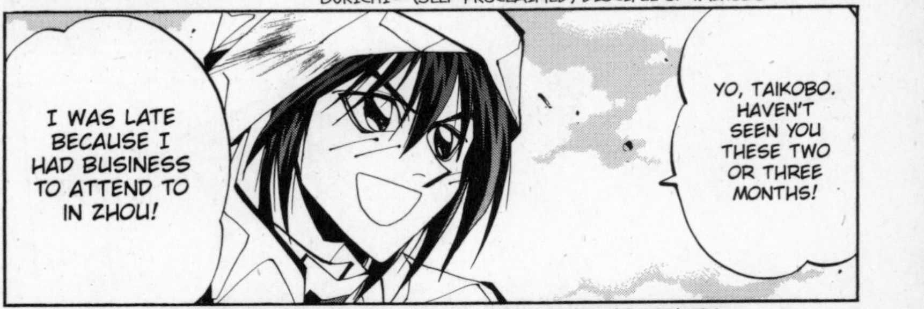
YO, TAIKOBO. HAVEN'T SEEN YOU THESE TWO OR THREE MONTHS!
I WAS LATE BECAUSE I HAD BUSINESS TO ATTEND TO IN ZHOU!
KING BU (HATSU KI)—KING OF ZHOU, WHICH IS AT WAR WITH YIN.

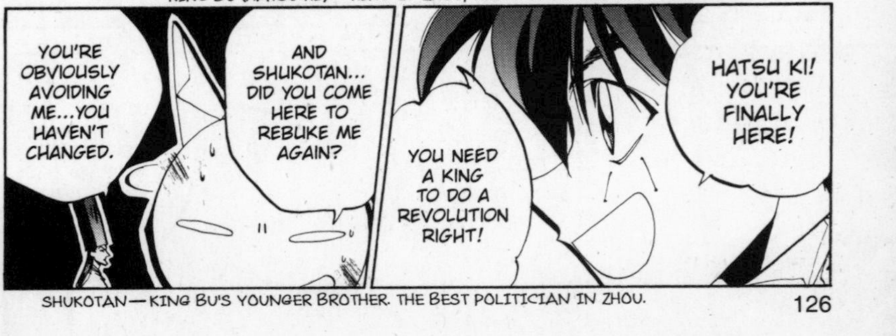
HATSU KI! YOU'RE FINALLY HERE!
YOU NEED A KING TO DO A REVOLUTION RIGHT!
AND SHUKOTAN... DID YOU COME HERE TO REBUKE ME AGAIN?
YOU'RE OBVIOUSLY AVOIDING ME...YOU HAVEN'T CHANGED.
SHUKOTAN—KING BU'S YOUNGER BROTHER. THE BEST POLITICIAN IN ZHOU.

READ THIS WAY

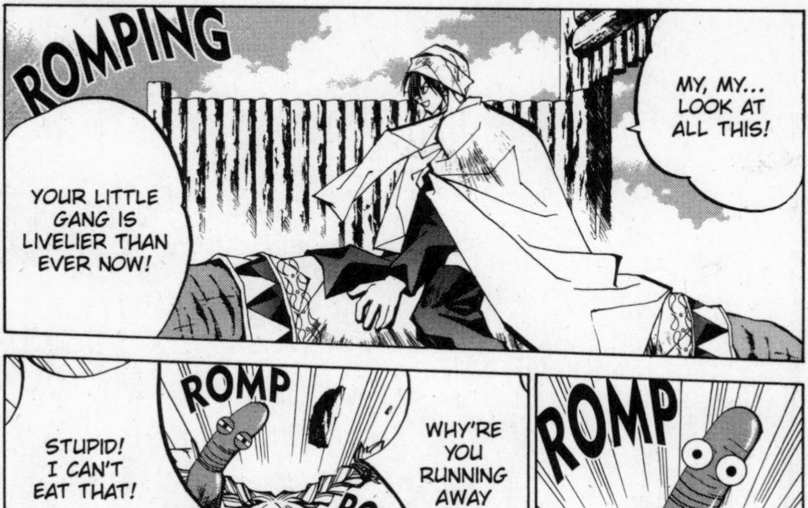
MY, MY... LOOK AT ALL THIS!
ROMPING
YOUR LITTLE GANG IS LIVELIER THAN EVER NOW!
ROMP
WRIGGLE
ROMP
DARLING! HERE'S YOUR MEAL!
ROMP
WHY'RE YOU RUNNING AWAY FROM ME?!
STUPID! I CAN'T EAT THAT!
ROMP
ROMP
ROMP
ROMP
BUT MOLES LOVE TO EAT EARTH-WORMS!

DOKOSON—A DOSHI WHO CAN DIVE AND MOVE UNDERGROUND.
TOH SENGYOKU—A FEMALE DOSHI WHO USED TO WORK FOR YIN. SHE SWITCHED SIDES AFTER FALLING IN LOVE WITH DOKOSON.

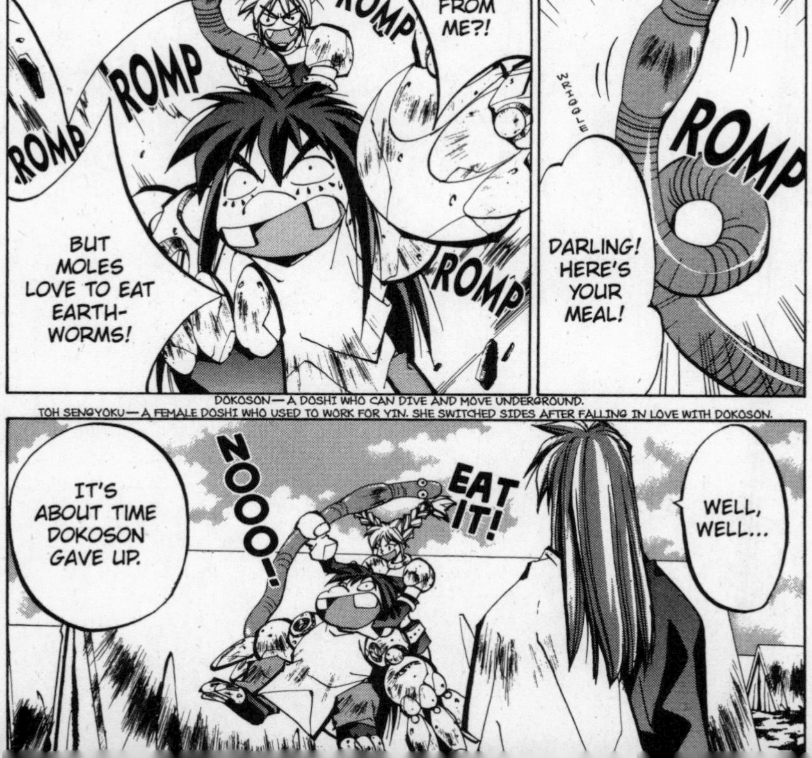
WELL, WELL...
EAT IT!
NOOO!
IT'S ABOUT TIME DOKOSON GAVE UP.

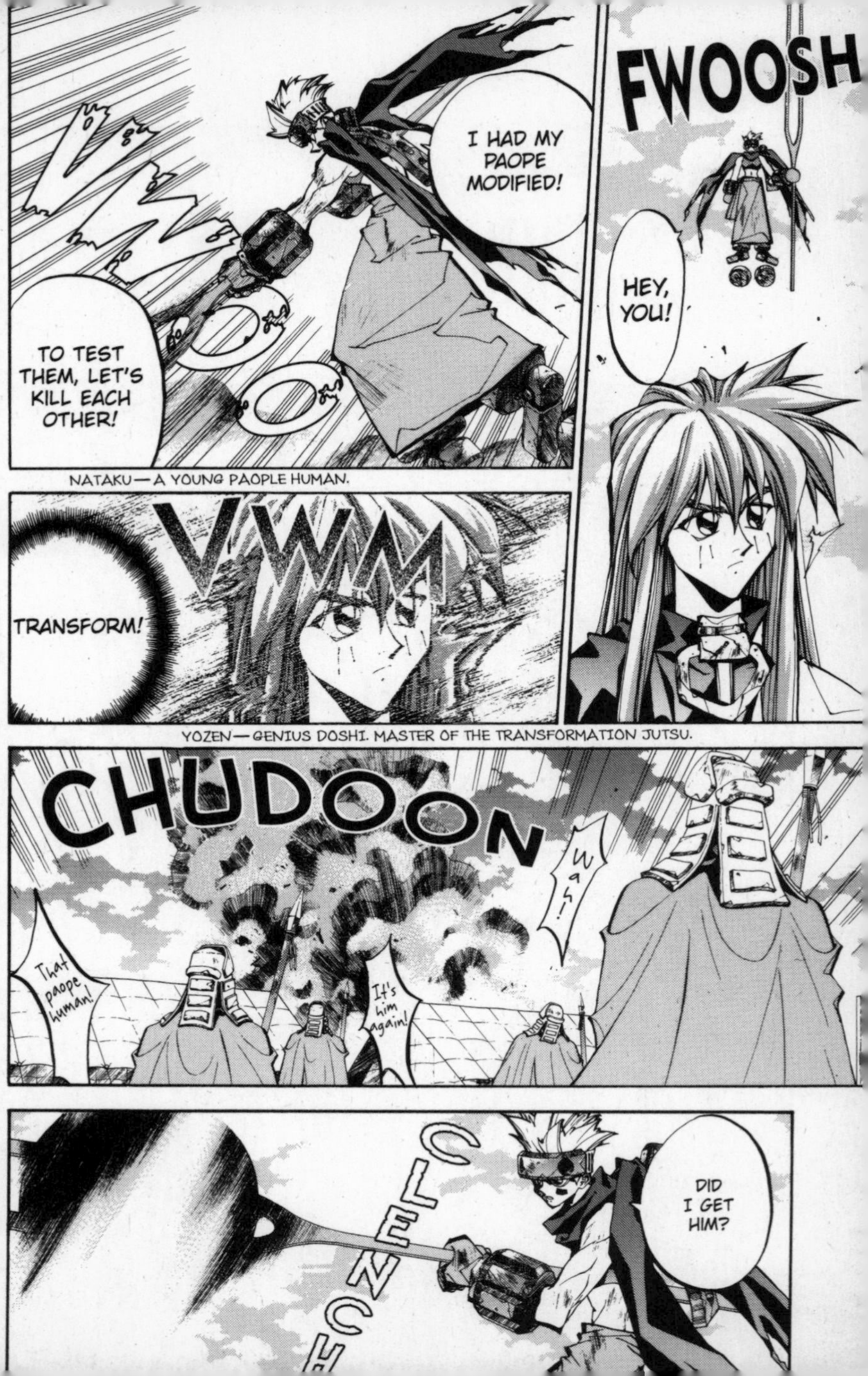
FWOOSH
HEY, YOU!
I HAD MY PAOPE MODIFIED!
TO TEST THEM, LET'S KILL EACH OTHER!
NATAKU—A YOUNG PAOPLE HUMAN.
VWM
TRANSFORM!
YOZEN—GENIUS DOSHI. MASTER OF THE TRANSFORMATION JUTSU.
CHUDOON
Wa-!
It's him again!
That paope human!
DID I GET HIM?
CLENCH

READ THIS WAY

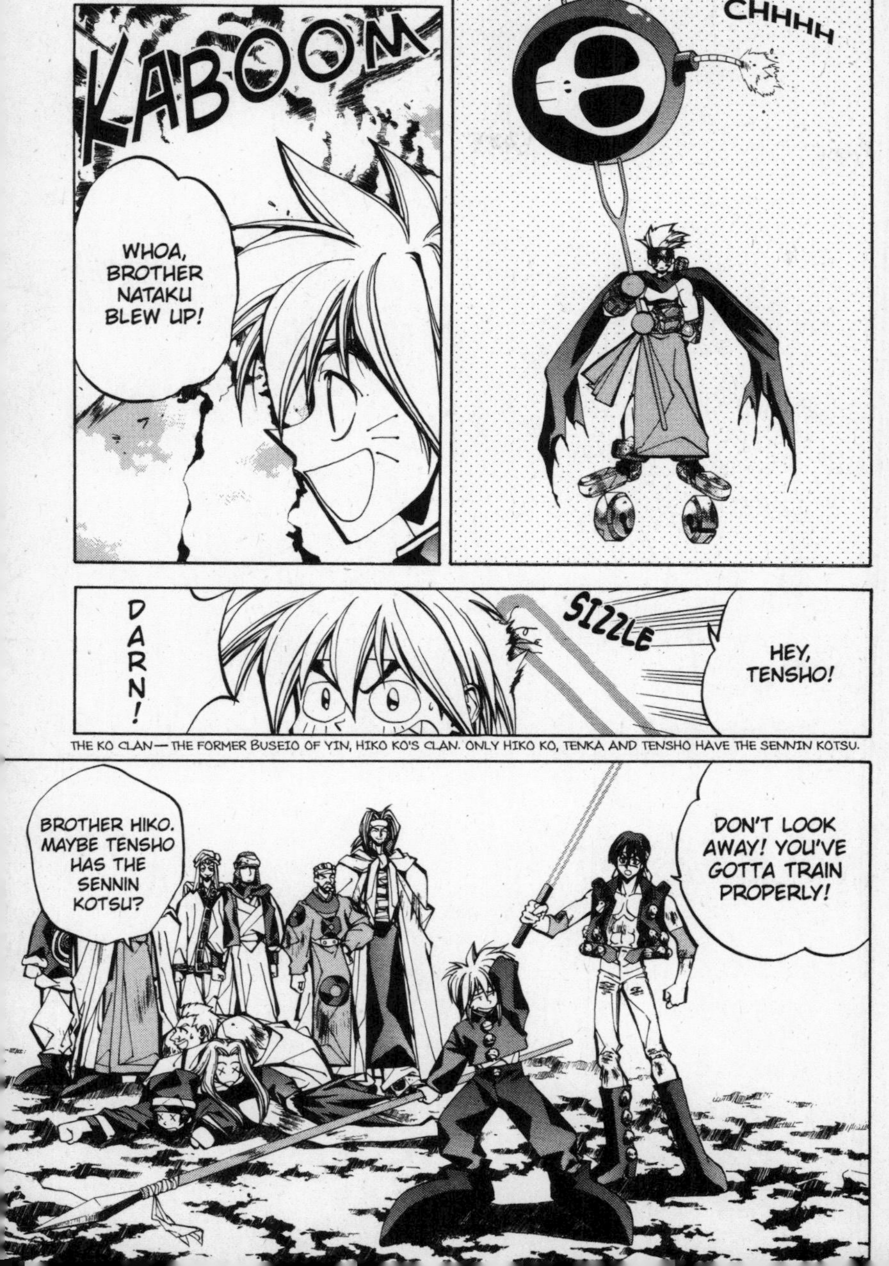
CHHHH
KABOOM
WHOA, BROTHER NATAKU BLEW UP!
HEY, TENSHO!
SIZZLE
DARN!
THE KO CLAN—THE FORMER BUSEIO OF YIN, HIKO KO'S CLAN. ONLY HIKO KO, TENKA AND TENSHO HAVE THE SENNIN KOTSU.
DON'T LOOK AWAY! YOU'VE GOTTA TRAIN PROPERLY!
BROTHER HIKO. MAYBE TENSHO HAS THE SENNIN KOTSU?

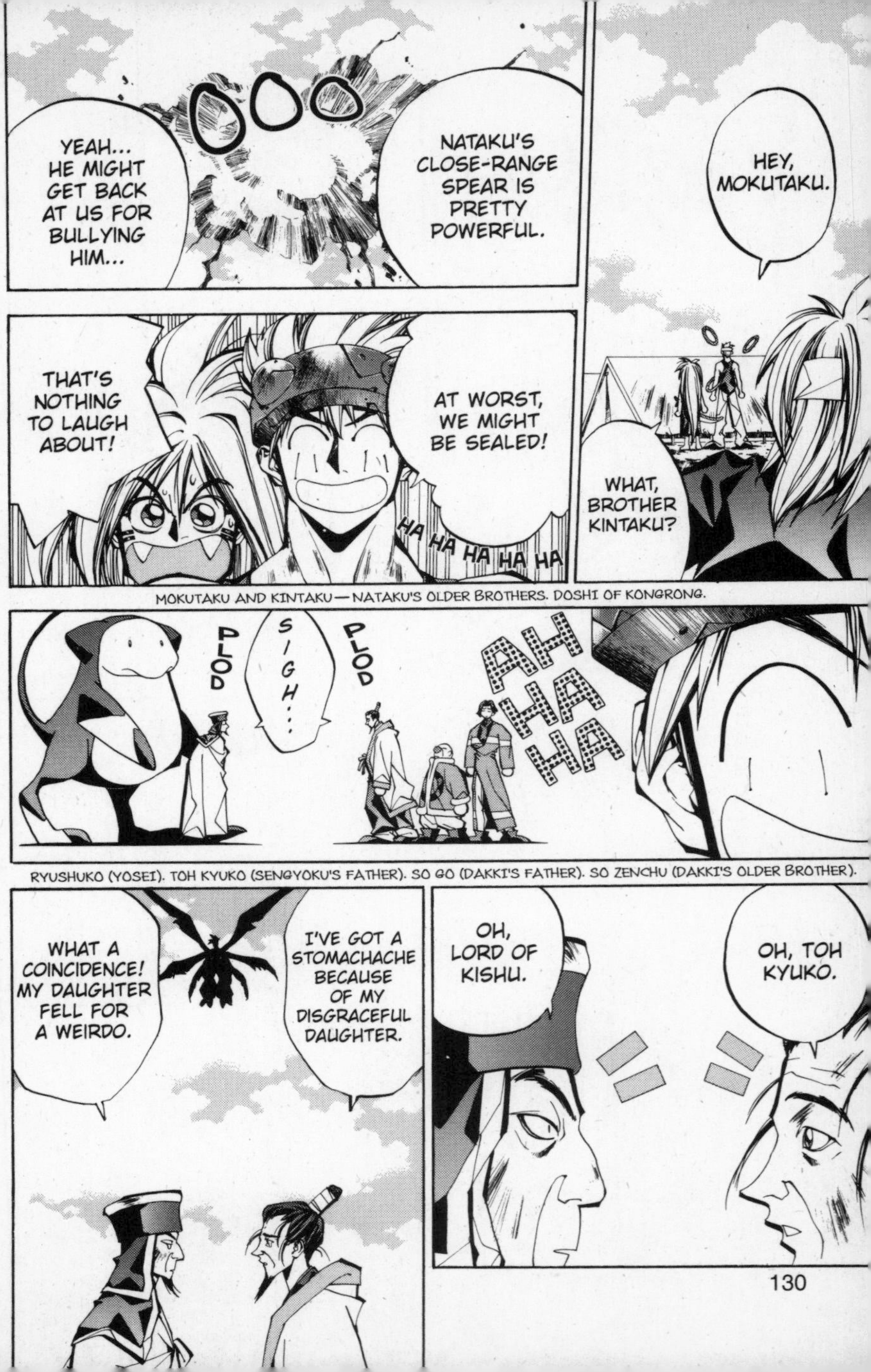
HEY, MOKUTAKU.
WHAT, BROTHER KINTAKU?
NATAKU'S CLOSE-RANGE SPEAR IS PRETTY POWERFUL.
YEAH... HE MIGHT GET BACK AT US FOR BULLYING HIM...
AT WORST, WE MIGHT BE SEALED!
HA HA HA HA HA
THAT'S NOTHING TO LAUGH ABOUT!
MOKUTAKU AND KINTAKU—NATAKU'S OLDER BROTHERS. DOSHI OF KONGRONG.
AH HA HA HA
PLOD
SIGH...
PLOD
RYUSHUKO (YOSEI). TOH KYUKO (SENGYOKU'S FATHER). SO GO (DAKKI'S FATHER). SO ZENCHU (DAKKI'S OLDER BROTHER).
OH, TOH KYUKO.
OH, LORD OF KISHU.
I'VE GOT A STOMACHACHE BECAUSE OF MY DISGRACEFUL DAUGHTER.
WHAT A COINCIDENCE! MY DAUGHTER FELL FOR A WEIRDO.

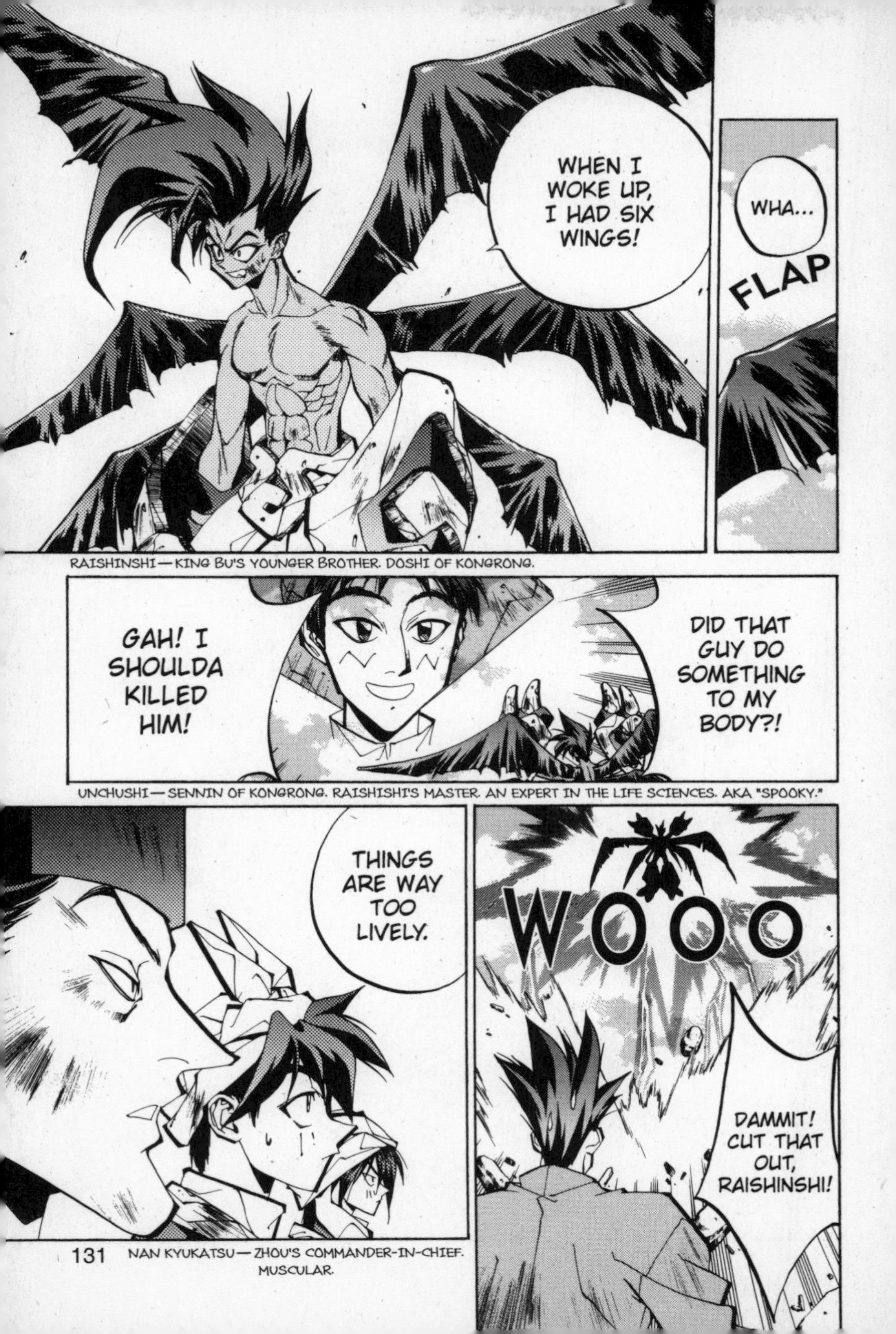
WHA...
FLAP
WHEN I WOKE UP, I HAD SIX WINGS!
RAISHINSHI—KING BU'S YOUNGER BROTHER. DOSHI OF KONGRONG.
DID THAT GUY DO SOMETHING TO MY BODY?!
GAH! I SHOULDA KILLED HIM!
UNCHUSHI—SENNIN OF KONGRONG. RAISHISHI'S MASTER. AN EXPERT IN THE LIFE SCIENCES. AKA "SPOOKY."
WOOO
DAMMIT! CUT THAT OUT, RAISHINSHI!
THINGS ARE WAY TOO LIVELY.
NAN KYUKATSU—ZHOU'S COMMANDER-IN-CHIEF. MUSCULAR.

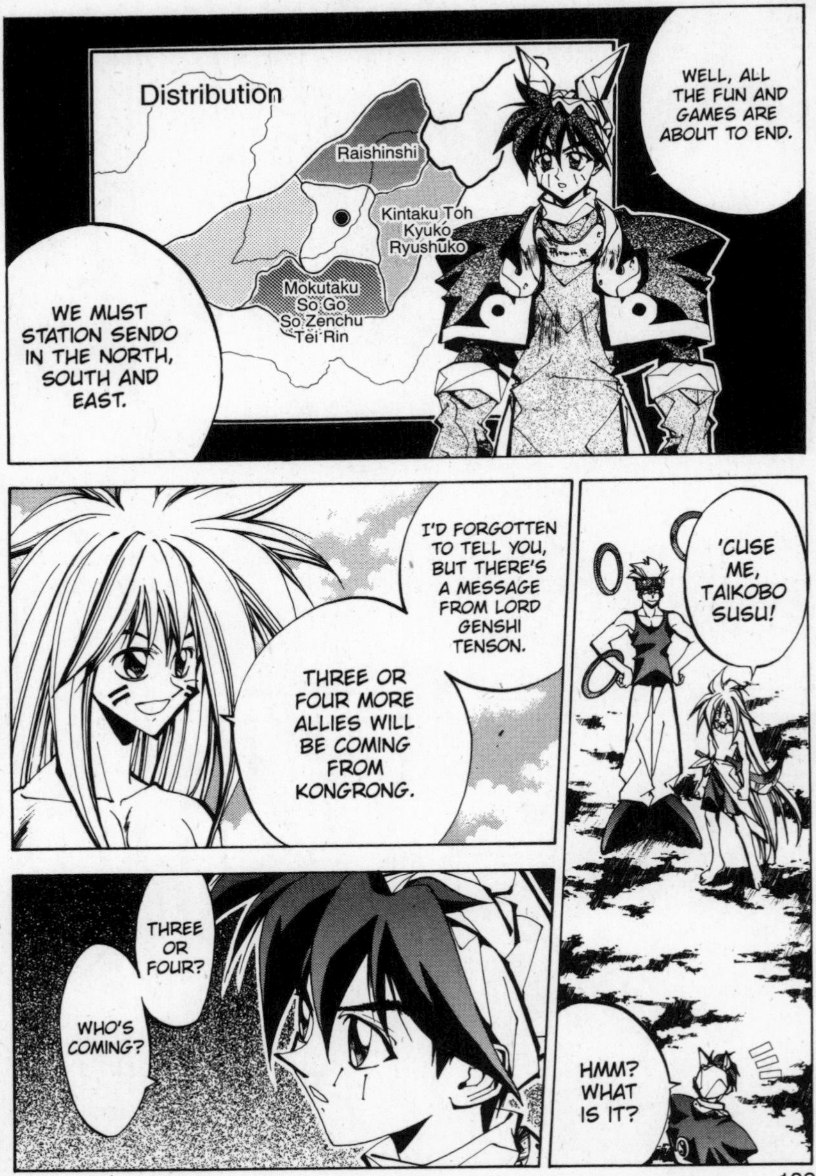
WELL, ALL THE FUN AND GAMES ARE ABOUT TO END.
Distribution
Raishinshi
Kintaku Toh
Kyuko
Ryushuko
Mokutaku
So Go
So Zenchu
Tei Rin
WE MUST STATION SENDO IN THE NORTH, SOUTH AND EAST.
'CUSE ME, TAIKOBO SUSU!
HMM? WHAT IS IT?
I'D FORGOTTEN TO TELL YOU, BUT THERE'S A MESSAGE FROM LORD GENSHI TENSON.
THREE OR FOUR MORE ALLIES WILL BE COMING FROM KONGRONG.
THREE OR FOUR?
WHO'S COMING?

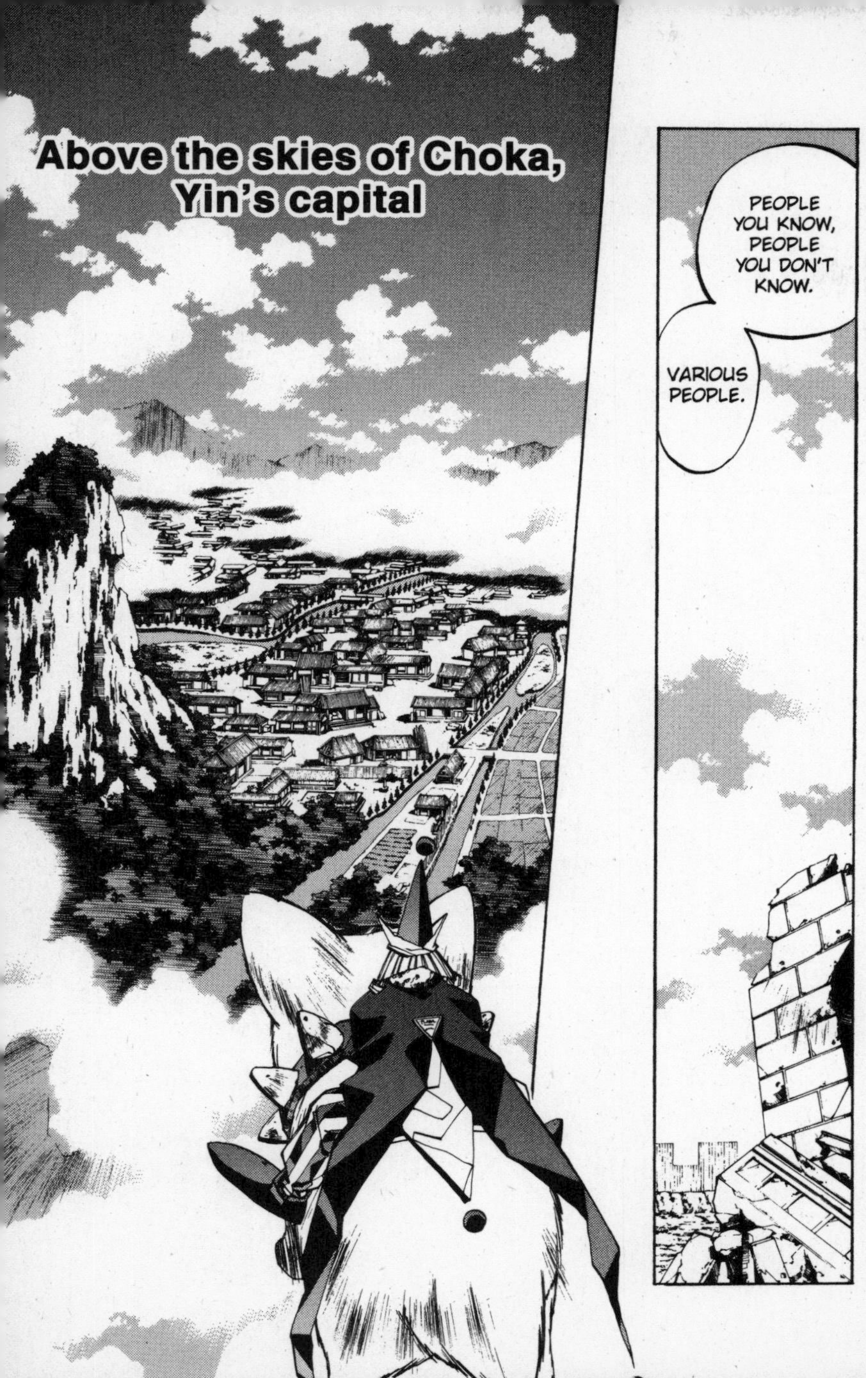
PEOPLE YOU KNOW, PEOPLE YOU DON'T KNOW.
VARIOUS PEOPLE.
Above the skies of Choka, Yin's capital

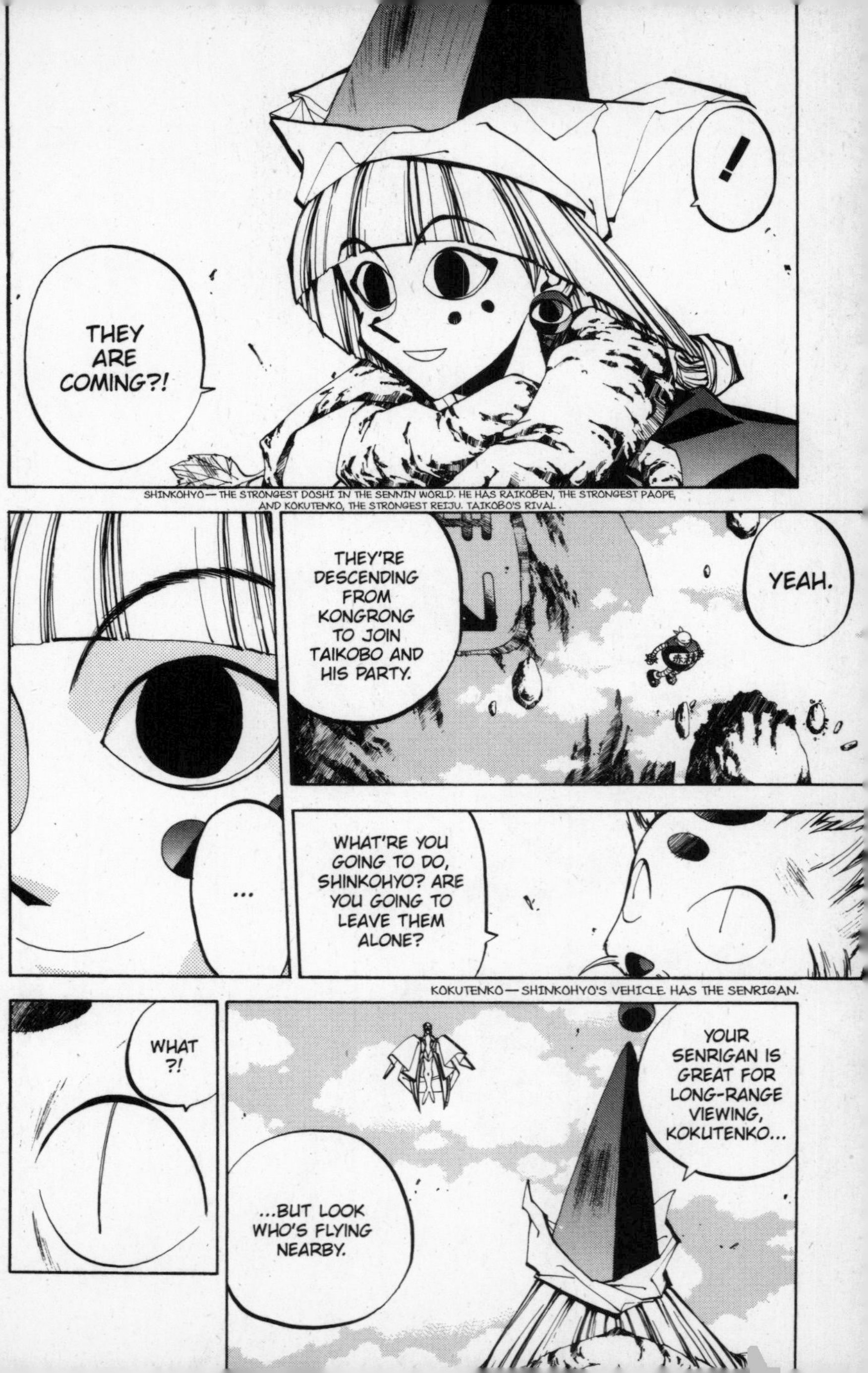
!
THEY ARE COMING?!
SHINKOHYO—THE STRONGEST DOSHI IN THE SENNIN WORLD. HE HAS RAIKOBEN, THE STRONGEST PAOPE, AND KOKUTENKO, THE STRONGEST REIJU. TAIKOBO'S RIVAL.
YEAH.
THEY'RE DESCENDING FROM KONGRONG TO JOIN TAIKOBO AND HIS PARTY.
WHAT'RE YOU GOING TO DO, SHINKOHYO? ARE YOU GOING TO LEAVE THEM ALONE?
...
KOKUTENKO—SHINKOHYO'S VEHICLE. HAS THE SENRIGAN.
YOUR SENRIGAN IS GREAT FOR LONG-RANGE VIEWING, KOKUTENKO...
...BUT LOOK WHO'S FLYING NEARBY.
WHAT ?!

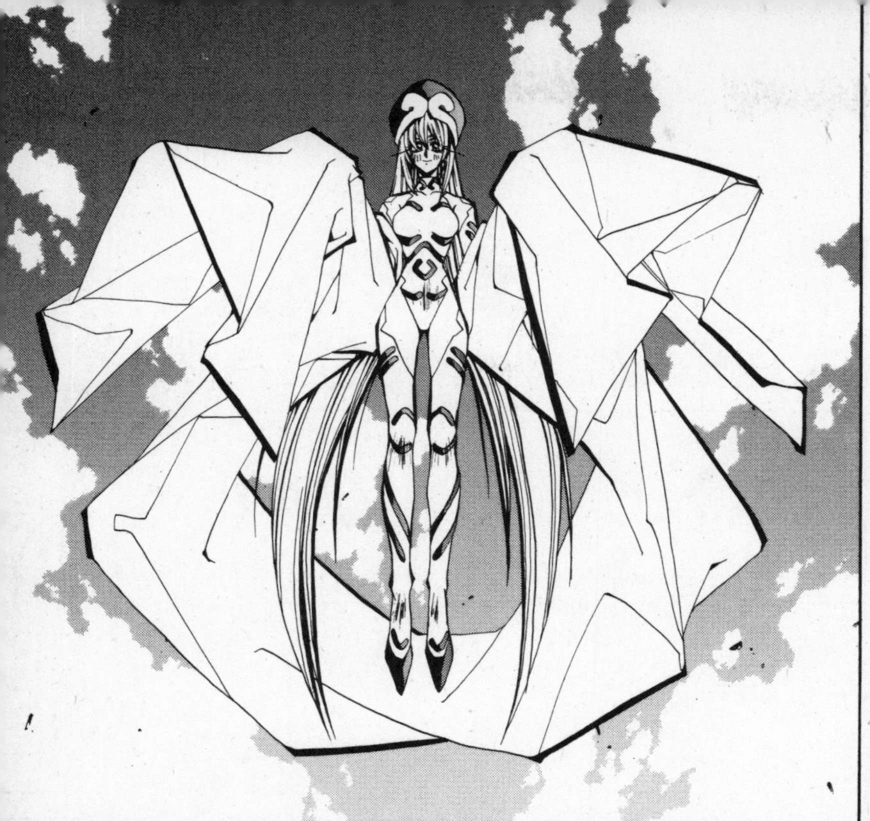

DAKKI—EMPRESS OF YIN. USED TO BE A SENNYO AT KINGO ISLAND. EFFECTIVELY CONTROLS YIN WITH HER PEERLESS BEAUTY AND THE PAOPE KEISEI GENJO. SHE HOLDS A LOT OF SECRETS.

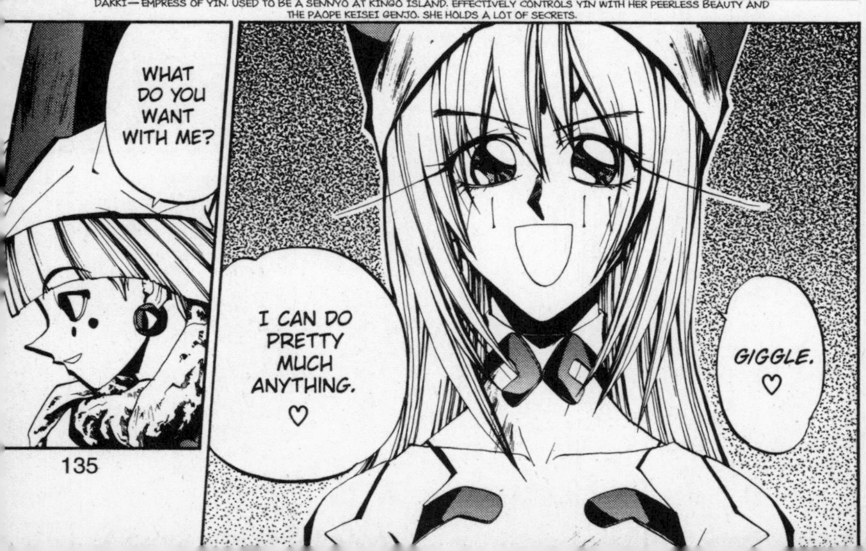
WHAT DO YOU WANT WITH ME?
I CAN DO PRETTY MUCH ANYTHING. ♡
GIGGLE. ♡

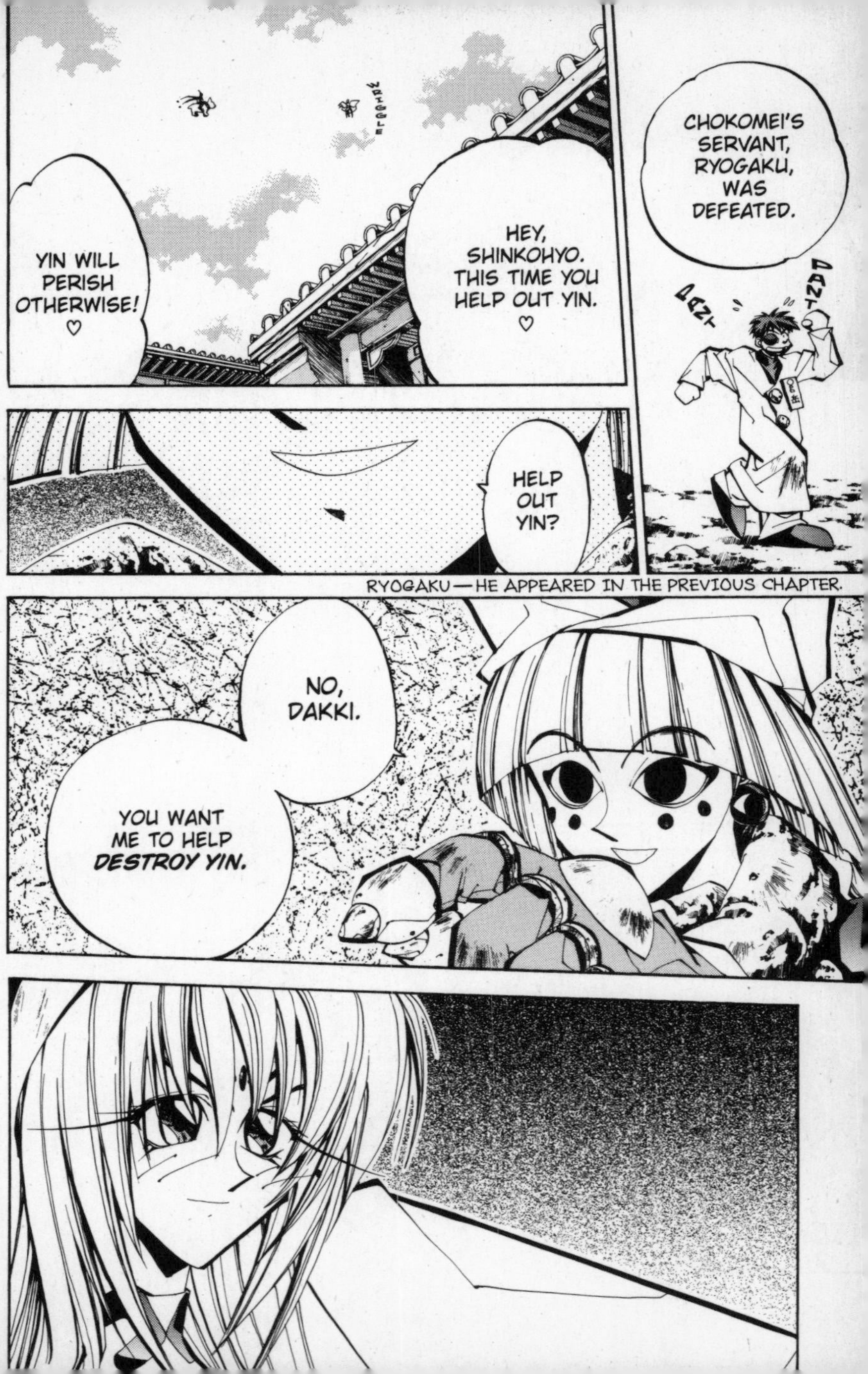
CHOKOMEI'S SERVANT, RYOGAKU, WAS DEFEATED.
PANT
WRIGGLE
HEY, SHINKOHYO. THIS TIME YOU HELP OUT YIN. ♡
YIN WILL PERISH OTHERWISE! ♡
HELP OUT YIN?
RYOGAKU—HE APPEARED IN THE PREVIOUS CHAPTER.
NO, DAKKI.
YOU WANT ME TO HELP **DESTROY YIN.**

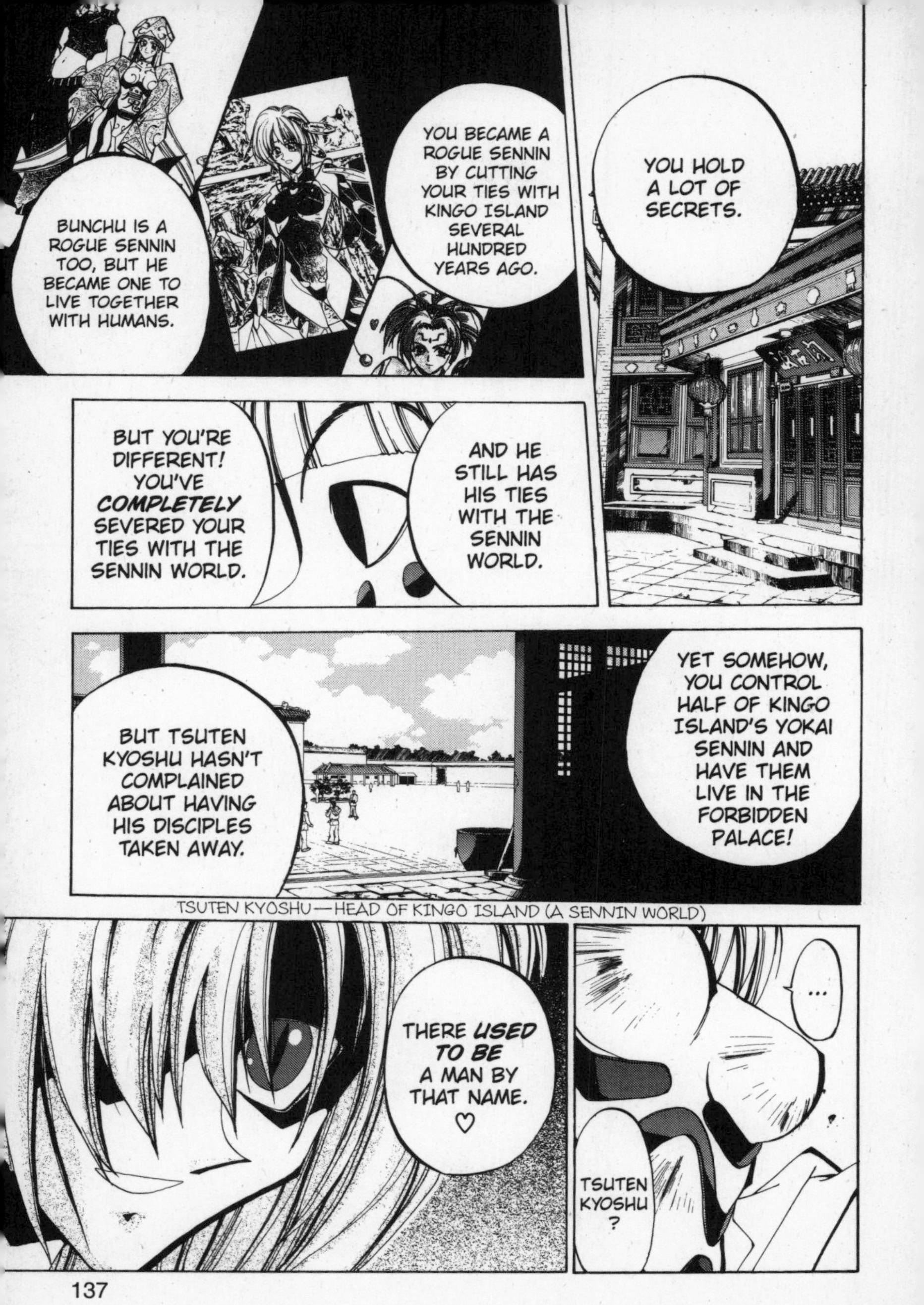
YOU HOLD A LOT OF SECRETS.
YOU BECAME A ROGUE SENNIN BY CUTTING YOUR TIES WITH KINGO ISLAND SEVERAL HUNDRED YEARS AGO.
BUNCHU IS A ROGUE SENNIN TOO, BUT HE BECAME ONE TO LIVE TOGETHER WITH HUMANS.
AND HE STILL HAS HIS TIES WITH THE SENNIN WORLD.
BUT YOU'RE DIFFERENT! YOU'VE *COMPLETELY* SEVERED YOUR TIES WITH THE SENNIN WORLD.
YET SOMEHOW, YOU CONTROL HALF OF KINGO ISLAND'S YOKAI SENNIN AND HAVE THEM LIVE IN THE FORBIDDEN PALACE!
BUT TSUTEN KYOSHU HASN'T COMPLAINED ABOUT HAVING HIS DISCIPLES TAKEN AWAY.
TSUTEN KYOSHU—HEAD OF KINGO ISLAND (A SENNIN WORLD)
...
TSUTEN KYOSHU?
THERE *USED TO BE* A MAN BY THAT NAME. ♡

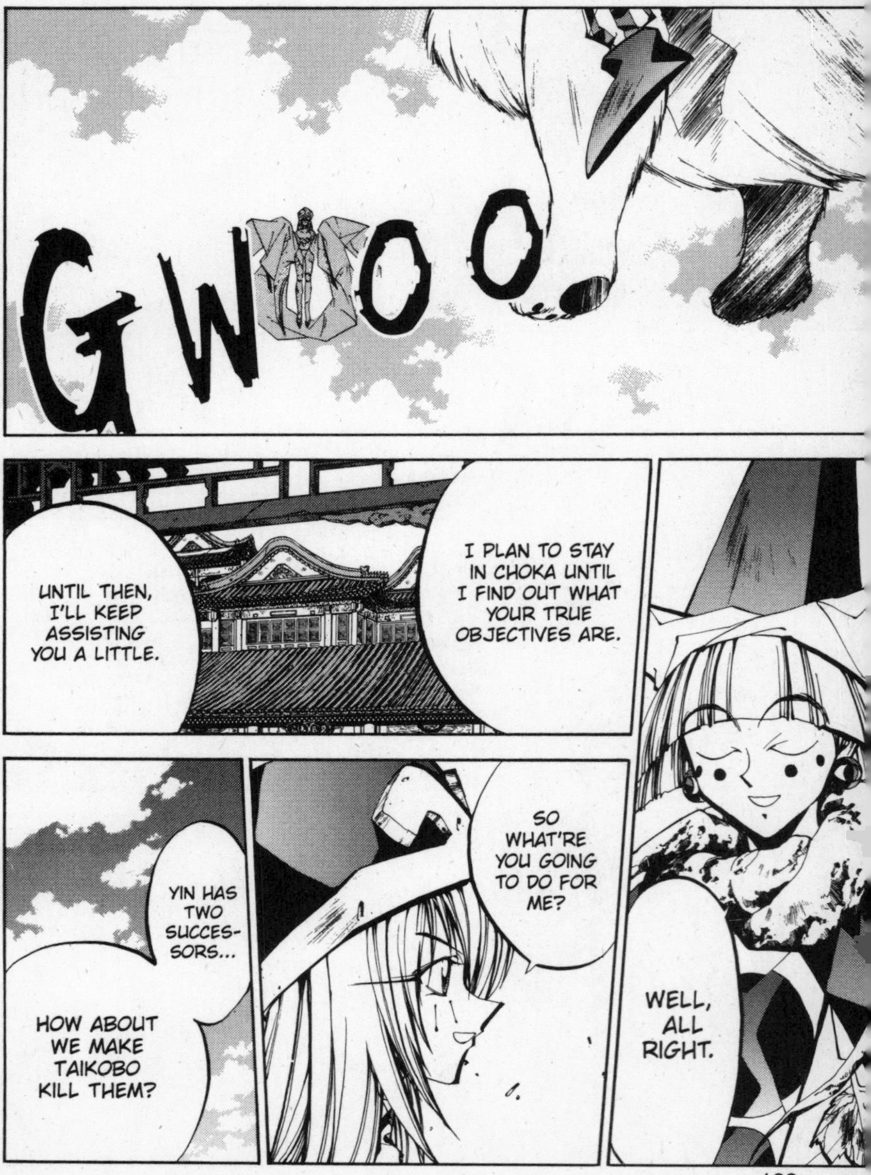
GWOOO
I PLAN TO STAY IN CHOKA UNTIL I FIND OUT WHAT YOUR TRUE OBJECTIVES ARE.
UNTIL THEN, I'LL KEEP ASSISTING YOU A LITTLE.
SO WHAT'RE YOU GOING TO DO FOR ME?
YIN HAS TWO SUCCES-SORS...
HOW ABOUT WE MAKE TAIKOBO KILL THEM?
WELL, ALL RIGHT.

READ THIS WAY

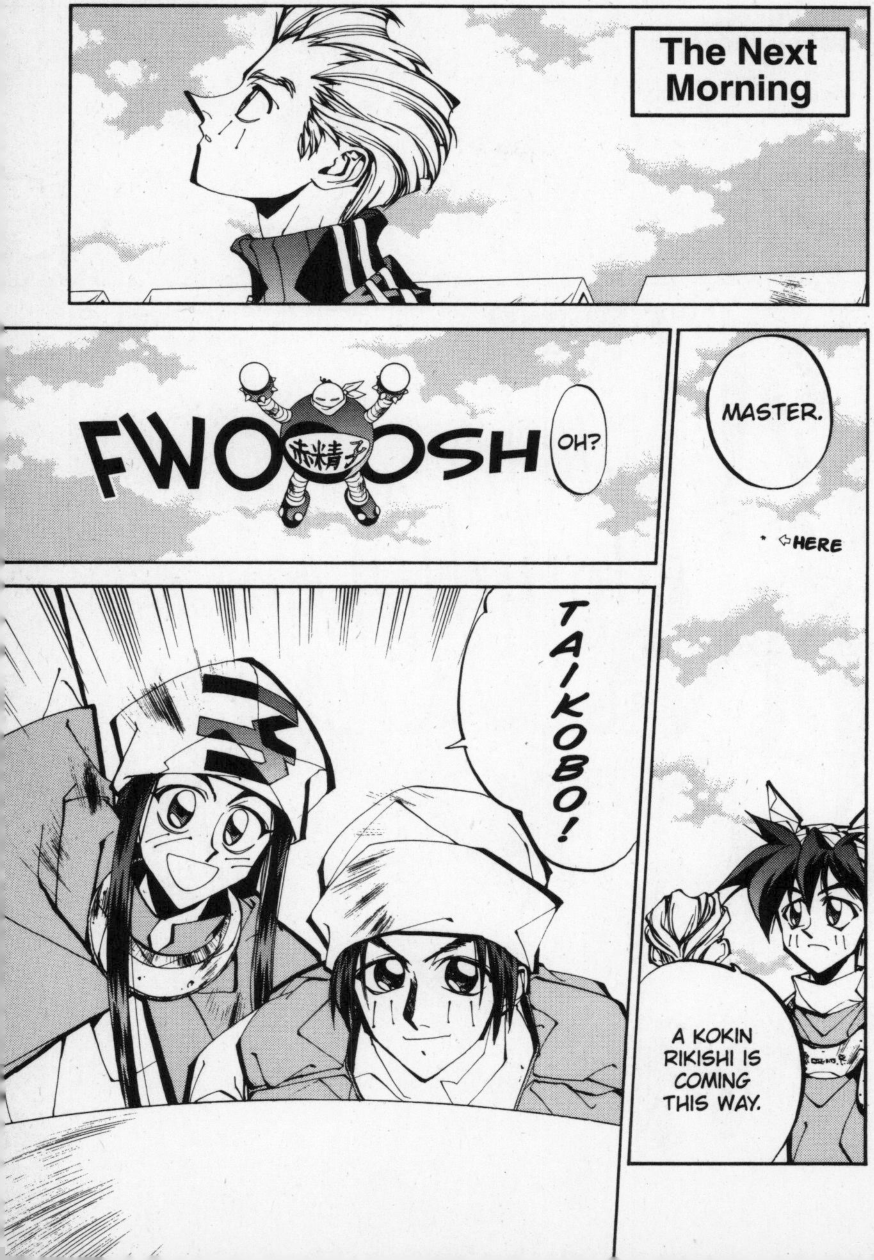
The Next Morning
MASTER.
HERE
A KOKIN RIKISHI IS COMING THIS WAY.
FWOOSH
赤精子
OH?
TAIKOBO!

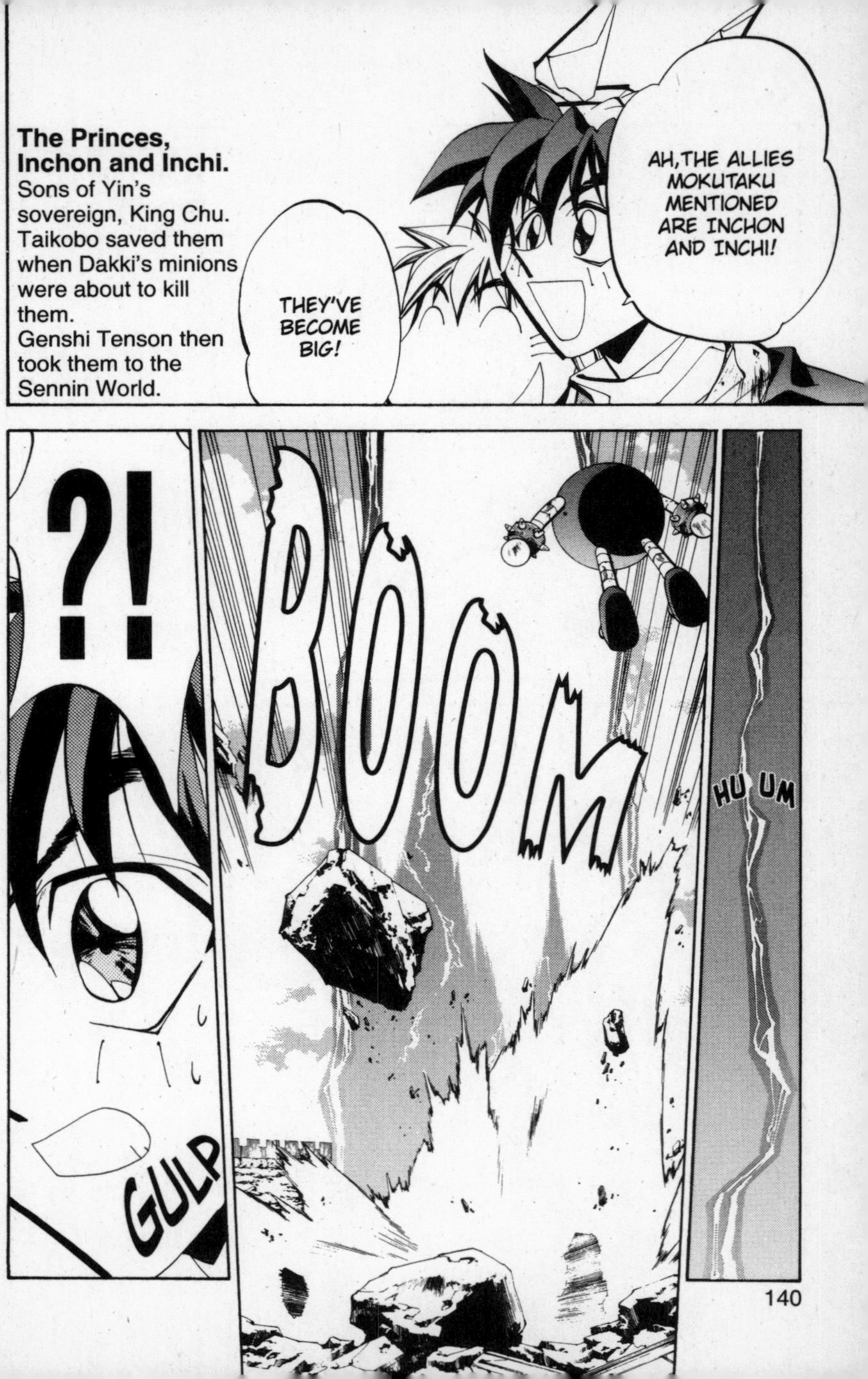
AH, THE ALLIES MOKUTAKU MENTIONED ARE INCHON AND INCHI!
THEY'VE BECOME BIG!
The Princes, Inchon and Inchi.
Sons of Yin's sovereign, King Chu. Taikobo saved them when Dakki's minions were about to kill them.
Genshi Tenson then took them to the Sennin World.
HU UM
BOOM
?!
GULP

READ THIS WAY

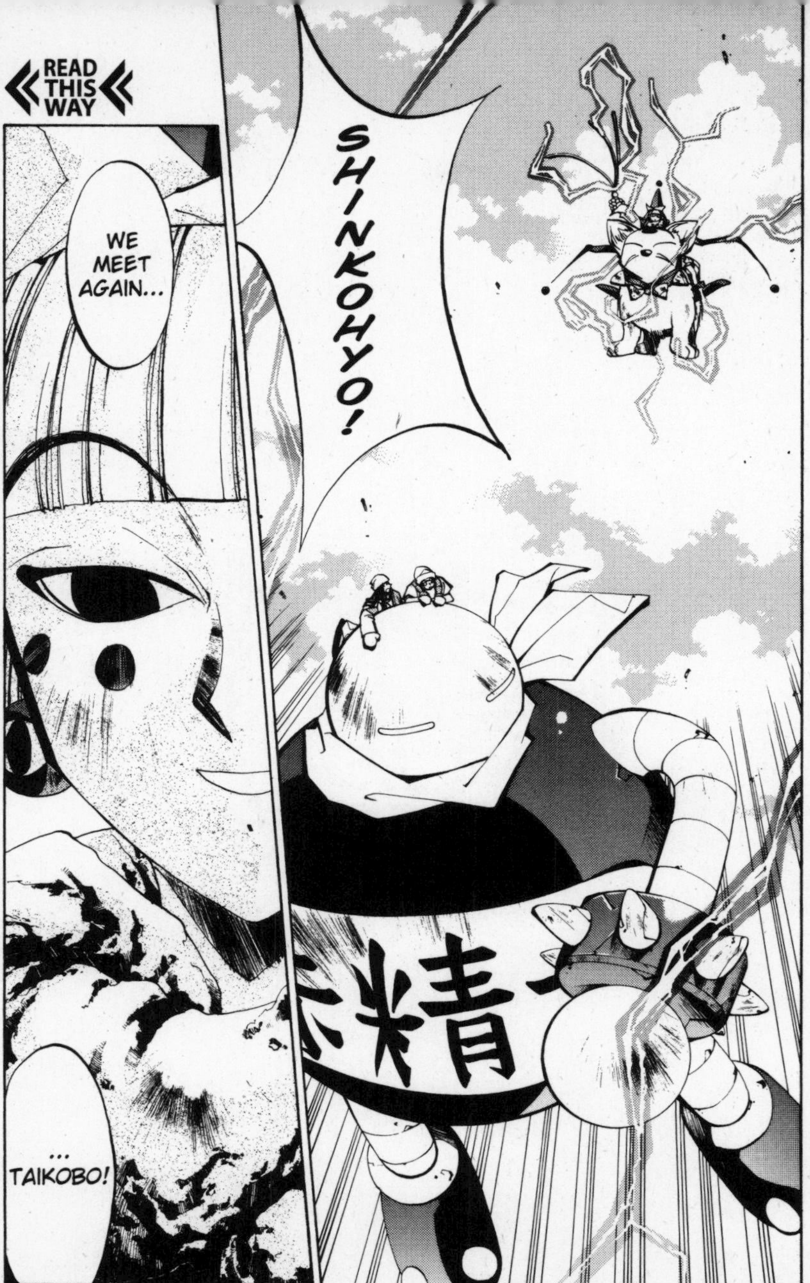
SHINKOHYO!
WE MEET AGAIN...
...TAIKOBO!

封神演義

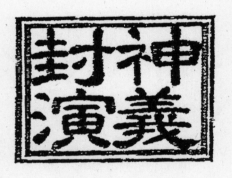

READ THIS WAY

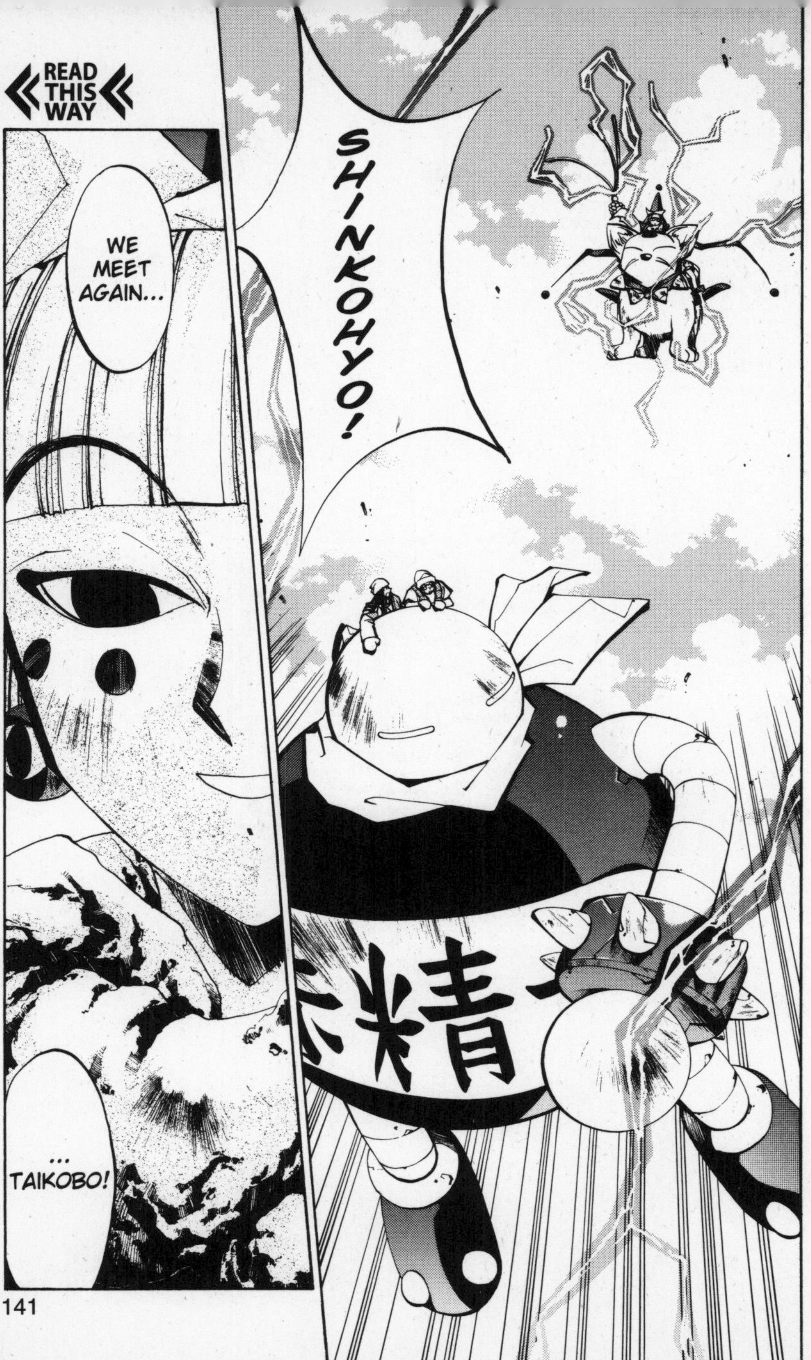
SHINKOHYO!
WE MEET AGAIN...
...TAIKOBO!

封神演義

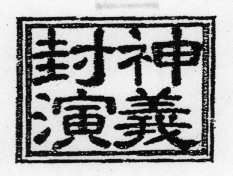

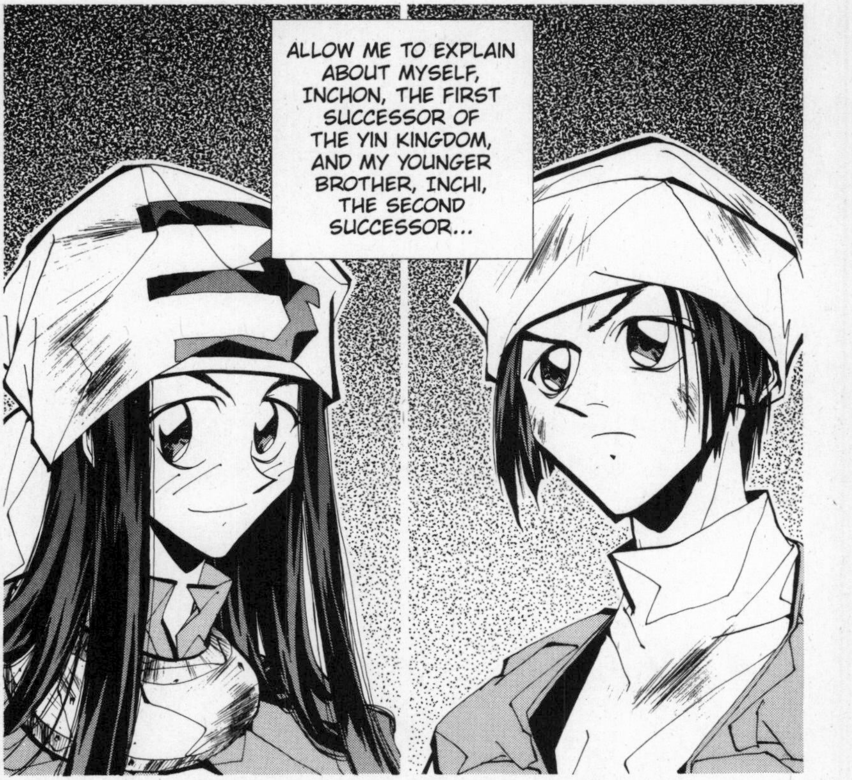
ALLOW ME TO EXPLAIN ABOUT MYSELF, INCHON, THE FIRST SUCCESSOR OF THE YIN KINGDOM, AND MY YOUNGER BROTHER, INCHI, THE SECOND SUCCESSOR...

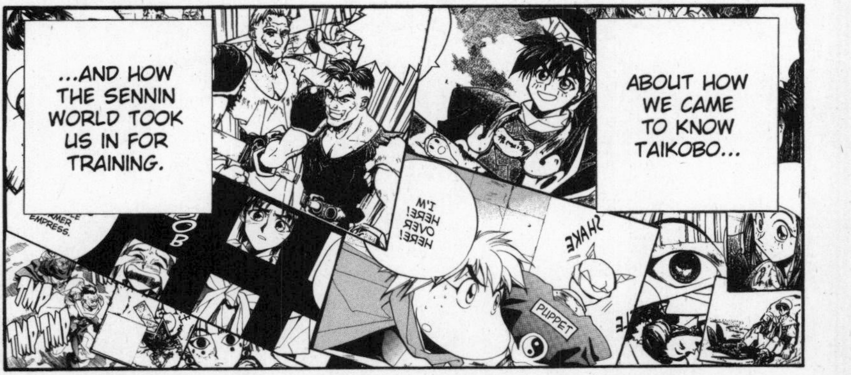
ABOUT HOW WE CAME TO KNOW TAIKOBO...
...AND HOW THE SENNIN WORLD TOOK US IN FOR TRAINING.

CHAPTER 77: THE PRINCES' CHOICE, PART 1

THE PRINCES' CHOICE, PART 1

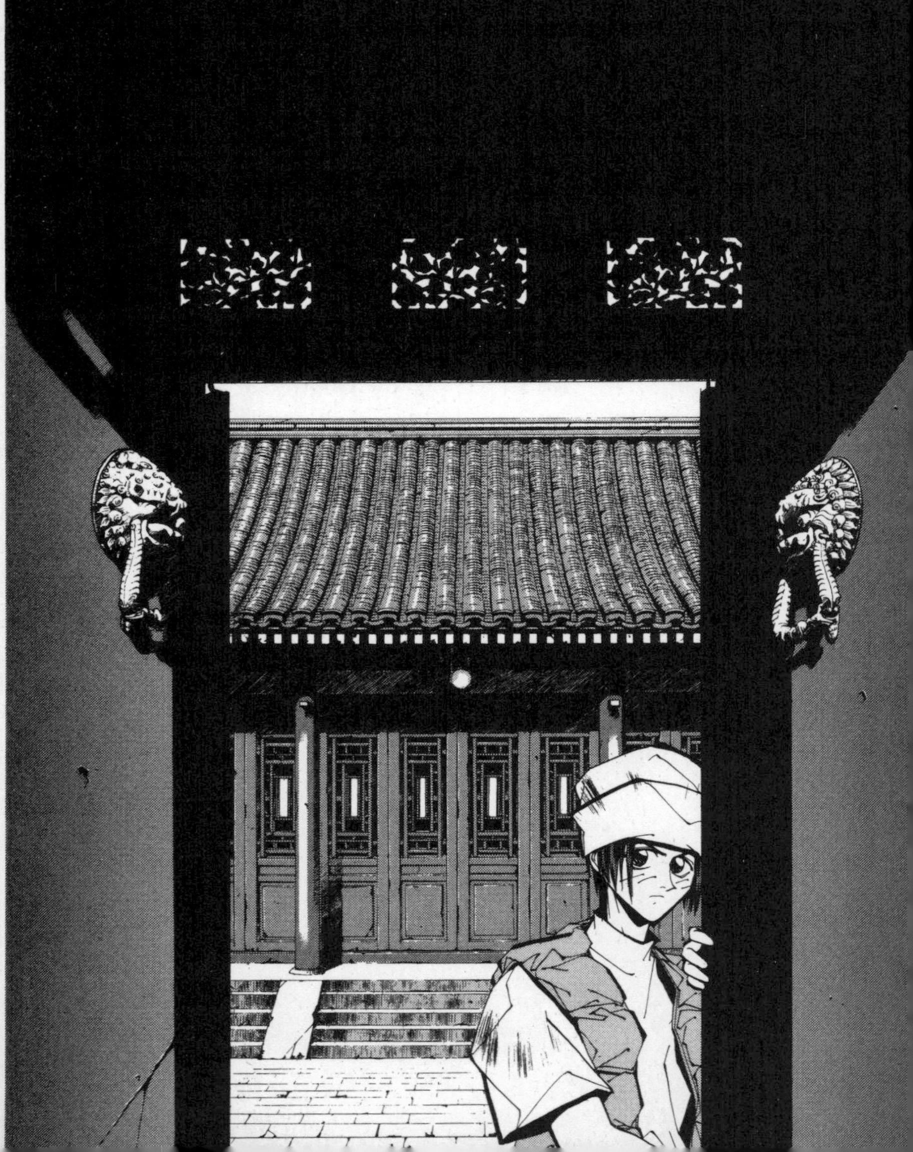

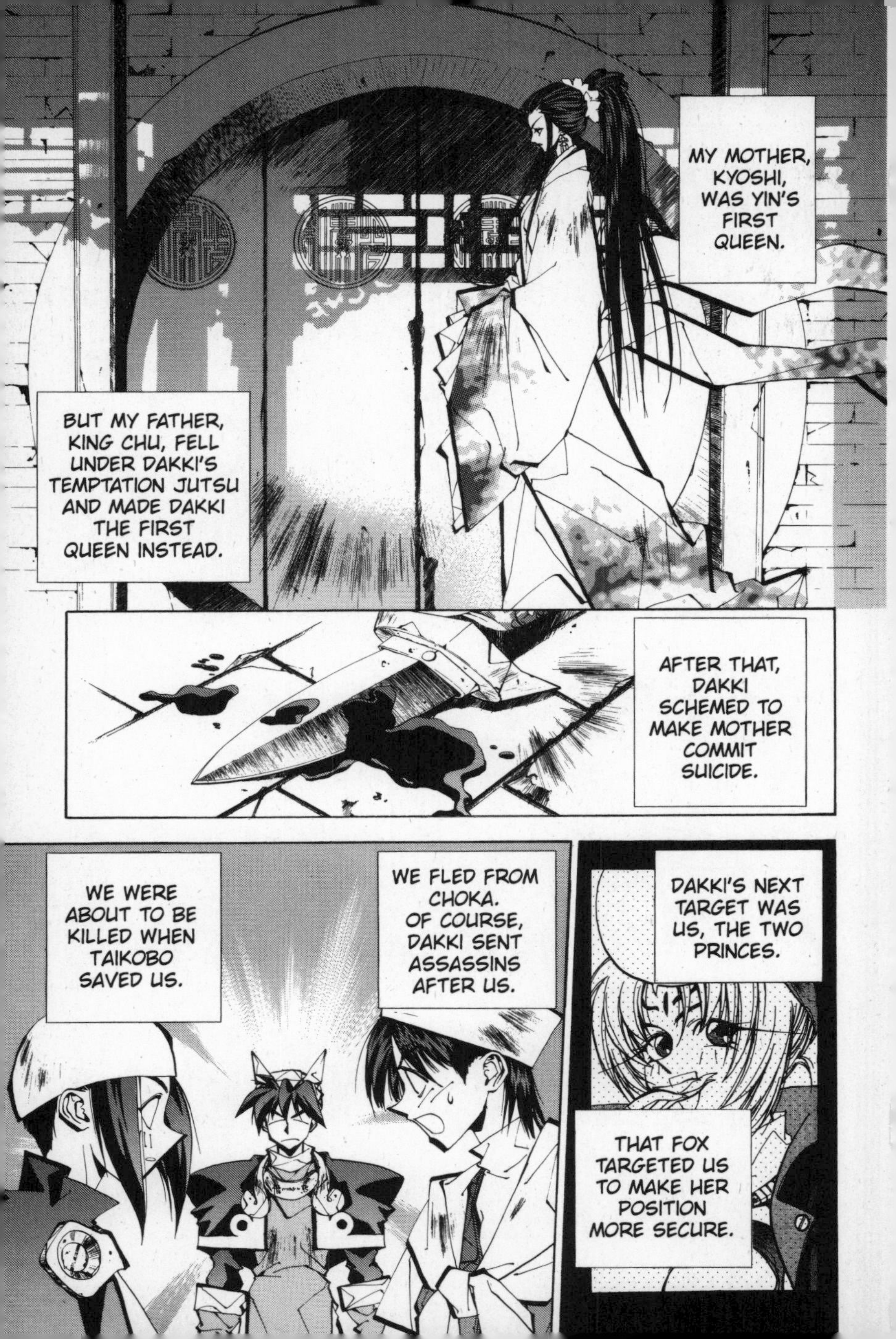
MY MOTHER, KYOSHI, WAS YIN'S FIRST QUEEN.
BUT MY FATHER, KING CHU, FELL UNDER DAKKI'S TEMPTATION JUTSU AND MADE DAKKI THE FIRST QUEEN INSTEAD.
AFTER THAT, DAKKI SCHEMED TO MAKE MOTHER COMMIT SUICIDE.
DAKKI'S NEXT TARGET WAS US, THE TWO PRINCES.
THAT FOX TARGETED US TO MAKE HER POSITION MORE SECURE.
WE FLED FROM CHOKA. OF COURSE, DAKKI SENT ASSASSINS AFTER US.
WE WERE ABOUT TO BE KILLED WHEN TAIKOBO SAVED US.

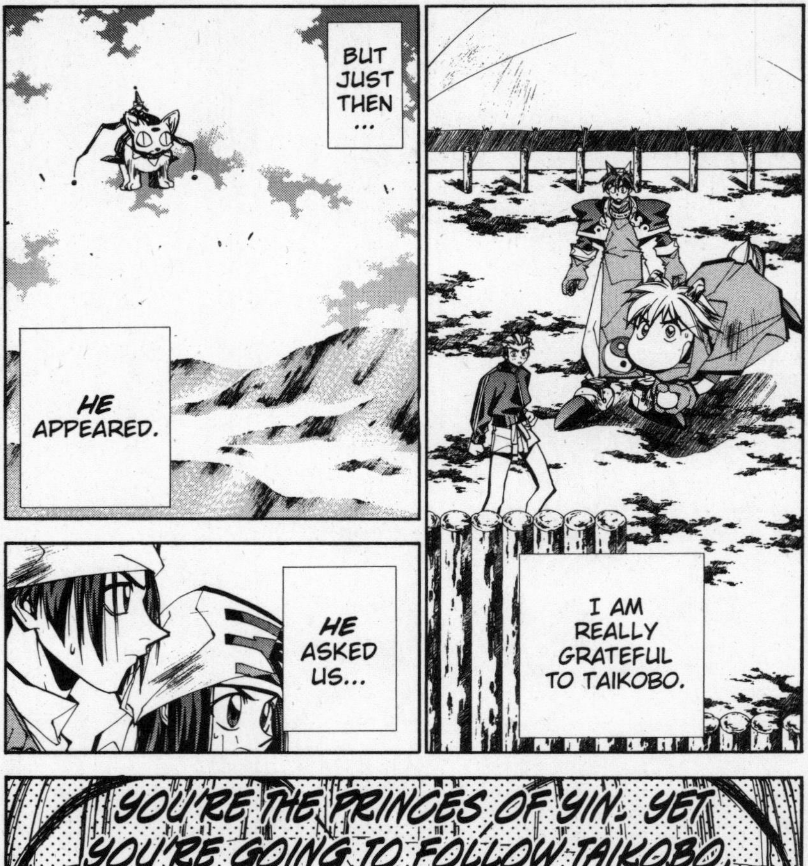
I AM REALLY GRATEFUL TO TAIKOBO.
BUT JUST THEN...
HE APPEARED.
HE ASKED US...
YOU'RE THE PRINCES OF YIN. YET YOU'RE GOING TO FOLLOW TAIKOBO.
WHO'S THE ENEMY OF YIN?

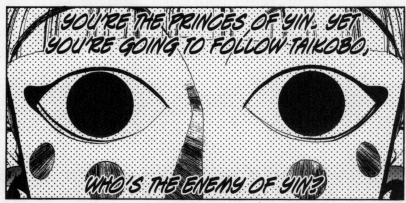

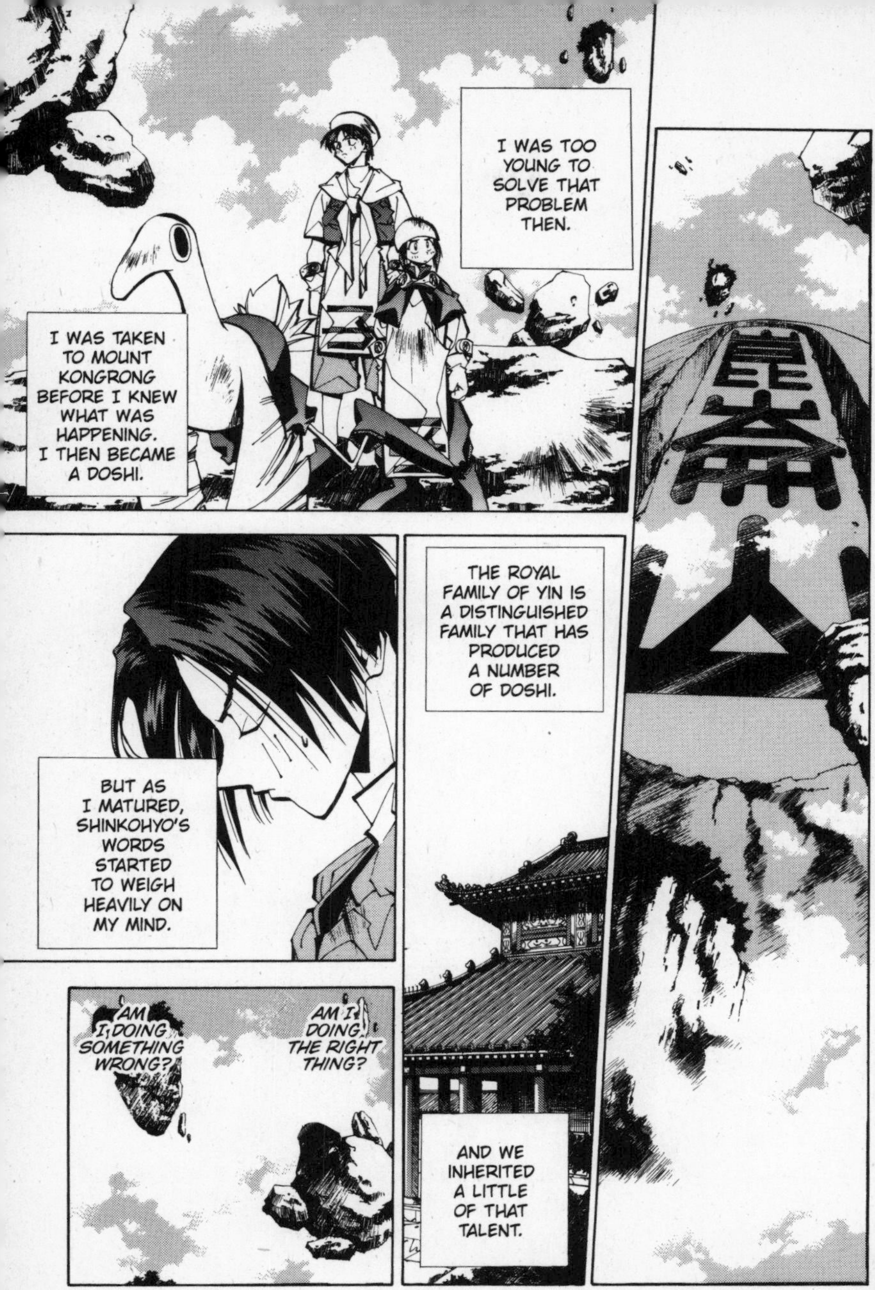
I WAS TOO YOUNG TO SOLVE THAT PROBLEM THEN.
I WAS TAKEN TO MOUNT KONGRONG BEFORE I KNEW WHAT WAS HAPPENING. I THEN BECAME A DOSHI.
THE ROYAL FAMILY OF YIN IS A DISTINGUISHED FAMILY THAT HAS PRODUCED A NUMBER OF DOSHI.
AND WE INHERITED A LITTLE OF THAT TALENT.
BUT AS I MATURED, SHINKOHYO'S WORDS STARTED TO WEIGH HEAVILY ON MY MIND.
AM I DOING THE RIGHT THING?
AM I DOING SOMETHING WRONG?

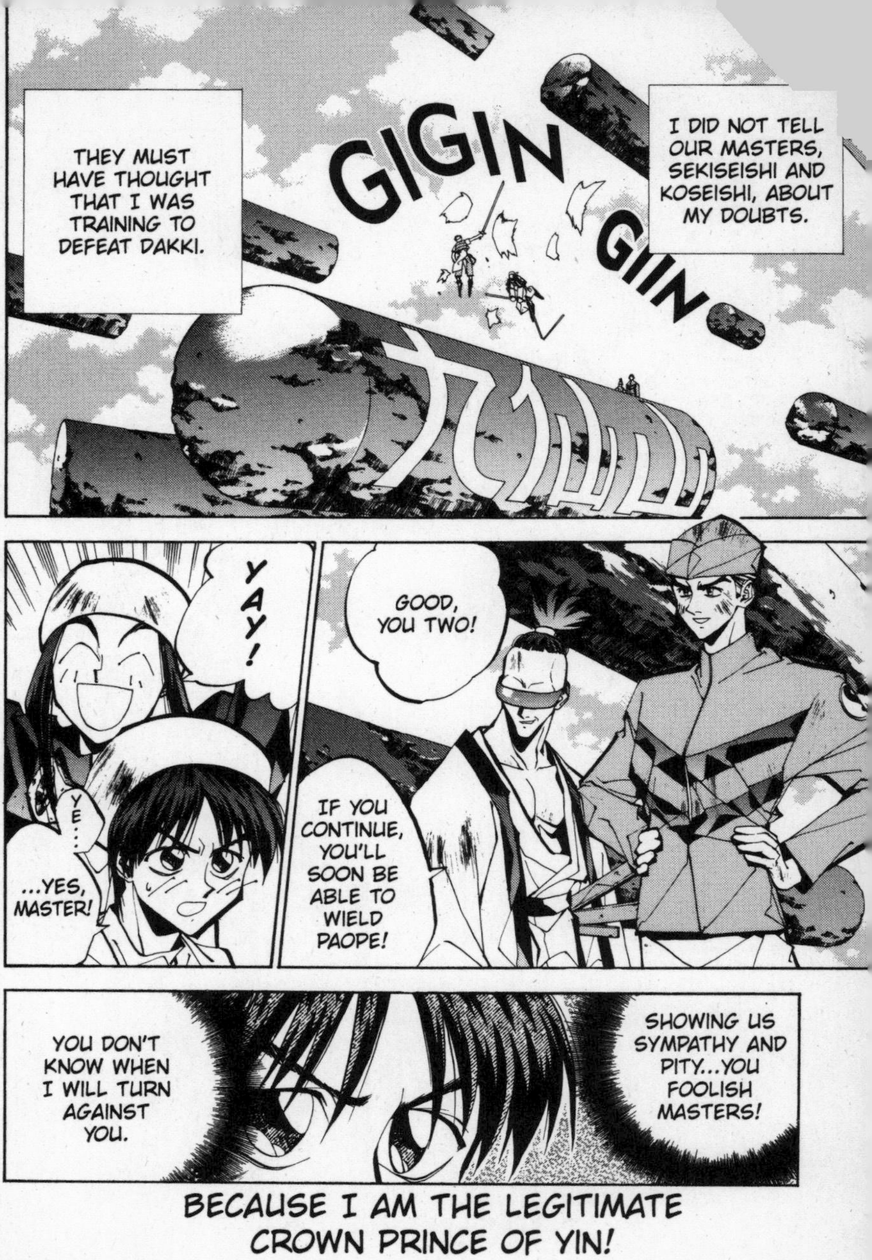
I DID NOT TELL OUR MASTERS, SEKISEISHI AND KOSEISHI, ABOUT MY DOUBTS.
GIGIN
GIIN
THEY MUST HAVE THOUGHT THAT I WAS TRAINING TO DEFEAT DAKKI.
GOOD, YOU TWO!
IF YOU CONTINUE, YOU'LL SOON BE ABLE TO WIELD PAOPE!
YAY!
YE...
...YES, MASTER!
SHOWING US SYMPATHY AND PITY...YOU FOOLISH MASTERS!
YOU DON'T KNOW WHEN I WILL TURN AGAINST YOU.

BECAUSE I AM THE LEGITIMATE CROWN PRINCE OF YIN!

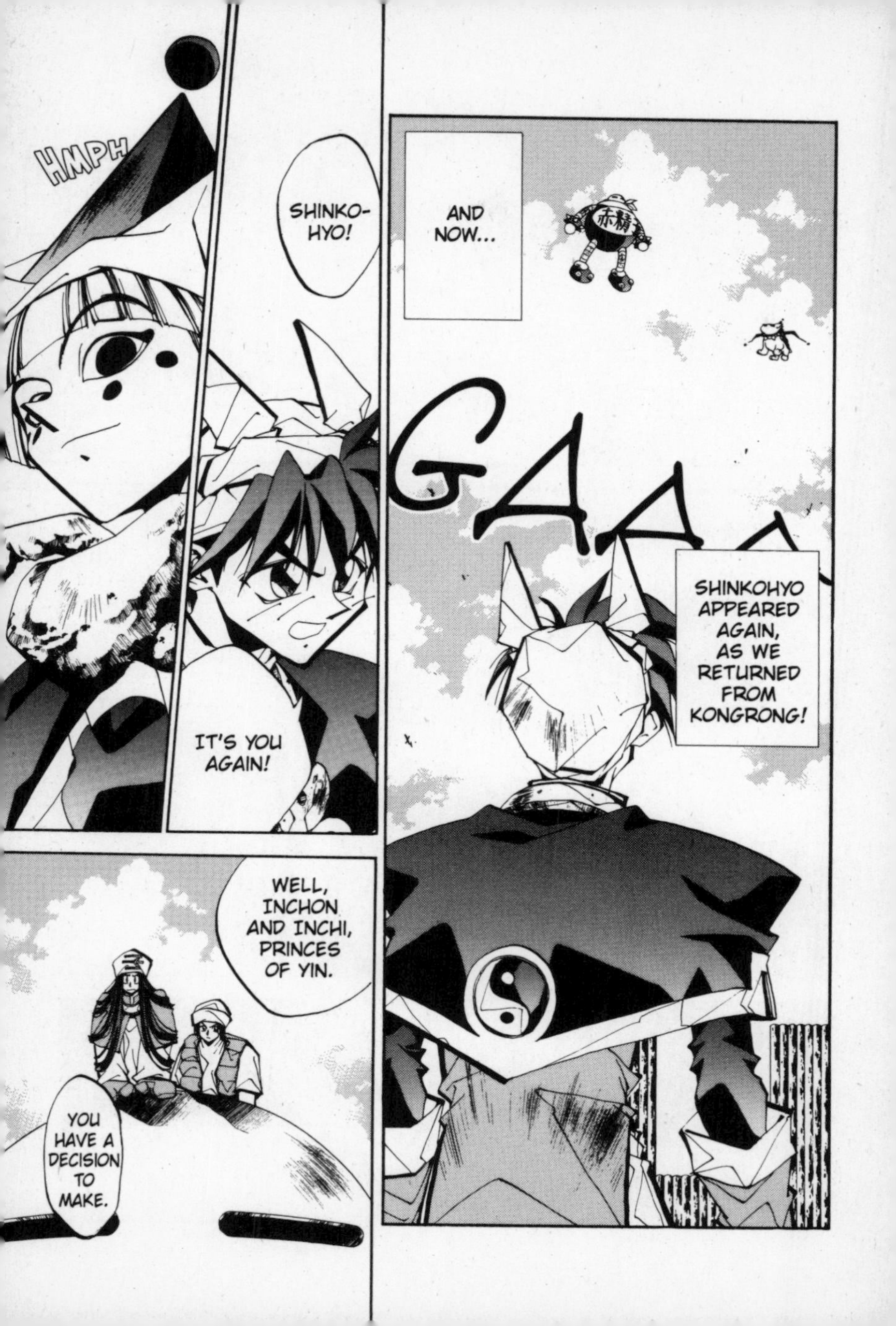
AND NOW...
GAA
SHINKOHYO APPEARED AGAIN, AS WE RETURNED FROM KONGRONG!
SHINKO-HYO!
IT'S YOU AGAIN!
HMPH
WELL, INCHON AND INCHI, PRINCES OF YIN.
YOU HAVE A DECISION TO MAKE.

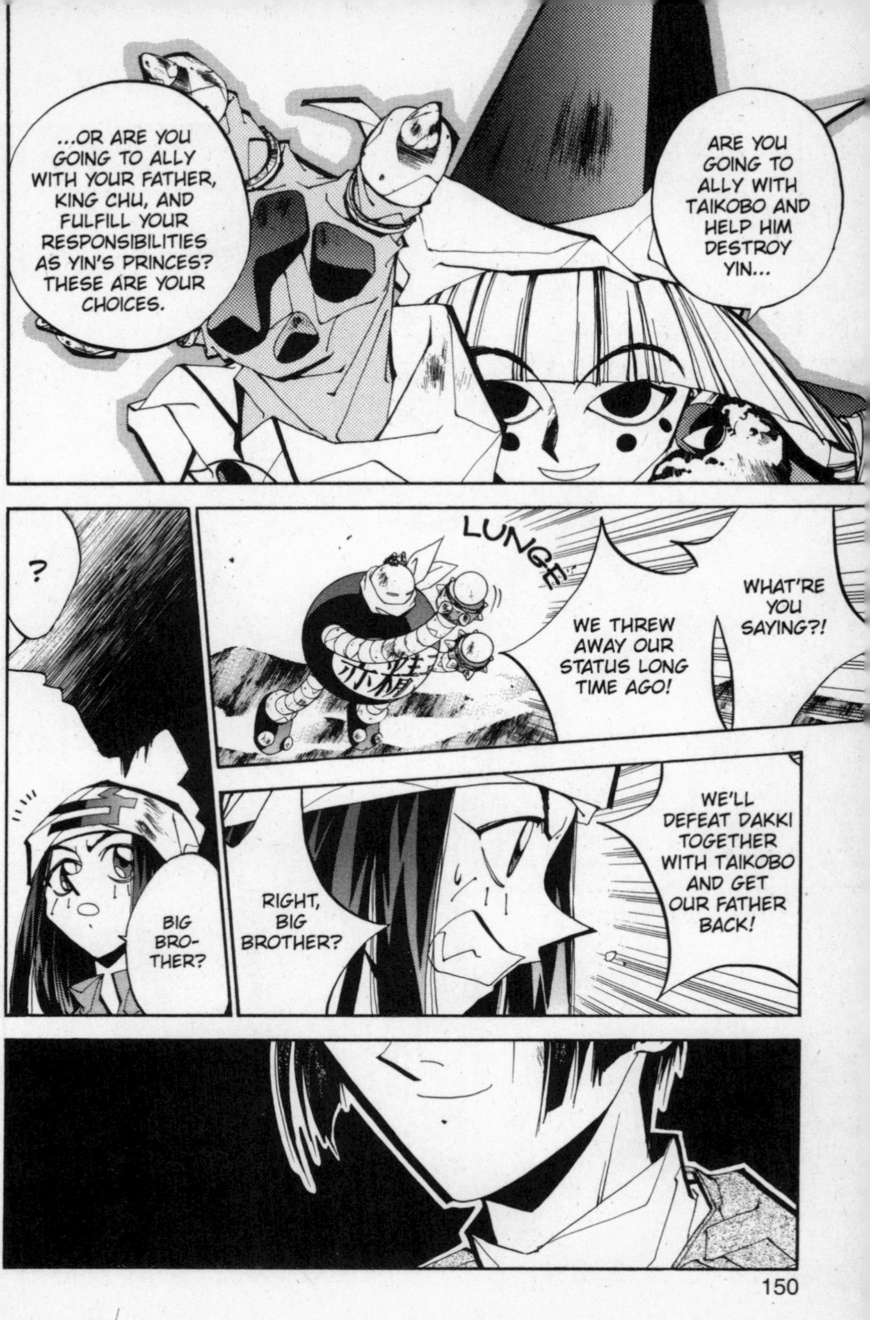
ARE YOU GOING TO ALLY WITH TAIKOBO AND HELP HIM DESTROY YIN...
...OR ARE YOU GOING TO ALLY WITH YOUR FATHER, KING CHU, AND FULFILL YOUR RESPONSIBILITIES AS YIN'S PRINCES? THESE ARE YOUR CHOICES.
LUNGE
WHAT'RE YOU SAYING?!
WE THREW AWAY OUR STATUS LONG TIME AGO!
WE'LL DEFEAT DAKKI TOGETHER WITH TAIKOBO AND GET OUR FATHER BACK!
RIGHT, BIG BROTHER?
?
BIG BRO-THER?

READ THIS WAY

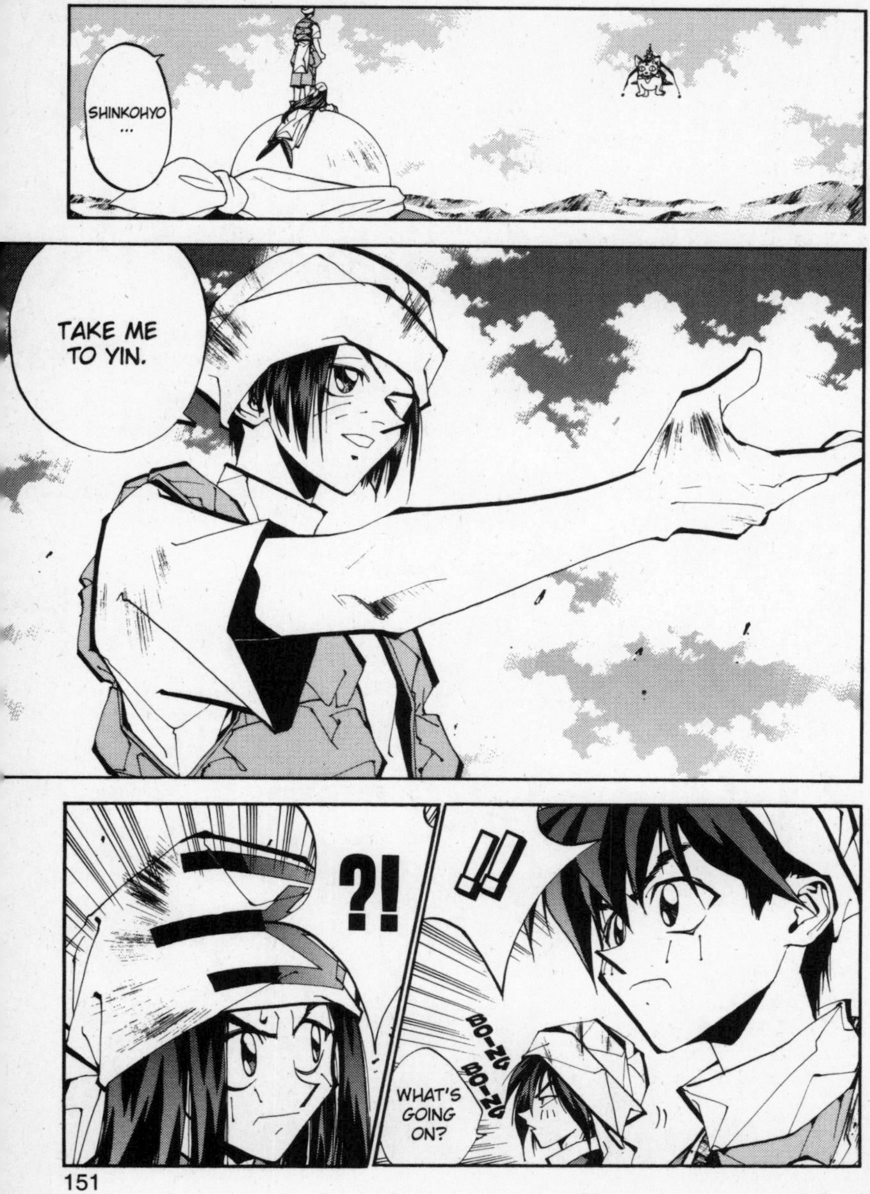
SHINKOHYO ...
TAKE ME TO YIN.
!!
BOING BOING
WHAT'S GOING ON?
?!

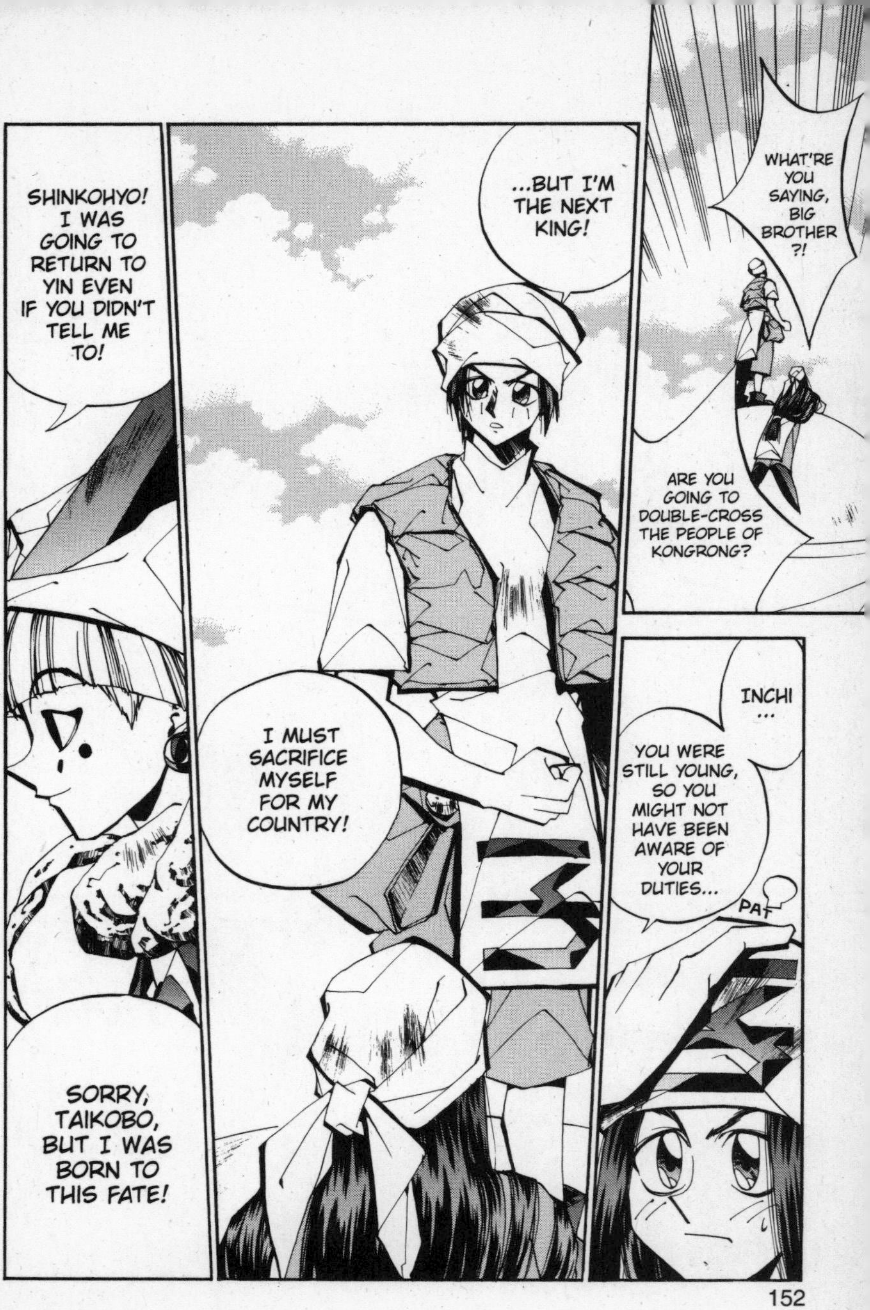
WHAT'RE YOU SAYING, BIG BROTHER ?!
ARE YOU GOING TO DOUBLE-CROSS THE PEOPLE OF KONGRONG?
INCHI ...
YOU WERE STILL YOUNG, SO YOU MIGHT NOT HAVE BEEN AWARE OF YOUR DUTIES...
PAT
...BUT I'M THE NEXT KING!
I MUST SACRIFICE MYSELF FOR MY COUNTRY!
SHINKOHYO! I WAS GOING TO RETURN TO YIN EVEN IF YOU DIDN'T TELL ME TO!
SORRY, TAIKOBO, BUT I WAS BORN TO THIS FATE!

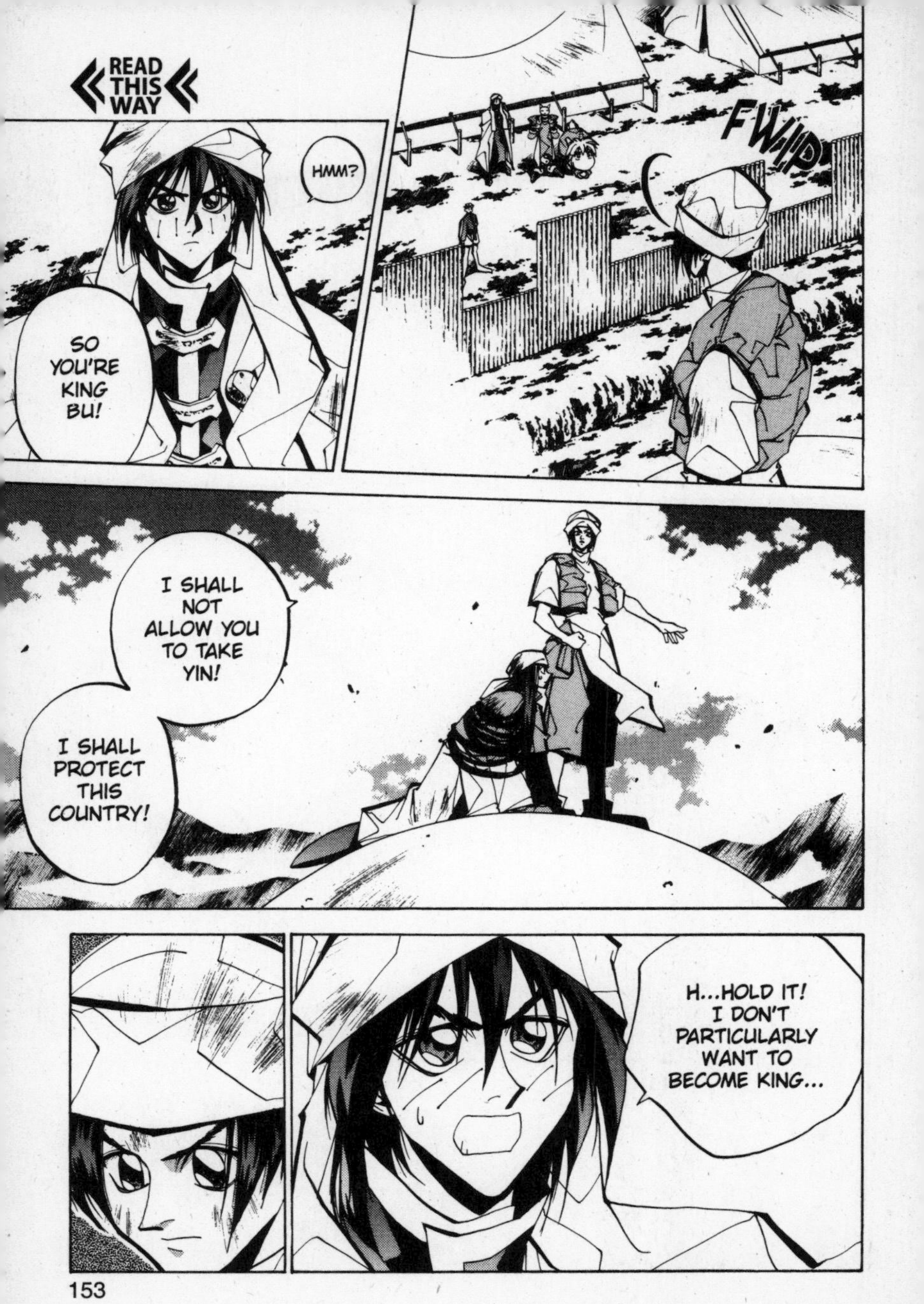
READ THIS WAY
FWIP
HMM?
SO YOU'RE KING BU!
I SHALL NOT ALLOW YOU TO TAKE YIN!
I SHALL PROTECT THIS COUNTRY!
H...HOLD IT! I DON'T PARTICULARLY WANT TO BECOME KING...

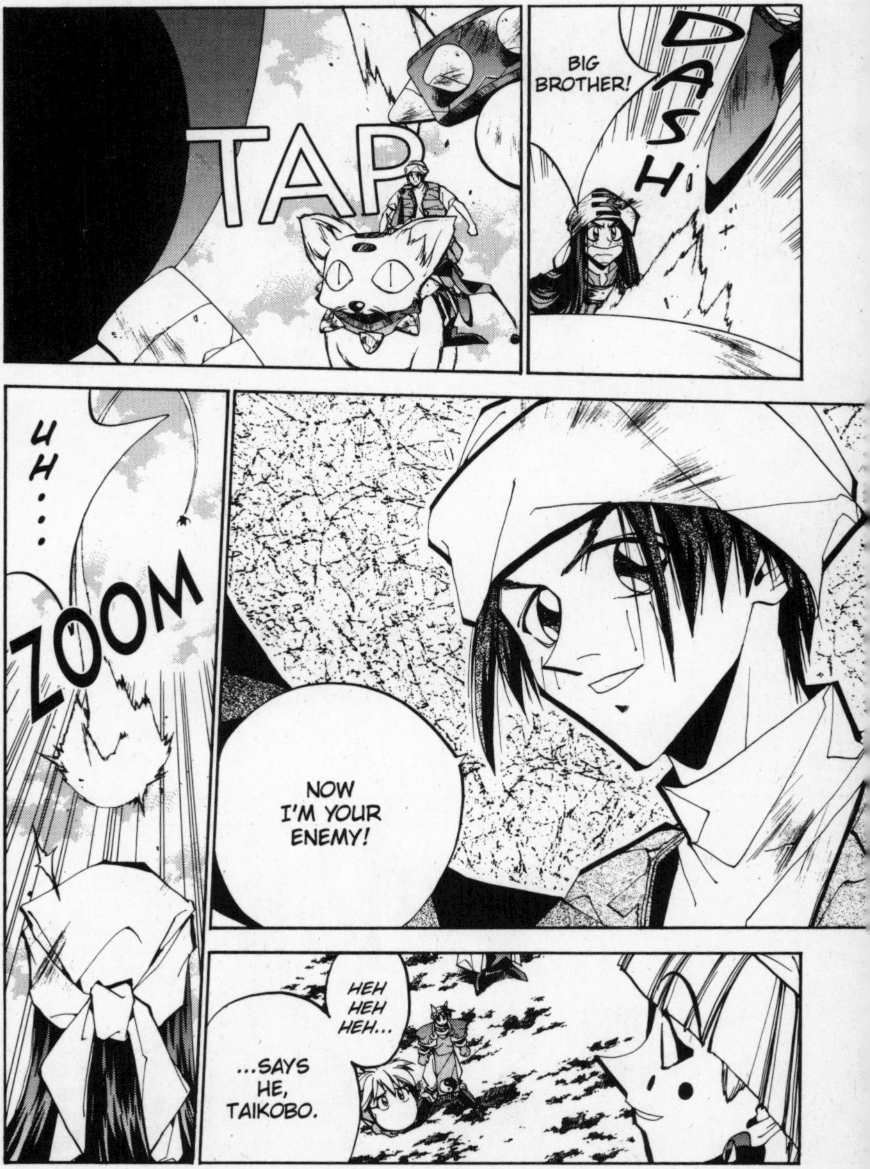
BIG BROTHER!
DASH
TAP
NOW I'M YOUR ENEMY!
HEH HEH HEH...
...SAYS HE, TAIKOBO.
UH...
ZOOM

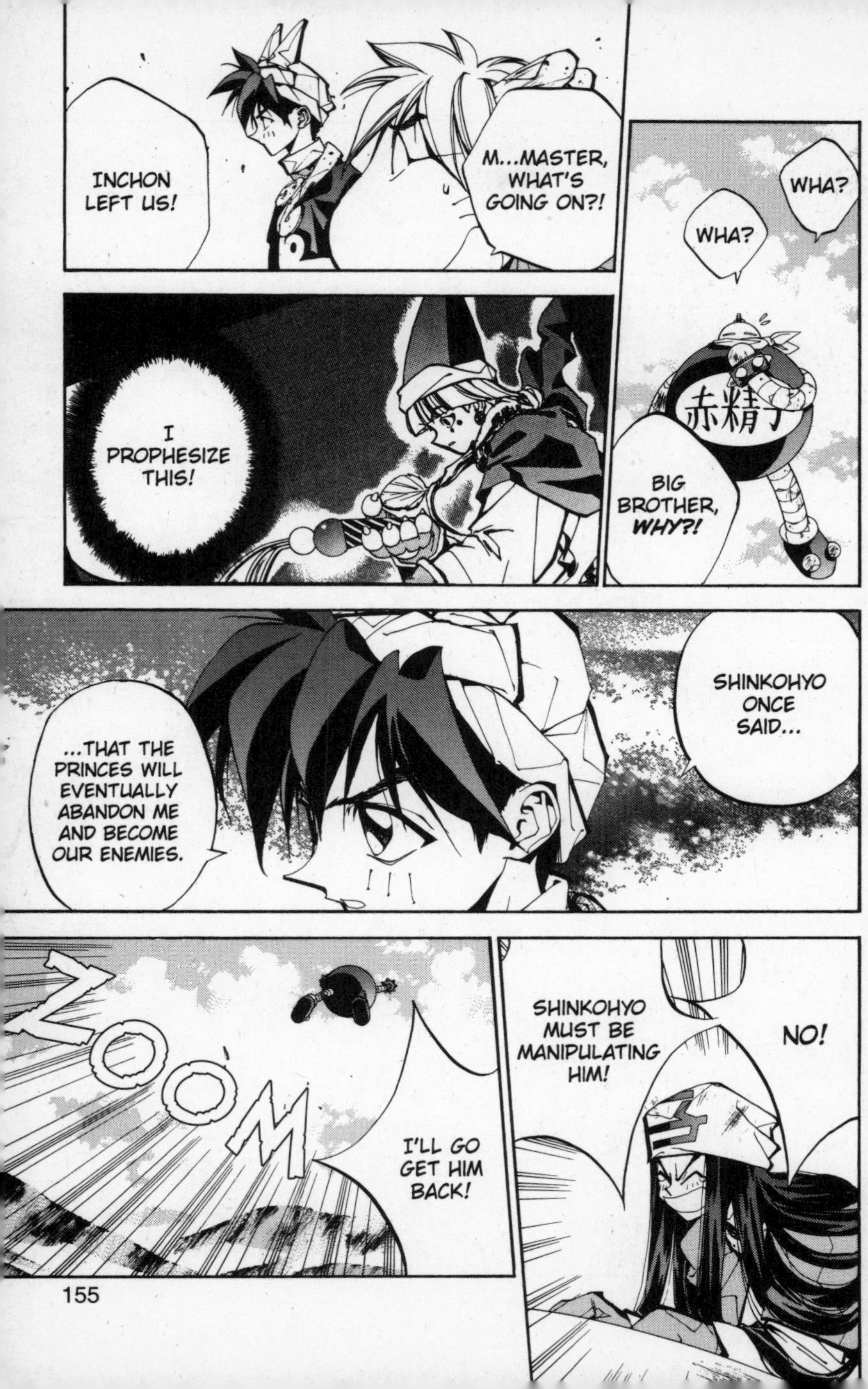
WHA?
WHA?
BIG BROTHER, WHY?!
M...MASTER, WHAT'S GOING ON?!
INCHON LEFT US!
I PROPHESIZE THIS!
SHINKOHYO ONCE SAID...
...THAT THE PRINCES WILL EVENTUALLY ABANDON ME AND BECOME OUR ENEMIES.
NO!
SHINKOHYO MUST BE MANIPULATING HIM!
I'LL GO GET HIM BACK!
ZOOM

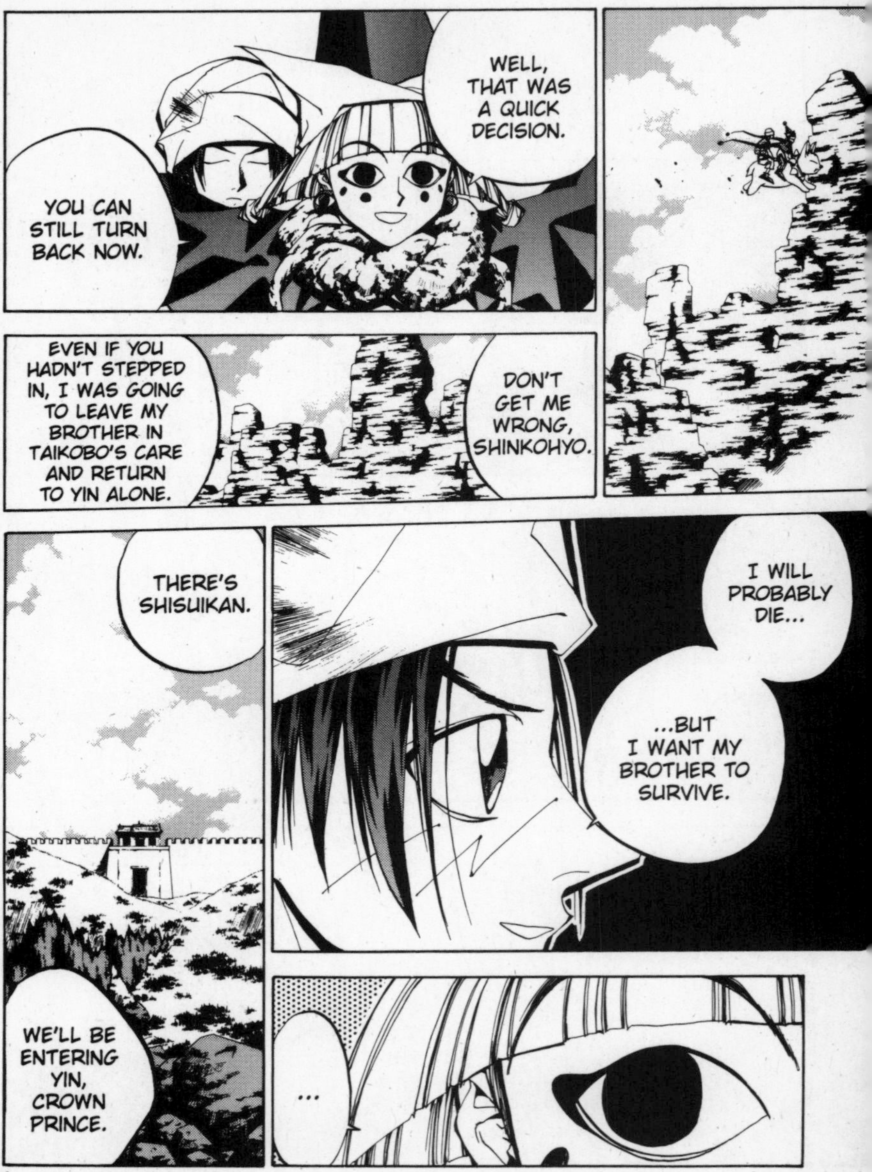

WELL, THAT WAS A QUICK DECISION.
YOU CAN STILL TURN BACK NOW.
DON'T GET ME WRONG, SHINKOHYO.
EVEN IF YOU HADN'T STEPPED IN, I WAS GOING TO LEAVE MY BROTHER IN TAIKOBO'S CARE AND RETURN TO YIN ALONE.
I WILL PROBABLY DIE...
...BUT I WANT MY BROTHER TO SURVIVE.
...
THERE'S SHISUIKAN.
WE'LL BE ENTERING YIN, CROWN PRINCE.

READ THIS WAY

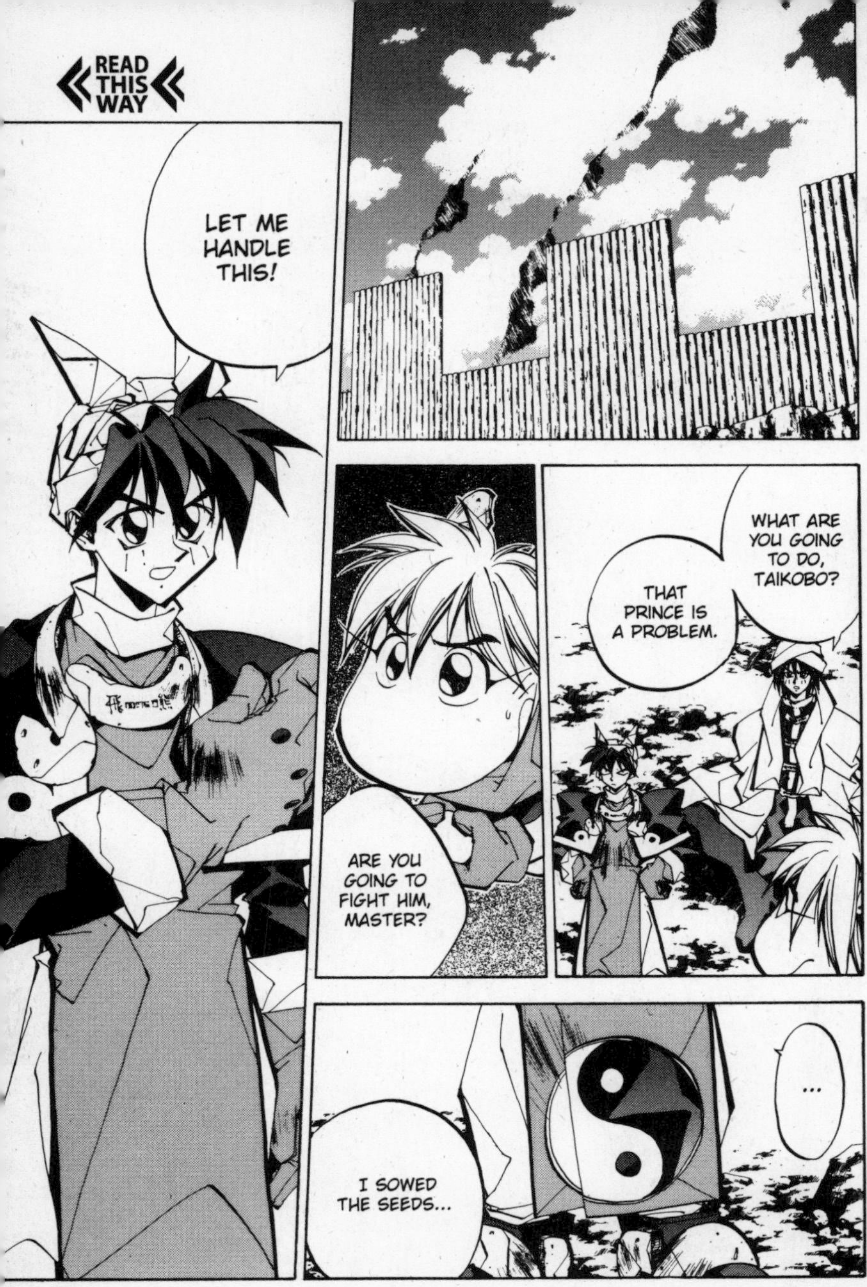
WHAT ARE YOU GOING TO DO, TAIKOBO?
THAT PRINCE IS A PROBLEM.
ARE YOU GOING TO FIGHT HIM, MASTER?
...
I SOWED THE SEEDS...
LET ME HANDLE THIS!

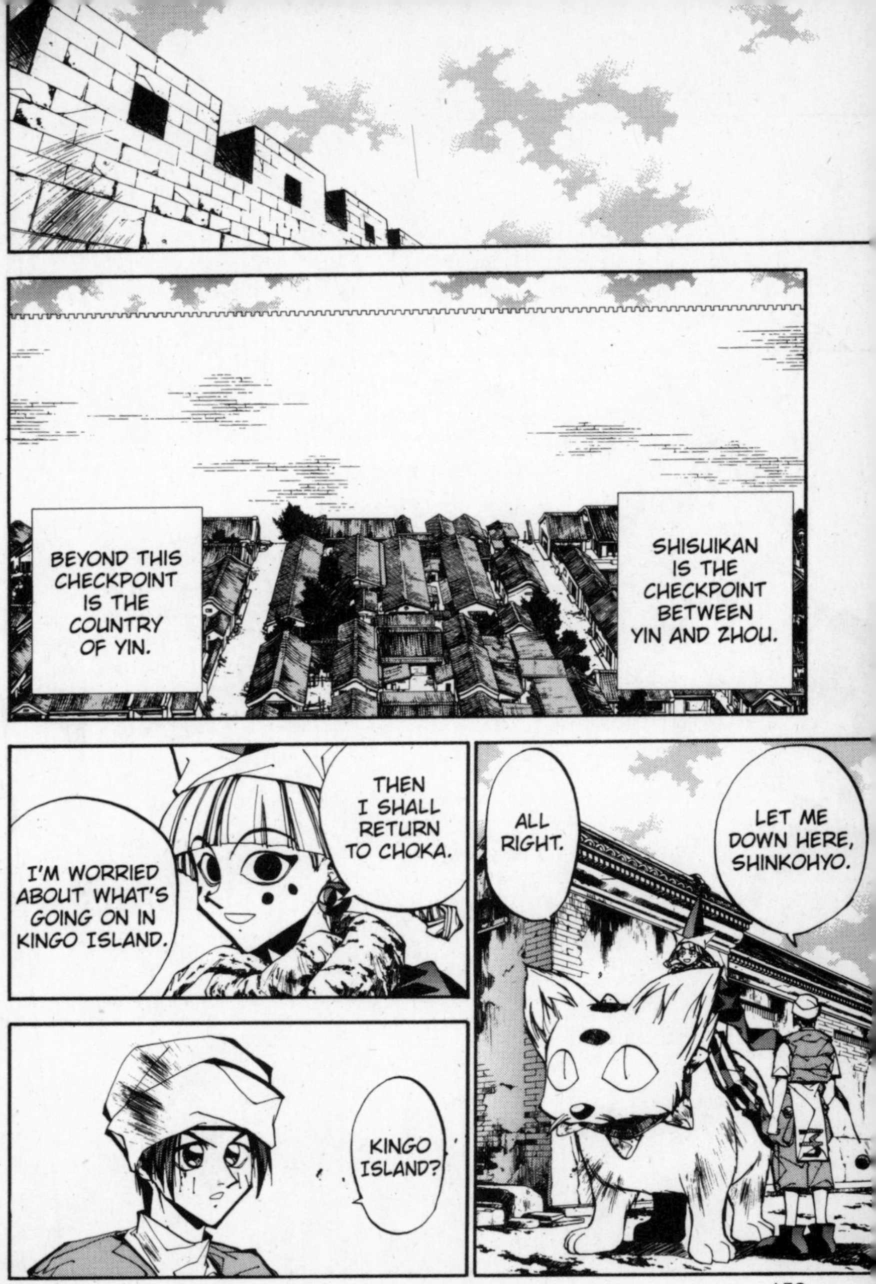
SHISUIKAN IS THE CHECKPOINT BETWEEN YIN AND ZHOU.
BEYOND THIS CHECKPOINT IS THE COUNTRY OF YIN.
LET ME DOWN HERE, SHINKOHYO.
ALL RIGHT.
THEN I SHALL RETURN TO CHOKA.
I'M WORRIED ABOUT WHAT'S GOING ON IN KINGO ISLAND.
KINGO ISLAND?

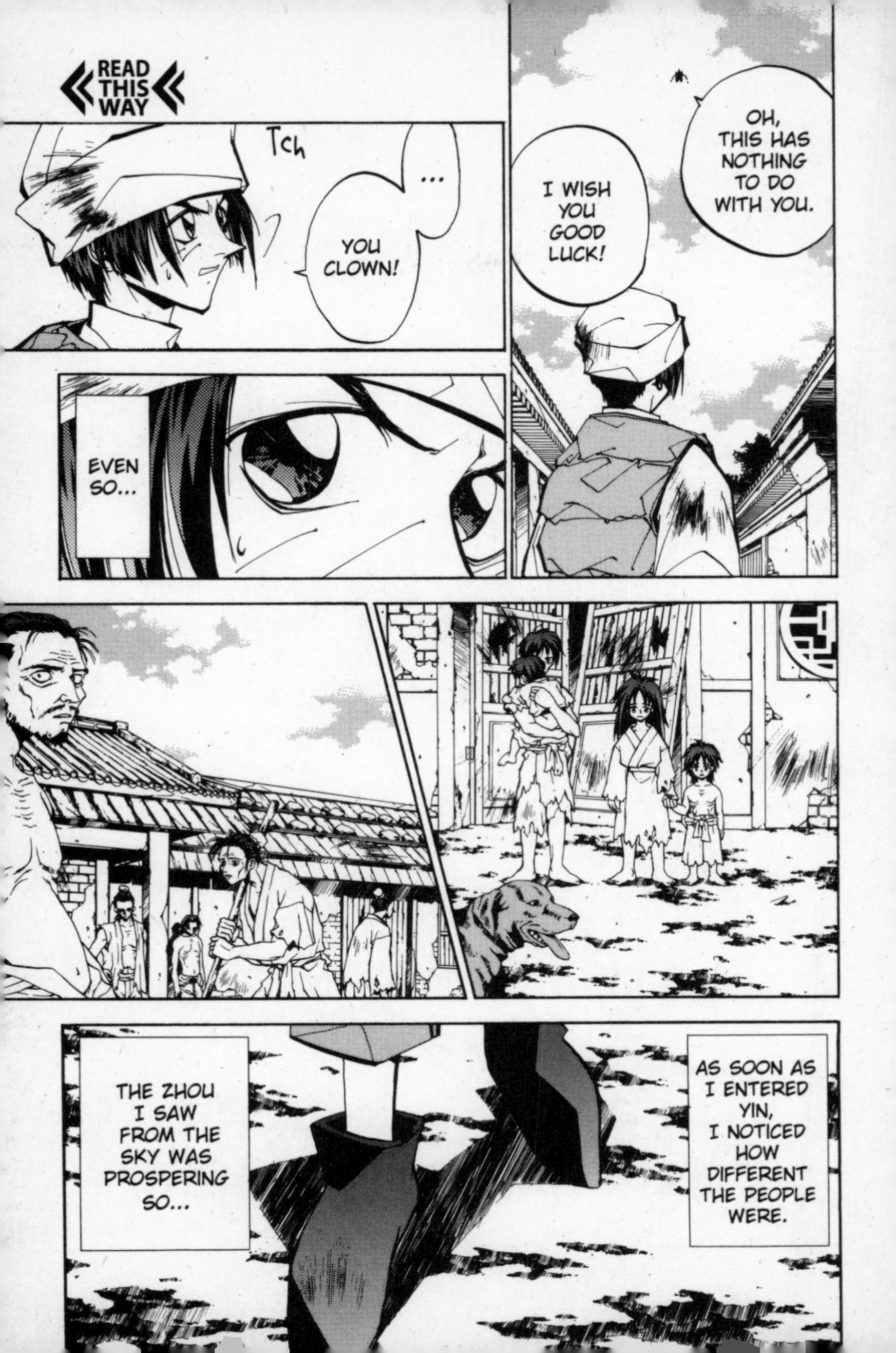
READ THIS WAY
OH, THIS HAS NOTHING TO DO WITH YOU.
I WISH YOU GOOD LUCK!
Tch
... YOU CLOWN!
EVEN SO...
AS SOON AS I ENTERED YIN, I NOTICED HOW DIFFERENT THE PEOPLE WERE.
THE ZHOU I SAW FROM THE SKY WAS PROSPERING SO...

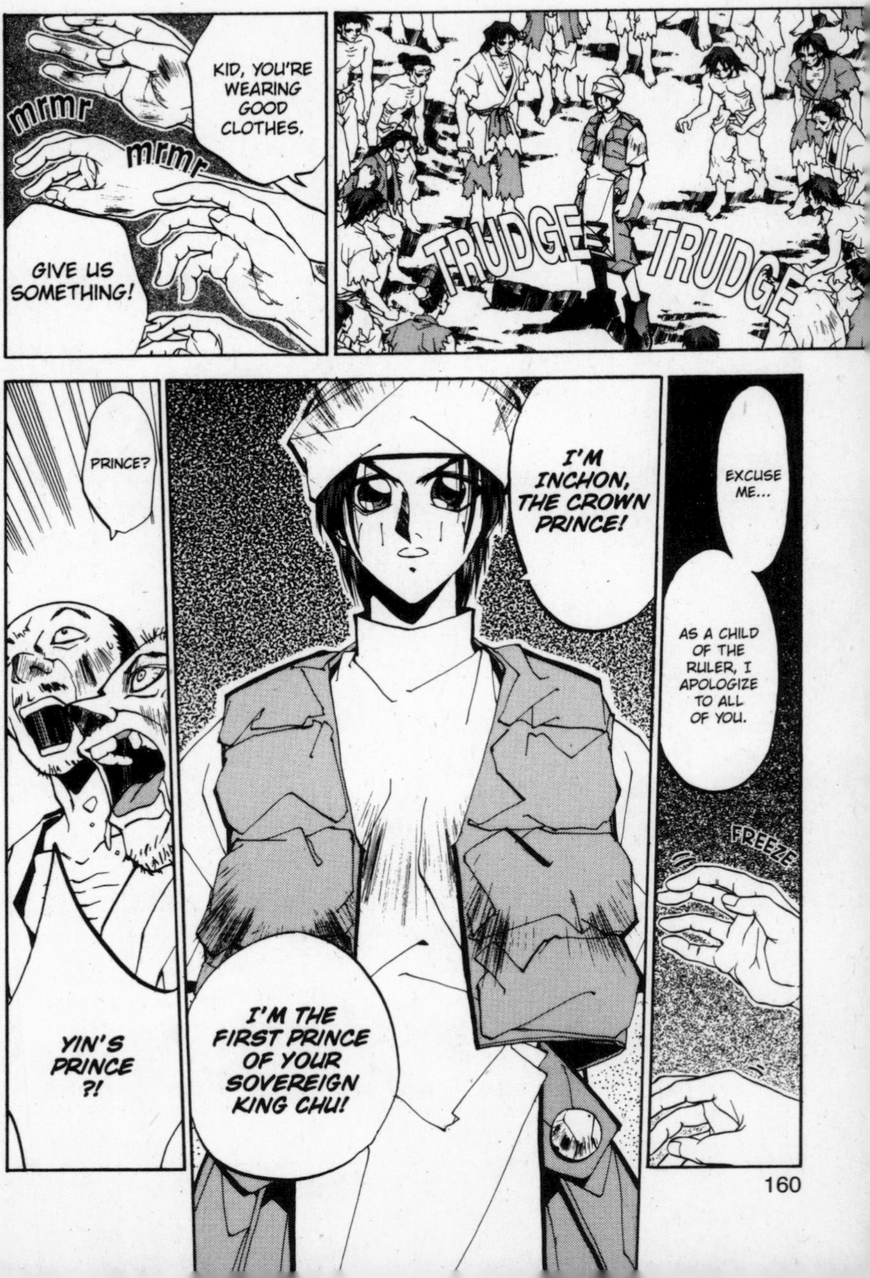
TRUDGE
TRUDGE
KID, YOU'RE WEARING GOOD CLOTHES.
mrmr
mrmr
GIVE US SOMETHING!
EXCUSE ME...
AS A CHILD OF THE RULER, I APOLOGIZE TO ALL OF YOU.
FREEZE
I'M INCHON, THE CROWN PRINCE!
I'M THE FIRST PRINCE OF YOUR SOVEREIGN KING CHU!
PRINCE?
YIN'S PRINCE ?!

READ THIS WAY

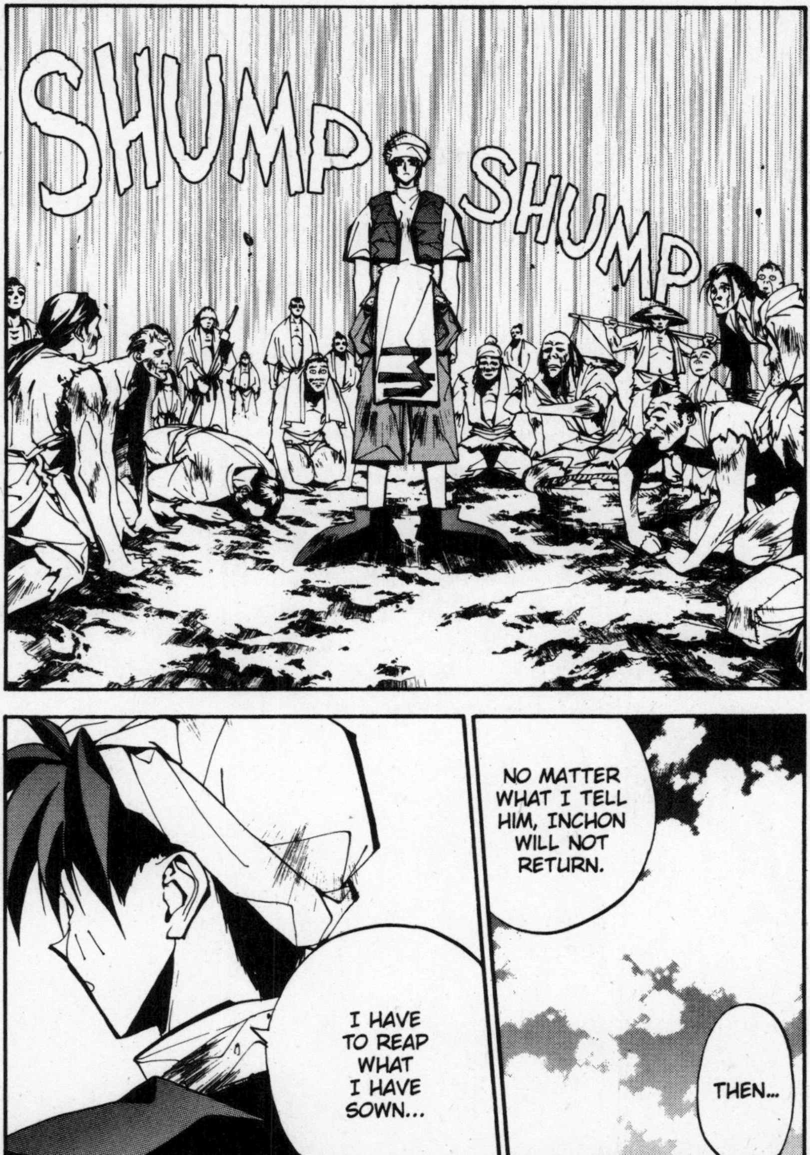

SHUMP
SHUMP
NO MATTER WHAT I TELL HIM, INCHON WILL NOT RETURN.
THEN...
I HAVE TO REAP WHAT I HAVE SOWN...

封神
演義

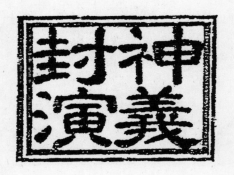

Chapter 78

THE PRINCES' CHOICE, PART 2

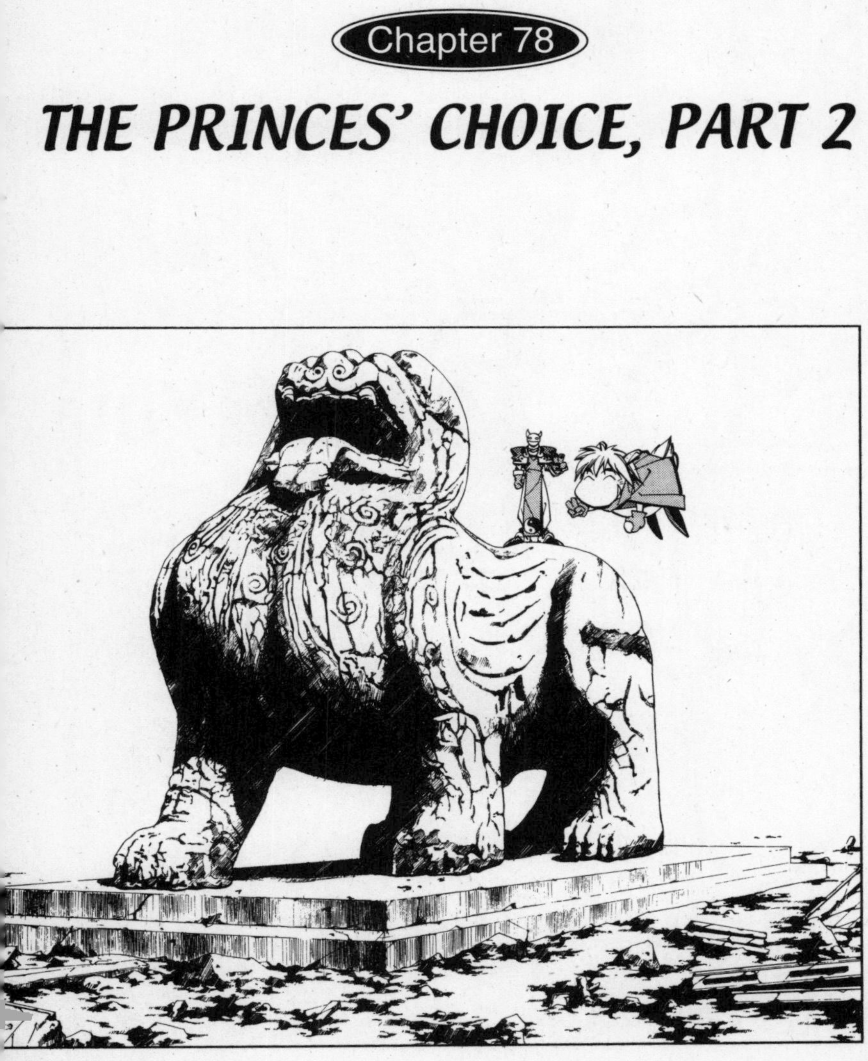

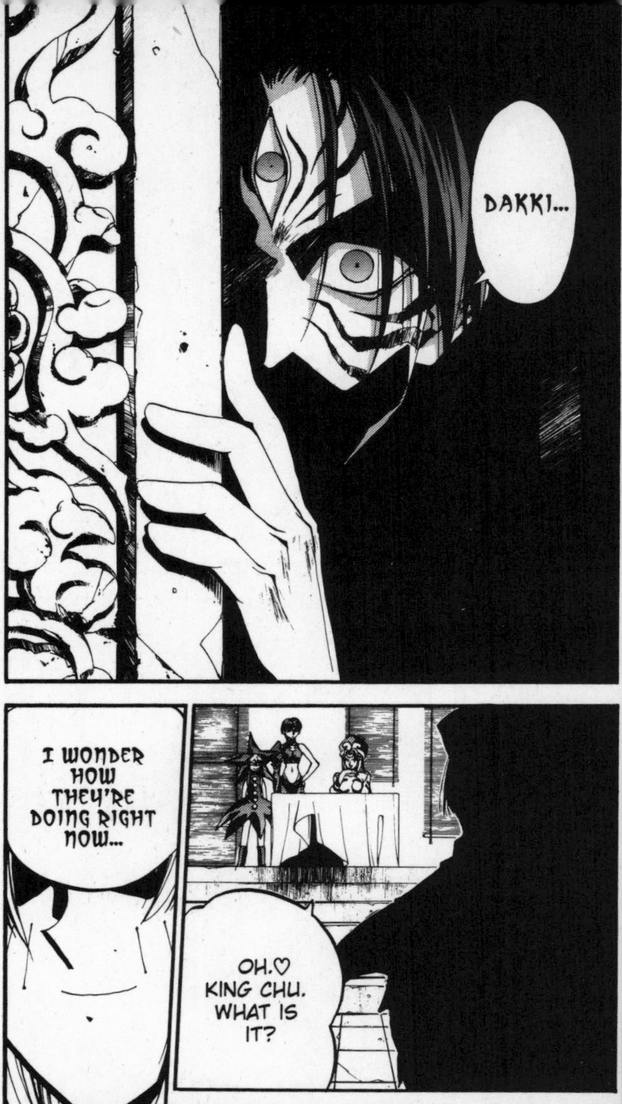
DAKKI...
OH.♡ KING CHU. WHAT IS IT?
MY CHILDREN... THE TWO PRINCES APPEARED IN MY DREAMS...
I WONDER HOW THEY'RE DOING RIGHT NOW...
CHUCKLE♡

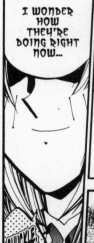

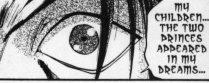

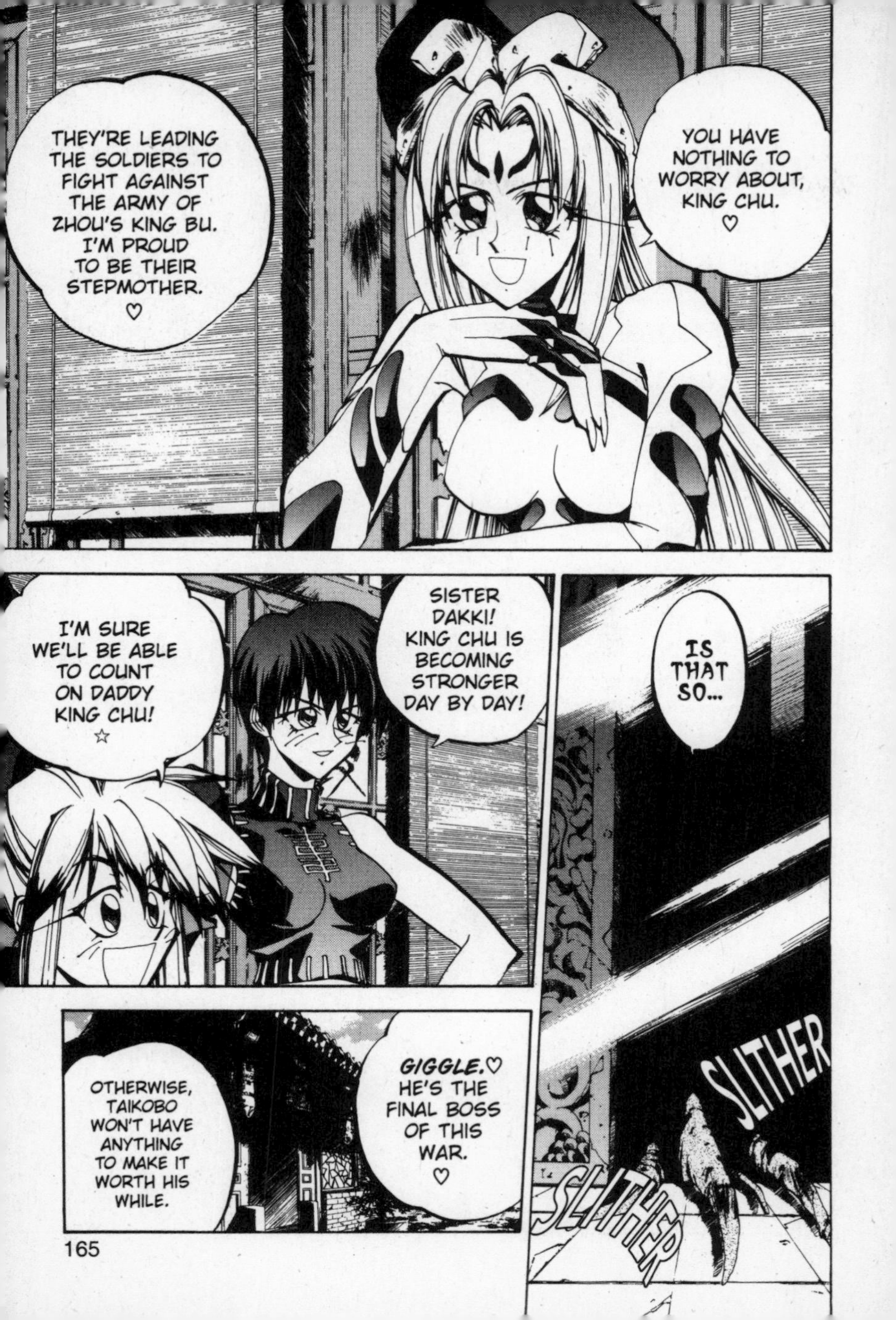

YOU HAVE NOTHING TO WORRY ABOUT, KING CHU. ♡
THEY'RE LEADING THE SOLDIERS TO FIGHT AGAINST THE ARMY OF ZHOU'S KING BU. I'M PROUD TO BE THEIR STEPMOTHER. ♡
IS THAT SO...
SLITHER
SLITHER
SISTER DAKKI! KING CHU IS BECOMING STRONGER DAY BY DAY!
I'M SURE WE'LL BE ABLE TO COUNT ON DADDY KING CHU! ☆
GIGGLE.♡ HE'S THE FINAL BOSS OF THIS WAR. ♡
OTHERWISE, TAIKOBO WON'T HAVE ANYTHING TO MAKE IT WORTH HIS WHILE.

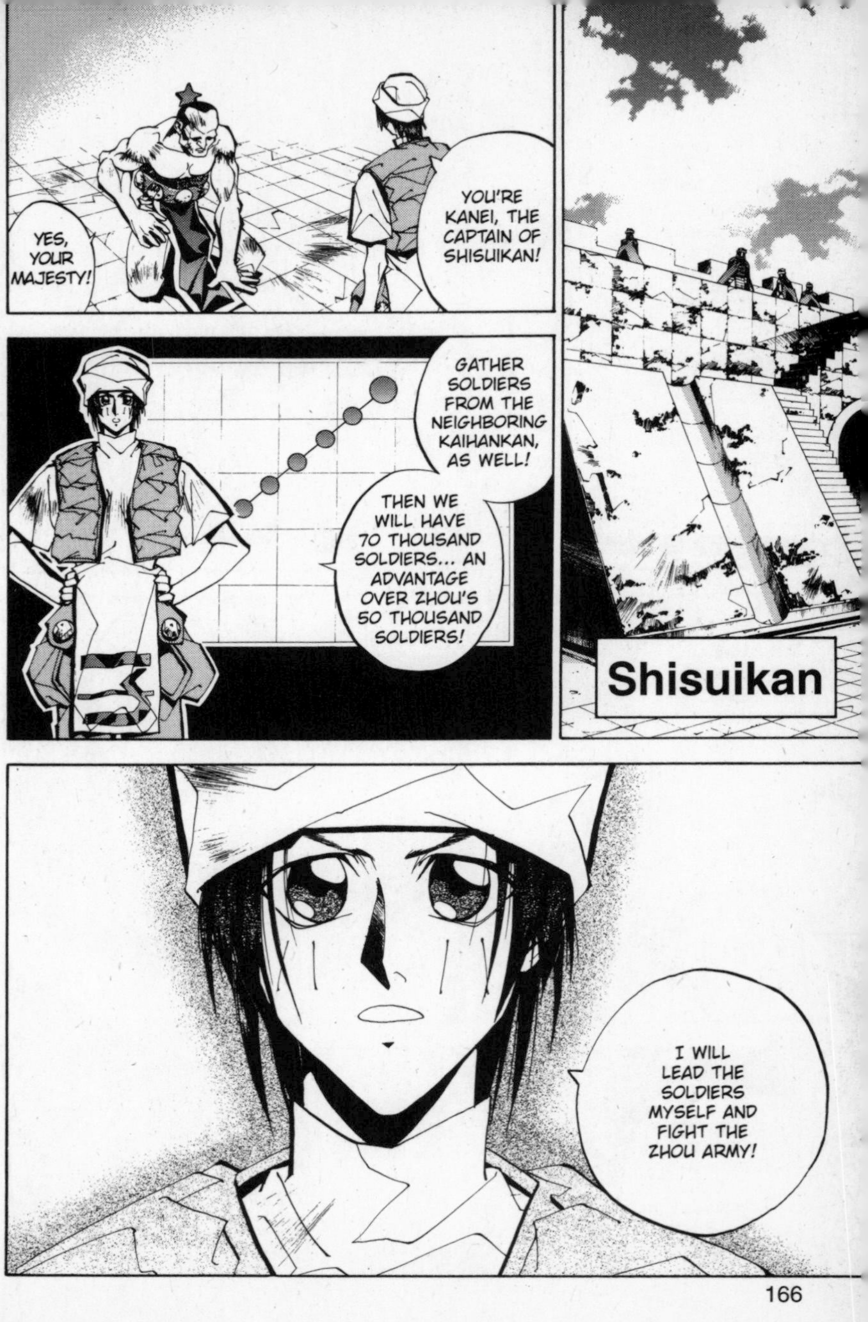
Shisuikan
YOU'RE KANEI, THE CAPTAIN OF SHISUIKAN!
YES, YOUR MAJESTY!
GATHER SOLDIERS FROM THE NEIGHBORING KAIHANKAN, AS WELL!
THEN WE WILL HAVE 70 THOUSAND SOLDIERS... AN ADVANTAGE OVER ZHOU'S 50 THOUSAND SOLDIERS!
I WILL LEAD THE SOLDIERS MYSELF AND FIGHT THE ZHOU ARMY!

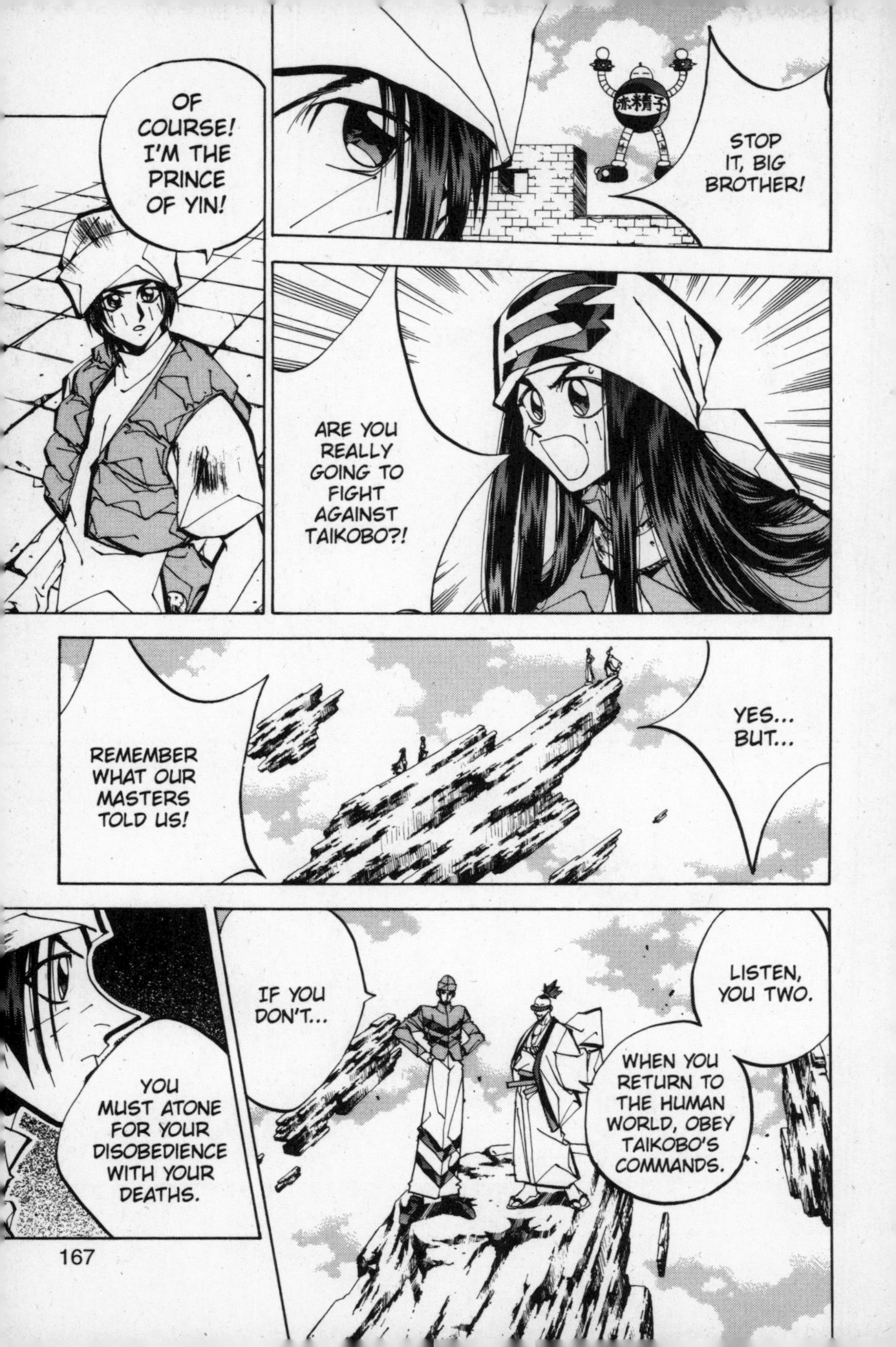
赤精子
STOP IT, BIG BROTHER!
ARE YOU REALLY GOING TO FIGHT AGAINST TAIKOBO?!
OF COURSE! I'M THE PRINCE OF YIN!
YES... BUT...
REMEMBER WHAT OUR MASTERS TOLD US!
LISTEN, YOU TWO.
WHEN YOU RETURN TO THE HUMAN WORLD, OBEY TAIKOBO'S COMMANDS.
IF YOU DON'T...
YOU MUST ATONE FOR YOUR DISOBEDIENCE WITH YOUR DEATHS.

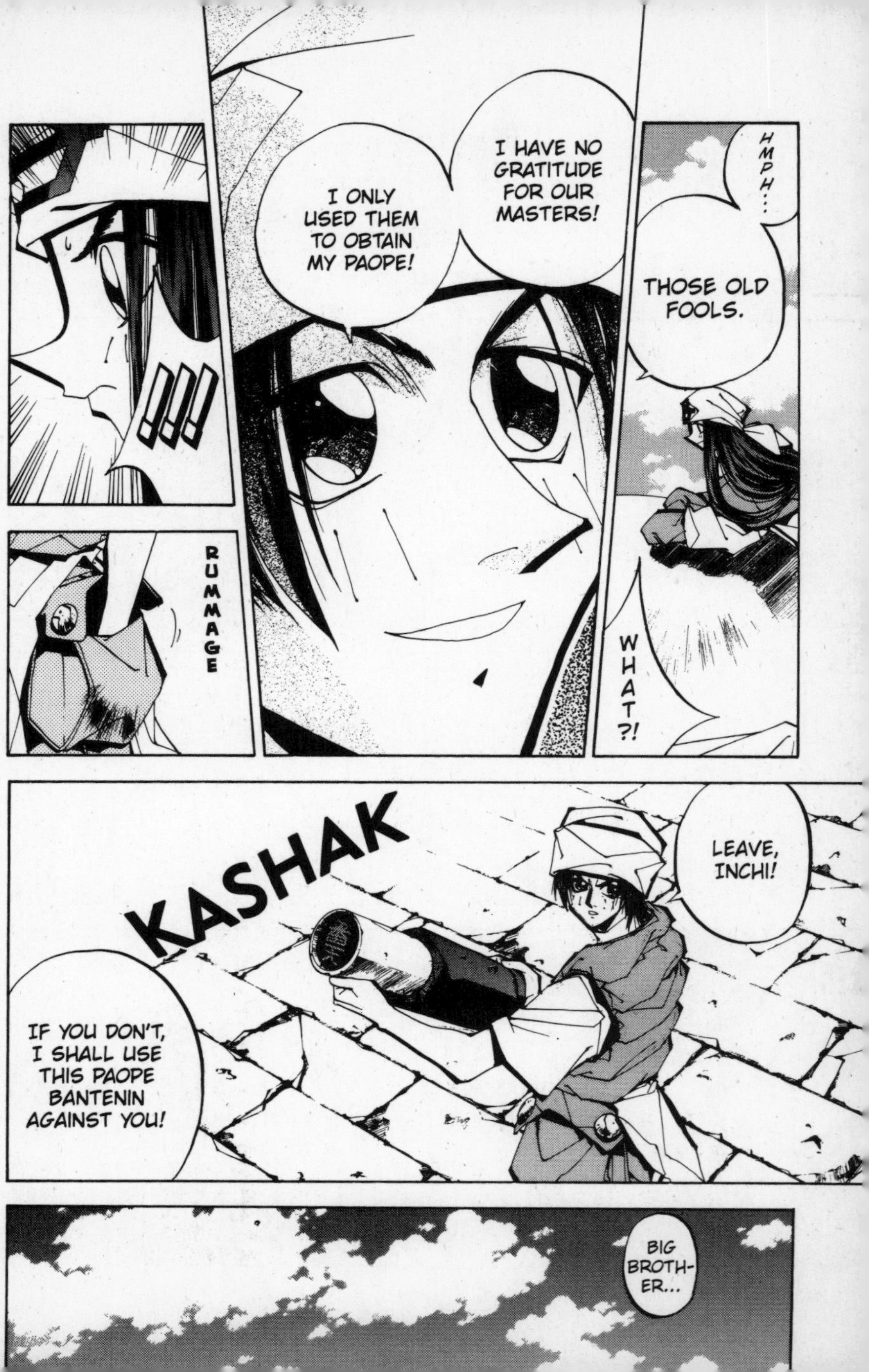
HMPH...
THOSE OLD FOOLS.
WHAT?!
I HAVE NO GRATITUDE FOR OUR MASTERS!
I ONLY USED THEM TO OBTAIN MY PAOPE!
!!!
RUMMAGE
LEAVE, INCHI!
KASHAK
IF YOU DON'T, I SHALL USE THIS PAOPE BANTENIN AGAINST YOU!
BIG BROTH-ER...

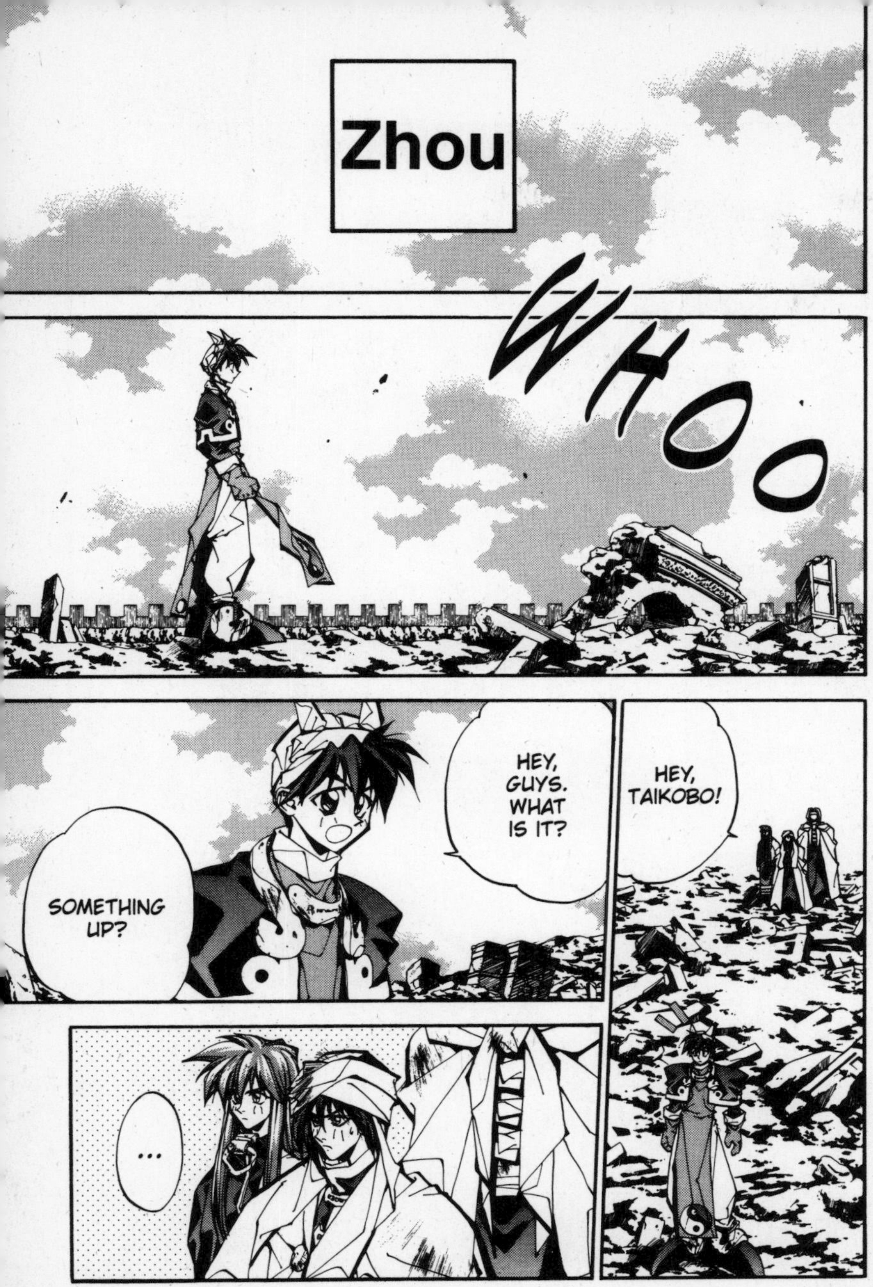
Zhou
WHOOO
HEY, TAIKOBO!
HEY, GUYS. WHAT IS IT?
SOMETHING UP?
...

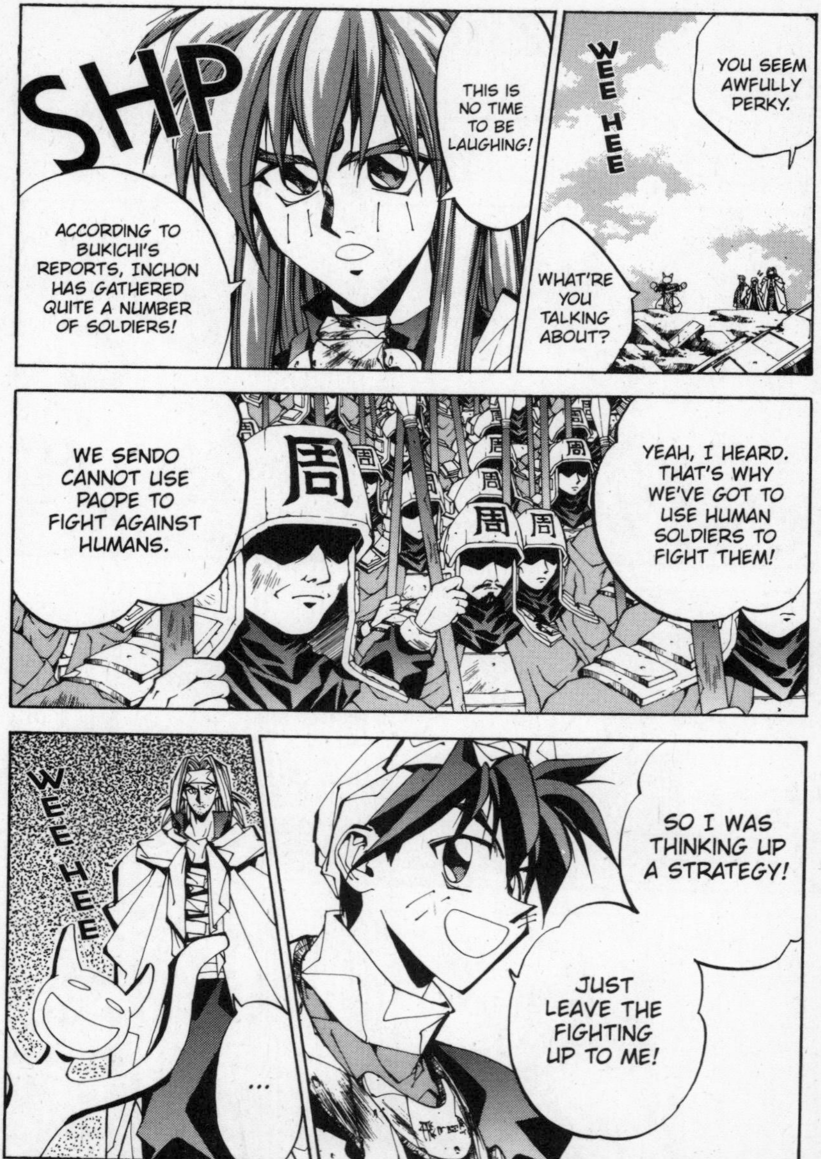
YOU SEEM AWFULLY PERKY.
WEE HEE
WHAT'RE YOU TALKING ABOUT?
THIS IS NO TIME TO BE LAUGHING!
SHP
ACCORDING TO BUKICHI'S REPORTS, INCHON HAS GATHERED QUITE A NUMBER OF SOLDIERS!
YEAH, I HEARD. THAT'S WHY WE'VE GOT TO USE HUMAN SOLDIERS TO FIGHT THEM!
WE SENDO CANNOT USE PAOPE TO FIGHT AGAINST HUMANS.
SO I WAS THINKING UP A STRATEGY!
JUST LEAVE THE FIGHTING UP TO ME!
WEE HEE
...

READ THIS WAY

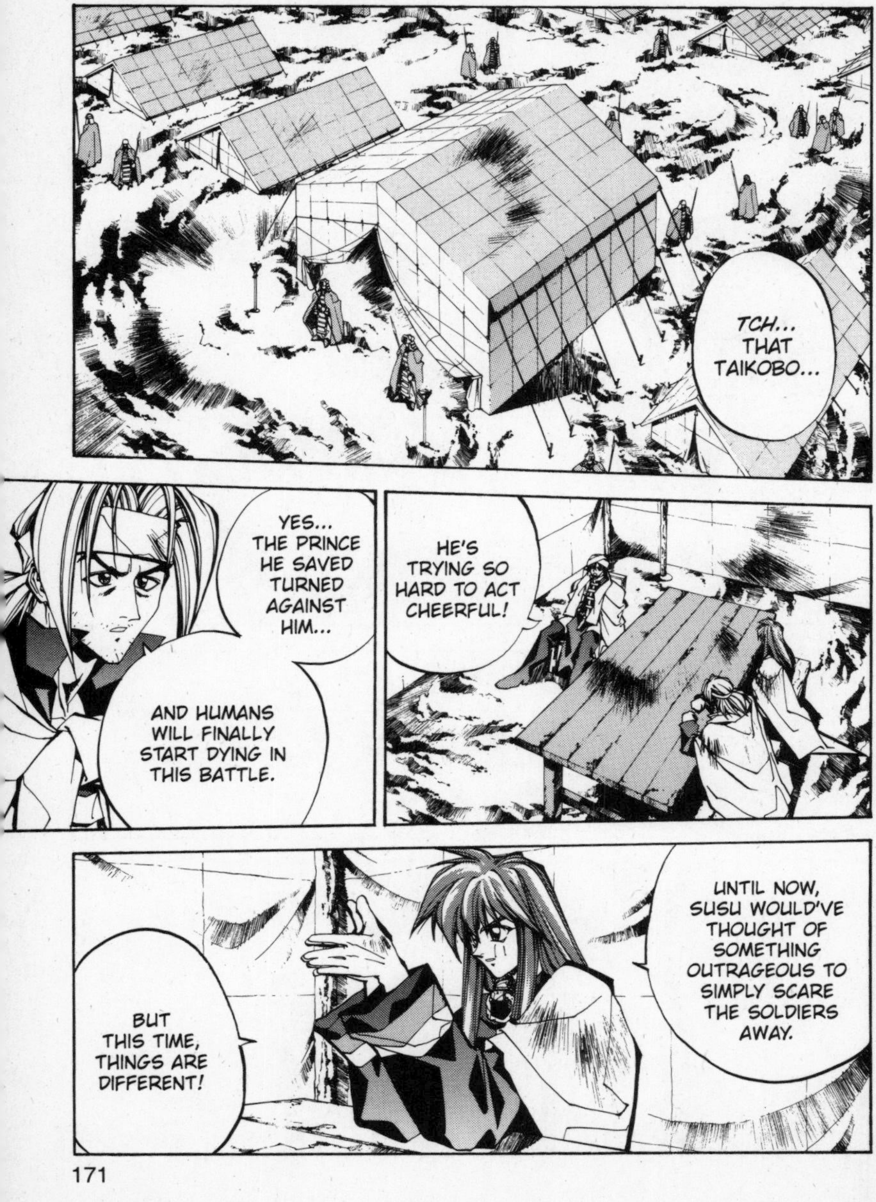
TCH... THAT TAIKOBO...
HE'S TRYING SO HARD TO ACT CHEERFUL!
YES... THE PRINCE HE SAVED TURNED AGAINST HIM...
AND HUMANS WILL FINALLY START DYING IN THIS BATTLE.
UNTIL NOW, SUSU WOULD'VE THOUGHT OF SOMETHING OUTRAGEOUS TO SIMPLY SCARE THE SOLDIERS AWAY.
BUT THIS TIME, THINGS ARE DIFFERENT!

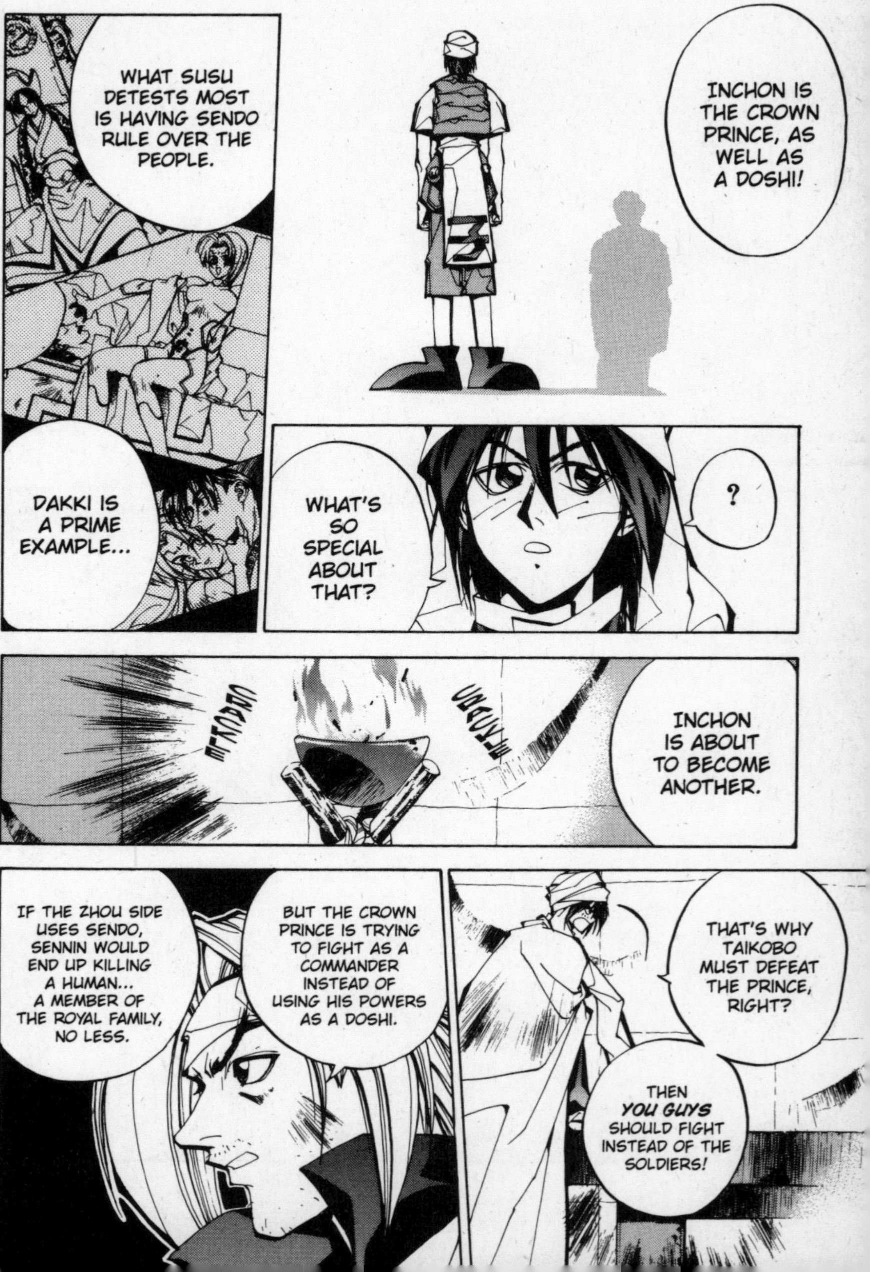
INCHON IS THE CROWN PRINCE, AS WELL AS A DOSHI!
?
WHAT'S SO SPECIAL ABOUT THAT?
WHAT SUSU DETESTS MOST IS HAVING SENDO RULE OVER THE PEOPLE.
DAKKI IS A PRIME EXAMPLE...
INCHON IS ABOUT TO BECOME ANOTHER.
THAT'S WHY TAIKOBO MUST DEFEAT THE PRINCE, RIGHT?
THEN *YOU GUYS* SHOULD FIGHT INSTEAD OF THE SOLDIERS!
BUT THE CROWN PRINCE IS TRYING TO FIGHT AS A COMMANDER INSTEAD OF USING HIS POWERS AS A DOSHI.
IF THE ZHOU SIDE USES SENDO, SENNIN WOULD END UP KILLING A HUMAN... A MEMBER OF THE ROYAL FAMILY, NO LESS.

READ THIS WAY

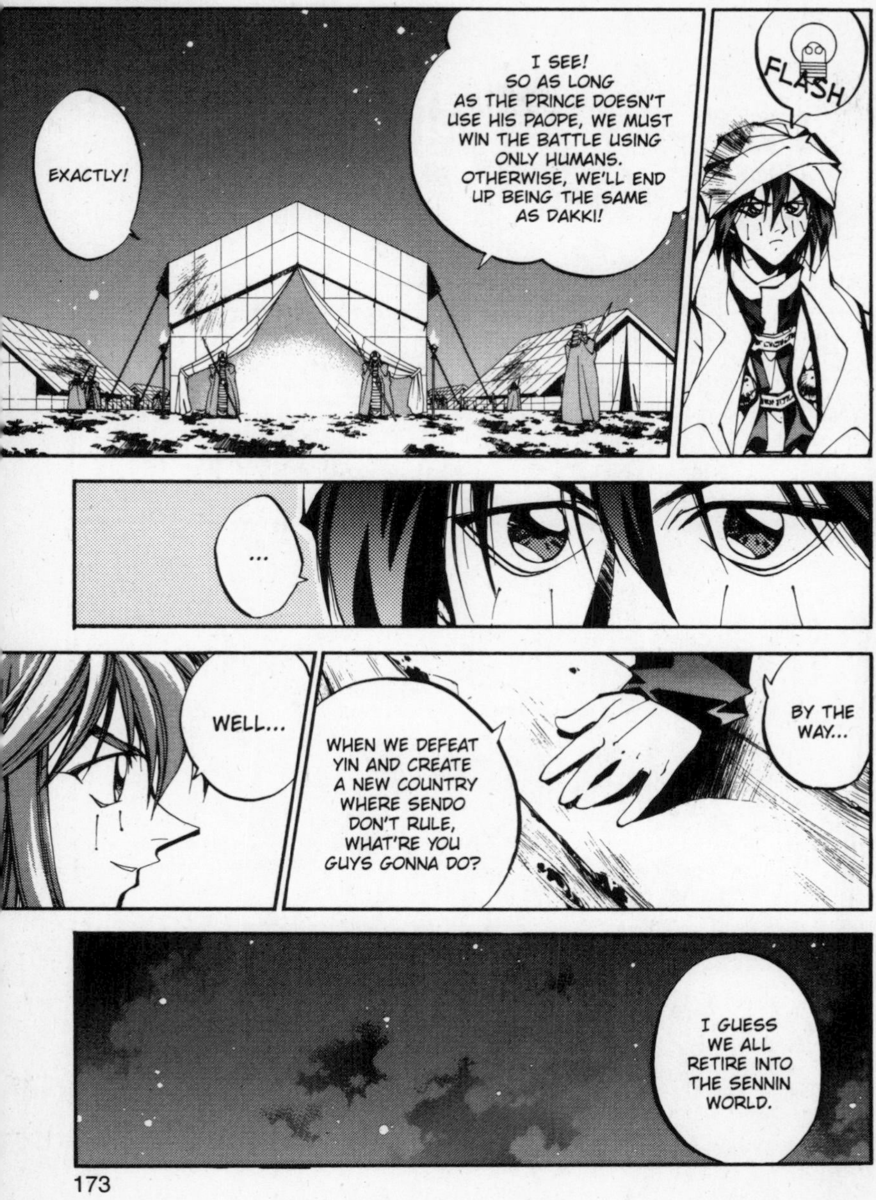
FLASH
I SEE! SO AS LONG AS THE PRINCE DOESN'T USE HIS PAOPE, WE MUST WIN THE BATTLE USING ONLY HUMANS. OTHERWISE, WE'LL END UP BEING THE SAME AS DAKKI!
EXACTLY!
...
BY THE WAY...
WHEN WE DEFEAT YIN AND CREATE A NEW COUNTRY WHERE SENDO DON'T RULE, WHAT'RE YOU GUYS GONNA DO?
WELL...
I GUESS WE ALL RETIRE INTO THE SENNIN WORLD.

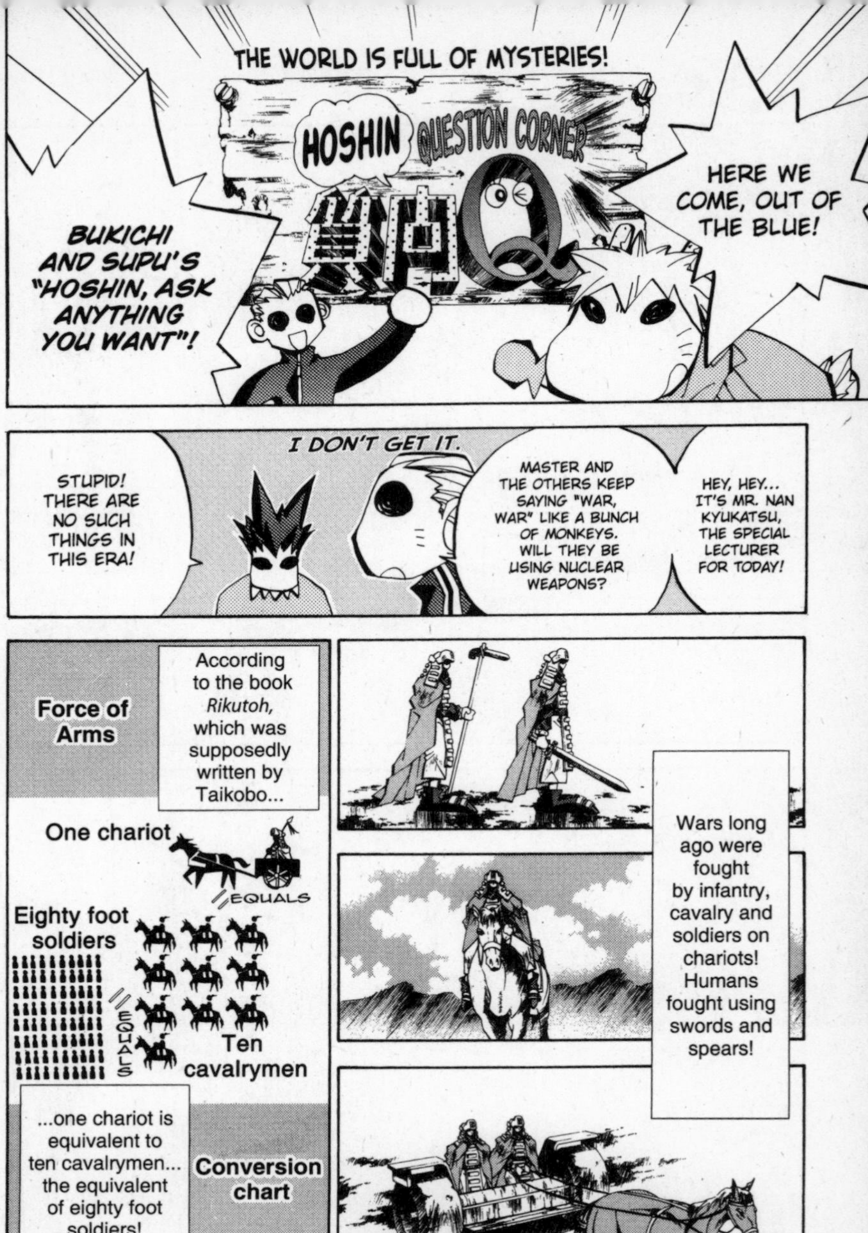
THE WORLD IS FULL OF MYSTERIES!
HOSHIN QUESTION CORNER
HERE WE COME, OUT OF THE BLUE!
BUKICHI AND SUPU'S "HOSHIN, ASK ANYTHING YOU WANT"!
HEY, HEY... IT'S MR. NAN KYUKATSU, THE SPECIAL LECTURER FOR TODAY!
MASTER AND THE OTHERS KEEP SAYING "WAR, WAR" LIKE A BUNCH OF MONKEYS. WILL THEY BE USING NUCLEAR WEAPONS?
I DON'T GET IT.
STUPID! THERE ARE NO SUCH THINGS IN THIS ERA!
Wars long ago were fought by infantry, cavalry and soldiers on chariots! Humans fought using swords and spears!
According to the book *Rikutoh,* which was supposedly written by Taikobo...
Force of Arms
One chariot
EQUALS
Eighty foot soldiers
EQUALS
Ten cavalrymen
Conversion chart
...one chariot is equivalent to ten cavalrymen... the equivalent of eighty foot soldiers!

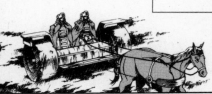

READ THIS WAY

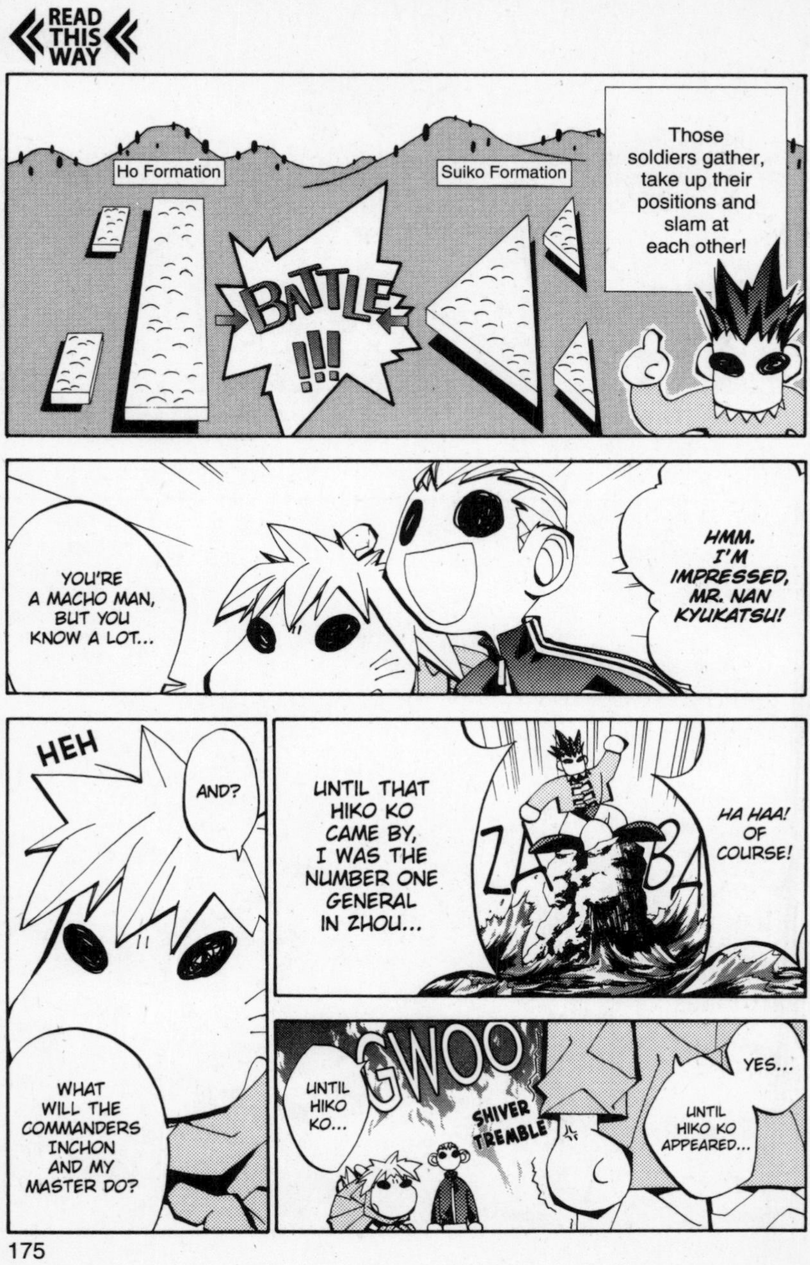

Those soldiers gather, take up their positions and slam at each other!
Suiko Formation
BATTLE!!!
Ho Formation
HMM. I'M IMPRESSED, MR. NAN KYUKATSU!
YOU'RE A MACHO MAN, BUT YOU KNOW A LOT...
HA HAA! OF COURSE!
UNTIL THAT HIKO KO CAME BY, I WAS THE NUMBER ONE GENERAL IN ZHOU...
YES...
UNTIL HIKO KO APPEARED...
SHIVER TREMBLE
GWOO
UNTIL HIKO KO...
HEH
AND?
WHAT WILL THE COMMANDERS INCHON AND MY MASTER DO?

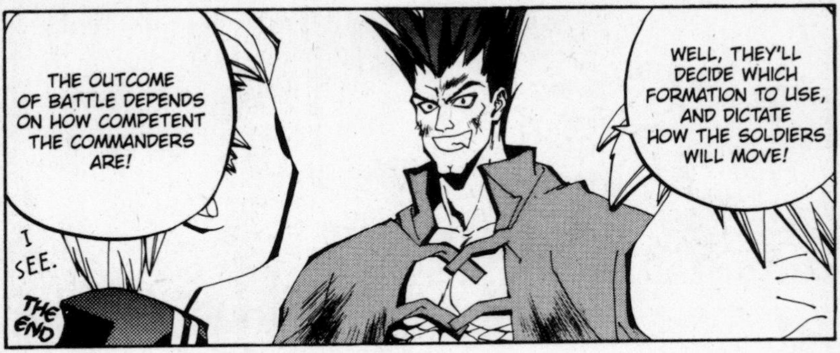
WELL, THEY'LL DECIDE WHICH FORMATION TO USE, AND DICTATE HOW THE SOLDIERS WILL MOVE!
THE OUTCOME OF BATTLE DEPENDS ON HOW COMPETENT THE COMMANDERS ARE!
I SEE.
THE END

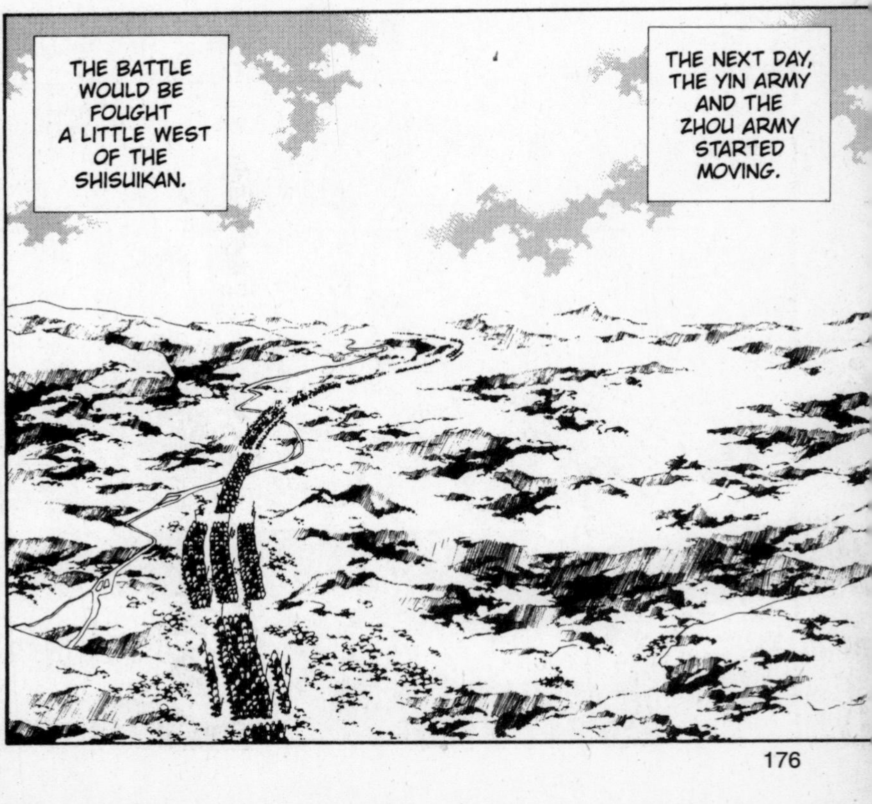
THE NEXT DAY, THE YIN ARMY AND THE ZHOU ARMY STARTED MOVING.
THE BATTLE WOULD BE FOUGHT A LITTLE WEST OF THE SHISUIKAN.

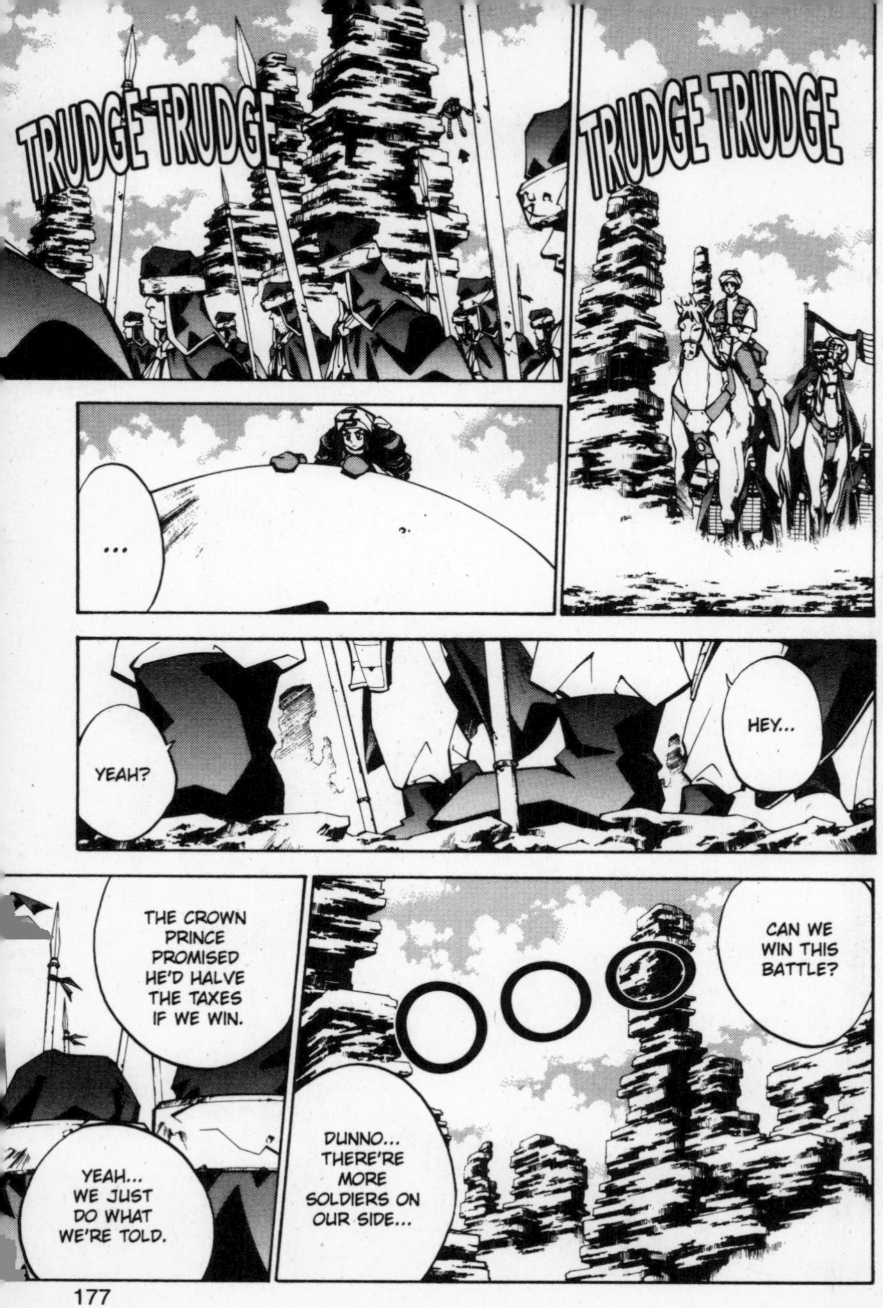
TRUDGE TRUDGE
TRUDGE TRUDGE
...
HEY...
YEAH?
CAN WE WIN THIS BATTLE?
DUNNO... THERE'RE MORE SOLDIERS ON OUR SIDE...
THE CROWN PRINCE PROMISED HE'D HALVE THE TAXES IF WE WIN.
YEAH... WE JUST DO WHAT WE'RE TOLD.

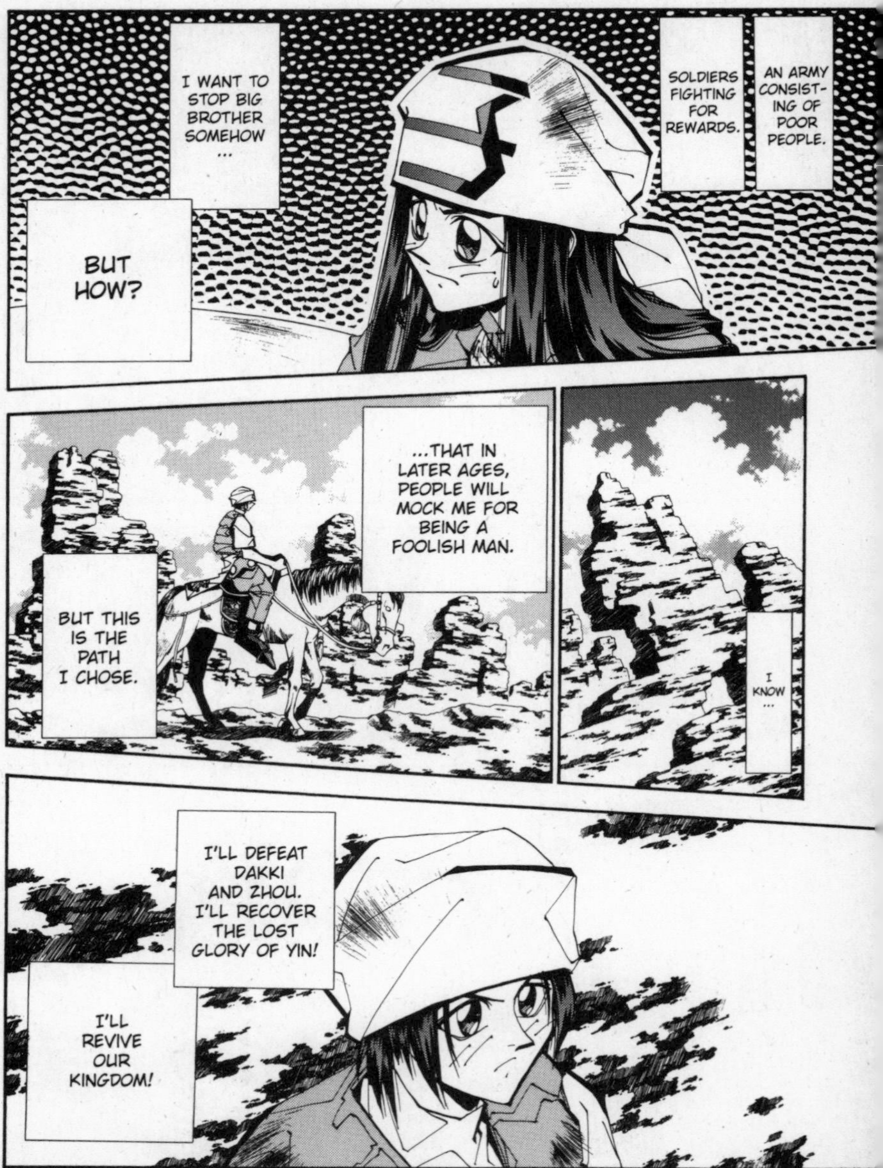
AN ARMY CONSISTING OF POOR PEOPLE.
SOLDIERS FIGHTING FOR REWARDS.
I WANT TO STOP BIG BROTHER SOMEHOW...
BUT HOW?
I KNOW...
...THAT IN LATER AGES, PEOPLE WILL MOCK ME FOR BEING A FOOLISH MAN.
BUT THIS IS THE PATH I CHOSE.
I'LL DEFEAT DAKKI AND ZHOU. I'LL RECOVER THE LOST GLORY OF YIN!
I'LL REVIVE OUR KINGDOM!

READ THIS WAY

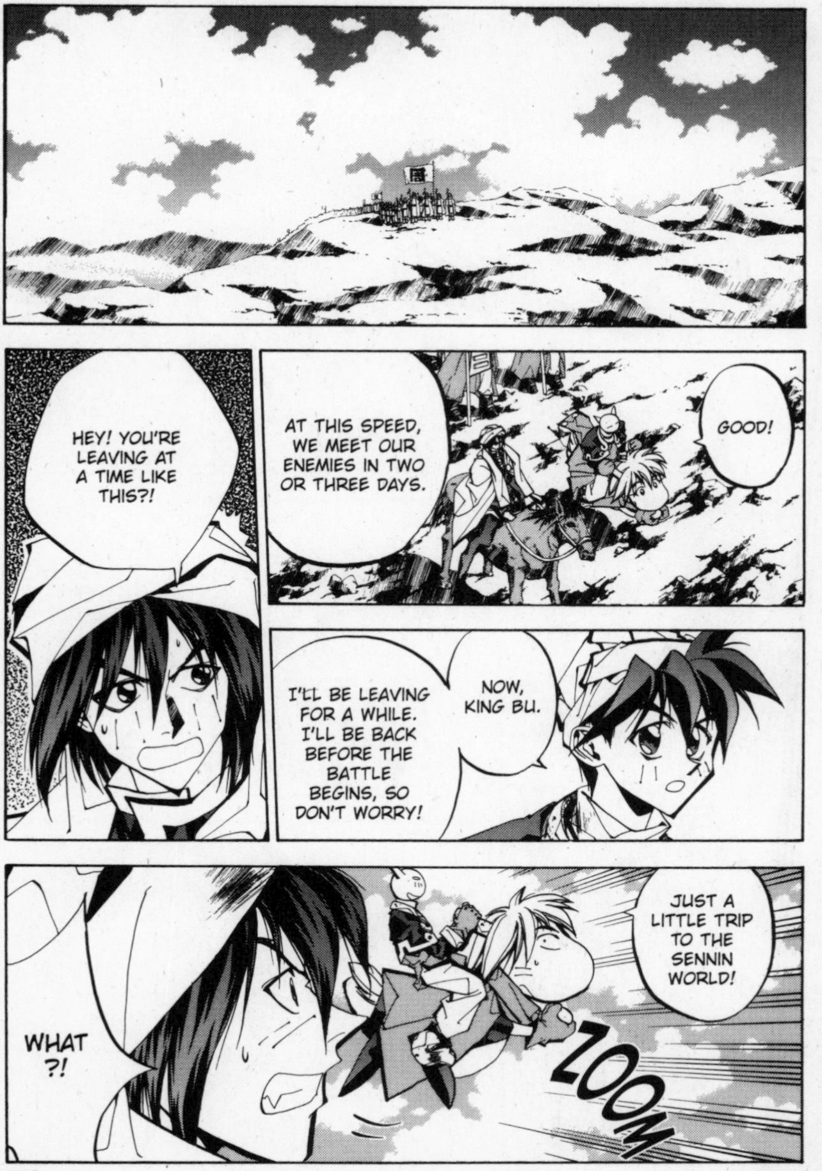
AT THIS SPEED, WE MEET OUR ENEMIES IN TWO OR THREE DAYS.
GOOD!
NOW, KING BU.
I'LL BE LEAVING FOR A WHILE. I'LL BE BACK BEFORE THE BATTLE BEGINS, SO DON'T WORRY!
HEY! YOU'RE LEAVING AT A TIME LIKE THIS?!
JUST A LITTLE TRIP TO THE SENNIN WORLD!
ZOOM
WHAT ?!

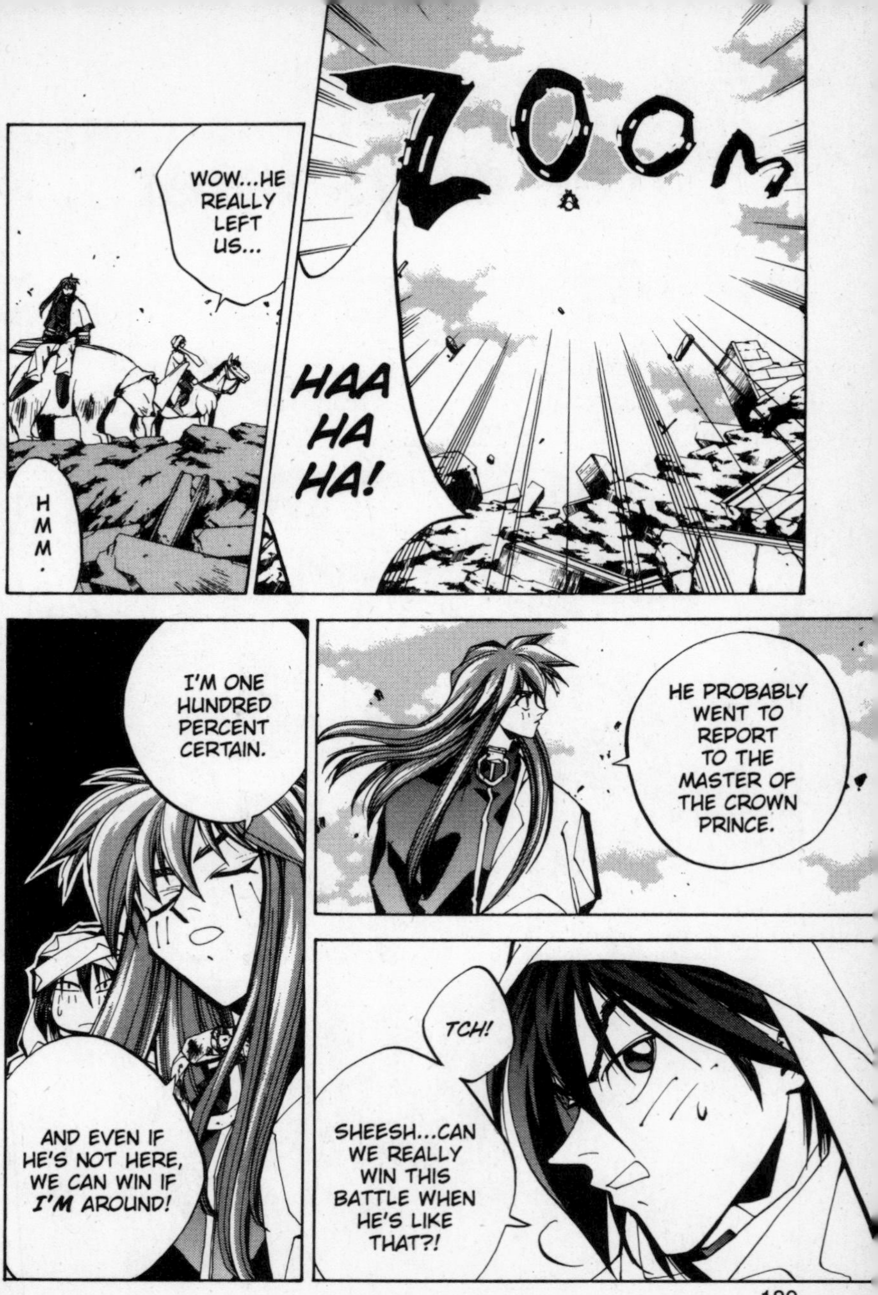
ZOOM
HAA HA HA!
WOW...HE REALLY LEFT US...
HMM.
HE PROBABLY WENT TO REPORT TO THE MASTER OF THE CROWN PRINCE.
TCH!
SHEESH...CAN WE REALLY WIN THIS BATTLE WHEN HE'S LIKE THAT?!
I'M ONE HUNDRED PERCENT CERTAIN.
AND EVEN IF HE'S NOT HERE, WE CAN WIN IF ***I'M*** AROUND!

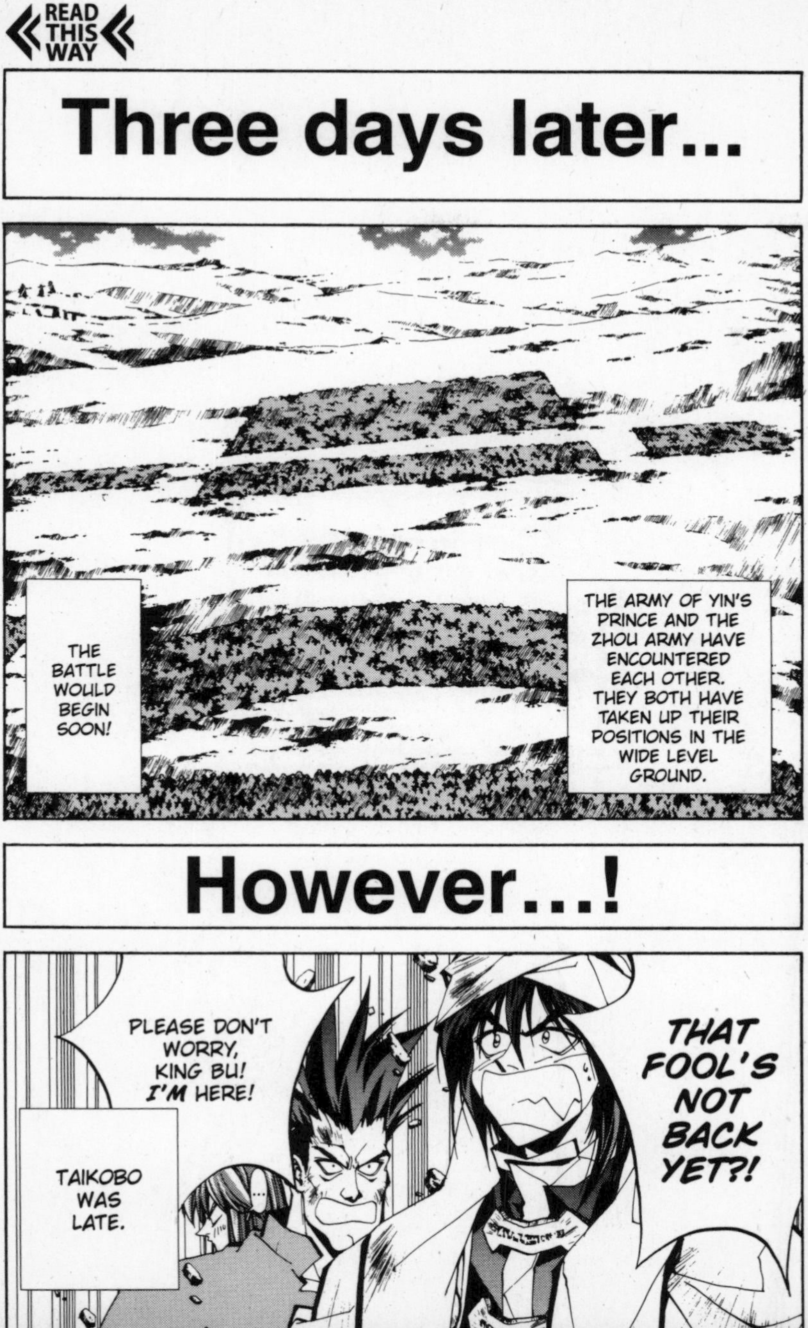
READ THIS WAY
Three days later...
THE ARMY OF YIN'S PRINCE AND THE ZHOU ARMY HAVE ENCOUNTERED EACH OTHER. THEY BOTH HAVE TAKEN UP THEIR POSITIONS IN THE WIDE LEVEL GROUND.
THE BATTLE WOULD BEGIN SOON!
However...!
THAT FOOL'S NOT BACK YET?!
PLEASE DON'T WORRY, KING BU! *I'M* HERE!
TAIKOBO WAS LATE.
...

封神演義

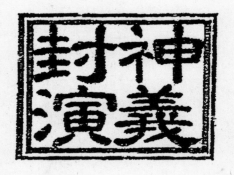

Chapter 79

THE PRINCES' CHOICE, PART 3

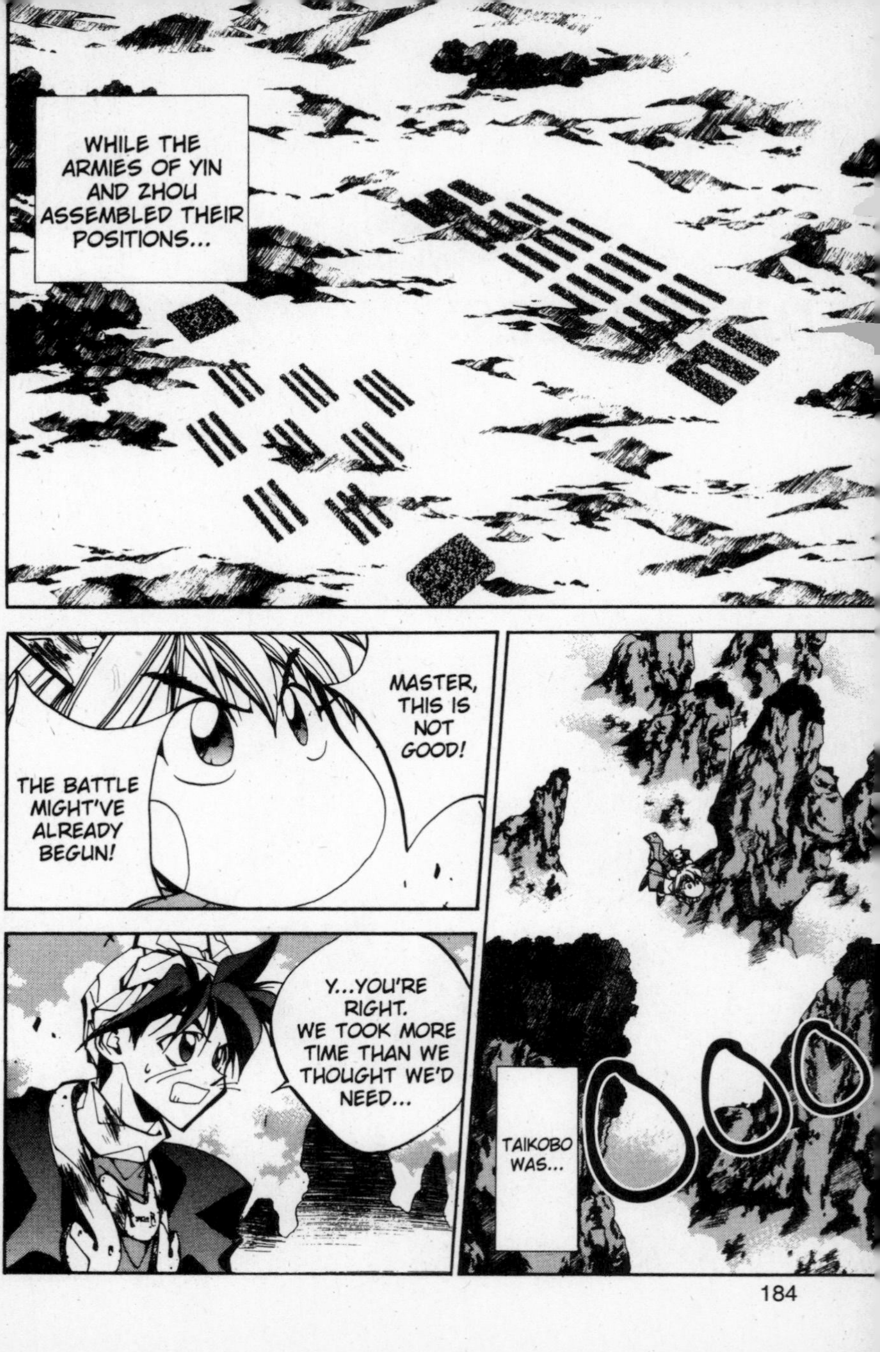
WHILE THE ARMIES OF YIN AND ZHOU ASSEMBLED THEIR POSITIONS...
TAIKOBO WAS...
MASTER, THIS IS NOT GOOD!
THE BATTLE MIGHT'VE ALREADY BEGUN!
Y...YOU'RE RIGHT. WE TOOK MORE TIME THAN WE THOUGHT WE'D NEED...

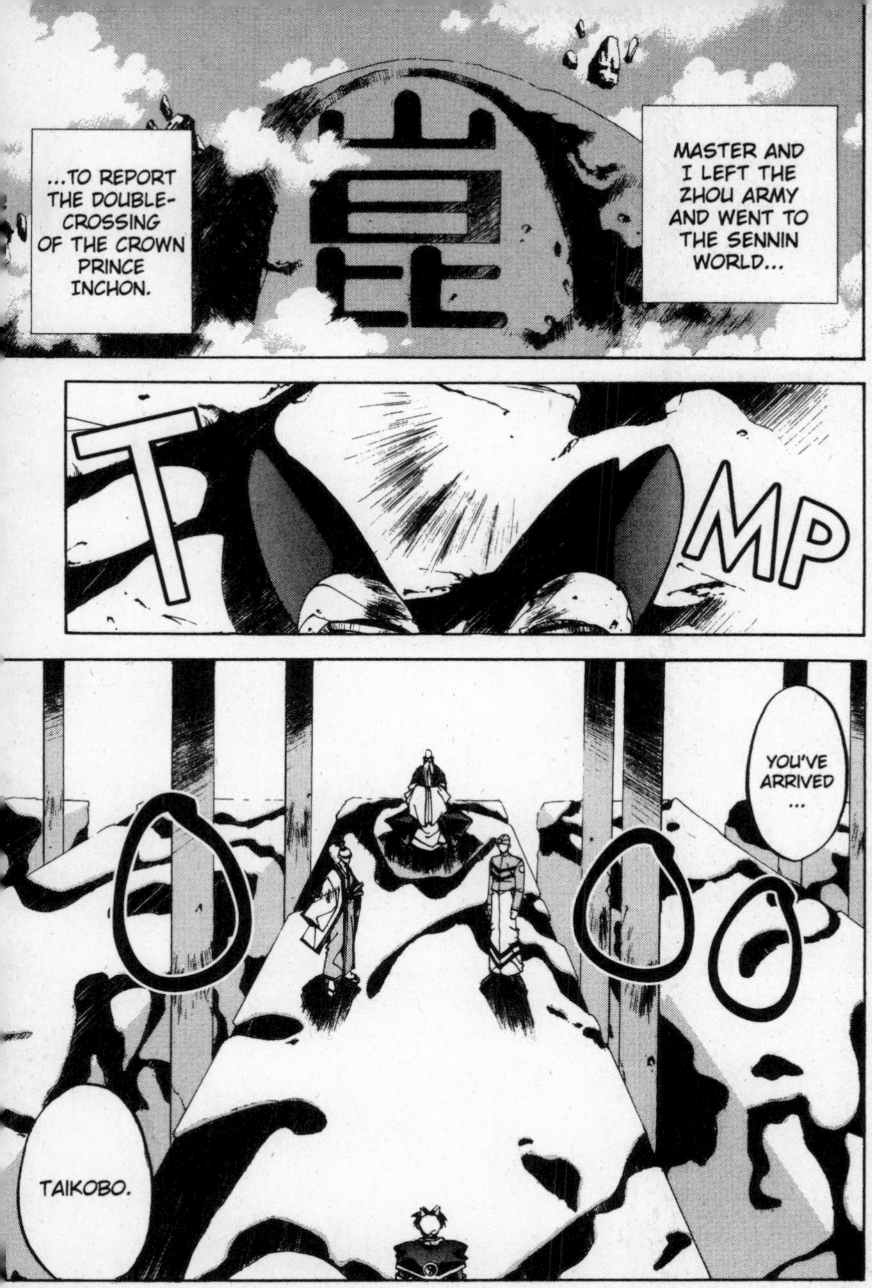
MASTER AND I LEFT THE ZHOU ARMY AND WENT TO THE SENNIN WORLD...
...TO REPORT THE DOUBLE-CROSSING OF THE CROWN PRINCE INCHON.
T MP
YOU'VE ARRIVED ...
TAIKOBO.

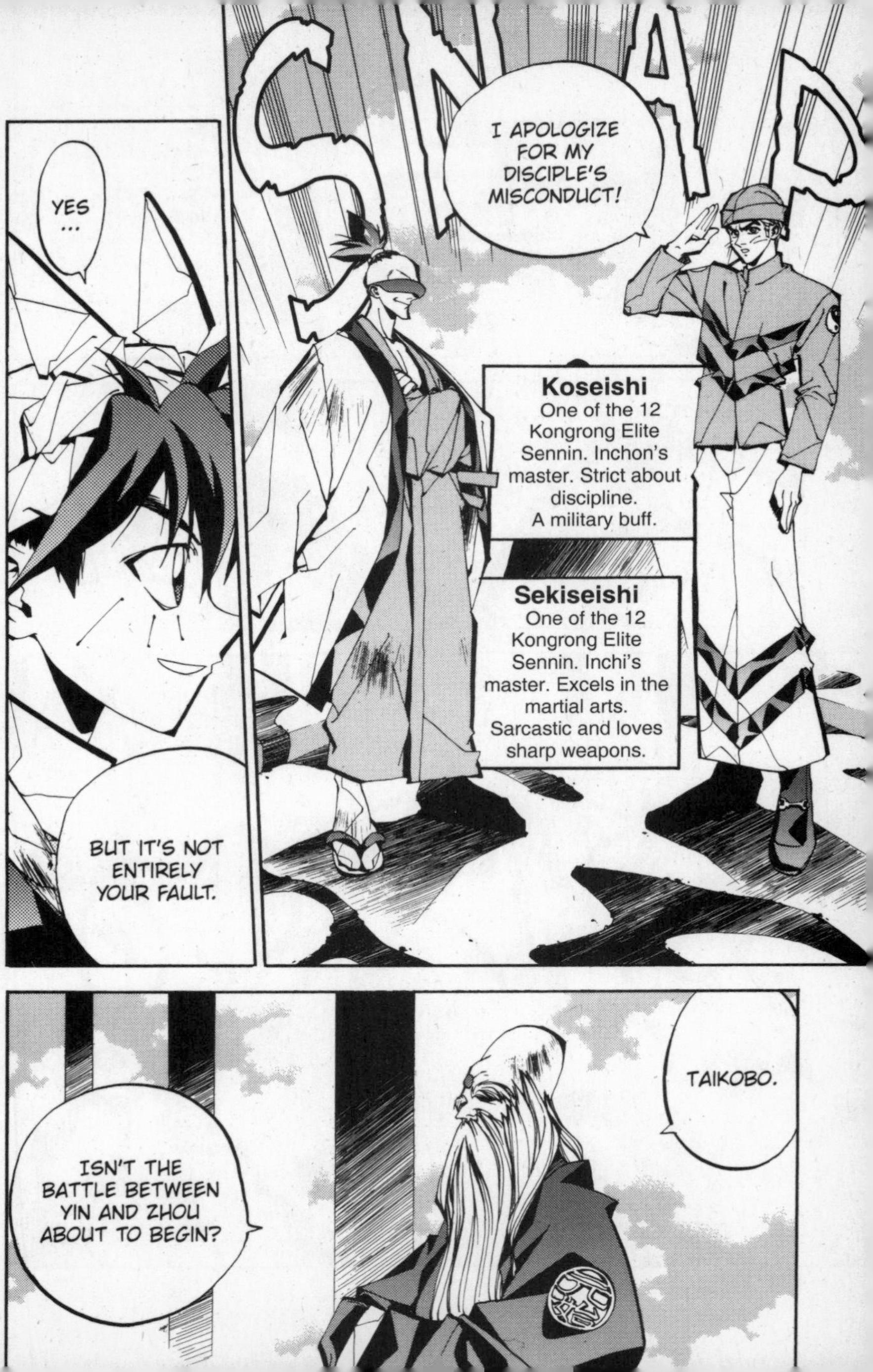
SNAP
I APOLOGIZE FOR MY DISCIPLE'S MISCONDUCT!
Koseishi One of the 12 Kongrong Elite Sennin. Inchon's master. Strict about discipline. A military buff.
Sekiseishi One of the 12 Kongrong Elite Sennin. Inchi's master. Excels in the martial arts. Sarcastic and loves sharp weapons.
YES ...
BUT IT'S NOT ENTIRELY YOUR FAULT.
TAIKOBO.
ISN'T THE BATTLE BETWEEN YIN AND ZHOU ABOUT TO BEGIN?

READ THIS WAY

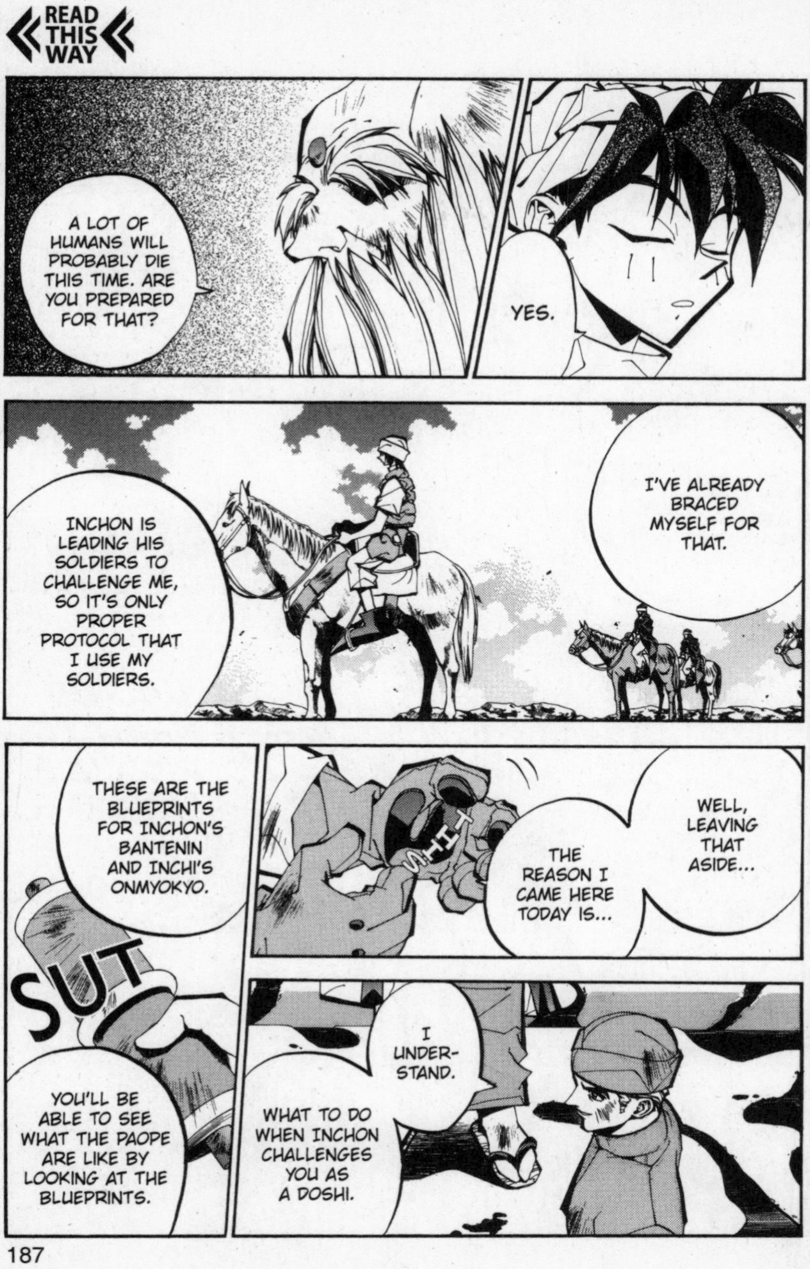
YES.
A LOT OF HUMANS WILL PROBABLY DIE THIS TIME. ARE YOU PREPARED FOR THAT?
I'VE ALREADY BRACED MYSELF FOR THAT.
INCHON IS LEADING HIS SOLDIERS TO CHALLENGE ME, SO IT'S ONLY PROPER PROTOCOL THAT I USE MY SOLDIERS.
WELL, LEAVING THAT ASIDE...
THE REASON I CAME HERE TODAY IS...
THIS
I UNDER-STAND.
WHAT TO DO WHEN INCHON CHALLENGES YOU AS A DOSHI.
THESE ARE THE BLUEPRINTS FOR INCHON'S BANTENIN AND INCHI'S ONMYOKYO.
SUT
YOU'LL BE ABLE TO SEE WHAT THE PAOPE ARE LIKE BY LOOKING AT THE BLUEPRINTS.

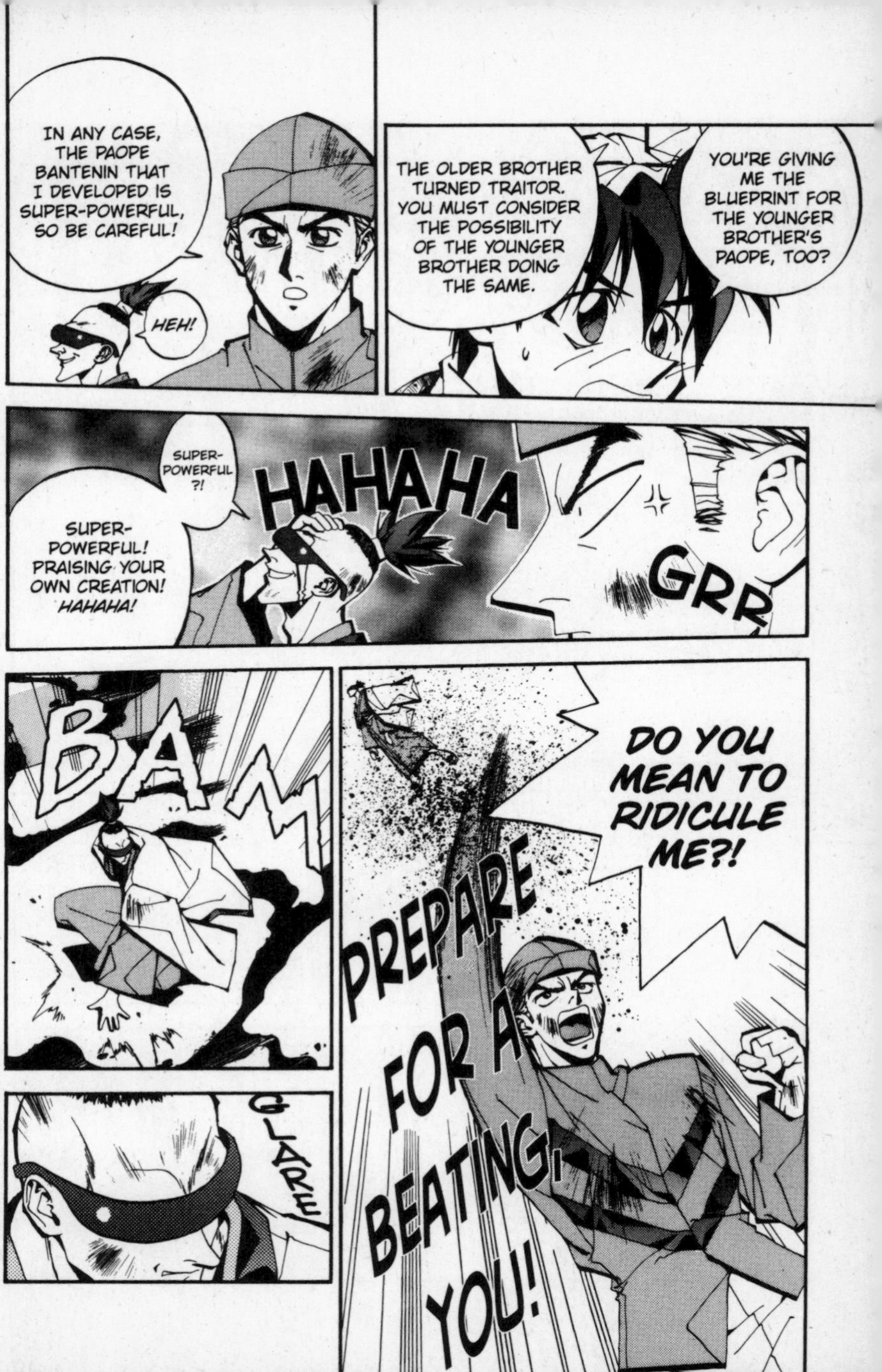
YOU'RE GIVING ME THE BLUEPRINT FOR THE YOUNGER BROTHER'S PAOPE, TOO?
THE OLDER BROTHER TURNED TRAITOR. YOU MUST CONSIDER THE POSSIBILITY OF THE YOUNGER BROTHER DOING THE SAME.
IN ANY CASE, THE PAOPE BANTENIN THAT I DEVELOPED IS SUPER-POWERFUL, SO BE CAREFUL!
HEH!
SUPER-POWERFUL?!
SUPER-POWERFUL! PRAISING YOUR OWN CREATION! HAHAHA!
HAHAHA
GRR
DO YOU MEAN TO RIDICULE ME?!
PREPARE FOR A BEATING, YOU!
BAM
GLARE

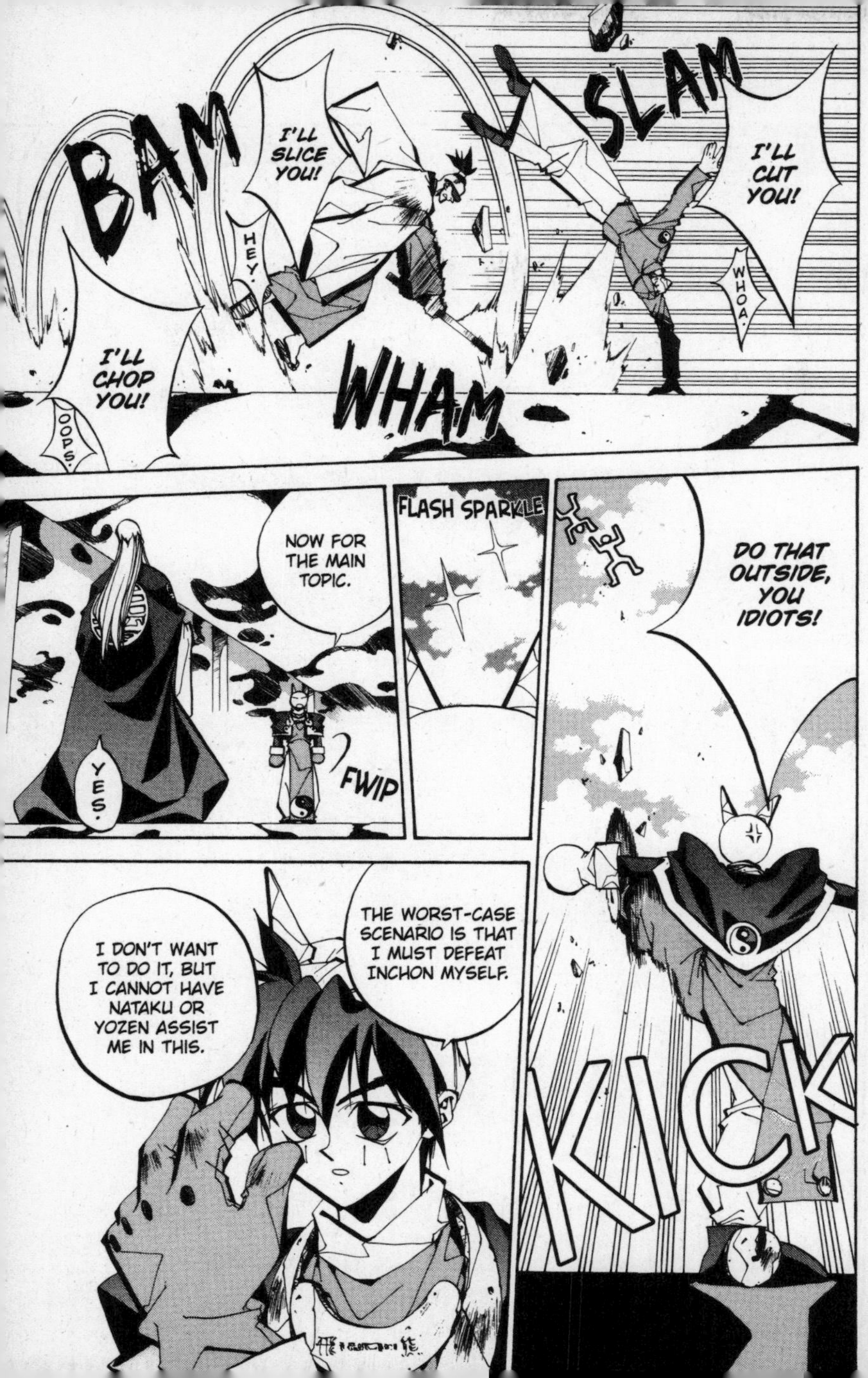
I'LL CUT YOU!
WHOA.
SLAM
I'LL SLICE YOU!
HEY.
BAM
WHAM
I'LL CHOP YOU!
OOPS.
DO THAT OUTSIDE, YOU IDIOTS!
KICK
FLASH SPARKLE
NOW FOR THE MAIN TOPIC.
YES.
FWIP
THE WORST-CASE SCENARIO IS THAT I MUST DEFEAT INCHON MYSELF.
I DON'T WANT TO DO IT, BUT I CANNOT HAVE NATAKU OR YOZEN ASSIST ME IN THIS.

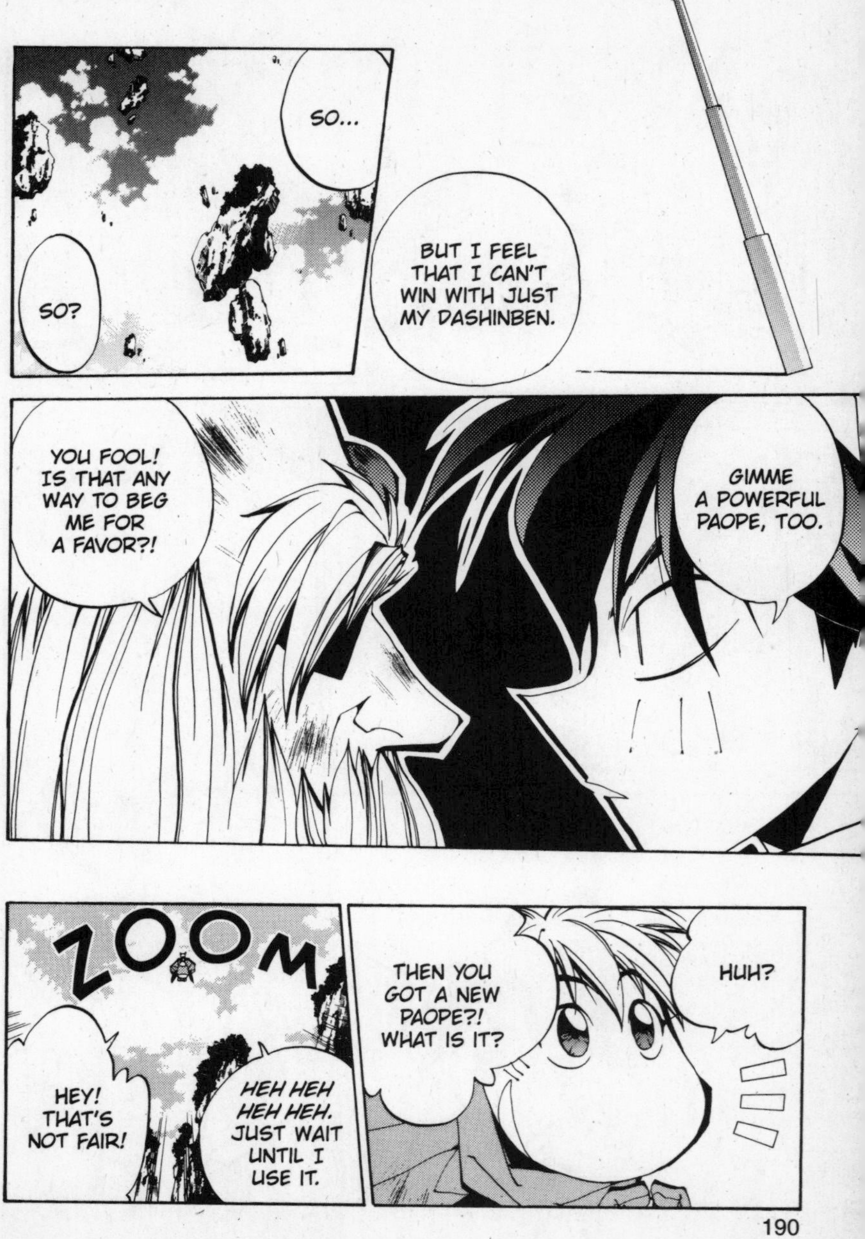
SO...
SO?
BUT I FEEL THAT I CAN'T WIN WITH JUST MY DASHINBEN.
GIMME A POWERFUL PAOPE, TOO.
YOU FOOL! IS THAT ANY WAY TO BEG ME FOR A FAVOR?!
HUH?
THEN YOU GOT A NEW PAOPE?! WHAT IS IT?
ZOOM
HEH HEH HEH HEH. JUST WAIT UNTIL I USE IT.
HEY! THAT'S NOT FAIR!

READ THIS WAY

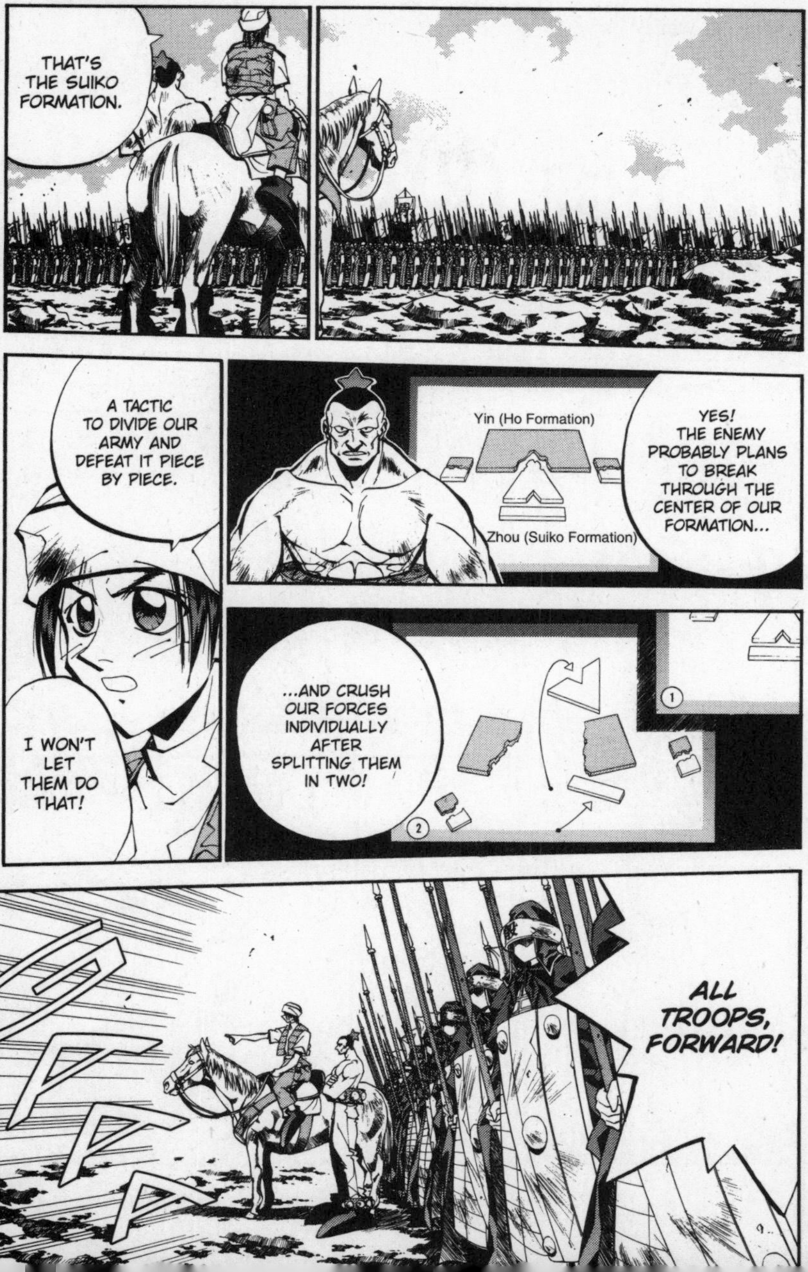
THAT'S THE SUIKO FORMATION.
Yin (Ho Formation)
Zhou (Suiko Formation)
YES! THE ENEMY PROBABLY PLANS TO BREAK THROUGH THE CENTER OF OUR FORMATION...
1
2
...AND CRUSH OUR FORCES INDIVIDUALLY AFTER SPLITTING THEM IN TWO!
A TACTIC TO DIVIDE OUR ARMY AND DEFEAT IT PIECE BY PIECE.
I WON'T LET THEM DO THAT!
ALL TROOPS, FORWARD!

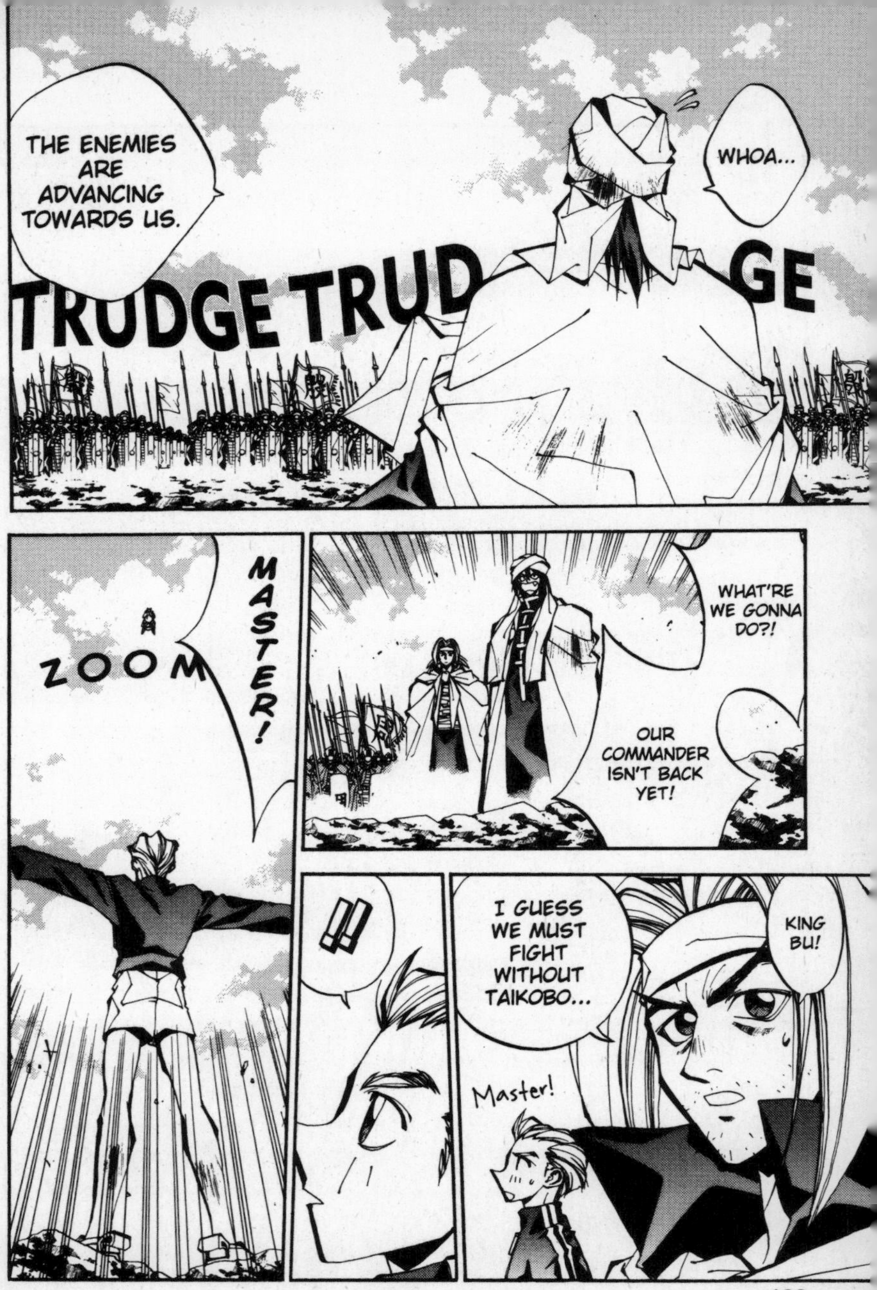
WHOA...
THE ENEMIES ARE ADVANCING TOWARDS US.
TRUDGE TRUDGE
WHAT'RE WE GONNA DO?!
OUR COMMANDER ISN'T BACK YET!
KING BU!
I GUESS WE MUST FIGHT WITHOUT TAIKOBO...
Master!
!!
MASTER!
ZOOM

READ THIS WAY

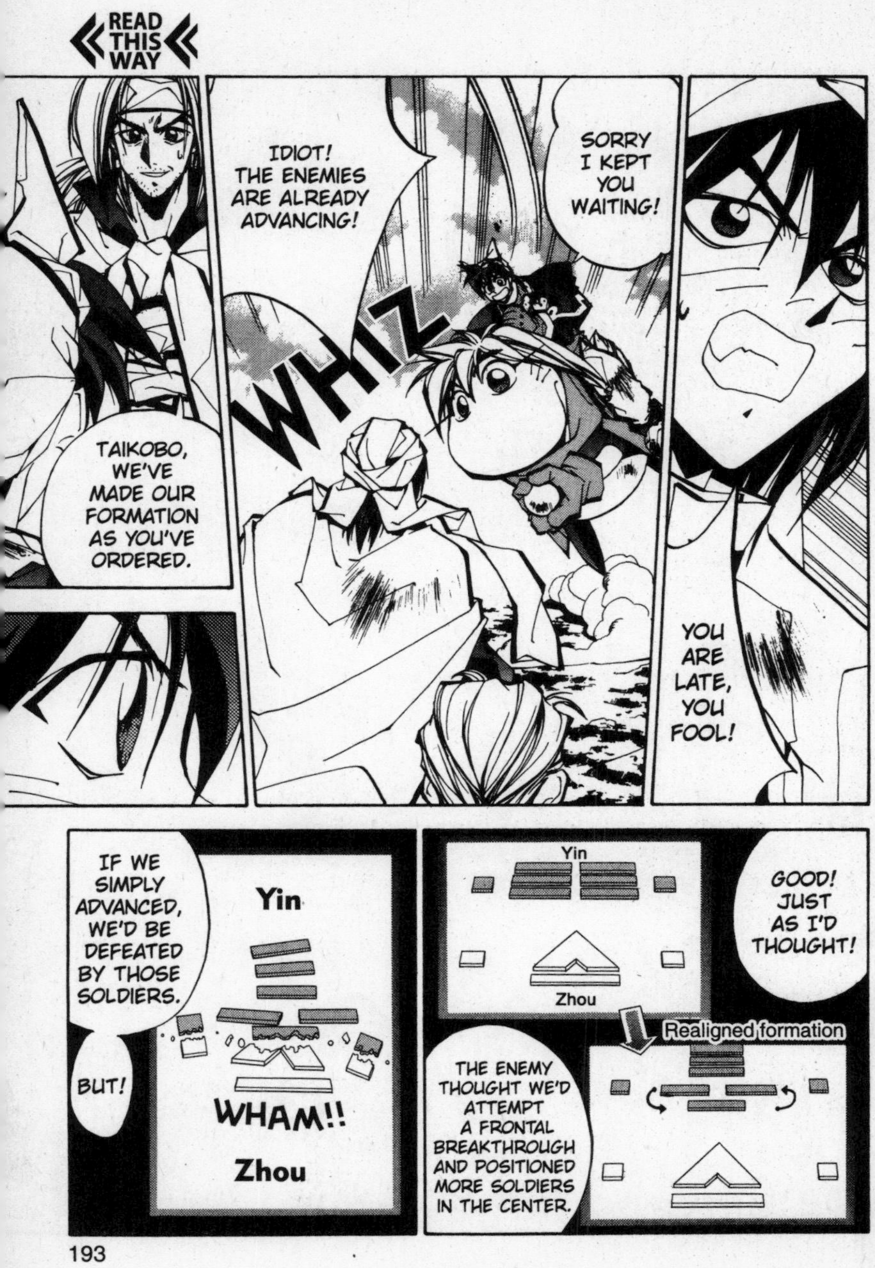
YOU ARE LATE, YOU FOOL!
SORRY I KEPT YOU WAITING!
IDIOT! THE ENEMIES ARE ALREADY ADVANCING!
WHIZ
TAIKOBO, WE'VE MADE OUR FORMATION AS YOU'VE ORDERED.
GOOD! JUST AS I'D THOUGHT!
Yin
Zhou
Realigned formation
THE ENEMY THOUGHT WE'D ATTEMPT A FRONTAL BREAKTHROUGH AND POSITIONED MORE SOLDIERS IN THE CENTER.
IF WE SIMPLY ADVANCED, WE'D BE DEFEATED BY THOSE SOLDIERS.
BUT!
Yin
WHAM!!
Zhou

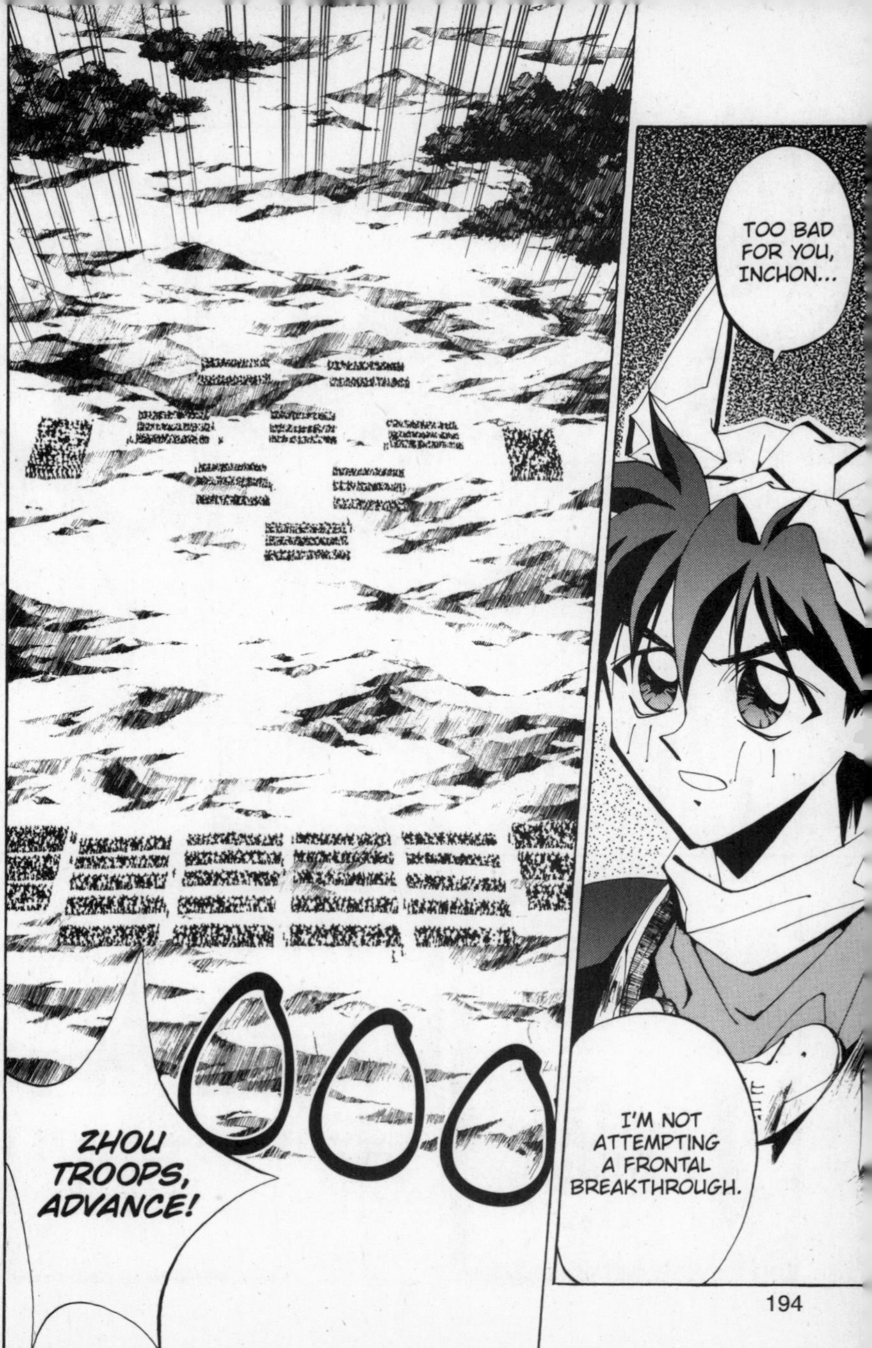
TOO BAD FOR YOU, INCHON...
I'M NOT ATTEMPTING A FRONTAL BREAKTHROUGH.
ZHOU TROOPS, ADVANCE!

« READ THIS WAY «

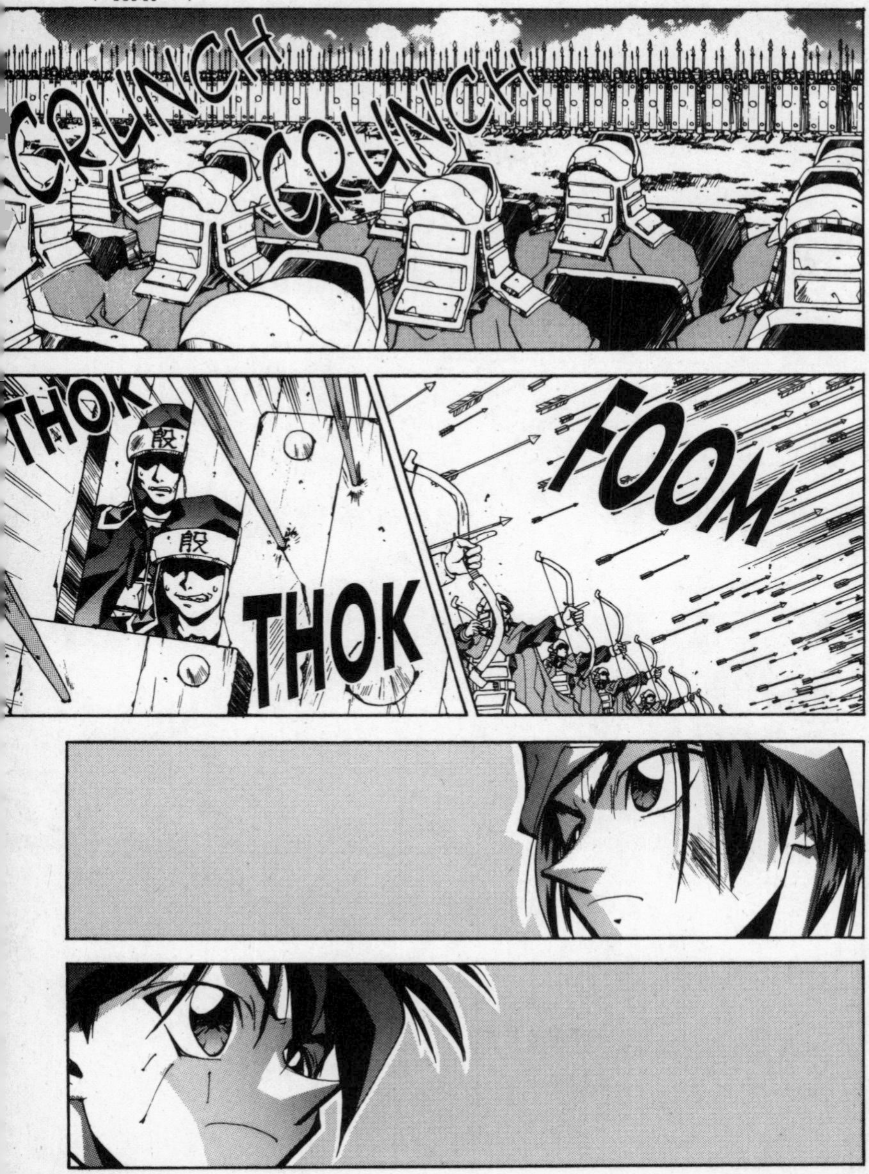
CRUNCH
CRUNCH
FOOM
THOK
殷
殷
THOK

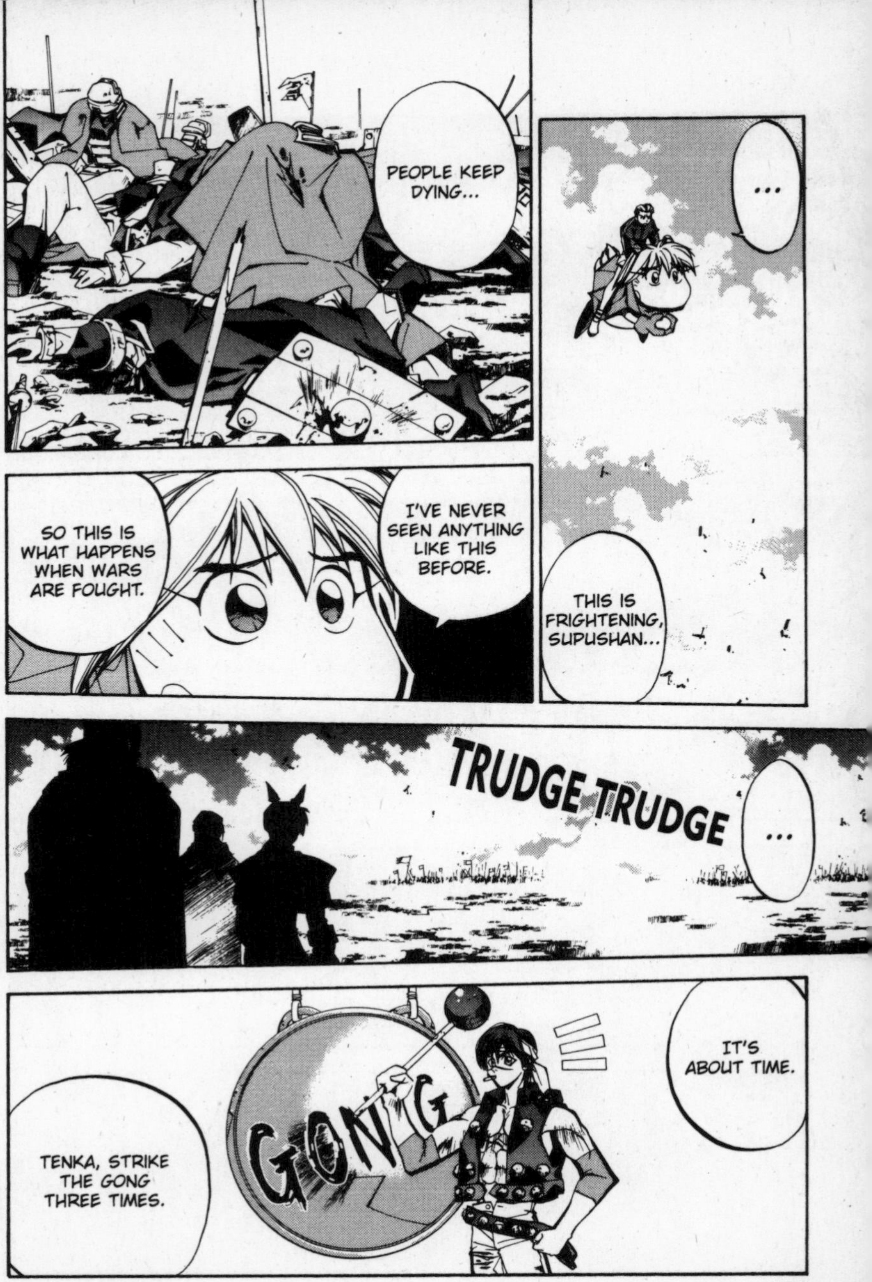
...
THIS IS FRIGHTENING, SUPUSHAN...
PEOPLE KEEP DYING...
I'VE NEVER SEEN ANYTHING LIKE THIS BEFORE.
SO THIS IS WHAT HAPPENS WHEN WARS ARE FOUGHT.
TRUDGE TRUDGE
...
IT'S ABOUT TIME.
GONG
TENKA, STRIKE THE GONG THREE TIMES.

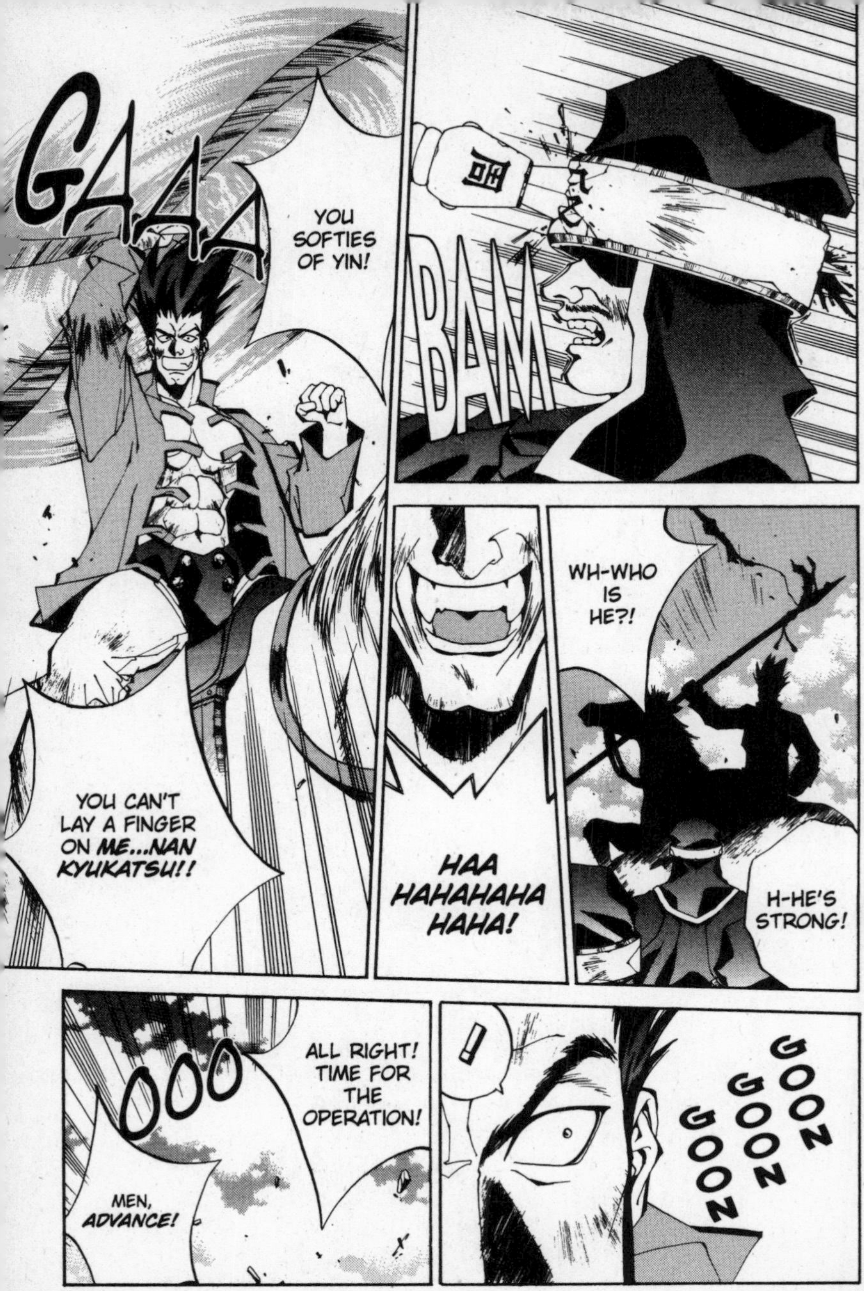
BAM
WH-WHO IS HE?!
H-HE'S STRONG!
HAA HAHAHAHA HAHA!
GAAA
YOU SOFTIES OF YIN!
YOU CAN'T LAY A FINGER ON *ME...NAN KYUKATSU!!*
!
GOON GOON GOON
OOO
ALL RIGHT! TIME FOR THE OPERATION!
MEN, *ADVANCE!*

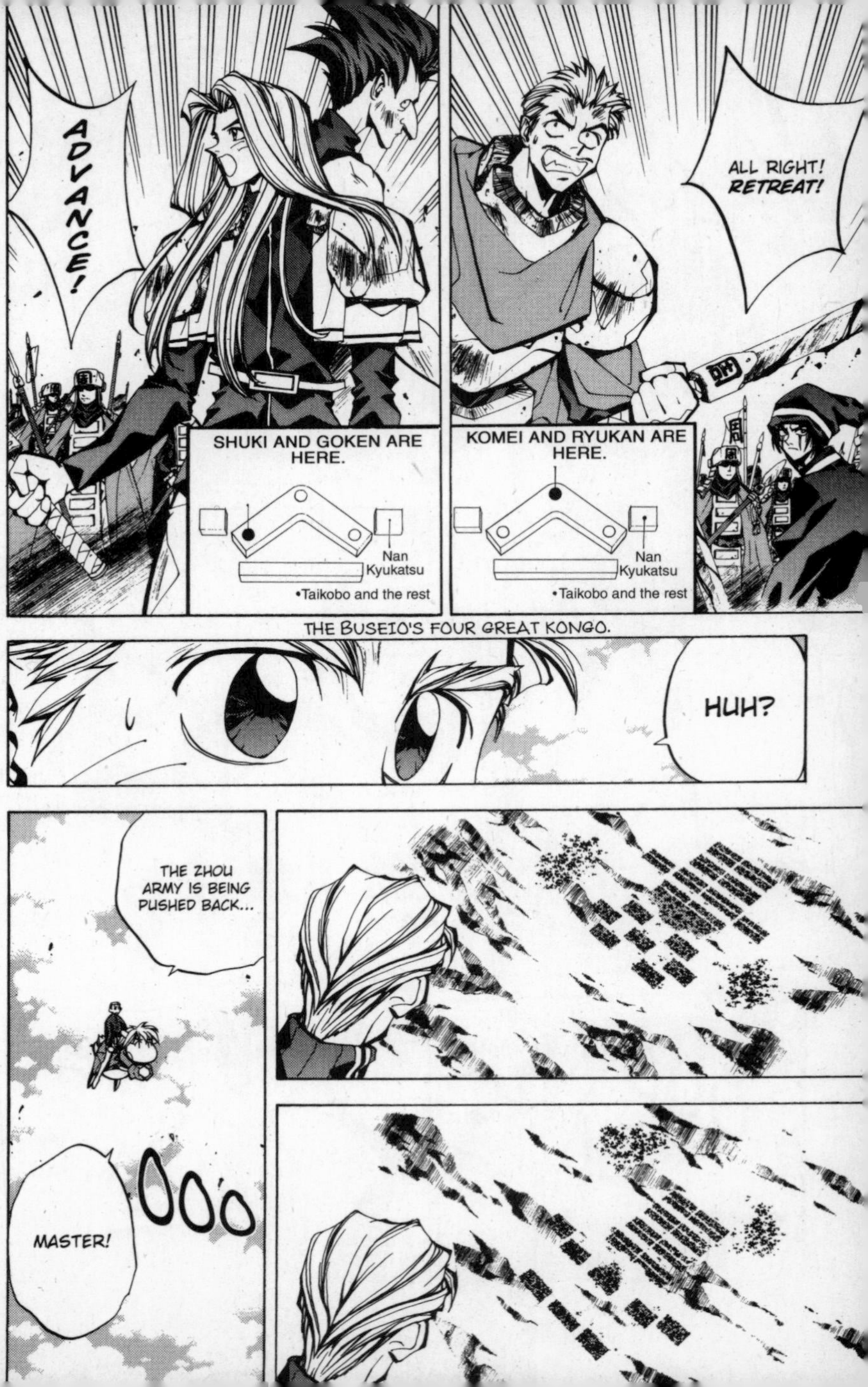
ALL RIGHT! RETREAT!
KOMEI AND RYUKAN ARE HERE.
Nan Kyukatsu
•Taikobo and the rest
ADVANCE!
SHUKI AND GOKEN ARE HERE.
Nan Kyukatsu
•Taikobo and the rest
THE BUSEIO'S FOUR GREAT KONGO.
HUH?
THE ZHOU ARMY IS BEING PUSHED BACK...
MASTER!

READ THIS WAY

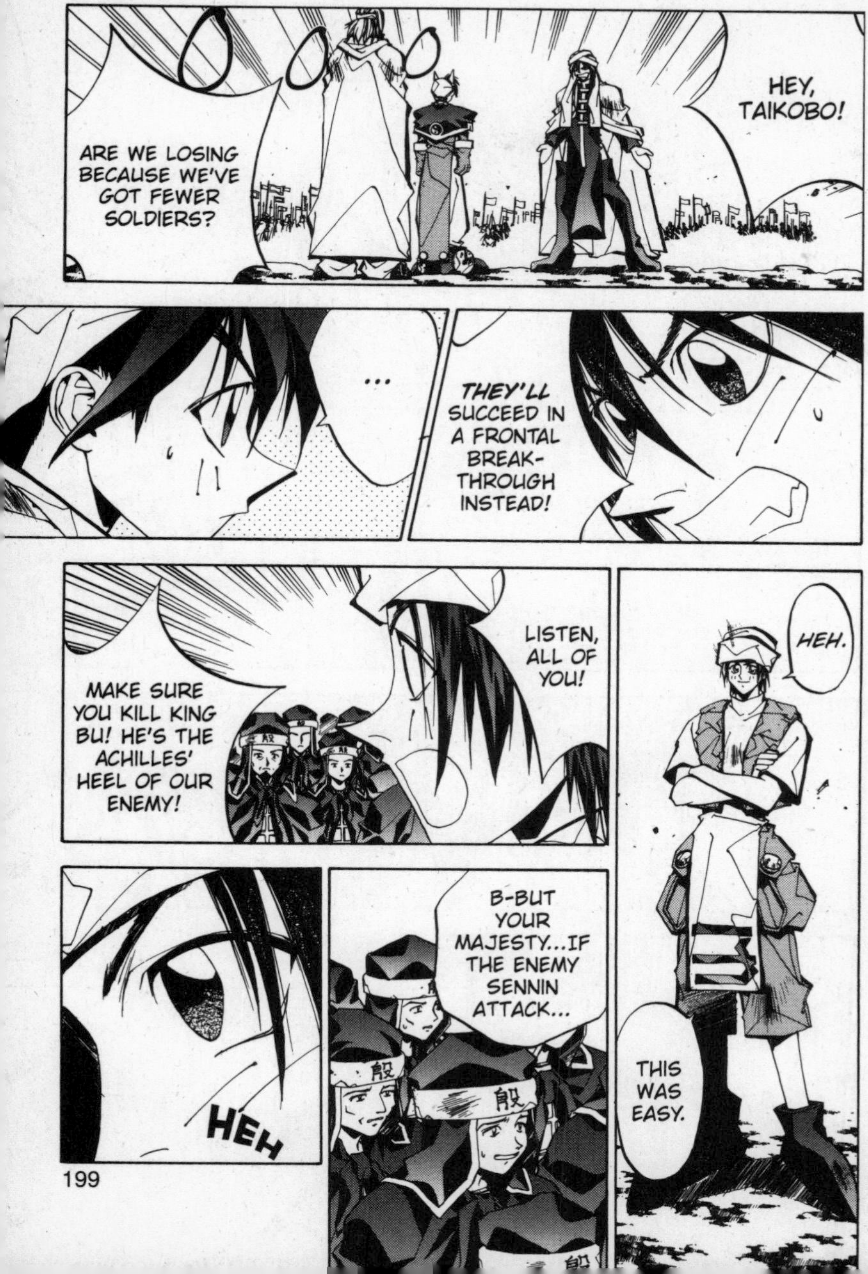
HEY, TAIKOBO!
ARE WE LOSING BECAUSE WE'VE GOT FEWER SOLDIERS?
THEY'LL SUCCEED IN A FRONTAL BREAK-THROUGH INSTEAD!
...
HEH.
THIS WAS EASY.
LISTEN, ALL OF YOU!
MAKE SURE YOU KILL KING BU! HE'S THE ACHILLES' HEEL OF OUR ENEMY!
B-BUT YOUR MAJESTY...IF THE ENEMY SENNIN ATTACK...
HEH

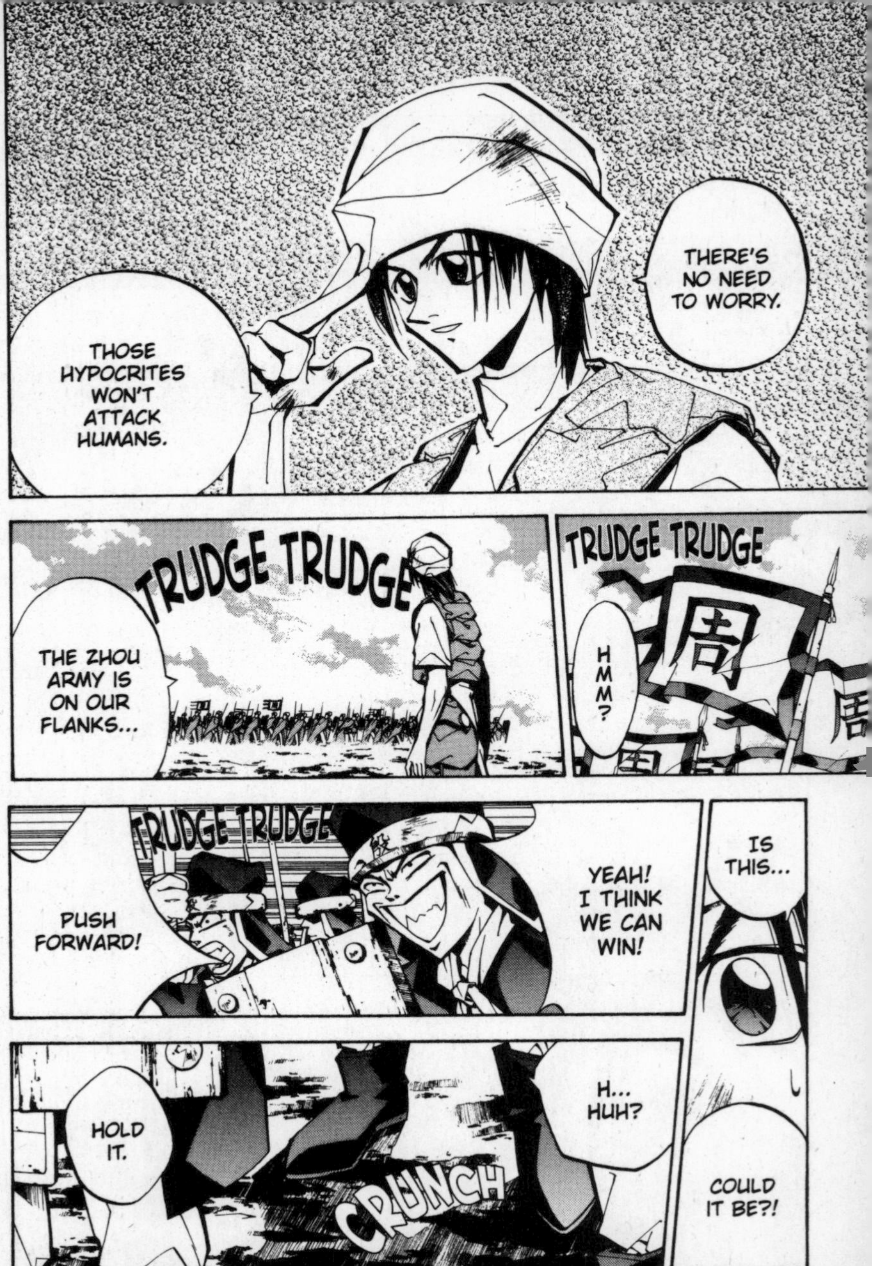
THERE'S NO NEED TO WORRY.
THOSE HYPOCRITES WON'T ATTACK HUMANS.
TRUDGE TRUDGE
HMM?
TRUDGE TRUDGE
THE ZHOU ARMY IS ON OUR FLANKS...
IS THIS...
COULD IT BE?!
YEAH! I THINK WE CAN WIN!
TRUDGE TRUDGE
PUSH FORWARD!
H... HUH?
CRUNCH
HOLD IT.

READ THIS WAY

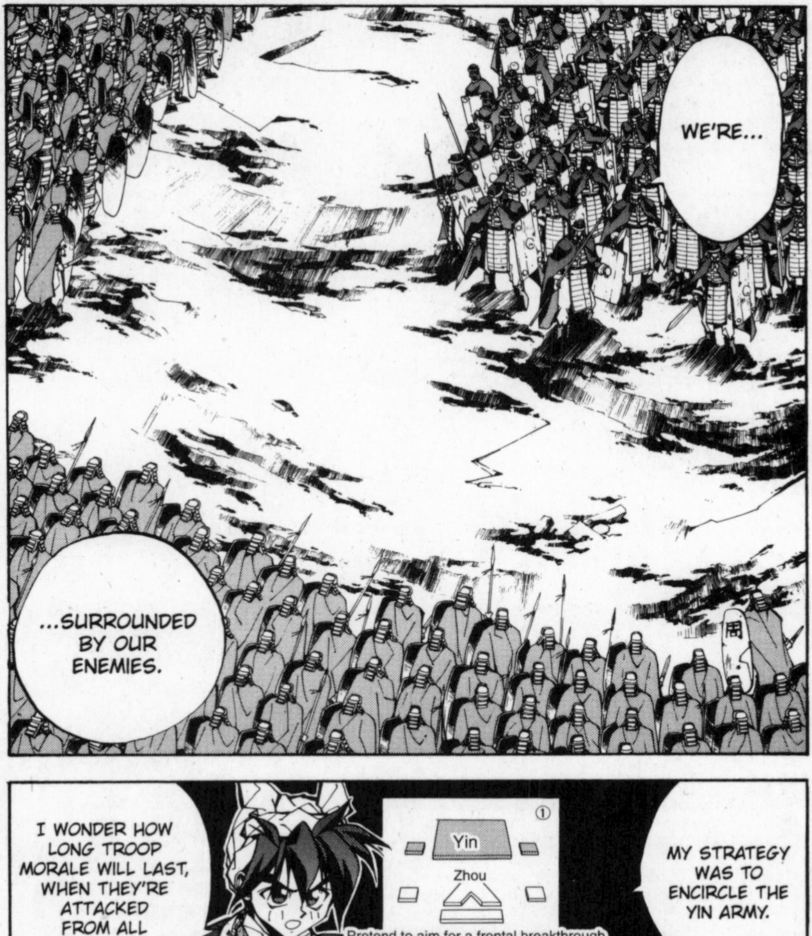
WE'RE...
周
...SURROUNDED BY OUR ENEMIES.

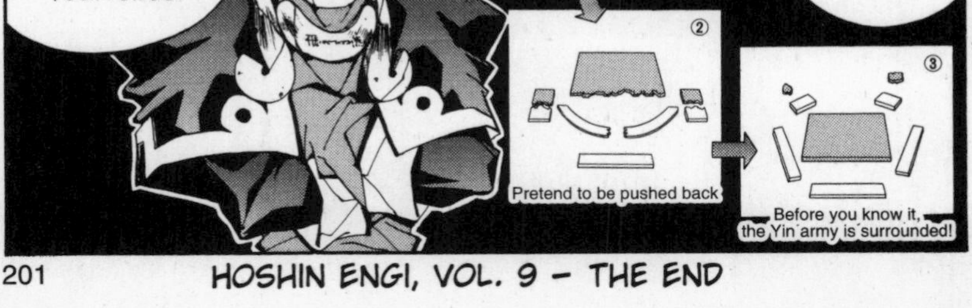
MY STRATEGY WAS TO ENCIRCLE THE YIN ARMY.
①
Yin
Zhou
Pretend to aim for a frontal breakthrough
②
Pretend to be pushed back
③
Before you know it, the Yin army is surrounded!
I WONDER HOW LONG TROOP MORALE WILL LAST, WHEN THEY'RE ATTACKED FROM ALL FOUR SIDES.

HOSHIN ENGI, VOL. 9 – THE END

He's the hero! Can he do it when it counts?! Taikobo Operations Encyclopedia!

I understand Master's cunning... I mean, his strength the best because I'm always watching from close by! I'll explain some of his operations!

I'll check them out!

Even his comrade Tenka Ko doubted Taikobo's abilities. However, Taikobo's specialty is his clever tactics. Check out the keenness of his operations!

Operation 1

Save the village from Chinto! The great drunken operation!

Situation: The Yokai Doshi Chinto headed toward the village of an alien tribe to hunt the villagers under Dakki's orders. Master realized it, yet he made the villagers drink sake and got them all drunk!

Operation and Result: The drunk villagers fell asleep and were all captured by Chinto. But that was Master's plan! Master defeated Chinto, and the enemy soldiers fled. Because the villagers did not resist, no one was hurt.

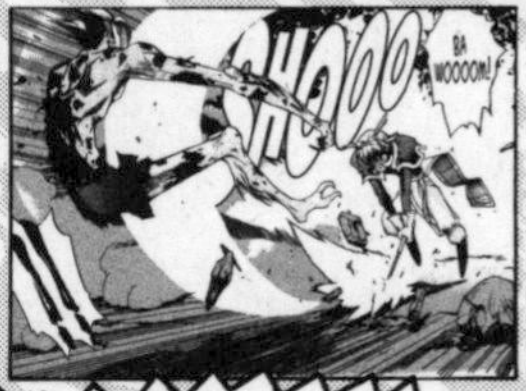
SHOOOO
BA WOOOOM!

He ran away from Chinto's Karyuhyo to surround Chinto with flames. He won the battle with his brains!

He defeated Chinto, a great success!

Operation 2

Defeat Okijin! A sneak attack operation!

Situation: The battle against Okijin. The Dashinben wasn't effective against the paope Shiju Hagoromo! Master quickly admitted defeat.

Operation and Result: Master asked permission to tell her fortune using firewood before he died...he used the wind on the sparks to burn the hagoromo.

It was a cheap trick, but he defeated Okijin!

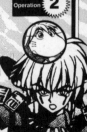

Kijin is strong, but is her personality is too simple?! She lost because she was duped.

Operation 3

Defeat Dakki! The King Chu kidnapping operation!

Situation: Master defeated Okijin and turned her back into a stone biwa lute. He then went into the Forbidden Palace where Dakki was. He gained favors with King Chu and became a court musician. But on the third day, in the early morning, Dakki came to Master's room...

Operation and Result: Master was waiting for a chance to attack Dakki when she came to attack him! He buried Dakki alive and tried to kidnap King Chu in the meantime, but...

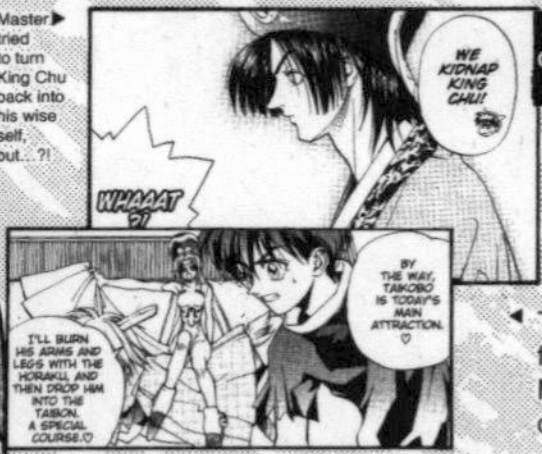
WE KIDNAP KING CHU!
WHAAAT ?!
BY THE WAY, TAIKOBO IS TODAY'S MAIN ATTRACTION. ♡
I'LL BURN HIS ARMS AND LEGS WITH THE HORAKU AND THEN DROP HIM INTO THE TAIBON. A SPECIAL COURSE.♡

Master tried to turn King Chu back into his wise self, but...?!

The operation failed! Master was captured.

Taikobo's first serious defeat!

YOU'RE NOT MY ENEMY YET ♡

Operation 4

Make Nataku an ally?! Mediate the father-son fight operation!

Situation: Master met a man named Sei Li, who was about to be killed by his son, Nataku. Nataku was wearing three paope, and Master thought up a plan to make him an ally...

Operation and Result: Master realized that Nataku didn't hate Sei Li completely and told Nataku to kill Sei Li. And when he saw his mother Inshi defend Sei Li, Nataku admitted defeat!

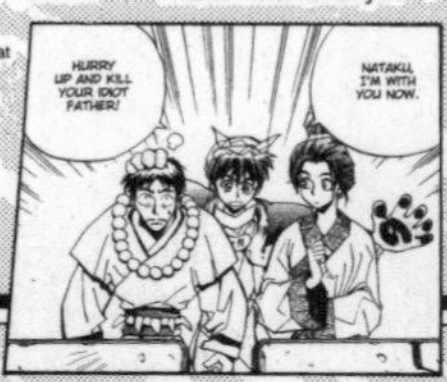
HURRY UP AND KILL YOUR IDIOT FATHER!
NATAKU, I'M WITH YOU NOW.

A low-down operation that used Sei Li and Inshi as shields?!

I haven't become your ally!

The two made up and Nataku became an ally!

Hoshin Why-What Question Box #3

Are paope and reiju different?

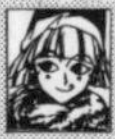

Basically, paope are weapons and protectors developed by *sennin*. Reiju are live beings. It is confusing because there's a paope like Yozen's Kotenken, but paope and reiju are completely different.
(By Shinkohyo)

By Kisosha

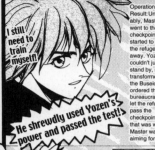

I still need to train myself!

He shrewdly used Yozen's power and passed the test!

Operation and Result: Unbelievably, Master went to the checkpoint and started to shoo the refugees away. Yozen couldn't just stand by, so he transformed into the Buseio and ordered the bureaucrats to let the refugees pass the checkpoint. And that was what Master was aiming for.

Situation: Yozen decided to test Master before becoming an ally. Yozen said that Master would pass the test if he could make all the refugees from Choka pass the checkpoint safely.

THEY HAVE ALL FLED CHOKA.

CAPTURE THAT SHADY DOSHI!
AAH!
KICK

The bureaucrats trust the Buseio Hiko Ko over Taikobo!

The people abandoned Choka because they could not endure the misrule anymore.

Operation 5

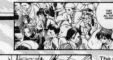

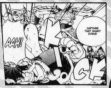

Yozen's test! Save the refugees operation!

Now you know how great I am!

I THINK I'VE CAUGHT A BIG ONE.
SMILE

Sho Ki heard about Master and came to see him. Just as Master had planned?!

Operation and Result: Master lectured Shukotan, who wouldn't forgive Bukichi's crime! As a result, Bukichi was pardoned, and Lord Sho Ki got interested in Master, eventually becoming an ally.

Situation: Master was looking for allies to fight against Yin together. He got to know Bukichi in Seiki. But Bukichi accidentally hurt Lord Sho Ki.

Operation 6

A godsend?! Make Sho Ki an ally operation!

Killing two birds with one stone! He saved Bukichi and was able to meet Sho Ki!

OOH

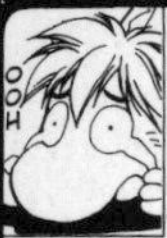

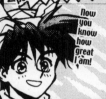

But still, I'm ashamed, Master.

He's good at using his brains, but Master sometimes fights hand-to-hand battles too. Master's favorite is the Drunken Fist, where you fight drunk. He wears an animal suit to go for someone's weak point. He's got no class at all...

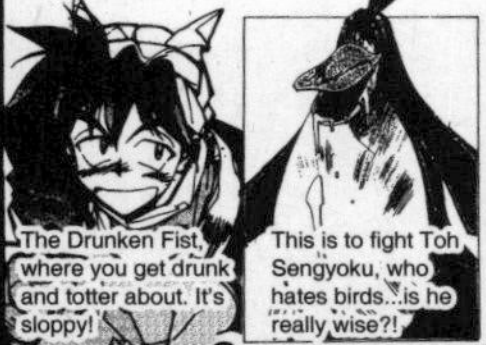

The Drunken Fist, where you get drunk and totter about. It's sloppy!

This is to fight Toh Sengyoku, who hates birds...is he really wise?!

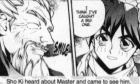

If Tenka was captured, we would've been in real danger. He thought ahead.

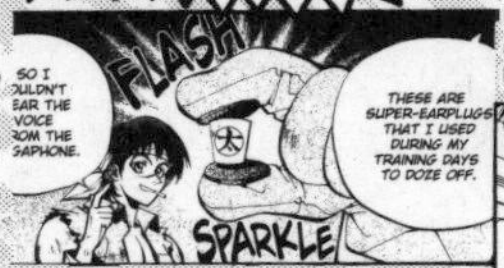

SO I COULDN'T HEAR THE VOICE FROM THE MEGAPHONE.
FLASH
THESE ARE SUPER-EARPLUGS THAT I USED DURING MY TRAINING DAYS TO DOZE OFF.
SPARKLE

He got captured right away and retired from the battle. How shameful!

YOU STUPID DOSHI! WHY'D YOU TELL THEM MY NAME?!
STEAM
HEH HEH HEH! NOW I'M NOT THE ONLY PRISONER!

Operation and Result: Master realized that the megaphone-shaped paope was something related to sound and gave Tenka his earplugs. Therefore Tenka wasn't captured, and we were able to fight back.

Situation: When Hiko Ko and his clan were heading for Seiki, the assassins Furin and Chokeiho appeared. They had strangely-shaped paope that we'd never seen before.

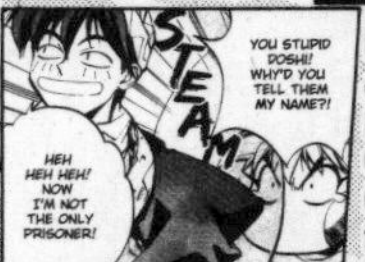

Operation 7

Battle against Furin and Chokeiho. Conquer the strange paope operation!

It looked as if he was useless! But he got the job done!

Su Kokuko was refusing to cooperate with Zhou because his older brother was in Yin.

ZOOM
GO, SHIN'YO!
CLICK

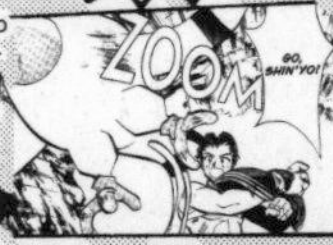

Dealing with Su Kokuko's bird reiju, Shin'yo would've been a hassle whether we fought or tried to talk to Su Kokuko. Master lured Shin'yo with super-strong bird feed and made Su Kokuko defenseless! But I had smelly bird feed dumped on my head...

Situation: Master went to Sujo, the capital of the north with some soldiers. This was so that the north would not attack from behind when Seiki attacked Yin. Master did not attack the castle, but instead camped outside. Lord Su Kokuko of Sujo lost patience and appeared in front of us.

Operation 8

Camping in front of the castle?! Make Su Kokuko an ally operation!

He ended up borrowing Sho Ki's help, but the north became an ally!

Editor S's Secret Story about *Hoshin*.

Part 3

About fan letters. I deliver them to sensei once a week. Most of them are people's impressions and encouraging letters, but sometimes there are complaints. Fans have sent in many requests, but I talk with sensei every week to outsmart everyone.

This article was published in Issue 51, 1997 of Weekly Shonen Jump.

Forecast! The Great Zhou vs. Yin War!

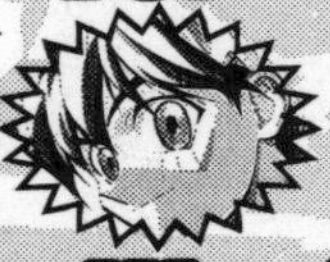

November is *Hoshin* Month! Four-weeks-in-a-row special.

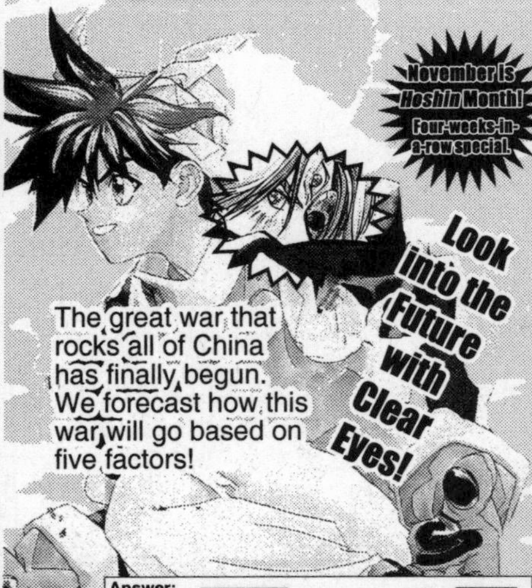

Look into the Future with Clear Eyes!

The great war that rocks all of China has finally begun. We forecast how this war will go based on five factors!

Hoshin Why-What Question Box (4)

Question: The brothers Inchon and Inchi, Kintaku and Mokutaku. Will characters that appeared previously reappear in the future?

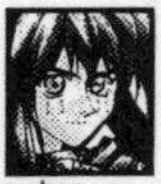

Answer: Dokoson, who was on Mount Kongrong, has reappeared. If the characters haven't been sealed, these other characters might appear again. It might be a good idea to read the manga again before these characters reappear. (By Yozen)

Factor: The King — (King Bu and King Chu)

They both love women, but...

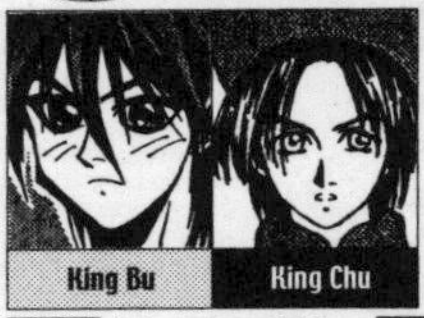

King Bu | King Chu

● King Bu became king although his older brother Hakuyuko was supposed to succeed Sho Ki. King Chu has fallen under Dakki's Temptation Jutsu, but he used to be known as a wise king. The difference in their experience as king is obvious. They both love women, though.

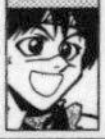

Tenka Ko: He's undependable, but you can't hate him! King Bu lacks experience because he just became king. But the people love him. He'll become a good king!

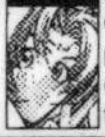

Dakki: King Chu is steadily changing. ♥ Due to my modification, King Chu has become powerful. ♥ He's even won against the Buseio. ♥

Summary: The deciding factor is King Chu's modification?!

● In Zhou, Shukotan and the others are mentally supporting King Bu. In Yin, Dakki is modifying King Chu's body! He'll be useful as a human weapon rather than as king!

Points: Zhou 3–5 Yin — Yin's Advantage!

Factor: The Gunshi — (Taikobo and Bunchu)

The flexible Taikobo and the firm Bunchu

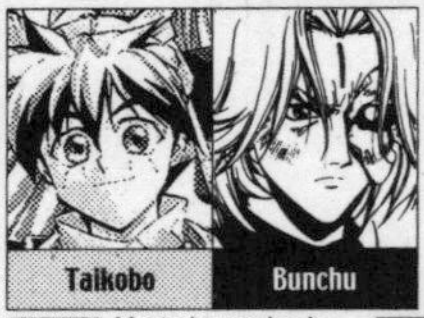

Taikobo | Bunchu

● Taikobo and Bunchu, the Gunshi of each country, are complete opposites. Taikobo uses teamwork and traps to make a power of one into a hundred. Bunchu crushes the enemy directly with overwhelming power!

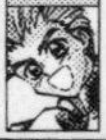

Bukichi: Master's cunning is guaranteed! Master isn't good at fighting, but he's always thinking ahead to come up with strategies. He holds everyone together!

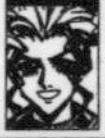

Chokomei: Bunchu is pretty upright! His loyalty to Yin is genuine. He can't leave King Chu's side for now, but he'll be heading for the front line soon.

Summary: Judging from his track record, Bunchu has an overwhelming advantage!

The two have fought before, but Taikobo, Yozen and Nataku together could not do anything against Bunchu. Bunchu is too strong!

Points: Zhou 3–5 Yin — Yin's Advantage!

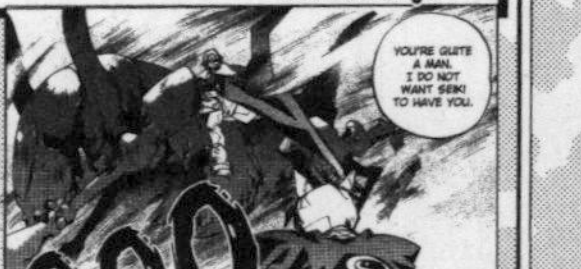
YOU'RE QUITE A MAN. I DO NOT WANT SEKI TO HAVE YOU.

➡ Taikobo could not do a thing against Bunchu's overwhelming strength!

Factor: The Sendo (Supporting Forces)

2) The 12 Kongrong Elite Sennin are cooperative.

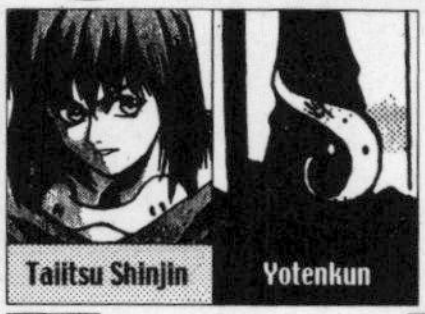
Taiitsu Shinjin
Yotenkun

● Mount Kongrong is supporting Zhou, with Taiitsu Shinjin treating Nataku, who was wounded in a fierce battle. On the other hand, the Juttenkun of Kingo Island haven't been completely cooperative, ignoring Bunchu's summons.

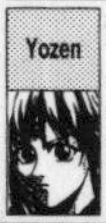
Yozen

We've got full support! The sennin of Mount Kongrong cannot participate conspicuously in a war between humans, but they are ready to fight as one.

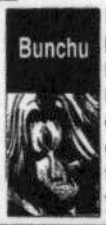
Bunchu

Everyone's giving me a headache! Lord Tsuten Kyoshu was supposed to have granted me the right of command over all sennin of Kingo Island...this is no time to be worrying about your pride, Juttenkun!

Summary The Zhou side is united!

The Zhou vs. Yin war is an extension of the Hoshin Project that Genshi Tenson of Mount Kongrong started. Thus, the Zhou side naturally has more solidarity than the Yin side!

Points Zhou 5–3 Yin
Zhou's Advantage!

Factor: The Sendo (Current Forces)

1) Zhou's solidarity is growing!

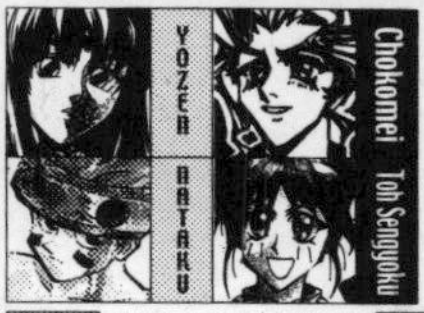
Yozen
Nataku
Chokomei
Toh Sengyoku

● The sendo on Zhou's side are all unique. It looked as if they were fighting on their own, but they started fighting as a team from when they fought the Maka Yonsho. Sendo on Yin's side hold strong fighting powers, but it looks as if they lack solidarity!

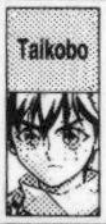
Taikobo

We have a long, hard fight ahead. There are limits to an individual's power, but if we fight as one, we may win! I can't believe Nataku would be obedient, though...

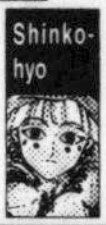
Shinko-hyo

I am apprehensive. The leaders Bunchu and Dakki don't trust each other, although Chokomei is mediating.

Summary You can't take them lightly, but the Yin side is at a disadvantage.

There are those who aren't too cooperative, but Zhou's Sendo share the common objective of defeating Yin. They have an advantage over Yin, whose Sendo are fueding among themselves.

Points Zhou 5–4 Yin
Zhou's Advantage!

Total Fighting Power

	Yin	Zhou
King	5	3
Gunshi	5	3
Sendo	4	5
Sendo	3	5
People	5	4
Total	22	20

● We predict the outcome of this war from these five factors and can analyze that Yin has a slight 2-point advantage! But the war situation changes moment by moment. Until a decisive battle is fought, both countries have the possibility of winning! How much can Zhou pare down Yin's fighting power in the beginning of the war, when Yin is lacking in solidarity?! That's what's important in the initial stages.

Zhou 20, Yin 22.
Yin has a slight advantage?!

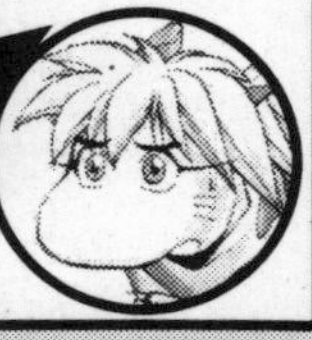

That's not true!

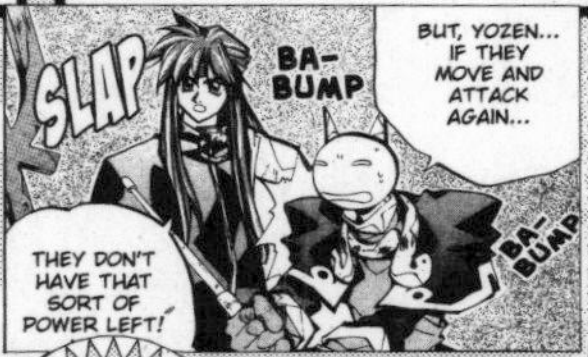
BUT, YOZEN... IF THEY MOVE AND ATTACK AGAIN...
BA-BUMP
SLAP
BA-BUMP
THEY DON'T HAVE THAT SORT OF POWER LEFT!

Sendo of Zhou really fought together for the first time when they fought against the Maka Yonsho. Taikobo, who brought everyone together dealt the final blow. This victory is worth more than all the previous wins!

Factor: The People (Common Soldiers)

The battle between merriness and the hungry spirit!

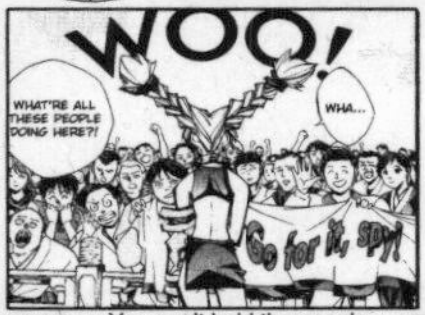
WOO!
WHAT'RE ALL THESE PEOPLE DOING HERE?!
WHA...
Go for it, spy!

● Because the Maka Yonsho destroyed Hoyu, the people of Zhou have become pro-war. On the other hand, the people of Yin are ready for war due to Dakki's Temptation Jutsu! The people of Zhou live comfortably in a wealthy environment. The people of Yin have been oppressed by misrule.

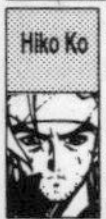
Hiko Ko

You can't hold the people together just by fear! Dakki does have her Temptation Jutsu, but what's moving the people of Yin is the fear that insubordination results in death. There's no way they can fight as one.

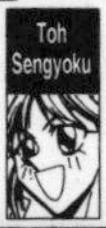
Toh Sengyoku

Zhou is too carefree! The people were watching my holy battle against Taikobo as if it were a festival ... there's a limit to how carefree you can be!

Summary Can the "iron ring" around Yin succeed?!

The Zhou army has 50,000 soldiers. The Yin army has a total of 700,000 soldiers! Yin has an overwhelming numerical advantage. The Zhou army bets everything on the encircling operation, attacking Yin from all four directions!

Points Zhou 4–5 Yin
Yin's Advantage!

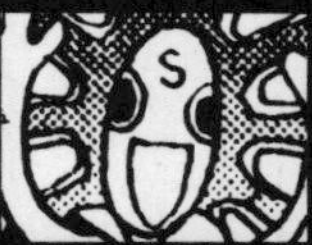

Editor S's Secret Story about *Hoshin*.

Part 4

This is the last week of the Hoshin Month. Thank you everyone for reading this! If you clip all these articles, I think you could enjoy future chapters of *Hoshin Engi* many times more. Finally, let me secretly tell you Fujisaki-sensei's weekly schedule. Sat: Meeting. Sun: Storyboards. Mon-Fri: Manuscripts. Sometimes the schedule is off by a day because of color pages. Oops, he...has no complete day off.

By Kisosha. This article was published in Issue 52, 1997 of Weekly Shonen Jump.

THE SHEER PRECIPICE, WHERE IS IT NOW? 12

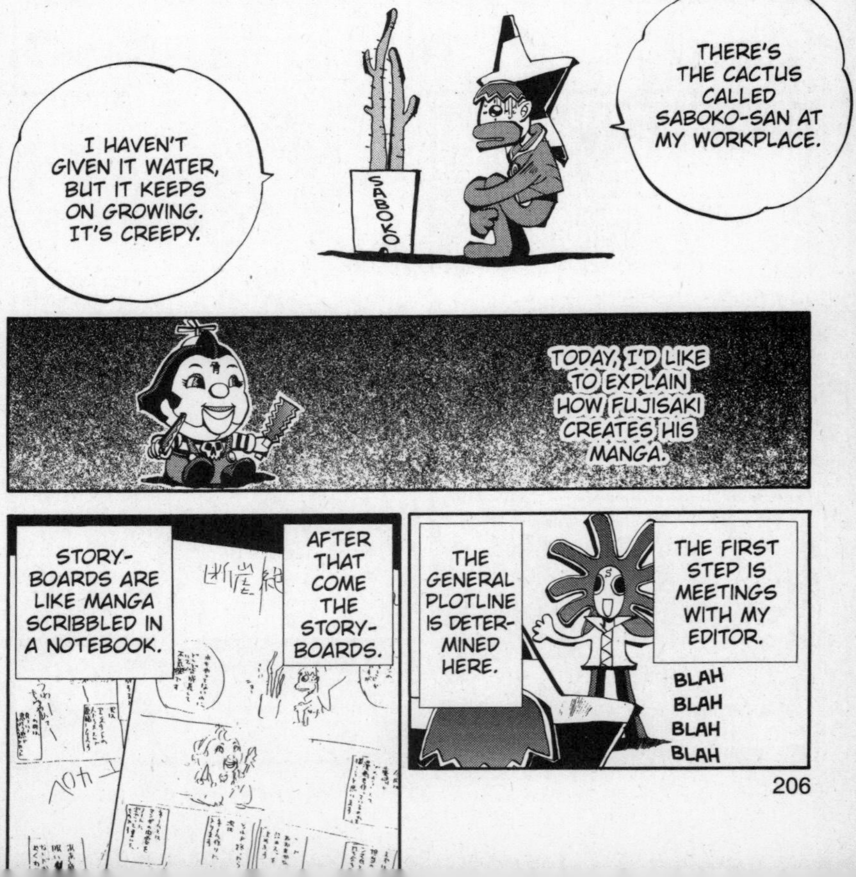
THERE'S THE CACTUS CALLED SABOKO-SAN AT MY WORKPLACE.
I HAVEN'T GIVEN IT WATER, BUT IT KEEPS ON GROWING. IT'S CREEPY.
SABOKO
TODAY, I'D LIKE TO EXPLAIN HOW FUJISAKI CREATES HIS MANGA.
THE FIRST STEP IS MEETINGS WITH MY EDITOR.
THE GENERAL PLOTLINE IS DETERMINED HERE.
BLAH BLAH BLAH BLAH
AFTER THAT COME THE STORYBOARDS.
STORYBOARDS ARE LIKE MANGA SCRIBBLED IN A NOTEBOOK.

READ THIS WAY

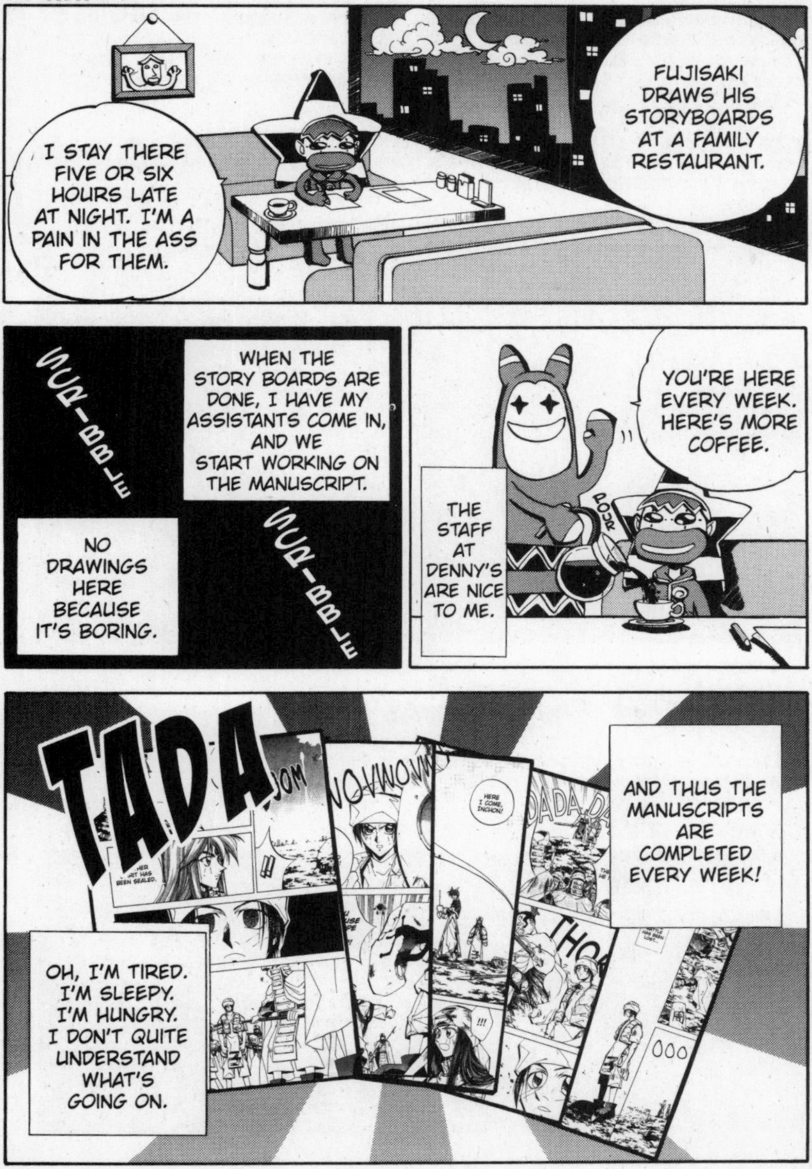

FUJISAKI DRAWS HIS STORYBOARDS AT A FAMILY RESTAURANT.
I STAY THERE FIVE OR SIX HOURS LATE AT NIGHT. I'M A PAIN IN THE ASS FOR THEM.
YOU'RE HERE EVERY WEEK. HERE'S MORE COFFEE.
POUR
THE STAFF AT DENNY'S ARE NICE TO ME.
WHEN THE STORY BOARDS ARE DONE, I HAVE MY ASSISTANTS COME IN, AND WE START WORKING ON THE MANUSCRIPT.
SCRIBBLE
SCRIBBLE
NO DRAWINGS HERE BECAUSE IT'S BORING.
AND THUS THE MANUSCRIPTS ARE COMPLETED EVERY WEEK!
HERE I COME, INCHON!
TADA
OH, I'M TIRED. I'M SLEEPY. I'M HUNGRY. I DON'T QUITE UNDERSTAND WHAT'S GOING ON.

Hoshin Engi: The Rank File!

You'll find as you read *Hoshin Engi* that there are titles and ranks that you are probably unfamiliar with. While it may seem confusing, there is an order to the madness that is pulled from ancient Chinese mythology, Japanese culture, other manga, and, of course, the incredible mind of *Hoshin Engi* creator Ryu Fujisaki.

Where we think it will help, we give you a hint in the margin on the page the name appears. But in addition, here's a quick primer on the titles you'll find in *Hoshin Engi* and what they mean:

Japanese	Title	Job Description
武成王	Buseio	Chief commanding officer
宰相	Saisho	Premier
太師	Taishi	The king's advisor/tutor
大金剛	Dai Kongo	Great Vassals
軍師	Gunshi	Military tactician
大諸侯	Daishoko	Great feudal lord
東伯侯	Tohakuko	Lord of the east region
西伯侯	Seihakuko	Lord of the west region
北伯侯	Hokuhakuko	Lord of the north region
南伯侯	Nanhakuko	Lord of the south region

Hoshin Engi: The Immortal File

Also, you'll probably find the hierarchy of the Sennin, Sendo and Doshi somewhat complicated. Here, we spell it out the easiest way possible!

Japanese	Title	Description
道士	Doshi	Someone training to become Sennin
仙道	Sendo	Used to describe both Sennin and Doshi
仙人	Sennin	Those who have mastered the way. Once you "go Sennin" you are forever changed.
妖孽	Yogetsu	A Yosei who can transform into a human
妖怪仙人	Yokai Sennin	A Sennin whose original form is not human
妖精	Yosei	An animal or object exposed to moonlight and sunlight for more than 1,000 years

Hoshin Engi: The Magical File

Paope (宝貝) are powerful magical items used by Sennin and Doshi. Sometimes they look like regular objects, like a veil or hat. These are just a few of the magical items, both paope and otherwise, that you'll encounter in *Hoshin Engi!*

Japanese	Magic	Description
打神鞭	Dashinben	Known as the God-Striking Whip, Taikobo's paope manipulates the air and wind.
霊獣	Reiju	A magical flying beast that Sennin and Doshi use for transportation and support. Taikobo's reiju is his pal Supu.
雷公鞭	Raikoben	Reduces an opponent to ashes with a huge clap of thunder.
哮天犬	Kotenken	The Howling Dog can fly and be used as an attack paope.
莫邪の宝剣	Bakuya no Hoken	Tenka's weapon, a light saber.
禁鞭	Kinben	A powerful whip that can attack anything in a diameter of several kilometers.
花狐貂	Kakoten	An object that consumes people and cities for its energy source.
青雲剣	Seiunken	A sword with a blade that splits into many blades when swung.
混元傘	Kongensan	Absorbs the enemy attacks and uses them against the attackers.
黒琵琶	Kurobiwa	A lute that manipulates the minds of those who hear it.
拌黄珠	Bankoju	A vehicle that shoots energy beams.
開天珠	Kaitenju	A missile that destroys anything it touches. Allows the user to fly.
紫綬羽衣	Shiju Hagoromo	Allows the user to fly, and emits a lethal poison moth powder.
傾世元禳	Keisei Genjo	An object that radiates the perfume of temptation.
鑽心釘	Sanshintei	Dagger-like version of Bakuya no Hoken.
五光石	Gokoseki	A rock that changes the face of whomever it strikes into a "weirdly macho-looking" face.
十絶陣	Juzetsujin	An alternate dimension that can envelop and conceal places in the real world.

Coming Next Volume:
Conquering Chokomei, Part 1

Dakki and Chokomei swoop in, capturing some of Taikobo's most trusted friends and carrying them off to Chokomei's magic tower. Now Taikobo and his allies must fight their way through the tower's gauntlet of death to rescue them!

AVAILABLE DECEMBER 2008!

Read Any Good Books Lately?

Hoshin Engi is based on *Fengshen Yanji* (*The Creation of the Gods*, written in the 1500s by Xu Zhonglin) one of China's four classical fantastical novels of adventure, magic and mystery. The other three are *Saiyuki* (*Journey to the West* by Cheng'en Wu, late 1500s), *Sangokushi Engi* (*Romance of the Three Kingdoms* by Guanzhong Luo), and *Shui Hu Zhuan* (*Outlaws of the Marsh*, by Shi Nai'an, mid-1500s).

Want to read these books? You can! They're all still in print, more than 500 years later!

These books are North American in-print editions only.

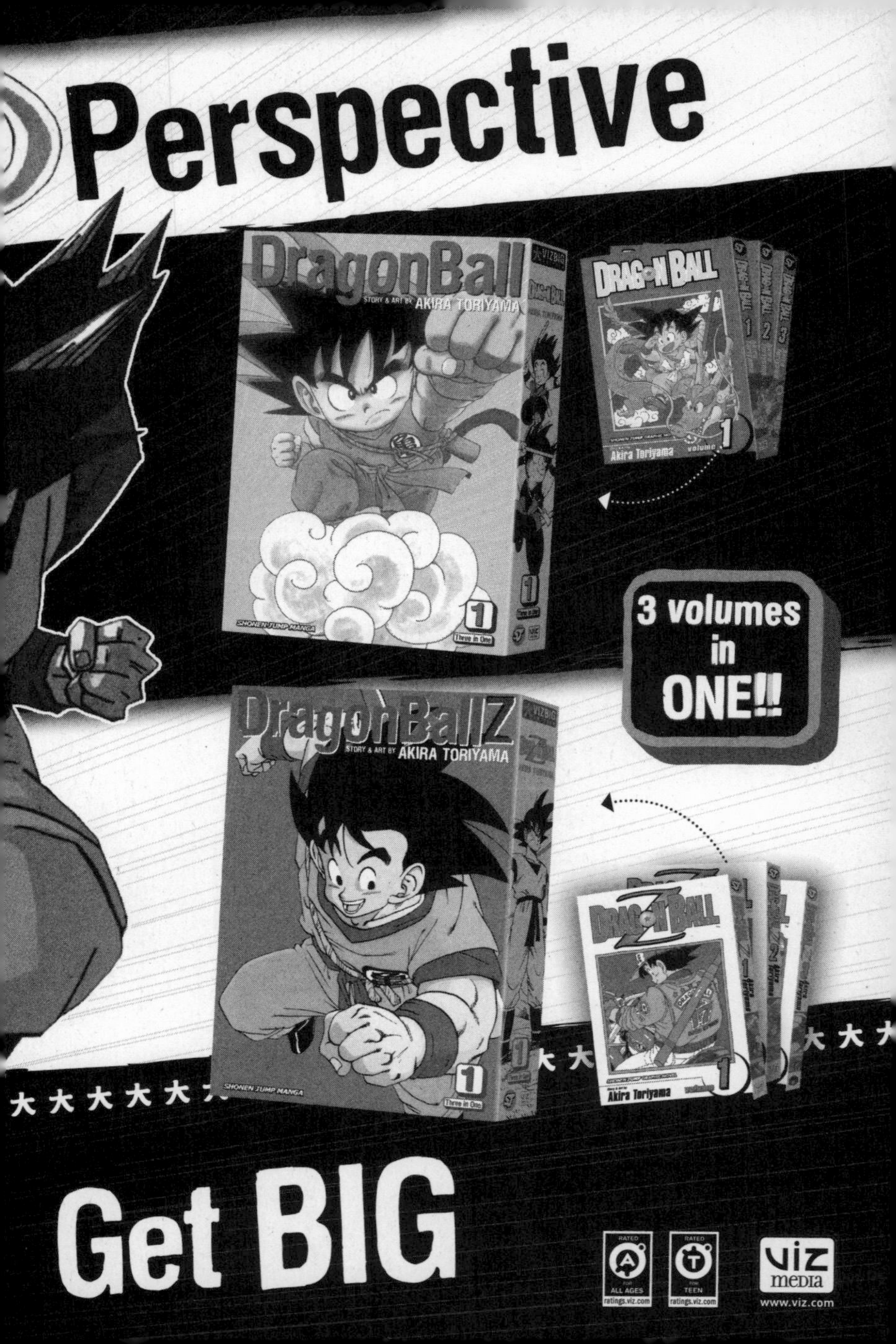
Perspective
DragonBall
STORY & ART BY AKIRA TORIYAMA
SHONEN JUMP MANGA
1
Three in One
DRAGON BALL
Akira Toriyama
volume 1
3 volumes in ONE!!
DragonBall Z
STORY & ART BY AKIRA TORIYAMA
SHONEN JUMP MANGA
1
Three in One
DRAGON BALL Z
Akira Toriyama
Get BIG
RATED A FOR ALL AGES ratings.viz.com
RATED T FOR TEEN ratings.viz.com
VIZ media
www.viz.com

Tell us what you think about SHONEN JUMP manga!

Our survey is now available online.
Go to: **www.*SHONENJUMP*.com/mangasurvey**

Help us make our product offering better!

THE REAL ACTION STARTS IN...

SHONEN JUMP

THE WORLD'S MOST POPULAR MANGA

www.shonenjump.com

ST ADVANCED

ST

VIZ media

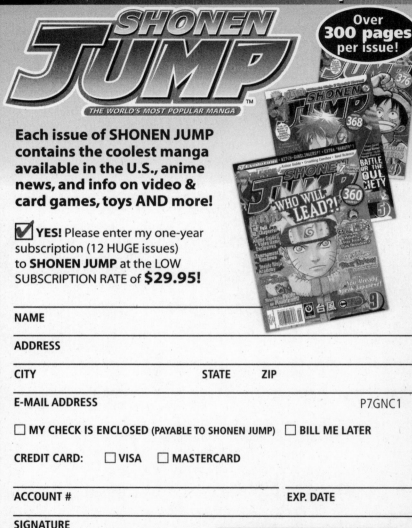